Mortgage Possession Proceedings

Other titles available from Law Society Publishing:

Bankruptcy (forthcoming, 2012)
Vernon Dennis

Consumer Credit (forthcoming, 2012)
Russell J. Kelsall

Conveyancing Handbook (18th edn)
General Editor: Frances Silverman

Conveyancing Protocol
The Law Society

Liquidation
Vernon Dennis

Litigation Funding Handbook (forthcoming, 2012)
General Editor: Neil Rose

Titles from Law Society Publishing can be ordered from all good bookshops or direct (telephone 0870 850 1422, email **lawsociety@prolog.uk.com** or visit our online shop at **www.lawsociety.org.uk/bookshop**).

MORTGAGE POSSESSION PROCEEDINGS

Timothy Powell

The Law Society

The author has asserted the right under the Copyright, Designs and Patents Act 1988 to be identified as author of this work.
Whilst all reasonable care has been taken in the preparation of this publication, neither the publisher nor the author can accept any responsibility for any loss occasioned to any person acting or refraining from action as a result of relying upon its contents.
The views expressed in this publication should be taken as those of the author only unless it is specifically indicated that the Law Society has given its endorsement.

© Timothy Powell 2012

Crown copyright material in Appendices A, B, C, E3 and E6 and in Precedents E3 and E6 on the accompanying disk is reproduced with the permission of the Controller of Her Majesty's Stationery Office. Extracts from the LSC Manual in Appendix D1 are copyright the Legal Services Commission.

ISBN-13: 978-1-85328-922-4

Published in 2012 by the Law Society
113 Chancery Lane, London WC2A 1PL

Typeset by Columns Design XML Ltd, Reading
Printed by CPI Group (UK) Ltd, Croydon, CR0 4YY

FSC
www.fsc.org
MIX
Paper from
responsible sources
FSC® C013604

The paper used for the text pages of this book is FSC® certified. FSC (the Forest Stewardship Council®) is an international network to promote responsible management of the world's forests.

Contents

Preface

Lambeth County Court in south London is one of the busiest courts in the country for housing possession claims. This book arose from my practical experience over many years as a duty solicitor in that court, representing mortgage borrowers and tenants.

The law of mortgages is complex, but the practice of defending mortgage possession claims is relatively straightforward. This book aims to equip legal advisers to carry out that task efficiently and effectively, whether they go to court or remain in the office.

If this whole book could be summarised in a few words of advice, they would be: 'buy time; effect change; never give up'.

It follows from this that legal advisers should, so far as possible, never agree to any kind of possession order, but always seek an adjournment either generally, or on terms. Of course, that will not always be possible, but it is by far and away the best starting point in dealing with mortgage possession claims. Remember, too, that in a meritorious case, an appeal will likely result in a thorough rehearing of the borrower's case.

The text of the book reflects my understanding of the law of England and Wales as at the end of August 2011. Any errors are mine. Comments on the contents of the book are welcome.

Tim Powell
September 2011

Acknowledgements

My thanks go to the staff at Powell Forster Solicitors in Brixton, London SW2, in particular my secretary and assistant Pam Griffiths for typing the book from sometimes disjointed dictation, to Jane Grant and Lynne Luck for their encouragement, and to my partner Deirdre Forster for her invaluable support and guidance, editorial advice and help in drafting a number of chapters and appendix materials.

I also wish to thank Robert Latham, a hugely experienced barrister in Doughty Street Chambers, London not only for reading and commenting on the chapter about human rights, but also for his advice and assistance with numerous possession claims over the years; and Duncan Forbes, housing solicitor and chief executive of Bron Afon Community Housing, Torfaen, Wales for reading and commenting on the chapter about the Mortgage Rescue Scheme in Wales.

I am grateful to all my colleagues and fellow members of the Housing Law Practitioners Association for providing me with opportunities to give presentations, seminars and workshops on defending mortgage possession claims, and for their comments and feedback. I would also mention the late Bob Lawrence, homelessness adviser at the Department of Communities and Local Government and erstwhile Chief Executive of the Empty Homes Agency, who was enthusiastic about my presentations and encouraged me to develop my work further.

Andrew Harrison at Blackfriars Advice Centre in south London deserves special mention for the advice and guidance he gave me in relation to mortgage possession claims and, indeed, so does everyone past and present who has been involved in administering the Lambeth County Court duty advice scheme. I am grateful to colleagues on that scheme, with whom I have discussed many difficult cases, and to the staff and judges at the court, who have been unfailingly polite, helpful and fair. Mark Batten and Brian Foxley at Centre 70 advice centre have given me invaluable advice over more than 20 years about debt management and welfare benefit issues.

Thanks too to Ben Mullane and the whole team at the Law Society for their enthusiasm, practical advice and helpful comments on early drafts of chapters, and for doing all the work necessary to deliver this book to print. I am also indebted to Kathryn Swift for her sterling work editing the initial manuscript and incorporating my many amendments.

Lastly, I give traditional thanks to my parents, John and Isabel Powell, without whom, as has been said so often by so many authors, none of this would have been possible.

Table of cases

Table of statutes

Table of statutory instruments

Table of European legislation

Abbreviations

AJA	Administration of Justice Act
AVS	assisted voluntary sale
CCA	Consumer Credit Act
CCJ	county court judgment
CLS	Community Legal Service
CPR	Civil Procedure Rules
CMI	current monthly instalment
CML	Council of Mortgage Lenders
DISP	Dispute Resolution: Complaints (in the FSA Handbook)
DWP	Department for Work and Pensions
ECHR	European Convention on Human Rights
ECtHR	European Court of Human Rights
FCA	Financial Conduct Authority
FOS	Financial Ombudsman Service
FSA	Financial Services Authority
FSMA 2000	Financial Services and Markets Act 2000
HA	Housing Act
HCA	Homes and Communities Agency
HPCDS	Housing Possession Court Duty Scheme
HRA 1998	Human Rights Act 1998
IA 1986	Insolvency Act 1986
LPA 1925	Law of Property Act 1925
LP(MP)A 1989	Law of Property (Miscellaneous Provisions) Act 1989
LRA 2002	Land Registration Act 2002
LSC	Legal Services Commission
LVT	Leasehold Valuation Tribunal
MCOB	Mortgages and Home Finance: Conduct of Business sourcebook (in the FSA Handbook)
MPPI	mortgage payment protection insurance
MR(PT)A 2010	Mortgage Repossessions (Protection of Tenants etc) Act 2010
OFT	Office of Fair Trading
PCOL	Possession Claim Online
RA 1977	Rent Act 1977

SA 1974	Solicitors Act 1974
SMI	Support for Mortgage Interest
SMOD	subject matter of dispute
SRB	sale and rent back
TLATA 1996	Trusts of Land and Appointment of Trustees Act 1996
UTCCR 1999	Unfair Terms in Consumer Contracts Regulations 1999

CHAPTER 1

Introduction

1.1 OVERVIEW

This chapter is aimed at the busy practitioner who needs an immediate overview of the available options when advising a mortgage borrower in difficulty. Its primary purpose is to assist advisers in situations where more urgent action is needed to protect the mortgage borrower's position.

1.2 KEEPING BORROWERS IN THEIR HOMES

Although there may be rare cases where the mortgage borrower's interests are best served by the making of an immediate order for possession, the vast majority of borrowers will want to hold on to their property, especially if it is their home.

1.2.1 The benefits of professional intervention

In practice, efforts to prevent the making of a possession order are usually worthwhile, especially if they are made at an early stage. Even so, it will rarely be too late to do anything on behalf of a mortgage borrower.

Advisers should not underestimate the likelihood of a successful outcome for the client arising from their ability to sift facts, order documents, identify trends and present proposals on behalf of mortgage borrowers. This is particularly so in circumstances where borrowers themselves have become mired in the detail of their cases and consequently ineffective in dealing with their affairs.

Lenders and the courts are receptive to professional intervention by practitioners, especially where a structured approach to dealing with mortgage arrears is proposed.

1.2.2 Finding time to improve the borrower's position

In nearly all cases, the imperative step is for the adviser to buy time for the mortgage borrower, so that they can rearrange their affairs, effect a change in their circumstances, improve their situation and, it is hoped, save their home.

1.3   PROCEEDINGS NOT YET ISSUED

If possession proceedings have not yet been issued, the adviser should immediately contact the lender directly, or its solicitors if already appointed, and seek a stay of further action for 14 or 28 days to enable instructions to be taken from the mortgage borrower.

1.3.1   The Mortgage Pre-Action Protocol

Advisers should make reference to the relevant provisions of the 'Pre-Action Protocol for Possession Claims based on Mortgage or Home Purchase Plan Arrears in Respect of Residential Property' (invariably referred to as the 'Mortgage Pre-Action Protocol' or simply 'the Protocol'). This will apply to most mortgage arrears. Fuller details will be found in **Chapter 7** and a copy of the Protocol is reproduced in **Appendix C5**.

Under the Protocol, para.5.2 the parties should take all reasonable steps to discuss with each other, or their representatives, the cause of the arrears, the borrower's financial circumstances and proposals for repayment of the arrears.

The court takes the view that starting a possession claim is usually a last resort and that such a claim should not normally be started when a settlement is still actively being explored (see the Protocol, para.7.1).

1.3.2   Calculate the equity in the property

Lenders may be more amenable to discussions if there is significant equity in the property concerned, as this will reassure lenders that their security is not unduly at risk if they agree to a delay in issuing court proceedings.

The mortgage borrower should be asked to provide a current valuation of their property if it were to be sold on the open market. A valuation can usually be provided swiftly by a local estate agent at no cost; and it is legitimate for the borrower to request this if one of their options might be to sell the property to pay off the mortgage and arrears.

Alternatively, there are several websites that provide details of recent sales of similar properties in any given area, which could give a valuable indication of the likely value of the mortgage borrower's property.

1.4   PROCEEDINGS HAVE BEEN ISSUED

If proceedings have already been issued, the ability to find time to improve the borrower's position may depend on when the first (or next) court hearing date is due to take place.

1.4.1 Agreeing an adjournment

If the adviser is instructed two or three weeks before the hearing date, it may be appropriate to ask the lender to agree to a short adjournment to take instructions and seek to formulate a proposal in respect of the mortgage arrears. Some lenders will agree to an adjournment, which can be arranged by both parties sending letters to the court (with copies to each other).

Alternatively, a lender may say that it intends to appear at the hearing, but will not object to an adjournment request, provided that some proposal is made for the payment of the current monthly instalment (CMI) and/or something towards the arrears.

As will be seen, it is not necessarily fatal to an adjournment application that the mortgage borrower cannot make payments at the current time, but the application will be strengthened if a proposal of some sort can be made.

1.4.2 Applying for an adjournment

If the lender rejects the request for an adjournment and/or the possession hearing is imminent (as will be the case where the adviser is representing a mortgage borrower on the day of the hearing, as part of a court duty advice scheme), then the application must be made to the judge (usually a district judge sitting in a private hearing). The powers of the court are set out below, but for case studies relating to adjournment applications, see **Appendices F1, F2** and **F3**.

1.4.3 Inherent jurisdiction to adjourn proceedings

The court has an inherent jurisdiction to grant adjournments 'which in the ordinary course of procedure may be desirable in circumstances such as temporary inability of a party to attend, and so forth': Russell J, in *Birmingham Citizens Permanent Building Society* v. *Caunt* [1962] Ch 883 at 912.

Examples of a temporary inability to attend are illness or temporary absence abroad. Where possible the judge should be given some documentary evidence relating to the inability to attend, for example a medical certificate or flight confirmation.

1.4.4 Civil Procedure Rules

More specifically, courts have the power to adjourn any hearing pursuant to their general case management powers under Civil Procedure Rules (CPR) rule 3.1(2)(b). Judges will take into account:

- the timing of the request;
- whether the mortgage borrower has previously sought advice and, if not, why not;
- the general merits of the borrower's case in the light of the level of arrears;

- the borrower's personal circumstances and likely ability to pay the CMI and/or arrears (particularly until the next hearing);
- what the borrower hopes to achieve in the time that would be provided by an adjournment; and
- what the risk may be to the lender of granting an adjournment, which usually entails an assessment of the likely equity in the property.

These issues will need to be addressed when making the adjournment application to the judge. The more that the mortgage borrower can offer to pay, the greater the likelihood that an adjournment will be granted.

If a good case can be made out, it would be unusual for an adjournment application to fail at a first hearing, but circumstances vary widely. Therefore, advisers must have a fallback position to make the best offer in relation to the arrears that the mortgage borrower can realistically make, in case the adjournment is refused and the judge proceeds to deal with the claim for possession.

If a possession order were to be made at a first hearing, the adviser should consider whether or not to apply for permission to appeal against the decision refusing an adjournment.

1.5   SUMMARY OF THE COURT'S POWERS

The court's powers are found in the two statutory regimes which govern mortgage possession proceedings:

- under the Administration of Justice Acts 1970 and 1973 (which cover most home purchase mortgages payable by instalments); and
- under the Consumer Credit Acts 1974 and 2006 (which cover regulated loans, often secured by second or third charges on property).

1.5.1   Administration of Justice Acts

Under the Administration of Justice Act (AJA) 1970, s.36 (as amended by AJA 1973, s.8) the court is given specific power to:

- adjourn mortgage possession proceedings, or
- stay or suspend execution of a judgment or possession order, or
- postpone the date for delivery of possession.

These powers are exercisable if the arrears are likely to be paid off within a 'reasonable period'. Fuller details are set out in **Chapter 8** and a copy of the relevant sections will be found in the **Appendices A1 and A2**.

4

1.5.2   Mortgages to which these powers apply

The court's powers under AJA 1970, s.36 apply equally to capital repayment mortgages and interest-only (endowment) mortgages, which are repayable by instalments. The different types of mortgage are dealt with in **Chapter 2**.

In general, the powers do not apply to the same extent to 'all monies charges', which secure loans such as a bank overdraft, for example. All monies charges tend to be repayable on demand, though there are some exceptions. These are dealt with in greater detail at **1.15** and in **Chapter 9**. Even with all monies charges the court may still adjourn for a short time, if there is a reasonable prospect of the borrower paying off the entire debt over a reasonable period.

Where the powers apply, the court can impose such conditions with regard to payment by the mortgage borrower or the remedying of any default, as it thinks fit. For example, the court could make a possession order suspended on terms that the borrower pays the CMI plus, say, £50 per month towards the arrears.

1.5.3   What is a reasonable period?

A 'reasonable period' means, *prima facie*, the remaining term of the mortgage: see *Cheltenham & Gloucester Building Society* v. *Norgan* [1996] 1 WLR 343, CA. In every single mortgage possession case, the adviser should calculate the minimum '*Norgan* offer' which is the amount required each month from the borrower to pay off the arrears by the end of the mortgage.

Example

The mortgage borrower has a 25-year mortgage which she took out five years ago, there now being 20 years left to the end of the mortgage term. She has £6,000 of mortgage arrears. Therefore, the minimum *Norgan* offer is: £6,000 ÷ 20 ÷ 12 = £25 per month. This is the sum which, if paid regularly by the mortgage borrower in addition to the CMI, would clear the mortgage arrears by the end of the remaining 20-year term of the mortgage.

In any case where a mortgage borrower can improve on the minimum *Norgan* offer, i.e. pay more than the minimum each month, that fact should be emphasised to the lender and to the judge. This information is crucial both at the point at which an adjournment application is made and at the point when a judge is considering whether or not to make a possession order against the borrower.

It will be the adviser's task to find ways to try to improve on the monthly offer, if time allows.

Any adjournment ranks as a success, and will effectively provide the mortgage borrower with much needed time, even if the adjournment is only very short.

1.5.4 Consumer Credit Act

Where a loan is a regulated agreement, the provisions of the Administration of Justice Acts 1970 and 1973 will not apply, but the Consumer Credit Act (CCA) 1974 provides a quite separate range of protections for borrowers. In particular, the court:

- may make a 'time order' under s.129; and if it does so,
- may make a further order under s.136 to reduce or vary interest, or otherwise amend the agreement; and
- may suspend a possession order under s.135; and
- may make a finding that a relationship between a creditor and a debtor is 'unfair' with a range of consequent orders that can then be made affecting the agreement and the parties.

Fuller details will be found below at **1.16** and in **Chapter 10**.

1.6 USING THE MORTGAGE PRE-ACTION PROTOCOL

The adviser's task of obtaining an adjournment will be made easier if they can identify a potential or actual breach of the Mortgage Pre-Action Protocol, a copy of which will be found in **Appendix C5**. Instructions need to be taken from the mortgage borrower, but the most common failures by lenders are:

- a failure to take all reasonable steps to discuss the cause of the arrears, the borrower's financial circumstances and proposals for repayment of the arrears (Protocol, para.5.2);
- a failure to consider a reasonable request from the borrower to change the date of regular payment or the method by which payment is made (Protocol, para.5.4);
- a failure to postpone the start of proceedings where the borrower has made a claim to the Department for Work and Pensions (DWP) for Support for Mortgage Interest (SMI) or to an insurer under a mortgage payment protection policy (provided there is a reasonable expectation of payment and an ability to pay a shortfall) (Protocol, para.6.1); and
- the lender has started possession proceedings when a settlement is still actively being explored, in particular where there has been inadequate or no discussion about a proposal by the borrower to extend the term of the mortgage, change the type of the mortgage, defer payment of interest due under the mortgage, or capitalise the arrears (i.e. add them to the principal loan) (Protocol, para.7.1 and **1.9.4**).

Where a potential or actual breach of the Protocol can be demonstrated, the court should be invited to adjourn the proceedings, not only to allow the adviser to assist the mortgage borrower to improve their situation, but also to enable the discussions that are envisaged by the Protocol to take place. Fuller details will be found in **Chapter 7**. For case studies involving the use of the Protocol, see **7.8.5** and **Appendix F3**.

1.7 PREPARING THE MORTGAGE BORROWER'S CASE

In advance of a mortgage possession hearing or having obtained an adjournment of an existing hearing, the adviser should take steps to evaluate any defence that the mortgage borrower may have and at the same time improve their position with regard to the mortgage and arrears. The aim is to avoid a possession order being made or, if this cannot be prevented, to ensure that any possession order is suspended.

1.8 DEFENCES TO A MORTGAGE POSSESSION CLAIM

In practice it is rare for an adviser to find circumstances that will establish a substantive defence to a mortgage possession claim. However, advisers need to be aware that the main defences which may arise are:

- the defendant did not sign the mortgage deed;
- the defendant signed only due to undue pressure;
- there has been some fraud; or
- there are technical deficiencies and/or unfair terms in the mortgage deed.

These substantive defences are dealt with in greater detail in **Chapter 3**. If a serious point arises, a defence should be prepared, or at least directions from the court should be obtained for the filing of a defence.

Advisers should note that where a counterclaim for damages against a lender is identified, this will not necessarily prevent a possession order being made.

1.9 IMPROVING THE BORROWER'S FINANCIAL POSITION

The adviser will want to explore all possibilities to improve the mortgage borrower's financial position, not only for the purpose of possession proceedings, but generally.

1.9.1 Mortgage payment protection policies

Many mortgage borrowers will have taken out a mortgage payment protection policy at the same time that the mortgage was granted. The adviser should establish whether such a policy exists and whether a claim has been made under it. Quite often the terms of such a policy are onerous, but late claims are still possible. The

7

adviser should consider complaining to the Financial Ombudsman Service (FOS) if an insurer refuses to pay. Complaints are dealt with at **23.3**.

1.9.2 Increasing income

In the short term, mortgage borrowers may seek contributions from other members of their family, either to make lump sum payments towards the arrears or to help them with the CMI and arrears payments.

A claim can be made to the DWP for SMI, which provides help towards mortgage interest payments and may be available if the borrower receives certain benefits.

There are several other ways that borrowers can increase their income, minimise mortgage payments and schedule other debts, which are dealt with in **Chapter 19**. In an appropriate case, specialist advice from a debt councillor may be obtained, for example from the National Debtline (**www.nationaldebtline.co.uk**).

1.9.3 Government help schemes

The government has created two schemes that may be of benefit to borrowers, which are dealt with in greater detail in **Chapter 20**:

- the Mortgage Rescue Scheme, which is aimed at vulnerable households facing repossession (i.e. those in 'priority need' for the purposes of the homelessness legislation); and
- the Homeowners Mortgage Support Scheme, which is aimed at those in work with a large, but temporary reduction in their income, and enables part of the interest payments under the mortgage to be deferred for up to two years. This scheme was closed to new applicants from 21 April 2011, but may be of importance to existing participants.

1.9.4 Negotiating with the lender

One of the quickest ways of reducing mortgage costs is to convert a capital repayment mortgage to an interest-only mortgage. Whilst this has the disadvantage that the capital borrowed under the mortgage does not reduce over time, there can be substantial savings in the CMI if payments are on an interest-only basis. Equally, in an appropriate case, lenders may be persuaded to capitalise the arrears, by which they are added to the existing capital loaned and the CMI is recalculated, in effect spreading the repayment of those arrears over the remaining period of the mortgage, usually at a beneficial interest rate.

In appropriate cases the mortgage borrower should apply to the lender immediately seeking these changes to the existing mortgage arrangements.

Some lenders will also agree to give borrowers a 'payment holiday', but usually only where it can be demonstrated that a reduction in income is a temporary problem, which will soon be resolved.

1.10   FINDING TIME TO PERMIT SALE OF THE PROPERTY

If the mortgage borrower's financial position is such that the only practical step is to sell the property on the open market, immediate instructions must be given to estate agents to put the property on the market, and to solicitors to facilitate any sale. Evidence of both will be needed at a future hearing if a court is to be persuaded to grant time for a sale to go ahead.

At the same time, it is often very helpful to have an up-to-date market valuation of the property concerned, to establish the level of equity that currently exists.

1.11   NEGOTIATING WITH THE LENDER

All negotiations with the lender should be pursued vigorously. Advisers should make reference to the appropriate paragraphs of the Mortgage Pre-Action Protocol and to the Financial Services Authority's (FSA) 'Mortgages and Home Finance: Conduct of Business sourcebook' (MCOB) which, amongst other things, requires lenders to:

- deal fairly with customers in arrears;
- issue possession proceedings only where all other reasonable attempts have failed;
- maintain adequate records; and
- provide customers with information.

Fuller details of MCOB will be found in **Chapter 5** and of the Protocol in **Chapter 7**.

If a repayment proposal can be made to a lender, which includes the CMI and a contribution to the mortgage arrears (usually at least the minimum *Norgan* amount) lenders will sometimes agree to adjourn proceedings either generally or on terms. If any such agreement is obtained, it must be in writing and a joint application to the court by letter for a general adjournment can be made.

Lenders will often offer terms provided their interest is secured by means of a suspended possession order. As a rule, advisers should seek to avoid the making of any possession order, even a suspended one, where at all possible. A general adjournment on terms is infinitely better. However, in a difficult case a mortgage borrower may be advised that a suspended possession order is the best outcome that can be obtained, although it represents a step closer to eviction if the terms of any suspension are breached (subject always to an application for a stay of execution of a warrant for possession – see **Chapter 14**).

1.12   PRESENTATION OF EVIDENCE

At the first or adjourned possession hearing the lender will give evidence by witness statement, which must have a statement of truth. However, there is no requirement for the borrower to do so. All judges should accept informal oral evidence at the hearing: see Nourse LJ in *Cheltenham & Gloucester Building Society* v. *Grant* (1994) 26 HLR 703, CA, who stated (at 707):

> It is not the function of this court to lay down rigid rules as to how busy district and county court judges should satisfy themselves of what they have to be satisfied for the purposes of sections 36 and 8. It must be possible for them to act without evidence, especially where, as here, the mortgagor is present in court and available to be questioned and no objection to the reception of informal material is made by the mortgagee. Clearly, it will sometimes be prudent for the mortgagor to put in an affidavit before the hearing.

Having said this, if time permits, a witness statement can usefully be prepared, to set out for the judge:

- a brief history of the past problem;
- the change in the borrower's circumstances, which has occurred (or which will occur soon) to enable the borrower to remedy the default; and
- the offer made to the court in relation to payment of mortgage arrears.

The above points should include details of the property, its occupants, the borrower's financial circumstances, the value of the property concerned and therefore any equity.

Whether or not a witness statement is prepared judges usually ask for documentary evidence of payments that the borrower has made, income that the borrower receives from work, a valuation of the property and, where the borrower is trying to sell the property, evidence of the sale transaction. The better the documentary evidence, the more convincing will be the mortgage borrower's case.

1.13 PROCEDURAL DEFICIENCIES

Lenders have many hurdles to jump in order to obtain possession of a property. Numerous procedural defects are often found in the court documents. These are detailed in **Chapter 6**, but advisers should be aware of the most common defects:

- failure to comply with an aspect of the Mortgage Pre-Action Protocol;
- an incomplete or inadequate schedule of mortgage arrears;
- failure to notify the occupiers of the property concerned within five days of receiving notification of the hearing by the court;
- inaccurate names, addresses and details in the particulars of claim; and
- conflicting details or figures in the court documents and the witness statement.

Advisers should make use of any procedural deficiencies, regardless of whether or not prejudice to the borrower can be shown. Judges are usually strict in ensuring that the court procedures are adhered to and that contradictions in court documents are resolved. Although in a serious case a judge may be persuaded to dismiss possession proceedings due to deficiencies, it is more likely that the judge will justify a (further) adjournment. For case studies relating to procedural deficiencies and the adjournments that may result from them, see **Appendix F1**.

1.14 THE HEARING

In every case the adviser is seeking to persuade the court to exercise one of its powers in AJA 1970, s.36, set out above and in greater detail in **Chapter 8**.

The considerations for the court are set out in *Cheltenham & Gloucester Building Society* v. *Norgan* (above) and are dealt with in detail at **8.3.6** onwards. However, the court will usually be most concerned with the following considerations:

- How much can the mortgage borrower reasonably afford to pay, both now and in the future?
- If the mortgage borrower has a temporary difficulty in meeting their obligations, how long is the difficulty likely to last?
- How much remains of the original term of the mortgage?
- Is it reasonable to expect the lender to recoup the arrears of interest over the remaining term of the mortgage, or within a shorter period?

Some judges claim not to be interested in the reason why the arrears have accumulated, but that is also one of the considerations highlighted by the Court of Appeal in *Norgan*. This should therefore form a significant part of any representations to the court, along with an explanation of the changing circumstances (now or in the future) that will persuade the court that the problem has been resolved (wholly or in part).

The court is also concerned with the amount of equity in a property to ensure that lenders have proper security if the court exercises its powers under AJA 1970, s.36. Advisers should aim for a general adjournment wherever possible, always accepting that the court may prefer to make a possession order, albeit suspended.

1.15 ALL MONIES CHARGES

An 'all monies charge' secures money loaned, for example on bank overdrafts or personal loans, which are repayable on demand. Payment is not deferred by instalments, as in a normal house purchase mortgage.

Although AJA 1970, s.36 still applies where the loan is secured on a dwelling-house, the court's powers are more limited than for instalment mortgages, because all monies charges do not benefit from the amendments brought about by AJA 1973, s.8. In effect, this means that, while retaining the power to adjourn proceedings, stay or suspend execution of the judgment or postpone the date for delivery of possession, the court may do so only if there is a reasonable prospect of the borrower paying off the entire debt within a reasonable period.

When deciding what is a reasonable term, the court will look at all the circumstances of the case. Unlike an instalment mortgage, there is no contractual term to consider as a starting point. The guidance from the courts is that the adjournment should be 'for a short time' to give the borrower time to pay off the lender in full or otherwise satisfy the lender: see *Birmingham Citizens Permanent Building Society* v. *Caunt* (above).

In addition, as with all possession proceedings, the court has power to adjourn a hearing for procedural reasons, for example if a party is temporarily unable to attend due to illness. Fuller details are found at **8.4** and in **Chapter 9**.

1.16   REGULATED AGREEMENTS UNDER THE CONSUMER CREDIT ACT 1974

The statutory regime which relates to regulated agreements under CCA 1974 is quite different to the regime under AJA 1970 and 1973, which relate to instalment mortgages.

Regulated agreements relevant to this book are credit agreements whereby traders lend money to individuals and are secured against that person's property. In practice, most residential first charge mortgages for the purchase of land are not regulated agreements and nor are top-up loans, for example for the improvement of a dwelling. However, most second or third charges will be regulated agreements under CCA 1974.

Where the agreement was made before 6 April 2008, a financial limit of £25,000 applies. Fuller details are set out in **Chapter 10**.

1.16.1   The need for proper execution

So far as advisers are concerned, the loan agreement will usually specify whether or not the arrangement is a regulated agreement. Regulated agreements that have not been properly executed and are not in the prescribed form will be enforceable only with the court's permission (which means that they may well be unenforceable).

1.16.2   Time orders

Before a regulated agreement can be enforced, the lender must serve a default notice on the borrower. The receipt of a default notice entitles the borrower to apply to the court for a 'time order'. This is an order which the court can make rescheduling the payment of money under the agreement over any length of time (whether it is greater than or less than the term of the original agreement).

Where an adviser considers that a time order may be appropriate, the court should be asked for an adjournment so that an application in the standard form may be made and for a witness statement in support to be filed, with a skeleton argument. Fuller details are found in **Chapter 10**.

1.16.3 Additional powers of the court

In addition to the power of the court to make a time order, the court has wide powers to interfere with regulated agreements that constitute an 'extortionate credit bargain' where the agreement was made before 6 April 2007 (and completed before 6 April 2008), or where the agreement amounts to an 'unfair relationship' at any time (including agreements made before 6 April 2007). The court's powers include setting aside obligations imposed on the debtor and altering interest rates. Fuller details are found in **Chapter 10**.

Once again, an adviser should seek an adjournment to enable a defence to be filed.

The possibility that any regulated agreement might contravene these provisions could be raised at the same time as seeking an adjournment to make an application for a time order.

1.17 UNFAIR CONTRACT TERMS

The Unfair Terms in Consumer Contracts Regulations 1999, SI 1999/2083 apply to standard mortgage terms. Fuller details are set out in **Chapter 3**, but advisers should be aware that:

- an unfair term is not binding on a borrower;
- a term may be unfair if it is not in plain English; and
- a term may be unfair if it causes a significant imbalance in the party's rights and obligations to the detriment of the consumer.

Decided cases have applied to the calculation of interest rates and redemption terms and conditions. Once again, an adviser should seek an adjournment to enable a defence to be filed raising any arguments that a term is unfair.

1.18 LAST-MINUTE STAYS OF EXECUTION

All of the powers open to the court on the hearing of a possession claim are available to the court on an application for a stay of execution of a warrant for possession.

The adviser should not hesitate to make an application for a stay of execution, even if there have been several such applications made previously. The adviser will look for evidence as to why the terms of a suspended order had not been adhered to and to show that the borrower can now make the proposed payments. If time permits, a witness statement is helpful, but otherwise the borrower can give oral evidence.

The court is often impressed by serious attempts to pay over time, even if they fall short of the amounts previously ordered.

Fuller details are found in **Chapter 14**.

1.19 TENANTS OF MORTGAGE BORROWERS

The Mortgage Repossessions (Protection of Tenants etc) Act 2010 offers protection to tenants of rental properties whose landlord has both defaulted on the mortgage and not notified the lender that the property is being let (i.e. an 'unauthorised tenancy'). The Act:

- gives the court power to postpone the delivery of a possession order, and to stay or suspend the execution of an existing possession order; and
- ensures that the tenant is given notice of the possession order before its execution.

Details of how to make such an application will be found in **Chapter 24**.

1.20 SUMMARY

In the majority of cases advisers should attempt to persuade the court not to make any kind of possession order in mortgage possession proceedings. It is not always possible to do this, but advisers can achieve remarkable success in obtaining adjournments through a combination of:

- focusing on failings by the lender to comply with myriad requirements of procedural regulations and substantive law;
- identifying and effecting change in a mortgage borrower's circumstances, through various means; and
- direct and assertive advocacy before the judge, with the benefit of a well-prepared case.

CHAPTER 2

Types of mortgage

2.1 OVERVIEW

Mortgages come in different forms, but they all essentially provide a lender with security for money loaned to the borrower. In the typical residential mortgage transaction, the borrower will receive money for the purchase or improvement of property, such as a house or flat, and personally contract with the lender to repay the debt, usually by instalments over time.

2.1.1 Creation of security over the property

In return for the loan, the mortgage borrower will create a security over the property (or another property) in favour of the lender. If the borrower redeems (i.e. pays off) the loan, the security will be removed from the property. However, if the borrower defaults on the instalment payments, the lender will attempt to enforce its security by repossessing the property and selling it to recover the money loaned.

The security may be by way of legal mortgage or equitable mortgage.

2.2 LEGAL MORTGAGES

A legal mortgage of land or an interest in land may take one of two forms:

- a mortgage by demise, where the lender becomes the owner of the mortgaged property until the borrower repays the loan, at which point the property is returned to the borrower; or
- a mortgage by legal charge, where the borrower remains the owner of the mortgaged property, but the lender acquires rights over the property to enforce the security if need be, for example by taking possession of and/or selling the property.

A mortgage by legal charge is by far the more common type of legal mortgage and, since the Land Registration Act (LRA) 2002, the only type of legal mortgage available for registered land: see LRA 2002, s.23.

2.2.1 Requirement for a deed

A legal mortgage of land or an interest in land must be created by deed (Law of Property Act (LPA) 1925, s.52(1)).

In the case of unregistered land the mortgage may either be by a demise for a term of years absolute, subject to a provision for cesser on redemption (i.e. the demise comes to an end when the loan is paid off) or by a charge by deed expressed to be by way of legal mortgage (LPA 1925, ss.85(1) and 86(1)).

Where the legal mortgage is for a term of years absolute, the demise is deemed to be a term of 3,000 years from the date of the mortgage, in the case of a first or only mortgage (LPA 1925, s.85(2)).

In the case of registered land the deed will create a charge 'expressed to be by way of legal mortgage' or will 'charge the estate at law with the payment of money' (LRA 2002, s.23(1)).

2.3 EQUITABLE MORTGAGES

An equitable mortgage may arise:

- by a mortgage of an equitable interest where, for example, one of two or more legal owners of a property grants a mortgage over their beneficial (or equitable) share in the property; or
- where the circumstances fall short of the creation of a legal mortgage, for example if the transaction to create a legal mortgage has not been completed, or a mortgage was entered into which fails to comply with the formalities for a legal mortgage, because of some defect in the mortgage documents or procedures (see **Chapter 3**).

Any mortgage that does not comply with the requirements for a legal mortgage will be an equitable mortgage, which is considered to be a contract to create a legal mortgage.

So far as the lender is concerned, there are important differences between the two. Whereas a legal mortgage properly entered into will automatically give the lender certain rights to enforce the security, for example by possession and sale, a lender with an equitable mortgage will need to apply to the court for consent to an order for sale.

2.3.1 Contracts for the sale or other disposition of land to be in writing

Prior to 27 September 1989 the deposit of the title deeds of property could also give a lender good security in equity, although there had to be additional proof beyond the mere deposit of the deeds to show an intention to create a charge.

However, since 27 September 1989, a contract made for a mortgage of or charge on land can only be made in writing, and only by incorporating all the terms, which the parties have expressly agreed in one document or, where contracts are exchanged in each (Law of Property (Miscellaneous Provisions) Act 1989, s.2). In addition, the document (or one of them if documents are exchanged) must be signed by or on behalf of each party to the contract.

Section 2 is limited to contracts for the creation or sale of interests in land and it is not concerned with documents that actually create or transfer such interests, such as an actual mortgage: see *Helden* v. *Strathmore Ltd* [2011] EWCA Civ 452.

2.4 IMMEDIATE RIGHT TO POSSESSION

A legal mortgage by demise operates as a transfer of the ownership of the land to the mortgage lender for a term of 3,000 years from the date of the mortgage, in the case of a first or only mortgage (LPA 1925, s.85(2)).

Where a legal mortgage of land is created by a charge by deed expressed to be by way of legal mortgage, the lender will have the same protection, powers and remedies as if a mortgage term of 3,000 years had been created in favour of the mortgage lender: LPA 1925, s.87(1) and, where the land is registered land, LRA 1925, s.27(1).

The effect of the above provisions is that the lender becomes entitled to immediate possession of the borrower's property at any time after the execution of the mortgage, by virtue of the estate that he has acquired. As Harman J famously observed in *Four-Maids Ltd* v. *Dudley Marshall (Properties) Ltd* [1957] Ch 317 at 320:

> The mortgagee may go into possession before the ink is dry on the mortgage unless there is something in the contract express or by necessary implication, whereby he has contracted himself out of that right.

Typically, the modern bank or building society mortgage does contain such a provision, whereby borrowers are entitled to retain possession of the property so long as they pay the monthly instalment repayments. However, if the borrower falls into arrears the full amount of the secured indebtedness becomes payable and the lender becomes entitled to take possession.

At common law the rule was, and remains, that once the mortgage lender has become entitled to take possession the court has only a very limited power to grant the borrower any relief: see *Birmingham Citizens Permanent Building Society* v. *Caunt* [1962] Ch 883 at 912. However, the common law position is modified by the enactment of AJA 1970, s.36 (as amended), which now gives the court statutory powers in such circumstances to adjourn, to postpone or to stay or suspend execution of any possession order.

2.5 THE EQUITY OF REDEMPTION

The 'equity of redemption' is the right of the mortgage borrower to pay off the loan secured on his property. The courts lean heavily on any obstacle to this right, i.e. on any 'clog on the equity of redemption'. When the borrower has repaid the loan, the mortgage is redeemed and freed from the security.

Where the purchase of residential property is concerned, it will usually be the case that the acquisition of the legal estate by the borrower is entirely dependent upon the provision of funds by the lender. In *Abbey National Building Society* v. *Cann* [1991] 1 AC 56, HL, Lord Oliver of Aylmerton, giving the leading judgment of the court, stated (at 93):

> The reality is that the purchaser of land who relies upon a building society or bank loan for the completion of his purchase never in fact acquires anything but equity of redemption, for the land is, from the very inception, charged with the amount of the loan without which it could never have been transferred at all and it was never intended that it should be otherwise.

2.6 THE THREE MAIN TYPES OF LEGAL CHARGE

The three main types of legal charge that the adviser is likely to come across are:

- instalment mortgages;
- all monies charges; and
- regulated agreements.

2.6.1 Mortgages repayable by instalments

The bulk of mortgage claims are brought by lenders with first legal charges on property, which are repayable by instalments. In most cases these will be purchase loans secured on the house in question by way of legal mortgage.

Some mortgages will be second, third or fourth charges, where loans have been taken out by borrowers for the improvement of the property, whether by repair, alteration or enlargement. From the adviser's point of view the essential characteristics of these mortgages is that they are repayable by instalments, because this brings into play important powers of the court under AJA 1970 and AJA 1973.

There are two main types of mortgage repayable by instalments: capital repayment mortgages and interest-only or endowment mortgages.

Capital repayment mortgages

The main feature of a capital repayment mortgage is that the monthly instalment payment includes repayment of both interest accrued and part of the capital sum borrowed. At the start of the mortgage, most of the repayments will comprise interest on the capital sum borrowed. As the capital sum reduces slowly over time, so the interest accrued each month reduces. The instalment payments gradually comprise a greater and greater proportion of capital repayment to interest accrued. The repayments are calculated so that the whole of the capital sum and thus the whole of the mortgage will be repaid by the end of the mortgage term.

Interest-only or endowment mortgages

As its name suggests, an interest-only mortgage involves the regular repayment only of the interest accrued each month, and not of any part of the capital sum. As a result, interest-only mortgages tend to be cheaper to maintain than capital repayment mortgages. However, the borrower will still owe the full capital sum at the end of the mortgage term and needs a way to pay this off at that stage.

The most common financial vehicle to achieve this is the endowment policy. This is a life insurance policy designed to pay a lump sum after a specified period of time, when it 'matures'. The borrower has to pay the insurance premiums towards the policy each month in addition to the interest on the mortgage. At the end of the mortgage term, the endowment policy will mature and, in theory, should provide a sufficient lump sum to pay off the capital that was originally borrowed from the lender.

In recent years endowment policies have fallen out of favour, as they often failed to realise sufficient money for this purpose on maturity, leaving the borrower with a remaining debt owed to the lender.

It is usually possible for a borrower to change his mortgage from an interest-only to a capital repayment basis. The opposite is also possible, but increasingly lenders place restrictions on doing so, because of the risk that the capital will not be repaid at the end of the mortgage term. Further details will be found in **Chapter 19**.

2.6.2 All monies charges

'All monies charges' also provide security to a lender for the repayment of a debt owed by the borrower, whether by loan or more commonly by way of bank overdraft. However, the crucial difference to a mortgage repayable by instalments is that the all monies charge is repayable on demand.

This means that although the lender may by concession have set up an arrangement for the repayment of the debt by instalments, the lender can bring that arrangement to an end at any time and can demand that the full amount of the loan is repaid at once. This distinction is important, because the court's powers to intervene in possession proceedings are much more limited and different considerations must be taken into account: see **Chapter 9**.

2.6.3 Regulated agreements

CCA 1974, as amended by CCA 2006, regulates the provision of most consumer credit to individuals. Many such credit agreements are secured by a legal charge on the borrower's property. Such agreements will be regulated by CCA 1974 provided they are within prescribed credit limits and are not exempt from regulation.

Prescribed limits

The prescribed limits are:

- £15,000 if the agreement is dated before 1 May 1998;
- £25,000 if the agreement is dated before 6 April 2008;
- no financial limit after 6 April 2008.

Exemptions

Amongst those exempt from regulation under CCA 1974 are:

- first charge mortgages, or home purchase plans, within the meaning of the Financial Services and Markets Act 2000 and regulated by the FSA (CCA 1974, s.16(6C));
- some second charge mortgages, depending upon the nature of the agreement and the identity of the lender (for example, an agreement where the creditor is a housing authority and the agreement is secured by a land mortgage of a dwelling) (CCA 1974, s.16(6A));
- business lending over £25,000, where the loan is wholly or predominantly for business purposes, although business lending up to £25,000 remains regulated (CCA 1974, s.16B; Consumer Credit (Exempt Agreements) Order 2007, SI 2007/1168, art. 6);
- lending to 'high net worth' individuals, whose net income exceeds £150,000 or whose net assets exceed £500,000 (CCA 1974, s.16A; 2007 Order, arts 2–5); and
- certain consumer credit agreements relating to investment properties – typically 'buy-to-let' agreements, where less than 40 per cent of the land is used, or is intended to be used, as or in connection with a dwelling by the debtor or by a person connected with the debtor (for example, a spouse or close relative) (CCA 1974, s.16C, as inserted by the Legislative Reform (Consumer Credit) Order 2008, SI 2008/2826).

It will be seen that most main first mortgages for the purchase of land are exempt agreements and therefore not covered by CCA 1974. Top-up loans from the same lender, which are used for the improvement of a dwelling, including repair, alteration or enlargement, are also exempt.

The court's powers under AJA 1970 and AJA 1973 do not apply where an agreement is regulated by CCA 1974. However, CCA 1974 provides separate and distinct powers to the court, which include the making of a 'time order' and reopening agreements which constitute an 'unfair relationship'. These are dealt with in greater detail in **Chapter 10**.

Mortgage documentation

Whatever type of mortgage is being considered, the adviser will want to look carefully at the documentation to ensure that it complies with legal requirements. The documentation usually makes it clear if the loan falls within CCA 1974. Whilst advisers can usually rely upon this, they should be aware that documentation can sometimes misstate the appropriate legal position.

Advisers will also want to check that any CCA 1974 secured loan agreement complies with the strict provisions of CCA 1974 as to the form and content of documentation. A failure to comply with the provisions may render the agreement unenforceable, so that a lender would not then be able to obtain a possession order against the borrower: see **Chapter 10**.

2.7 MORTGAGES REGULATED BY THE RENT ACT 1977

Advisers are unlikely to come across mortgages regulated by the Rent Act (RA) 1977, but should be aware that they exist.

Such regulated mortgages are legal mortgages of land consisting of or including a dwelling-house let on or subject to a regulated tenancy, which is binding on the lender.

The relevant provisions are contained within RA 1977, ss.129, 131 and 132. They apply to regulated mortgages created before the 'relevant date', being 8 December 1965, or such later date as specified in RA 1977, s.129, depending on the precise circumstances of the case.

2.7.1 Application to the court

In relation to RA 1977 regulated mortgages, a mortgage borrower can apply to the court to mitigate hardship in certain circumstances (RA 1977, s.132). The application has to be made within 21 days, or such longer time as the court may allow, after the occurrence of one of the following events:

- an increase in the rate of interest under the mortgage; or
- a reduction in the registered rent in respect of the tenancy of the property; or
- the lender demanding repayment of the principal money or taking steps to enforce the security.

Application is to the county court, unless the mortgage borrower makes an application in pursuance of any step taken by the mortgagee in the High Court, in which case the application is to the High Court (RA 1977, s.132(6)).

Although the CPR do not deal with such applications, it is suggested that claimants may use the Part 8 procedure, since they will be seeking 'the court's decision on a question which is unlikely to involve a substantial dispute of fact' (CPR rule 8.1(2)(a)). The application would therefore be made on Form N208 – Claim Form (CPR Part 8).

2.7.2 Powers of the court

If the court is satisfied on any such application that, by reason of the event in question, the borrower would suffer financial hardship unless relief were given, the court may by order make such provision as it thinks appropriate:

- limiting the rate of interest;
- extending the time for the repayment of the principal money; or
- otherwise varying the terms of the mortgage or imposing any limitation or condition on the exercise of any right or remedy in respect thereof.

2.8 HOME PURCHASE PLANS (OR 'ISLAMIC MORTGAGES')

A 'home purchase plan' provides a consumer with finance for buying a home and to this extent it serves the same purpose as an ordinary mortgage. However, the home purchase plan avoids the payment of interest, which is contrary to Islamic law. Instead, the plan creates a sale and lease arrangement between the home purchaser and the firm providing the finance, known as a 'home purchase provider' (the provider).

2.8.1 Conditions to be met

The plan must meet several conditions:

- the provider buys a qualifying interest in land or an undivided share of a qualifying interest in land;
- the interest is held on trust for the provider and the purchaser as beneficial tenants in common;
- there is an obligation on the purchaser to buy the interest bought by the provider during the course of or at the end of a specified period; and
- the purchaser or an individual who is a beneficiary of a trust where the purchaser is a trustee, or a related person, is entitled under the arrangement to occupy at least 40 per cent of the land in question as or in connection with a dwelling during that period and intends to do so.

2.8.2 Regulation

Lenders who offer home purchase plans are regulated by the FSA. Such plans are expressly covered by the 'Mortgages and Home Finance: Conduct of Business source book' (MCOB), which forms part of the 'Business Standards' section of the FSA Handbook: see **Chapter 5** for fuller details.

2.8.3 How the plans operate

There are two main types of home purchase plan: the *Ijara* and the *Musharaka* (or 'diminishing' *Musharaka*), which are described below. Details of a third type of plan, the *Murabaha*, are dealt with at the end of this section, as its features are different.

Although the home purchaser typically makes a 10 per cent contribution to the purchase price, the property itself is bought by the provider (usually a bank or other lender) on behalf of the borrower. The provider will be registered as the proprietor of the freehold title at the Land Registry.

The property is then held on trust for the purchaser, who will take a lease of the property from the provider for an agreed number of years. The purchaser will be registered as the proprietor of the leasehold title and will grant a first legal charge to the provider, against that title.

The purchaser will make monthly repayments over the agreed term. The repayments consist of a small proportion of the sum borrowed and a payment of rent to the provider in exchange for the purchaser or a member of their family living in the property. At the end of the term the purchaser becomes the legal owner of the property provided that all required payments have been made. At this stage, the freehold title to the property will be transferred to the purchaser's name and the legal charge removed from the leasehold title.

The arrangements surrounding home purchase plans tend to be more complex than conventional mortgages. As a result, home purchase plans also tend to be more expensive.

Although home purchase plans vary considerably in detail according to the provider, the main differences between plans are outlined below.

The Ijara ('lease-to-own')

Under the *Ijara* home purchase plan monthly repayments are fixed over a typical 25-year term. In addition the purchaser makes monthly rent payments, which are adjusted each year. A minimum 10 per cent 'deposit' or advance contribution towards the purchase price is usually required at the outset. Purchasers are often allowed to make lump sum payments, which go to reduce future monthly repayments.

The purchaser's share of the property remains the same throughout the term, regardless of the payments made. Purchasers only become the legal owner once they have paid the last instalment.

The (diminishing) Musharaka ('reducing partnership')

As with the *Ijara*, under the *Musharaka* the monthly repayments are fixed, but typically over a shorter period of 15 rather than 25 years. The 'deposit' or contribution to the purchase price will also be larger, at around 20 per cent of the purchase price. The property belongs to the provider until the purchaser has paid the agreed 'total amount repayable' and, once again, the purchaser has to pay rent in return for living in the property during the term.

The *Musharaka* differs from the *Ijara* in that each of the monthly payments to the provider results in the purchaser acquiring an extra share of the property, so that the purchaser's share increases and the provider's share decreases each month, until the purchaser owns the whole property. As the purchaser's share in the property increases, so the rent that the purchaser pays for the use of the provider's share will decrease.

Murabaha ('cost-plus sale with deferred repayment')

The third type of home purchase plan is the *Murabaha*. Under this plan the property is purchased by the provider and then immediately either sold to the purchaser and registered in the purchaser's name (in a second transaction at a higher price), or it is registered in the name of a trust with the sale between the purchaser and the provider being recorded in the *Murabaha* contract.

The first payment to the provider is made on the day of completion and is the purchaser's initial contribution, being an amount often between 17 and 35 per cent of the purchase price. Payments for the balance of the capital borrowed are then fixed for the rest of the payment term, usually a much shorter period of 5 to 15 years, though longer periods are possible.

2.8.4 Protecting the purchaser's interests

The home purchase plan should make provision to protect the purchaser's interest in the property. This includes the purchaser's right to occupy the property throughout the term of the plan, in the event that the provider sells any of its obligations or rights under the plan (including its legal interest in the property) to a third party, or the provider goes into liquidation.

Purchasers should make sure that the lease granting them the right to live in the property has been properly registered with the Land Registry or they may lose their right to live there.

2.8.5 Possession proceedings

Should the purchaser breach any of the terms of the plan, particularly but not limited to those relating to payments, then the purchaser faces the risk of losing his or her right to stay in the property. Where purchasers have financial difficulties, they may fall behind both in the payment of the monthly contribution to the purchase price and in relation to the monthly payment of rent. In the case of such default, the powers of the lender will depend on the terms of the contract with the purchaser.

Mortgage Pre-Action Protocol

As well as falling under the FSA's MCOB (see **2.8.2**), home purchase plans are expressly covered by the provisions of the Mortgage Pre-Action Protocol, even though they differ from conventional mortgage products. Where purchasers of home purchase plans fall into arrears, they should be accorded the same treatment under the Protocol as a normal mortgage borrower: see **Chapter 7**.

Relevant documentation

As there are likely to be several related agreements governing the relationship between provider and purchaser, advisers should obtain copies at the earliest opportunity, together with office copy entries of the relevant titles. The documentation may include:

- an offer letter setting out the terms and conditions upon which the offer was made;
- an *Ijara*, *Musharaka* or *Murabaha* agreement (according to the type of plan used);
- a lease agreement; and
- a legal charge.

Advisers are referred to **Chapter 3** in relation to potential defences that may be available in relation to possession claims. In particular, advisers may wish to consider the comments of Laws LJ in *Ladjadj* v. *Bank of Scotland* [2000] EWCA Civ 21, [2000] 2 All ER (Comm) 583 about confusing contractual documentation (see **3.3**) and the provisions of the Unfair Terms in Consumer Contracts Regulations 1999, SI 1999/2083 (see **3.4**).

Possession proceedings may be brought for breach of the lease and/or by way of enforcement of any charge registered against the purchaser's title. To this extent, the position of the purchaser may be similar to the borrower under a shared ownership scheme, at least in respect of the *Ijara* or *Musharaka*-type plans (see **Chapter 18**).

2.9   SHARED OWNERSHIP SCHEMES

A number of registered providers of social housing in England and registered social landlords in Wales (commonly referred to as housing associations) offer shared ownership schemes. These are part purchase, part rent schemes, where the borrower purchases part of the property and takes out a mortgage to finance the purchase, and the other part of the property is owned by the housing association. Borrowers pay mortgage payments on the share that they own to the lender, and rent payments to the housing association for the part which they do not own.

The arrangement allows for 'staircasing' whereby borrowers can increase or decrease the share of the property that they own, with a corresponding decrease or increase in their rental payments.

Problems arise where borrowers fall into financial difficulties. The borrower may then face possession proceedings by the lender for non-payment of the mortgage and/or proceedings by the housing association for non-payment of the rent. Further details are found in **Chapter 18**.

CHAPTER 3

Defences

3.1 OVERVIEW

Human rights defences are dealt with in **Chapter 17**. It is uncommon for an adviser to come across other substantial defences to a mortgage possession action. However, the adviser needs to be aware of circumstances which may mean that the mortgage is not binding on a defendant. This will entail consideration of the facts surrounding the creation of the mortgage and the associated documentation, in the light of those facts.

Wherever a substantive defence is identified, the adviser will aim to file and serve a detailed defence, and obtain any necessary time for this purpose. A successful defence to a mortgage claim on one of these substantive grounds will prevent a possession order being made and may result in some or all of the loan being irrecoverable from the borrower. A precedent defence and counterclaim, which can be adapted as necessary, will be found in **Appendix E2**.

3.2 VOID AND VOIDABLE MORTGAGES

A void mortgage has no legal effect. This will be the case where the mortgage deed lacks an essential element, such as identifiable premises. Where the mortgage is void, the lender will not have a right to possession if the borrower defaults. The lender may be able to obtain a money judgment for the amount loaned and then register it as a charge against the property. However, if the lender applies for an order for sale, the court will have a wide discretion as to whether to grant the application.

A mortgage is voidable if, unlike a void mortgage, it has legal effect but it may be avoided by one or other of the parties. Situations where a mortgage may be voidable are where there has been some misrepresentation, a mistake, undue influence or duress, fraud or where one of the parties is legally incapable of contracting (for example due to unsoundness of mind). If the mortgage contract does not comply with requirements of a statute, then it may also be voidable. The most compelling example would be a failure to comply with the strict requirements of CCA 1974.

Individual clauses in the mortgage agreement may not be binding on a borrower, where they constitute 'unfair terms' under the Unfair Terms in Consumer Contracts Regulations (UTCCR) 1999, SI 1999/2803 (see **3.4**).

In practice, the adviser will most commonly come across situations where:

- the borrower did not sign the mortgage deed;
- the borrower signed the mortgage deed, but only because of undue pressure from someone else (typically, a spouse or partner, or mortgage adviser, but not limited to these categories); and
- there are technical deficiencies in mortgage deed/unfair terms.

3.2.1 The borrower did not sign the mortgage deed

Where the adviser examines mortgage documentation and discovers that the borrower has not signed the mortgage, it may be unenforceable as against the borrower.

Legal mortgages

Since the coming into force of LPA 1925, s.85, a legal mortgage can only be created by a demise for a term of years absolute or by a charge by deed expressed to be by way of legal mortgage. Accordingly, the document creating the legal charge must be signed by the mortgage borrower.

Section 1 of the Law of Property (Miscellaneous Provisions) Act (LP(MP)A) 1989 adds that an instrument shall not be a deed unless it makes it clear on its face that it is intended to be a deed by the person making it and is validly executed as a deed by that person. The person making the deed must sign it in the presence of at least one witness.

Equitable mortgages

Until 27 September 1989 an equitable mortgage (which commonly is a transaction which falls short of the formal requirements of the legal mortgage) could be created by the deposit of the title deeds with the mortgage lender.

Since that date a contract for the sale or other disposition of an interest in land can only be made in writing (LP(MP)A 1989, s.2). The document concerned must incorporate all the terms which the parties have expressly agreed and it must be signed by or on behalf of each party to the contract (though more than one document may be signed where contracts are exchanged between the parties).

3.2.2 Technical deficiencies in the mortgage deed

Similarly, if any essential ingredient in the mortgage deed is missing, for example the identification of the property or the operative clauses of the deed, that may also afford an opportunity to the borrower to challenge the enforceability of the mortgage.

However, essential terms may be incorporated into a document by reference to another document (LP(MP)A 1989, s.2(2)).

3.2.3 Requirements of the Consumer Credit Act 1974

A failure to comply with strict requirements of CCA 1974 may render the mortgage unenforceable. Regulated agreements and their requirements are dealt with in detail in **Chapter 10**, together with defences which may be applicable to possession claims brought in respect of them. Precedent defences will be found in **Appendices E9** and **E10**.

3.2.4 Undue influence

Over recent decades there have been numerous cases before the courts where a mortgage borrower has sought to defend possession proceedings on the basis that the mortgage deed had been signed under the undue influence of another party. Perhaps the most well-known leading case is the House of Lords decision in *Barclays Bank plc* v. *O'Brien* [1994] 1 AC 180.

In this case husband and wife were joint owners of the matrimonial home. The husband offered a guarantee to the bank in respect of the debts of a company in which he was interested. Mr O'Brien falsely represented to his wife that the charge was to secure only £60,000 and that even this liability would be discharged in a short time when the house was remortgaged. In reality the potential liability was more than double this amount.

Mrs O'Brien signed a legal charge at the bank's premises securing those debts against the matrimonial home. She was given no explanation of the effect of the documents and was not told to take independent advice. She did not read the documents, but simply signed the legal charge. She was not given a copy of the guarantee. Although she was effectively acting as a surety for her husband's debts, the nature of the transaction was not explained to her.

When the bank claimed an order for possession of the matrimonial home, Mrs O'Brien raised a defence that the bank was on notice that her conduct during the transaction was a result of her husband's undue influence.

In giving the judgment of the court that there had been undue influence in this case, Lord Browne-Wilkinson said (at 196):

> Therefore in my judgment a creditor is put on inquiry when a wife offers to stand surety for her husband's debts by the combination of two factors: (a) the transaction is on its face not to the financial advantage of the wife; and (b) there is a substantial risk in transactions of that kind that, in procuring the wife to act as surety, the husband has committed a legal or equitable wrong that entitles the wife to set aside the transaction.

He continued that:

It follows that unless the creditor who is put on inquiry takes reasonable steps to satisfy himself that the wife's agreement to stand surety has been properly obtained, the creditor will have constructive notice of the wife's rights.

The House of Lords held that the bank should have been put on inquiry as to the circumstances in which Mrs O'Brien had agreed to stand surety for the debt of her husband. There was a failure to warn her about the risks she was undertaking by signing the documents and a failure to recommend that she take legal advice. In the circumstances the bank (having failed to take reasonable steps) was fixed with constructive notice of the wrongful misrepresentations made by Mr O'Brien. Mrs O'Brien was therefore entitled as against the bank to set aside the legal charge on the matrimonial home.

3.2.5 Loan to husband and wife

In the case of *CIBC Mortgages plc* v. *Pitt* [1994] 1 AC 200, a judgment was given on the same day by the same appellate committee of the House of Lords as *O'Brien* but with a different outcome. Money had been advanced to husband and wife jointly, pursuant to an application for a loan signed by both of them. So far as the bank was concerned, the loan was being made for joint purposes, to purchase a holiday home. In reality, however, Mr Pitt had applied pressure on Mrs Pitt amounting to actual undue influence to borrow money on the security of the house and to use a loan to buy shares on the stock market. In this case, the bank was not put on inquiry, because the bank was not aware that the loan was being made for the husband's purposes, as distinct from their joint purposes.

3.2.6 Father and son

In *Lloyd's Bank Ltd* v. *Bundy* [1975] QB 326 the defendant mortgaged his farm in order to guarantee the debts of his son's company. The guarantee and charge documents were signed at the farm, on the first visit by the bank manager, without the defendant being advised or given the opportunity to take independent legal advice.

Setting aside the possession order, the court noted that the relationship between the bank and the defendant was one of trust and confidence. However, the bank failed in that trust and had sought further security for the company's debt purely for its own benefit. Similarly, the relationship between father and son was such that the son had a large amount of influence on his father. It was clear that had the defendant been advised to take independent advice, he would not have allowed the bank 'to have swept up his sole remaining asset' for nothing.

3.2.7 Employee and employer

A more extreme example, which serves to show that any close relationship may give rise to undue influence arose in *Credit Lyonnais Bank Nederland NV* v. *Burch*

[1997] 1 All ER 144. In that case Miss Burch's employer persuaded Miss Burch to give a guarantee for his company's overdraft facility supported by a second charge on her one-bedroom flat. The court had no difficulty in deciding that the employer had procured the security through undue influence: the bank knew that Miss Burch was only an employee of the company, that the transaction was manifestly to her disadvantage and that all of these matters constituted notice of facts which put the bank on inquiry. Accordingly, the transaction as against the bank was set aside.

3.2.8 The evidential burden

Eight conjoined appeals relating to undue influence were decided by the House of Lords in *Royal Bank of Scotland* v. *Etridge* [2001] UKHL 44, [2002] 2 AC 773. In each case the wife had charged her interest in the home in favour of a bank as security for her husband's indebtedness or the indebtedness of company through which he carried on business. The wife later asserted that she signed the charge under the undue influence of her husband. The bank claimed an order for possession of the matrimonial home. The wife raised the defence that the bank was on notice that her concurrence in the transaction had been obtained as a result of her husband's undue influence.

The House of Lords took the opportunity to review the previous cases relating to undue influence. Their Lordships noted certain common features, none of them conclusive in themselves, such as: the close relationship between the parties, the betrayal of trust placed by one person in another and a person's dependence or vulnerability which had been exploited. While disadvantage is not a necessary ingredient of the cause of action, the issue is likely only to arise when, in some respect, the transaction was disadvantageous either from the outset or as matters turned out.

The burden of proving an allegation of undue influence rests upon the person who claims to have been wronged. Proof that the complainant placed trust and confidence in the other party in relation to the management of the complainant's financial affairs, coupled with a transaction which calls for explanation, will normally be sufficient, failing satisfactory evidence to the contrary to discharge the burden of proof.

At that point the evidential burden shifts to the other party to produce evidence to counter the inference that, in the absence of a satisfactory explanation, the transaction can only have been procured by undue influence.

The fact that a complainant received advice from a third party before entering into the transaction is only one of the matters that a court takes into account when weighing all the evidence.

A bank or other creditor is put on inquiry whenever a wife offers to stand surety for her husband's debt. The position is the same if the husband stands surety for his wife's debts (and presumably for civil partners). Similarly, the bank is on inquiry in the case of unmarried couples, whether heterosexual or homosexual, where the bank is aware of the relationship. Cohabitation is not essential.

Where the bank has been put on inquiry, it must take reasonable steps to bring home to the wife the risk she is running by acting as a surety and it must advise her to take independent advice.

A lender satisfies these requirements if it insists that the wife attend a private meeting with its representatives at which she is told of the extent of her liabilities as surety, warned of the risk she is running and urged to take independent legal advice. In exceptional cases the lender, to be safe, has to insist that the wife is separately advised.

The court set out the scope of the responsibilities of the solicitor who is advising the wife, listing the 'core minimum' requirements (see at [64] and [65]). The solicitor's discussion with the wife should take place at a face-to-face meeting.

3.3 UNCLEAR TERMS IN MORTGAGE DOCUMENTS

Where mortgage terms are difficult for a lay person to understand, they will be construed *contra proferentem*, i.e. any doubt or contradiction will be construed in favour of the borrower and against the lender who drafted the mortgage documents and offered them to the borrower for signature: *Ladjadj* v. *Bank of Scotland* [2000] EWCA Civ 21, [2000] 2 All ER (Comm) 583.

In that case, the lender and borrower could not agree on the level of the mortgage arrears. There was a very large discrepancy between the rival figures – £80,000 and £40,000. The borrower's appeal against a possession order was upheld, against a background of mortgage documentation being described as 'disgracefully sloppy and well capable of creating confusion'. Laws LJ added:

> ... the very fact that there are four separate contractual documents is bad enough. At some points they are by no means easy to reconcile one with another. What a lay person would be supposed to make of them I cannot begin to imagine. In such a situation I consider that the *contra proferentem* rule of construction possesses special force. I regard it as nothing short of scandalous that a major lending institution should foist this jigsaw puzzle of a contract on the borrowing public.

3.4 UNFAIR TERMS

UTCCR 1999 apply to mortgage deeds and provide that a term in a mortgage will not be binding on the borrower (referred to as 'a consumer' in the regulations) if a number of conditions are met (the regulations are reproduced in **Appendix A7**).

Date of the mortgage

The regulations revoke and replace previous regulations which came into effect in 1995. It follows that only mortgages executed on or after 1 July 1995 will benefit.

Consumers and sellers

Regulation 3 defines a 'consumer' as: 'any natural person who is acting for purposes which are outside his trade, business or profession'. A borrower who has taken out a mortgage to buy a home will therefore be a consumer for the purpose of the regulations. The situation will be less clear for a buy-to-let mortgage borrower. A person who owns perhaps one or two properties held in his own name and whose main source of income is another trade or profession might be able to argue that he is a consumer. A borrower who has several buy-to-let properties or is holding them in the name of a limited company is unlikely to have the benefit of the regulations.

In *Evans* v. *Cherrytree Finance Ltd* [2008] EWCA Civ 331 the claimant borrowed money on commercial premises with the stated purpose of paying his wife her share of a divorce settlement. He was held to be a consumer for the purposes of the regulations.

The only mortgage lender that will not be considered a 'seller' will be a natural person who lends money unconnected with trade or business; for example, parents who lend money to their son and daughter-in-law and who protect the loan by way of a charge on their house. In such circumstances UTCCR 1999 will not apply.

Core terms

Regulation 6(2) excludes terms that define the main subject matter of the contract or the 'adequacy of the price as against the goods or services supplied in exchange'. As a result the borrower cannot use UTCCR 1999 to challenge the initial interest rate or the amount of repayments in a mortgage. An important exception is where such core terms are not written in 'plain intelligible language' in which case they can be found to be unfair (UTCCR 1999, reg.6(2)).

In *Director General of Fair Trading* v. *First National Bank* [2001] UKHL 52, [2002] 1 AC 481, a term providing for default interest was held to be 'subsidiary' and not a term expressing the 'substance of the bargain'. Lord Steyn stated that the predecessor to reg. 6(2) 'must be given a restrictive interpretation' (at [34]).

Lord Steyn went on to state that 'price escalation clauses' are not core terms and are subject to the regulations: 'It would be a gaping hole in the system if such clauses were not subject to the fairness requirement.' It follows that a term providing for an increase in the interest rate is not a term relating to the 'adequacy of the price' and as such is a term which is open to challenge, if unfair. A mortgage that provides for the interest rate to increase to reflect market fluctuations is, however, likely to be fair, see below.

Fairness

Regulation 5 states that a contractual term shall be regarded as unfair if: 'contrary to the requirement of good faith, it causes a significant imbalance in the parties' rights and obligations arising under the contract, to the detriment of the consumer'.

Schedule 2 to the regulations contains an indicative and non-exhaustive list of examples of terms which may be considered unfair. The examples most likely to be relevant to advising a person in mortgage arrears are set out in Sched.2, para.1:

(e)   requiring any consumer who fails to fulfil his obligation to pay a disproportionately high sum in compensation [i.e. penalty clauses];

...

(i)   irrevocably binding the consumer to terms with which he had no real opportunity of becoming acquainted before the conclusion of the contract [i.e. hidden terms];

(j)   enabling the seller or supplier to alter the terms of the contract unilaterally without a valid reason [but this will not include alterations due to fluctuations in interest];

...

(m)   giving the seller ... the exclusive right to interpret any term of the contract;

(n)   limiting the seller's ... obligation to respect commitments undertaken by his agents or making his commitments subject to compliance with a particular formality;

(o)   obliging the consumer to fulfil all his obligations where the seller or supplier does not perform his;

(p)   giving the seller or supplier the possibility of transferring his rights and obligations under the contract, where this may serve to reduce the guarantees for the consumer, without the latter's agreement.

Although not listed in Sched. 2, an onerous mortgage exit clause is also likely to be considered unfair (see FSA Report, *Terms Providing for the Variation of Charges in Mortgage Contracts* (August 2008)).

Under reg.6, all the circumstances at the time the mortgage was executed and all the other terms of the mortgage deed have to be taken into account.

In the *First National Bank* case (above) Lord Bingham stated at [17]:

> The requirement of significant imbalance is met if a term is so weighted in favour of the supplier as to tilt the parties' rights and obligations under the contract significantly in his favour. This may be by the granting to the supplier of a beneficial option or discretion or power, or by the imposing on the consumer of a disadvantageous burden or risk or duty ... The requirement of good faith in this context is one of fair and open dealing. Openness requires that the terms should be expressed fully, clearly and legibly, containing no concealed pitfalls or traps. Appropriate prominence should be given to terms which might operate disadvantageously to the customer. Fair dealing requires that a supplier should not, whether deliberately or unconsciously, take advantage of the consumer's necessity, indigence, lack of experience, unfamiliarity with the subject matter of the contract, weak bargaining position or any other factor listed in or analogous to those listed in ... the regulations. Good faith in this context is not an artificial or technical concept; nor, since Lord Mansfield was its champion, is it a concept wholly unfamiliar to British lawyers. It looks to good standards of commercial morality and practice. Regulation ... [5(1)] ... lays down a composite test, covering both the making and the substance of the contract, and must be applied bearing clearly in mind the objective which the regulations are designed to promote ...

In the *First National* case the mortgage provided that, contrary to the County Court (Interest on Judgment Debts) Order 1991, SI 1991/1184, interest under the mortgage would continue to accrue after judgment until the borrower had paid the debt in full. The Director General of Fair Trading applied for an injunction obliging the bank to amend this term. The bank defended the case on two grounds: (a) that the term was a core term and therefore exempt, and (b) that in any event the term was not unfair. Whilst the bank lost on the first argument, the House of Lords held that there was nothing unbalanced or detrimental in a borrower's obligation to pay the principal in full with contractual interest (Lord Bingham at [20] and [24]).

Plain intelligible language

Regulation 7 requires that any written term of a contract is expressed in plain, intelligible language. If there is doubt about the meaning of a written term, the interpretation which is most favourable to the borrower prevails (essentially, a restatement of the *contra proferentem* rule).

In *Evans* v. *Cherrytree Finance Ltd* (above) the Court of Appeal decided one narrow issue. Other decisions made by the High Court were not appealed and are reported at [2007] EWHC 3527 (Ch). The High Court heard that the borrower fell behind with his payments and the lender had obtained possession. The lender realised the amounts due under the agreement, including a six-month early redemption penalty. The borrower, relying on UTCCR 1999 then applied to have the redemption clause struck out and for an order for the return of the amount of the penalty. Judge Kaye QC, sitting as a Deputy High Court Judge in Leeds, found that a term providing for payment of a substantial early redemption penalty in a secured credit agreement was 'opaque', 'unclear' and therefore unfair and gave judgment for the claimant for repayment of the penalty of £33,939.85 plus interest.

The FSA considers any term that requires a borrower to pay charges 'on an indemnity basis' to be unfair because 'indemnity' is a technical word not easily understood by a borrower (see FSA Report, *Terms Providing for the Variation of Charges in Mortgage Contracts* (August 2008)).

Individual negotiation

UTCCR 1999 only apply to standard terms which have not been 'individually negotiated' (reg.5(1)).

Regulation 5(2) states that: 'A term shall always be regarded as not having been individually negotiated where it has been drafted in advance and the consumer has therefore not been able to influence the substance of the term.'

In *UK Housing Alliance (North West) Ltd* v. *Francis* [2010] EWCA Civ 117, [2010] Bus LR 1034, it was held that the fact that a consumer or his legal representative had the opportunity of considering the terms of an agreement does not mean that it has been individually negotiated.

Under reg.5(4) the burden is on the supplier to prove that a relevant term was individually negotiated and not caught by the regulations.

It will therefore be rare for a mortgage term to be exempt from UTCCR 1999.

Enforcement

The FSA regulates first mortgages whereas the Office of Fair Trading supervises second and buy-to-let mortgages. Where one of these regulators considers a term to be unfair, it invites the lender to amend the term and then inform all borrowers of new, fairer provision. If the lender refuses to amend the provision, the regulator can apply to the High Court for an injunction and if the court agrees that the term is unfair, the lender will be compelled by court order to amend the provision.

An individual consumer can apply to the court for a declaration that an unfair term be struck out from his agreement. Alternatively, if facing possession proceedings, the borrower can invite the court not to apply the offending clause. This may significantly reduce the amount owing, for example where interest has been increased unfairly or where unfair penalties have added to the debt.

Advisers should not assume that a mortgage drawn up by a large corporate lender is unassailable, see **3.3** above. The FSA published a report in June 2008 giving examples of good and bad practice. Of the 20 mortgage contracts reviewed, 15 had at least one term that the FSA considered to be unfair (FSA, *Fairness of Terms in Consumer Contracts* (June 2008) para.3.37).

3.5 COUNTERCLAIMS

The general rule is that the existence of a counterclaim does not affect a lender's right to possession: see, for example, *Barclays Bank plc* v. *Tennet* (unreported, CA (Civ Div), 6 June 1984, CA Transcript 242). However, it may do so in certain circumstances.

Set-off against the bank's money claim

In *Royal Bank of Scotland* v. *O'Shea* [1998] EWCA Civ 138, the bank brought possession proceedings against the borrowers, Mr and Mrs O'Shea, and also claimed a money judgment against them. Mr O'Shea, acting in person, submitted a counterclaim, which was held by the Court of Appeal to be available as a set-off against the bank's money claim.

The court held that although this may not be a defence to the claim for possession, it would be a defence to the money judgment. If the borrowers applied under AJA 1970, s.36, the court was entitled to take into account that they may have a valid counterclaim, which would be sufficient to satisfy the money judgment. In those circumstances the court would exercise its discretion under s.36 not to give effect to any order for possession. Giving the leading judgment of the court, Stuart-Smith LJ said:

> Accordingly, it seems to me that the defendant has an arguable defence to this money claim and grounds in contending that no order for possession should be made, or at least it should be stayed under the provisions of s.36 of the 1970 Act.

The appeal was allowed, the possession order set aside and the matter remitted to the county court for rehearing.

Need to pay off the arrears within a reasonable period

For a contrary decision, see *Citibank Trust Ltd* v. *Ayivor* [1987] 1 WLR 1157. In that case the borrowers accepted a mortgage offer and purchased a house, unaware that a survey which the lender arranged to be carried out revealed evidence of rising damp and dry rot. A copy of the report was not sent to the borrowers although they were required to pay for the survey. When they later obtained a copy of the report, the borrowers refused to pay the instalments due under the mortgage and the lender applied for possession of the property.

The borrowers submitted a counterclaim for more than £9,000, being the cost of repairs. Mervyn Davies J held that although AJA 1970, s.36 modifies the rule that a mortgage lender is entitled to possession, where the borrower is in arrears it may exercise such powers only 'if it appears to the court that in the event of its exercising the power the mortgagor is likely to be able within a reasonable period to pay any sums due under the mortgage ...'. He was not willing to give weight to the possibility that the counterclaim may result in a substantial sum being owed by the bank to the lender within a year. To do so:

> might nullify or circumvent the rule that the existence of a counterclaim does not prevent the mortgagee from obtaining possession. The wording of section 36 does not seem to impinge on that rule. But however that may be, in this particular case, I do not, on the evidence, find myself able to say that the existence of the counterclaim means that the defendants are likely 'to be able within a reasonable period' to pay off the arrears. Even if I assume that the defendants' prospects of success on the counterclaim are good that does not justify me in concluding that the defendants are likely soon to reduce the arrears by paying over any damages they may recover. (at 1164)

Accordingly, the possession order was upheld and the bank's appeal against a stay of execution pending pursuit of the counterclaim was allowed.

CHAPTER 4

Overriding interests

4.1 OVERVIEW

When granting a mortgage, a lender will be subject to certain pre-existing equitable interests in the property (i.e. interests in land that a person may have, but which are not necessarily registered against the title of the property or, in unregistered land, against the name of the owner of property).

The most common example is the interest of the person in actual occupation of the property at the time of the mortgage. Such a person may be the spouse or civil or unmarried partner of the owner of the land, but anyone in actual occupation of the property may have an interest, which they can assert against a lender.

Certain short leases may also constitute pre-existing equitable interests in the property.

4.2 THE POSITION WHERE THE LAND IS UNREGISTERED

In the case of unregistered land the equitable interest of the person in actual occupation will bind a lender who has notice of that interest, whether it is express, constructive or imputed notice.

Certain interests may be protected against an unregistered title by the registration of a land charge registered against the name of the owner of the property. For example, matrimonial home rights under the Family Law Act 1996 are registrable as a Class F land charge (Family Law Act 1996, s.30).

Registration of a land charge will constitute actual notice to the lender of the interest (LPA 1925, s.198).

A lender will not be bound by a registrable right that has not been registered as a land charge unless it is within the lender's knowledge, or the knowledge of his solicitor or agent, or would have been 'if such inquiries and inspections had been made as ought reasonably to have been made by him' or by the solicitor or other agent (LPA 1925, s.199(1)(ii)).

In practical terms, this provision requires the lender to make inquiries as to the persons who are in actual occupation of the land before making an advance under a mortgage.

Where any existing right of occupation is non-registrable as a land charge (for example, a right of occupation by someone other than a spouse or civil partner), the lender will be bound by any actual, constructive or imputed notice of that person's occupation. Once again, a failure to make sufficient inquiries may mean that the lender is bound by that person's pre-existing right of occupation. This would enable such a person to intervene in the possession proceedings in order to put in a defence.

4.3 THE POSITION WHERE THE LAND IS REGISTERED

In the case of registered land, the rights of persons in actual occupation are protected by virtue of LRA 1925, s.70(1)(g) for mortgages granted before 13 October 2003, and by LRA 2002, Scheds.1 and 3 for mortgages granted after that date.

Despite the change, the case law in respect of LRA 1925, s.70(1)(g) is still considered to be good law.

In addition, it should be noted that leases granted for a term not exceeding 21 years may be overriding interests under LRA 1925, s.70(1)(k) for mortgages granted before 13 October 2003, and leases granted for a term not exceeding seven years (with certain exceptions) may be overriding interests under LRA 2002, Scheds.1 and 3 for mortgages granted after that date.

4.3.1 Mortgages granted before 13 October 2003

The default position for mortgages granted before 13 October 2003 under LRA 1925, s.70(1)(g), is that all registered land shall be deemed to be subject to 'the rights of every person in actual occupation of the land or in receipt of the rents and profits thereof, save where enquiry is made of such person and the rights are not disclosed'.

The proper meaning of LRA 1925, s.70(1)(g)

In the case of *Bank of Scotland* v. *Hussain* [2008] EWHC 1669 (Ch) the High Court considered the test to be applied to determine whether the mortgage lender has made adequate inquiry within LRA 1925, s.70(1)(g).

First, the bank must make an inquiry as to whether any person would be in actual occupation of the property at or after completion. If so, the lender must make an inquiry directed to the person who would be in actual occupation at or after completion as to the rights that he or she claimed. Geoffrey Vos QC (at [21]) summarised the position as follows:

> In my judgment, looked at as a matter of pure construction:
>
> (1)   The overriding interest in question under Section 70(1)(g) is the '*rights of every person in actual occupation of the land*'.

(2)   The proviso to Section 70(1)(g) abrogates the overriding interest of '*every person in actual occupation*' if '*enquiry is made of such person and the rights are not disclosed*'.

(3)   Thus, to be protected, the Bank's first task is to enquire whether there will be persons in actual occupation.

(4)   How the Bank finds out if there will be persons in actual occupation is not prescribed in the section.

(5)   More importantly, if the Bank fails to establish that a person is in actual occupation and make the enquiry in the section, it will be bound by that person's rights.

(6)   The proviso comes at a second stage, once the Bank has ascertained that a person will be in actual occupation.

(7)   Section 70(1)(g) provides that, at that stage, the overriding interest will not prevail if '*enquiry is made of such person and the rights are not disclosed*'.

(8)   The enquiry then envisaged is an enquiry as to the rights that he claims in the property or entitling him to occupy the property: e.g: a tenancy or a right to avoid the contract of sale. This is a mechanical enquiry, but the question must be directed so as to obtain an answer which does or does not disclose the rights which the person in actual occupation claims. (emphasis in original)

Sole registered proprietor

In *Williams and Glyn's Bank Ltd* v. *Boland* [1981] AC 487, the wife contributed a substantial sum of her own money towards the purchase of the matrimonial home. As a result she acquired an equitable interest in the home to the extent of her contribution. The house, which was registered land, was transferred into the sole name of her husband who became its registered proprietor. Later, the husband mortgaged the house by legal mortgage to the bank, which made no inquiries of the wife. The husband defaulted on the mortgage; the bank started possession proceedings with a view to sale and the judge made an order for possession. On appeal, the question was whether the legal and registered mortgage took effect against the matrimonial home, or whether the wife's beneficial interest had priority over it.

The House of Lords held that a spouse, living in a house, has an actual occupation capable of protection as an overriding interest under LRA 1925, s.70(1)(g). Furthermore, the wife's equitable interest, subsisting in reference to the land, was by the fact of occupation also made into an overriding interest and was so protected by s.70(1)(g).

As a result, the mortgage took effect subject to the overriding interest of the wife, even though her interest was not registered. The bank was not entitled to a possession order.

Overreaching rights under a trust – two or more registered proprietors

Where an equitable interest can be attached to the proceeds of sale, then the purchaser can overreach that interest if he pays the purchase price to two trustees who represent the interest of all those who have an interest in the property (LPA 1925, s.27).

In *City of London Building Society* v. *Flegg* [1988] 1 AC 54, HL, four people contributed to the purchase price of a property: two parents, their daughter and son-in-law. All four of them lived at the property, but only two of them – the daughter and son-in-law – were registered as the registered proprietors of the property.

The registered proprietors granted a legal mortgage to the lender and kept the money advanced for their own use. The parents knew nothing about it. The House of Lords held that the mortgage was subject to the actual occupation of the parents in the property, but any 'overriding interest' that the parents may have had under LRA 1925, s.70(1)(g) had been overreached because the mortgage monies had been paid to two trustees.

LPA 1925, s.27 provides that where the proceeds of sale are paid to two or more persons, the purchaser need not concern himself with any trusts affecting the land; effectively the mortgage lender was treated as a purchaser. The House of Lords distinguished the earlier case of *Williams and Glyn's Bank Ltd* v. *Boland* (above), since in that case the lender had advanced capital monies to a sole trustee, namely the husband who was the sole proprietor of the registered land.

Indivisible transaction

In *Abbey National Building Society* v. *Cann* [1991] 1 AC 56, HL, Mr Cann purchased a house with the aid of a mortgage from a building society on the footing that the house was for his own occupation, whereas in truth it was to be occupied by his mother and her husband-to-be (whom she subsequently married). When Mr Cann later defaulted on the mortgage repayments, the building society brought proceedings for possession against Mr Cann, his mother and her husband.

Mr Cann took no part in the proceedings, but his mother resisted the claim for possession on the basis that since, by chance, she was in actual occupation of the house at the time when completion took place, she had an overriding interest under LRA 1925, s.70(1)(g), with the result that her equitable interest took priority over the interest of the building society.

This defence was founded on the proposition that since the charge to the building society was executed after the transfer of the title to the house to Mr Cann, there was a moment in time between the execution of the two deeds during which the legal title to the house vested in Mr Cann free from any charge. As a result, the mother argued, by the time the charge came to be executed she had acquired an equitable interest in the house which, by virtue of the fact that she was in actual occupation of the house, constituted an overriding interest which took priority to the building society's charge.

The House of Lords rejected the 'moment in time' argument. It held that where a purchaser relied on a bank or building society loan for the completion of his purchase, the transactions of acquiring the legal estate and granting the charge were one indivisible transaction, at least where (as in this case) there had been a prior agreement to charge the legal estate when obtained; that in substance Mr Cann had never acquired anything more than a equity of redemption in the house, subject to the charge; and that there was no moment in time at which it could be said that the legal estate was vested in Mr Cann free from the charge so that the mother acquired an overriding interest that would be binding on the building society.

Tenants of mortgage borrowers

The position of tenants of mortgage borrowers is dealt with in **Chapter 24**. However, it is worth mentioning at this point the decision in *Woolwich Building Society* v. *Dickman* [1996] 3 All ER 204, CA, where the defendant purchased a leasehold flat with registered title and thereafter granted a tenancy, protected by the Rent Acts, to his parents-in-law. He subsequently applied for a loan on the flat from the building society, making it clear that the property was occupied by others. The society mistakenly treated the tenants as informal co-sharers and required them to sign a consent form postponing their rights to the rights of the society as first mortgagee. When the borrower later defaulted under the mortgage, the society brought proceedings for possession of the property.

The tenants opposed the proceedings. The Court of Appeal held that while the consents signed by the tenants were valid despite the misunderstanding by the society, as they were persons in actual occupation of the flat, the consents could have no effect upon the mandatory rights the tenants enjoyed under LRA 1925, s.70(1)(g) ('unless a provision to that effect was expressed on the register', which it was not).

In *Barclays Bank plc* v. *Zaroovabli* [1997] Ch 321, a Rent Act tenancy created after the grant of the mortgage (and in breach of its terms), but before the mortgage was registered, was held to constitute an overriding interest by virtue of LRA 1925, s.70(1)(k) and binding on the bank. The fact that the contractual tenancy had expired and had been replaced with a statutory tenancy before registration of the mortgage did not affect the protection afforded by RA 1977.

4.3.2 Mortgages granted on or after 13 October 2003

Unregistered interests overriding first registration

On a first registration of unregistered land after 13 October 2003, the interest of a person in actual occupation of land will (as above) override any new mortgage created after that date: LRA 2002, Sched.1, para.2.

Unregistered interests which override registered dispositions

Where the land is already registered, the unregistered interests which will override a mortgage granted on or after 13 October 2003 are set out in LRA 2002, Sched.3. The provisions of that Schedule are more restricted than the wide provisions of LRA 1925, s.70(1)(g), which apply in respect of mortgages granted before that date (see **4.3.1**).

By LRA 2002, Sched.3 unregistered interests which override registered dispositions on or after 13 October 2003 include an interest belonging at the time of the disposition to a person in actual occupation, relating to land of which he is in actual occupation, with certain exceptions (LRA 2002, Sched.3, para.2).

The relevant exceptions are:

- an interest of a person of whom inquiry was made (i.e. by the mortgage lender) before the disposition and who failed to disclose the right when he or she could reasonably have been expected to do so;
- an interest which belongs to a person whose occupation would not have been obvious on a reasonably careful inspection of the land (i.e. by the mortgage lender) at the time of the disposition, and of which the person to whom the disposition is made (again, the mortgage lender) does not have actual knowledge at that time.

Under these newer provisions, the onus is on the person on whom inquiry is made to disclose the existence of the interest of a person in actual occupation. Alternatively, if the mortgage lender makes a reasonably careful inspection of the land and does not have actual knowledge of the interest of a person in actual occupation, the lender will not be bound by that interest. These provisions strengthen the position of lenders and reduce the scope of the overriding interest of a person in actual occupation of the land.

Meaning of 'a person in actual occupation'

In *Link Lending Ltd* v. *Bustard* [2010] EWCA Civ 424, [2010] 2 EGLR 55, the defendant, Ms Bustard, had been taken into psychiatric care more than a year before a legal charge was acquired by the lender from a fraudulent third party, without the defendant's knowledge. She claimed to be 'a person in actual occupation' of registered land and thus enjoy the priority protection of an overriding interest, pursuant to LRA 2002, Sched.3, para.2.

The Court of Appeal upheld the judge's conclusion that there was evidence 'of a sufficient degree of continuity and permanence of occupation, of involuntary residence elsewhere, which was satisfactorily explained by objective reasons, and of a persistent intention to return home when possible, as manifested by her regular visits to the property'. She was therefore 'in actual occupation' for the purposes of LRA 2002.

The Court of Appeal endorsed a passage from the judgment of Lewison J in *Thompson* v. *Foy* [2009] EWHC 1076 (Ch), [2010] 1 P & CR 16 summarising the law in relation to 'actual occupation'. The passage in question (at [127]) reads as follows:

Before addressing the question of Mrs Thompson's actual occupation directly, it is necessary to say a little more about 'actual occupation':

(i)   The words 'actual occupation' are ordinary words of plain English and should be interpreted as such. The word 'actual' emphasises that physical presence is required: *Williams & Glyn's Bank v Boland* [1981] AC 487 per Lord Wilberforce at 504;

(ii) It does not necessarily involve the personal presence of the person claiming to occupy. A caretaker or the representative of a company can occupy on behalf of his employer: *Abbey National BS v Cann* [1991] 1 AC 56 per Lord Oliver at 93;

(iii) However, actual occupation by a licensee (who is not a representative occupier) does not count as actual occupation by the licensor: *Strand Securities Ltd v Caswell* [1965] Ch 958 per Lord Denning MR at 981;

(iv) The mere presence of some of the claimant's furniture will not usually count as actual occupation: *Strand Securities Ltd v Caswell* [1965] Ch 958 per Russell LJ at 984;

(v)   If the person said to be in actual occupation at any particular time is not physically present on the land at that time, it will usually be necessary to show that his occupation was manifested and accompanied by a continuing intention to occupy . . .

4.4   SALE AND RENT BACK ARRANGEMENTS

Sale and rent back arrangements (also known as 'sale and leaseback' or 'sell-to-rent-back' arrangements) are dealt with in detail in **Chapter 21**. There have recently been inconsistent decisions of the courts which, at the time of writing, are pending a decision of the Court of Appeal.

In *Redstone Mortgages plc* v. *Welch & Jackson* [2009] 3 EGLR 71, CC, the Jacksons had been registered proprietors of a property in Shrewsbury. Being in financial difficulty, they had entered into a sale and rent back arrangement with a third party, Miss Welch. Under that arrangement, Miss Welch bought the property from the Jacksons, paid off their mortgage and arrears, and granted a tenancy back to them, to enable them to stay in their home. Miss Welch charged the property to the lender, which later brought possession proceedings against the Jacksons.

Judge Worster found that the Jacksons were entitled as against Miss Welch to an agreement to grant an assured tenancy (not an assured shorthold tenancy) and a right to set aside the sale for fraud. As against the lender, the agreement for a tenancy was 'indissolubly bound up with the agreement to sell the property'. As it was never intended that Miss Welch should have more than a title encumbered by the Jackson's right to a tenancy, the Jacksons' equitable rights had priority over the mortgage. They arise prior to registration and were protected by the Jacksons' actual occupation pursuant to the priority provisions in LRA 2002, Sched.3, para.2. The judge distinguished and declined to follow *Abbey National Building Society* v. *Cann* (above).

In the subsequent case of nine conjoined appeals known as *Re North East Property Buyers Litigation* [2010] EWHC 2991 (Ch), registered proprietors had sold their homes to nominees of North East Property Buyers (NEPB) under a sale and rent back scheme in return for lump sum payments and promises as to their right to occupy the properties as tenants. The nominees mortgaged the properties on a 'buy-to-let' basis. Exchange of contracts between the occupiers and the nominees, completion of the transfers and the execution of the mortgages all took place on the same day. Subsequent to completion the nominees granted tenancies to the occupiers. The lenders brought possession proceedings based on mortgage arrears and joined the occupiers as defendants.

Judge Behrens, sitting as a judge of the High Court in Leeds, declined to follow and disapproved of the decision in *Redstone*, although the facts were almost 'indistinguishable'. Instead, he preferred to follow *Abbey National Building Society* v. *Cann* (above) holding that (at [52]):

> once two different dispositions (or grants) by the purchaser are introduced into the picture, the question necessarily arises as to the priority between the interests thereby created. There cannot in law be a 'dead heat' between two mutually inconsistent and competing interests over a legal estate in land. There must be a priority as between them. Whilst it is true ... that the vendors' assumed equitable right to a lease back is bound up with the sale of their properties to NEPB, the sale is equally bound up with the charge in favour of the mortgagees which funded the transaction. The solution in *Cann* and the other cases that follow it is that mortgagee gets priority ...

The decision of Judge Behrens is under appeal to the Court of Appeal under the name *Rooftop Mortgages Ltd* v. *Old* (A3/2011/0199) and is expected to be heard in December 2011.

4.5 CONCLUSION

Asserting pre-existing equitable rights against a lender is particularly important for those affected by mortgage possession claims who are not themselves borrowers.

Case law continues to develop in relation to those who are former property owners, who have entered sale and rent back arrangements.

CHAPTER 5

Regulation of the mortgage industry

5.1 OVERVIEW

Between July 1997 and October 2004 the mortgage industry regulated itself by means of a voluntary 'Mortgage Code'. That was superseded from 31 October 2004 by government regulation through the Financial Services Authority (FSA).

The key document is the FSA's 'Mortgages and Home Finance: Conduct of Business sourcebook' (MCOB), which forms part of the 'Business Standards' section of the FSA Handbook (**http://fsahandbook.info/FSA/html/handbook/ MCOB**).

5.2 GENERAL APPLICATION OF MCOB

MCOB sets out the requirements which apply to firms with mortgage business customers. In particular, the sourcebook applies to every firm that:

- carries on a home finance activity (subject to the business loan application provisions); or
- communicates or approves a financial promotion of qualifying credit, of a home purchase plan, of a home reversion plan or of a regulated sale and rent back agreement (MCOB 1.2.1).

A 'home finance activity' is defined widely as being 'any home finance mediation activity, home finance providing activity or administering a home finance transaction'.

5.2.1 Activities covered

MCOB applies to activities carried out in respect of all types of product: regulated mortgage contracts (which includes lifetime mortgages), home purchase plans, home reversion plans and regulated sale and rent back agreements. Together, these products are referred to as 'home finance transactions', although lifetime mortgages and home reversion plans are also together referred to as 'equity release transactions'.

5.2.2 Firms covered

MCOB applies to four types of firm: lenders/providers; administrators; arrangers; and advisers (the latter together referred to as 'intermediaries'). It also includes those firms that provide business loans to customers under regulated mortgage contracts. A single firm may fall into more than one of these types (MCOB 1.2.2).

5.2.3 Regulated agreements

MCOB does not apply to regulated loan agreements under the Consumer Credit Acts, for which see **Chapter 10**.

5.3 AREAS OF REGULATION

MCOB sets out rules covering all aspects of the promotion and provision of mortgage finance. These include:

- advising and selling standards (MCOB 4);
- disclosure of information pre-application, at the offer stage and at the start of a contract, and after sale (MCOB 5–7);
- equity release products (MCOB 8–9);
- the annual percentage rate (MCOB 10);
- the financing of home purchase plans (MCOB 11); and
- charges (MCOB 12).

5.4 HIGH LEVEL STANDARDS: THE PRINCIPLES

The FSA Handbook begins by setting out 'high level standards' and a series of principles applicable to all firms. Amongst others, these principles require a firm to conduct its business with integrity and with due skill, care and diligence.

Principle 6 states that 'a firm must pay due regard to the interests of its customers and treat them fairly'. Principle 7 states that 'a firm must pay due regard to the information needs of its clients, and communicate information to them in a way which is clear, fair and not misleading'.

These provisions may be of importance where an adviser is reviewing the past conduct of the mortgage lender, either in relation to the promotion or provision of a mortgage product. However, the main provisions of MCOB that will be of use in relation to court action by lenders are found in MCOB 13, which relates to 'Arrears and repossessions: regulated mortgage contracts and home purchase plans'.

5.5 THE PROVISIONS OF MCOB 13

The latest edition of MCOB 13, which deals with arrears and repossessions, was revised with effect from 6 April 2011 (**http://fsahandbook.info/FSA/html/hand book/MCOB**).

MCOB 13 amplifies principle 6 (referred to above) in respect of the information and service provided to customers who have payment difficulties or face a sale shortfall (MCOB 13.2.1).

Advisers will want to scrutinise the detailed provisions of MCOB 13 wherever there are concerns that a mortgage lender is being unhelpful or obstructive, or is behaving unreasonably in relation to a borrower's needs.

5.5.1 Requirement to deal fairly

MCOB 13.3.1 is explicit in stating that 'a firm must deal fairly with any customer who is in arrears on a regulated mortgage contract or home purchase plan; has a sale shortfall, or is otherwise in breach of a home purchase plan'. (A 'sale shortfall' is defined as 'the outstanding amount due to the home finance provider, under a home finance transaction, following the sale of the property that is its subject', which is a subject covered in **Chapter 21**.)

5.5.2 Customers in payment difficulties

A firm's policies and procedures must reflect the actions that a firm will take when dealing with any customer in payment difficulties. In such a situation, amongst other things, a firm must:

- make reasonable efforts to reach an agreement with the customer over the method of repaying any payment shortfalls;
- allow a reasonable time for the payment shortfall to be repaid;
- grant, unless it has a good reason not to do so, a customer's request for a change to:

    (a) the date on which payment is due; or
    (b) the method by which payment is made;

    and give the customer a written explanation of its reasons if it refuses the request;
- where no reasonable payment arrangement can be made, allow the customer to remain in possession for a reasonable time to effect a sale; and
- not to repossess the property unless all other reasonable attempts to resolve the position have failed (MCOB 13.3.2A).

With regard to the latter point, MCOB specifies what other reasonable attempts might be taken to resolve the position, to avoid repossessing the property. By MCOB 13.3.4A, a firm must consider whether, given the individual circumstances of the customer, it is appropriate to do one or more of the following in relation to the regulated mortgage contract or home purchase plan with the agreement of the customer:

- extend its term; or
- change its type; or
- defer payment of interest due on the regulated mortgage contract or of sums due under the home purchase plan; or
- treat the payment shortfall as if it were part of the original amount provided (but a firm must not automatically capitalise the payment shortfalls); or
- make use of any government forbearance initiatives (for example, the Home-owners Mortgage Support Scheme) in which the firm chooses to participate.

A firm must give customers adequate information to understand the implications of any proposed arrangement and make customers aware of the existence of any applicable government schemes to assist borrowers in payment difficulties.

5.5.3   Maintaining adequate records

A mortgage lender or administrator must make and retain an adequate record of its dealing with a customer whose account is in arrears, to show its compliance. That record must include a recording of all telephone conversations between the firm and the customer, which discuss the sums due and the records should be kept for three years (MCOB 13.3.9).

5.5.4   Provision of information

If a customer falls into arrears on a regulated mortgage contract, a firm must as soon as possible, and in any event within 15 days of becoming aware of that fact, provide the customer with the following in a durable medium (MCOB 13.4.1):

- the current Money Advice Service information sheet called 'Problems paying your mortgage' (a copy of which can been found on **www.money adviceservice.org.uk**; copies can also be obtained by calling 0300 500 5000);
- a list of the due payments either missed or only paid in part;
- the total sum of the payment shortfall;
- the charges incurred as a result of the payment shortfall;
- the total outstanding debt, excluding charges that may be added on redemption;
- an indication of the nature (and where possible the level) of charges the customer is likely to incur unless the payment shortfall is cleared.

5.5.5 Steps to be taken before repossession action

Importantly, MCOB 13.4 sets out the steps that are required before any action is taken for repossession of property. Before commencing action for repossession, a firm must:

- provide written updated information as set out above;
- ensure that the customer is informed of the need to contact the local authority to establish whether the customer is eligible for local authority housing after his property is repossessed; and
- clearly state the action that will be taken with regard to repossession (MCOB 13.4.5).

5.5.6 Requirement for regular written statements

By MCOB 13.5.1 where an account is in arrears, and the payment shortfall is attracting charges, a firm must provide the customer with a regular written statement (at least once a quarter) of the payments due, the actual payment shortfall, the charges incurred and the debt. MCOB 13.5.1 also applies to situations where there is a 'sale shortfall': see **5.5.7** and **Chapter 21**.

5.5.7 Sale shortfalls

MCOB 13.5.1 (above) and 13.6.3 to 13.6.5 apply to a situation where, after the sale of a repossessed property, the proceeds of sale are less than the amount due under the regulated mortgage or home purchase plan, i.e. there is a 'sale shortfall' (see **21.6**).

Where that happens, by MCOB 13.6.3, the firm must ensure that, as soon as possible after the sale, the customer is informed in a durable medium of:

- the amount of the sale shortfall; and
- where relevant, the fact that the sale shortfall may be pursued by another company (for example, a mortgage indemnity insurer).

If the decision is made to recover the sale shortfall, the firm must ensure that the customer is notified of this intention within six years of the date of the sale (MCOB 13.6.4).

However, a firm is not required to recover a sale shortfall if, for example, the sums involved make action for recovery unviable (MCOB 13.6.5).

5.5.8 Complaints to the Financial Ombudsman Service

The procedures for making complaints against firms are set out in 'Dispute Resolution: Complaints' (DISP) which forms part of the 'Redress' section of the FSA Handbook (**http://fsahandbook.info/FSA/html/handbook/DISP**).

Any breach of the requirements of the FSA Handbook may be referred to the Financial Ombudsman Service (FOS) under its compulsory jurisdiction, if it relates to an act or omission by a firm in carrying out (amongst other things) regulated activities, consumer credit activities and lending money secured by a charge on land (DISP 2.3.1).

Complaints to the FOS are dealt with in **Chapter 23**. Advisers should not be slow to present a complaint where a mortgage lender appears to have breached the provisions of MCOB. As will be seen in relation to **Chapter 7** on the Mortgage Pre-Action Protocol, the existence of a genuine complaint to the FOS is one of the circumstances in which a lender should consider postponing the start of possession proceedings (Protocol, para.8.1 (see **7.5**)).

The provisions of MCOB remain in force and effect notwithstanding the later introduction of the Mortgage Pre-Action Protocol.

5.6 FUTURE DEVELOPMENTS

On 16 June 2011 the government published a financial regulation White Paper, *A new approach to financial regulation: a blueprint for reform* (Cm 8083), which includes a draft Financial Services Bill, with a view to creating a new Financial Conduct Authority (FCA) to replace the Financial Services Authority (FSA) in the regulation of financial firms providing services to consumers.

The government has indicated a commitment to retaining an independent alternative dispute resolution body in the shape of the FOS, though changes to legislation will impose greater clarity around how the proposed FCA and the FOS cooperate and share information (White Paper, para.2.200).

CHAPTER 6

Procedural requirements that the lender must satisfy

6.1 INTRODUCTION

It is important to be aware of all the legal and procedural requirements that a lender must meet to bring a successful possession claim. The formalities are set out in CPR Part 55, together with Practice Directions 55A and 55B (see relevant extracts in **Appendices C1, C2** and **C3**). There is also a protocol relating to mortgage possession proceedings, which is dealt with **Chapter 7**.

Any failure to comply with the formalities required by the CPR could result in the dismissal of the claim, sanctions and/or delay.

This chapter deals with the requirements of CPR Part 55 and identifies common errors made by lenders and generally by the courts. Lenders will of course have taken care to avoid such errors, but those advising borrowers will no doubt wish to take tactical advantage of their mistakes.

6.2 CPR PART 55

CPR Part 55 relates to making a possession claim, which is defined as meaning 'a claim for the recovery of the possession of land (including buildings or parts of buildings)' (see **Appendix C1**). A 'mortgage' is defined as including 'a legal or equitable mortgage and a legal or equitable charge and "mortgagee" is to be interpreted accordingly' (CPR rule 55.1). Section I of CPR Part 55 contains the general rules which apply to possession claims, including a possession claim brought by a mortgage lender.

6.3 THE APPROPRIATE COURT

The vast bulk of mortgage possession claims are brought in the county court, and must be for dwelling-houses situated outside of Greater London (County Courts Act 1984, s.21(3)), although practitioners will come across High Court possession claims from time to time.

CPR rule 55.3(1) requires the claim to be started in the county court for the district in which the land is situated, unless the lender can justify starting the claim in the High Court or an enactment provides otherwise. By CPR rule 55.3(2) the claim may be started in the High Court if the claimant lender files with his claim form a certificate stating the reasons for bringing the claim in that court verified by a statement of truth. Paragraphs 1.3 and 1.4 of Practice Direction 55A set out circumstances which may justify starting a claim in the High Court, namely:

- there are complicated disputes of fact;
- there are points of law of general importance; or
- the claim is against trespassers and there is a substantial risk of public disturbance or of serious harm to persons or property which properly require immediate determination.

The value of the property and the amount of any financial claim may be relevant circumstances, but these factors alone will not normally justify starting the claim in the High Court.

Paragraph 1.1 of Practice Direction 55A makes it clear that only exceptional circumstances justify starting a claim in the High Court. If a lender does so, but the court decides that the proceedings should have been started in the county court, the High Court will normally either strike the claim out or transfer it to the county court on its own initiative (para.1.2). This is likely to result in delay for the claim and the court will normally disallow the costs of starting the claim in the High Court and of any transfer.

High Court claims for the possession of land subject to a mortgage are assigned to the Chancery Division.

6.4 ISSUING THE CLAIM

Practice Direction 4 – Forms requires all possession claims to be issued using Form N5 (see **Appendix B2**). The particulars of claim must be in Form N120 (see **Appendix B3**), which are specifically designed for mortgaged residential premises.

Copies of the forms can be found on the Ministry of Justice website (**www. justice.gov.uk**) using a 'Forms' link on the home page. Versions of the forms in the Welsh language are also available on this site.

6.4.1 Particulars of claim

The particulars of claim in Form N120 require the claimant lender to provide detailed information about the property of which possession is claimed, about the mortgage, about the defendant borrower and about any tenancy that may have been entered into between the borrower and the lender. The contents of the form mirror the requirements of paras.2.1 and 2.5 of Practice Direction 55A.

All of the relevant sections of Form N120 must be completed or deleted if they are not appropriate to the claim. With regard to the mortgage, the lender claimant must specify:

- the date of the mortgage;
- the persons currently in possession of the property;
- whether or not the agreement is a regulated consumer credit agreement and, if so, the date that notice of default was given to the defendant(s);
- the ground upon which the claimant is seeking possession;
- the amount loaned;
- the current terms of repayment;
- the total amount required to repay the mortgage in full at a given date (not more than 14 days after the claim was issued) and the amount included for solicitors' costs and administration charges;
- any additional payments also required under the terms of the mortgage;
- details of the arrears;
- the total amount secured;
- interest rates which have been applied to the mortgage at different times; and
- any steps which have already been taken to recover the money secured by the mortgage.

In addition to confirming who is currently in possession of the property, Form N120 requires the lender to give information as to what is known about the defendant's circumstances, in particular whether the defendant(s) is (are) in receipt of social security benefits and whether any payments are made directly to the claimant. The form requires the lender to indicate whether notice of proceedings will be given to any person who has a registered interest in the property under specified provisions of the Family Law Act 1996, the Matrimonial Homes Act 1983 or the Matrimonial Homes Act 1967.

The particulars of claim must be verified by a statement of truth, as to which see below.

6.4.2   Statement of truth

Practice Direction 22, para.3 sets out the persons who may sign any statement of truth (whether on a claim form, particulars of claim, Mortgage Pre-Action Protocol checklist or any other document containing a statement of truth).

The claimant lender's legal representative may sign the statement of truth on his behalf (para.3.7). However, it is often the case that court documents are prepared by mortgage lenders themselves. In this case, para.3.4 states that where a document is to be verified on behalf of a company or other corporation, the statement of truth must be signed by a person holding a senior position in the company or corporation. That person must state the office or position held. The meaning of 'senior position' is set out in para.3.5 of Practice Direction 22 (which repeats the provisions of para.6.2 of Practice Direction 6A). In respect of a registered company or corporation, persons hold a senior position if they are a director, the treasurer, secretary, chief executive, manager or other officer of the company or corporation.

In the event that the claimant lender is a partnership rather than a company or corporation, the statement of truth may be signed by any of the partners or a person having the control or management of the partnership business (para.3.6).

Paragraph 3.11 of Practice Direction 22 gives examples of who may sign a statement of truth verifying statements in documents other than a witness statement. With reference to companies and paras.3.4 and 3.5, the court would expect a manager signing the statement of truth to have personal knowledge of the content of the document (in a smaller company) or to be responsible for managing those who have that knowledge of the content (in a large company).

The individual who signs the statement of truth must print his full name clearly beneath his signature (para.3.9) and a legal representative must sign in his own name, not that of his employer (para.3.10).

A party may not rely on the contents of a statement of case as evidence unless it has been properly verified by a statement of truth (para.4.1). Therefore, if the statement of truth has not been completed properly or at all, or the provisions of Practice Direction 22 have not been complied with, a borrower's representative may seek a stay or adjournment of the possession claim until the error has been rectified. More seriously, para.4.2 allows any party to apply to the court to strike out a statement of case unless, within a period specified by the court, the statement of case is verified by the service of a statement of truth.

More seriously still, CPR rule 32.14(1) provides for proceedings to be brought against a person for contempt of court if he makes, or causes to be made, a false statement in a document verified by a statement of truth without an honest belief in its truth. The penalties for contempt include imprisonment and a fine.

6.4.3   Contents of the particulars of claim

The particulars of claim for mortgaged residential premises in Form N120 reflect the requirements for particulars of claim in Practice Direction 55A (see **Appendix C2**). In particular, para.2.1 states that the particulars of claim must:

- identify the land to which the claim relates;
- state whether the claim relates to residential property;
- state the ground on which possession is claimed;
- give full details about any mortgage or tenancy agreement; and
- give details of every person who, to the best of the claimant's knowledge, is in possession of the property.

If a claim is brought by a lender, para.2.5 of Practice Direction 55A requires the particulars of claim to include additional information, namely:

- If the claim relates to residential property, whether notices have been registered under specified sections of the Matrimonial Homes Act 1967, Matrimonial Homes Act 1983 or Family Law Act 1996, and confirming where applicable that the claimant will serve notice of the claim on the persons on whose behalf the land charge is registered or the notice of caution entered.
- Specified information as to the state of the mortgage account.
- A schedule of arrears (see below for more detail).
- Whether or not the loan is a regulated consumer credit agreement and, if so, the date on which any notice required by CCA 1974, s.76 or 87 was given (see **Chapter 10**).
- If appropriate, details that show the property is not one to which CCA 1974, s.141 applies (see **Chapter 10**).
- Any relevant information about the defendant's circumstances, in particular whether the defendant is in receipt of social security benefits and whether any payments are made directly on his behalf to the claimant.
- Give details of any tenancy entered into between the borrower and lender (including any notices served).
- State any previous steps which the claimant has taken to recover the money secured by the mortgage or the mortgaged property and, in the case of proceedings, give details of previous claims and any orders made.

A failure to comply with the mandatory requirements of either para.2.1 or 2.5 may result in the court adjourning proceedings for corrections to be made and re-service or, where there is serious default, in the dismissal of the claim.

6.4.4 Schedules attached to particulars of claim

Where a possession claim is brought because of a failure to pay the periodic payments under a mortgage when due, details of the arrears must be contained in schedule form. The relevant provisions depend upon whether the proceedings had been issued by delivering documents to a court, or by issuing proceedings online, using the Possession Claim Online (PCOL) service.

6.4.5 Proceedings issued at court

By para.2.5(3) of Practice Direction 55A the schedule of arrears must specify:

- the dates and amounts of all payments due and payments made under the mortgage agreement or mortgage deed for a period of two years immediately preceding the date of issue, or
- if the first date of default occurred less than two years before the date of issue from the first date of default, and
- a running total of the arrears.

Paragraph 2.5A of Practice Direction 55A provides that if the claimant wishes to rely on a history of arrears which is longer than two years, he should state this in his particulars and exhibit a full (or longer) schedule to a witness statement.

6.4.6 Possession Claim Online

Most institutional lenders make use of the online possession scheme. The Possession Claim Online (PCOL) scheme enables claimants and their representatives to start certain possession claims under CPR Part 55 by requesting the issue of a claim form electronically via the PCOL website (**www.possessionclaim.gov.uk/pcol**). The rules governing the scheme are laid out in Practice Direction 55B (see **Appendix C3**).

By para.5.1 of Practice Direction 55B, in relation to land subject to a mortgage, a claim may be started online if:

- it is brought under Section I of Part 55 (which includes possession claims brought by mortgage lenders);
- it includes a possession claim for residential property by a mortgagee against a mortgagor, solely on the ground of default in the payment of sums due under a mortgage, relating to land within the district of a specified court;
- it does not include a claim for any other remedy except for payment of money due under a mortgage, interest and costs;
- the defendant has an address for service in England and Wales; and
- the claimant is able to provide a post code for the property.

By para.5.2 a claim must not be started online if the defendant is known to be a child (unlikely in the context of mortgage possession proceedings) or a protected party, namely someone who lacks capacity to conduct the proceedings (CPR rule 21.1(2)).

Claim form

The website makes provision for a claimant to complete an online claim form and to pay the issue fee electronically. PCOL fees are lower than for other claims, to encourage the use of the online service.

By Practice Direction 55B, para.6.2, the particulars of claim must be included in the online claim form and may not be filed separately. It is not necessary to file a copy of the mortgage deed or mortgage agreement with the particulars of claim.

History of the mortgage account

By paras.6.3, 6.3A, 6.3B, 6.3C and 6.4 of Practice Direction 55B, provisions are made for to provide the defendant with a history of the mortgage account in schedule form (these provisions are considered in detail below).

When the claimant issues a claim form PCOL serves a printed version and a defence form on the defendant and sends the claimant notice of issue. The claim form has a unique customer identification number or a password by which the defendant may access the claim on the PCOL website.

Defence and counterclaim

A defendant wishing to file a defence or a counterclaim may, instead of filing a written form, do so by completing the relevant online form at the PCOL website (and paying any appropriate fee in respect of the counterclaim electronically). A defence is filed when the online defence form is received by the court's computer system.

Statement of truth

With regard to the requirements in CPR Part 22 for a statement of case to be verified by a statement of truth, para.9.1 of Practice Direction 55B provides that any provision of the CPR which requires a document to be signed by a person is satisfied by that person entering his name on an online form.

Applications made online

Certain applications in relation to a possession claim started online may be made electronically by completing the appropriate online application form on the PCOL website.

Where the court has made an order for possession in a claim started online and the claimant is entitled to the issue of a warrant of possession without requiring the permission of the court, the claimant may request the issue of a warrant by completing an online request form at the PCOL website and paying the appropriate fee electronically.

Similarly, the defendant may apply electronically for the suspension of the warrant, provided that the application is made at least five clear days before the appointment for possession and the defendant is not prevented from making such an application without the permission of the court.

6.4.7   Schedule of arrears in PCOL cases

Paragraph 6.3 of Practice Direction 55B repeats the requirement in para.2.5(3) of Practice Direction 55A in that the particulars of claim must include a history of the mortgage account, in schedule form setting out:

- the dates and amounts of all payments due and all payments made under the mortgage deed or mortgage agreement either from the first date of default if

that date occurred less than two years before the date of issue or for a period of two years immediately preceding the date of issue; and
- a running total of arrears.

However, in the case of PCOL claims this requirement is subject to paragraphs 6.3A and 6.3B. These allow a claimant, in place of the information required by paragraph 6.3, to include in his particulars of claim a summary only of the arrears.

Summary of arrears

The ability to include a summary of the arrears only applies where (by Practice Direction 55B, para.6.3A) the claimant has, before commencing proceedings, provided the defendant in schedule form with details of the dates and amounts of all payments due and payments made under the mortgage deed or mortgage account:

(a) for a period of two years immediately preceding the date of commencing proceedings; or
(b) if the first date of default occurred less than two years before that date, from the first date of default; and
(c) a running total of the arrears.

The summary which the claimant may provide under para.6.3B must contain at least the following information:

- the amount of arrears at the date of the claimant's letter before action;
- the dates and amounts of the last three payments in cleared funds made by the defendant or, if less than three payments have been made, the dates and amounts of all payments made;
- the arrears at the date of issue, assuming that no further payments are made by the defendant.

Procedure following service of a summary of arrears

Where a claimant avails himself of the ability to serve a summary only of the arrears under Practice Direction 55B, para.6.3B, the claimant must (by para.6.3C):

- serve on the defendant not more than seven days after the date of issue, a full, up-to-date arrears history containing at least the information required by para.6.3; and
- either:
  (a) make a witness statement confirming that he has complied with para.6.3A, and including or exhibiting the full arrears history, or
  (b) verify by way of oral evidence at the hearing that he has complied with para.6.3A and also produce and verify the full arrears history.

Where a claimant makes use of a witness statement, it must be filed and served at least two days before the hearing: CPR rule 55.8(4).

However, by para.6.4, if the claimant wishes to rely on a history of arrears which is longer than two years, he should state this in his particulars and exhibit a full (or longer) schedule to a witness statement.

6.5 COMMON PROCEDURAL DEFECTS

As will be seen from the above, there are numerous requirements which claimant lenders must comply with in order to issue and serve effective proceedings upon a defendant successfully. Any failure to comply with CPR Part 55, Practice Direction 55A or Practice Direction 55B may, in a serious case, justify an application to dismiss the possession claim, although often the court will simply adjourn proceedings to enable the defect to be rectified. For case studies covering adjournment applications arising from PCOL procedural defects, see **Appendix F1**.

The court will take care to ensure that the requirements of the CPR are adhered to. Advisers acting for borrowers should therefore not hesitate to rely upon any technical defect to secure at least an adjournment of the proceedings, since in most cases time bought for the borrower can be used to good advantage to improve the borrower's position.

6.5.1 Problems with the issue and service of proceedings

Common problems with court documents are as follows:

- The claim form is not in Form N5. This is especially so with smaller, non-institutional lenders.
- The particulars of claim are not in Form N120 and/or they fail to give the details set out in Practice Direction 55A, para.2.5.
- The claim has been started in the wrong court, i.e. not in the court for the area in which the property is situated. (CPR rule 30.2(1) authorises proceedings to be transferred from one county court to another.)
- An incorrect address for the property has been given.
- An incorrect address for service of the defendant has been given (especially where the defendant does not reside in the property subject to the proceedings).
- The schedule attached to the particulars of claim does not set out all of the payments due and made for the two years prior to issue or from the date of the first defaulting payment if this occurred less than two years before issue and/or there is no running total of arrears.

6.5.2 Common problems with Possession Claim Online

Although early teething problems with the PCOL website and online procedures have been ironed out, the issue of proceedings online still causes problems to arise from time to time. Examples are:

- Proceedings issued in the wrong court – this does not prevent the court in which the claim is issued making a possession order, but the case will have to be transferred to the correct court for enforcement.
- Duplicate proceedings are issued in the same court or different courts.
- Where claim forms are retyped by the court service, they may contain errors as to the parties' names or addresses and/or the address of the property.
- Schedules of arrears entered by the claimant, but not attached to the particulars of claim, on the court file or served on the defendant.
- There are no copies of previous orders as drawn, including any possession order, on the court file.

6.5.3 Common defects in schedules and mortgage statements

Schedules and mortgage statements are often incomplete. Common defects which advisers will encounter are:

- missing entries (especially a failure to credit payments which the borrower has made);
- a one-line arrears figure, rather than details of previous payments;
- schedules showing the last three payments due, not the last three payments made;
- schedules which do not add up, have no running total and/or do not record all payments made;
- a full statement has not been served on the defendant and/or is not exhibited to the claimant's witness statement.

CHAPTER 7

The Mortgage Pre-Action Protocol

7.1 OVERVIEW

'The Pre-action Protocol for Possession Claims based on Mortgage or Home Purchase Plan Arrears in Respect of Residential Property' applies to all mortgage and home purchase plans based on arrears issued on or after 19 November 2008. The latest version of the Protocol is dated April 2011.

A copy of the Protocol will be found at **Appendix C5** and online on the Ministry of Justice website (**www.justice.gov.uk**).

7.2 ARREARS TO WHICH THE PROTOCOL APPLIES

The Protocol applies to arrears on:

- first charge residential mortgages and home purchase plans regulated by the FSA under the Financial Services and Markets Act 2000;
- second charge mortgages over residential property and other secured loans regulated under CCA 1974 on residential property; and
- unregulated residential mortgages.

7.3 AIM OF THE PROTOCOL

The aims of the Protocol are twofold, namely:

- to ensure that the lender and borrower act fairly and reasonably with each other in resolving any matter concerning mortgage or home purchase plan arrears; and
- to encourage more pre-action contact between the parties in an effort to seek agreement between them.

The Protocol describes the behaviour the court will normally expect of the parties prior to the start of a possession claim (para.1.1), but it does not alter the parties' rights and obligations (para.1.2). The provisions of the Protocol mirror many of the requirements imposed on mortgage companies by the FSA 'Mortgages and Home Finance: Conduct of Business sourcebook' (MCOB) dealt with in **Chapter 5.**

7.4 INITIAL CONTACT AND PROVISION OF INFORMATION

Where either party is required to communicate and provide information to the other, reasonable steps should be taken to do so in a way that is clear, fair and not misleading (para.2.2). If the lender is aware that the borrower may have difficulties in reading or understanding the information provided, the lender should take reasonable steps to ensure that information is communicated in a way the borrower can understand.

Where the borrower falls into arrears, the lender should provide the borrower with:

- the required regulatory information sheet or the National Homelessness Advice Service booklet on mortgage arrears (para.5.1(1)); and
- the amount of the arrears, the amount outstanding on the mortgage or the home purchase plan and whether interest or charges will be added, with details of or an estimate of the amounts that may be payable (para.5.1(2)).

In addition, the parties should take all reasonable steps to discuss with each other the cause of the arrears, the borrower's financial circumstances and proposals for repayment of the arrears. The Protocol gives an example that the parties should consider whether the causes of the arrears are temporary or long-term and whether the borrower may be able to pay the arrears in a reasonable time (para.5.2). The lender should:

- advise the borrower to make early contact with the housing department of the borrower's local authority;
- consider a reasonable request from the borrower to change the date of regular payment or the method by which payment was made (giving the borrower a written explanation of its reasons for any refusal, within a reasonable period of time) (para.5.4);
- respond promptly to any proposal for payment made by the borrower (giving reasons in writing for any disagreement within 10 days of the proposal) (para.5.5);
- give the borrower a reasonable period of time in which to consider a proposal for payment made by the lender (which should have sufficient detail to enable the borrower to understand the implications of the proposal) (para.5.6);
- give the borrower 15 business days' notice in writing of its intention to start a possession claim, if the borrower fails to remedy the breach of any agreement which may have been reached.

7.5 POSTPONING THE START OF PROCEEDINGS

In addition to encouraging initial contact and the provision of information, the Protocol (para.6.1) also requires that a lender should consider not starting a possession claim for mortgage arrears where the borrower can demonstrate to the lender that the borrower has:

- submitted a claim to the Department for Works and Pensions (DWP) for Support for Mortgage Interest (SMI); or
- claimed on insurance under a mortgage payment protection policy, and has provided all the evidence required to process the claim; or
- approached a participating local authority for support under a Mortgage Rescue Scheme and has provided all the evidence required to process a claim.

In each of the above cases, the borrower must have provided all the evidence required to process a claim. In addition, there must be a reasonable expectation of payment.

In the case of the first two situations, the borrower must also be able to pay any mortgage instalment which is not covered by a claim to the DWP or to the insurer.

A lender should also consider postponing starting a possession claim:

- if a borrower can demonstrate that reasonable steps have been or will be taken to market a property (para.6.2); or
- where the borrower has made a genuine complaint to the Financial Ombudsman Service (FOS) about the potential possession claim (para.8.1). See **Chapter 23** for details of how to make a complaint to the FOS.

7.5.1 Marketing the property

Where a borrower is seeking to market the property it must be at an appropriate price in accordance with reasonable professional advice. The borrower must take active steps to find a buyer and keep the lender informed about details of any purchase offers received. The borrower should also give the lender details of the estate agent and the conveyancer instructed to deal with the sale, and authorise them to communicate with the lender about the progress of the sale and the borrower's conduct during the sale.

In every case where the lender decides not to postpone the start of a possession claim it should inform the borrower of the reasons for this decision at least five business days before starting proceedings (para.6.4).

7.6 ALTERNATIVE DISPUTE RESOLUTION

The Protocol states explicitly that 'starting a possession claim is usually a last resort' and should not normally be started when settlement is still actively being explored (para.7.1).

By encouraging initial contact and the provision of information and specifying circumstances when the start of the possession claim should be postponed, the Protocol attempts to steer the parties into an alternative resolution of the mortgage arrears problem, and to avoid court proceedings. Discussion of proposals for repayment of the arrears, which is referred to in para.5.2 of the Protocol may include options such as:

- extending the term of the mortgage;
- changing the type of the mortgage;
- deferring payment of interest due under the mortgage; or
- capitalising the arrears (i.e. adding the arrears to the principal loan) (para.7.1).

The absence of pre-action discussion about these issues and, more importantly, a failure by a lender to address proposals surrounding these issues made by the borrower will often provide a fruitful source of adjournment applications to the borrower (see case studies at **7.8.5** and in **Appendix F3**).

7.7　COMPLIANCE AND SANCTIONS

Paragraph 9 of the Mortgage Pre-Action Protocol states that the parties should be able, if requested by the court, to explain the actions that they have taken to comply with the Protocol.

In the context of a court hearing, a lender's representative can simply be asked to explain whether and/or how the lender has complied either with the whole of the Protocol or with a specific paragraph of it. Lender's representatives often produce a completed proforma list or schedule stating the ways in which the specific provisions of the Protocol have been complied with but, on closer examination, this may include insufficient or inaccurate information that will not satisfy the court.

To an extent, such proforma documents have been superseded by the requirement of lenders to present a Mortgage Pre-Action Protocol checklist to the court on the day of the hearing (which is dealt with below).

7.7.1　Practice Direction – pre-action conduct

There are no specific sanctions for non-compliance with the Mortgage Pre-Action Protocol in the Protocol itself. To find specific sanctions for non-compliance, the adviser must refer to the Practice Direction – Pre-Action Conduct (see **Appendix C6**; the Practice Direction can also be found online on the Ministry of Justice website (**www.justice.gov.uk**)). The latest version of the Practice Direction is dated April 2010.

Section II of the Practice Direction sets out the approach of the courts to compliance. In particular, the court may take into account the extent of the parties' compliance with any relevant pre-action protocol when giving directions for the management of claims and making orders about who should pay costs (para.4.1). There is an expectation that the parties will have complied with any relevant pre-action protocol and where there has been a failure of compliance the court may ask that party to provide an explanation (para.4.2). Guidance is given about assessing the degree of compliance (para.4.3) and examples are given of what might constitute non-compliance (para.4.4).

7.7.2 Sanctions

When deciding whether to impose sanctions, the court will look at the overall effect of non-compliance on the other party (para.4.5). However, if in the opinion of the court there has been non-compliance, the sanctions which the court may impose include:

- staying (that is suspending) the proceedings until steps which ought to have been taken have been taken (this is of course the sanction of most use to a borrower);
- ordering that a party at fault pays the costs, or part of them, of the other party (including on an indemnity basis); and
- an order that the claimant is deprived of interest and/or that interest is awarded at a lower rate on any future judgment sum; or (if the party at fault is a defendant)
- an order that the defendant pay interest at a higher rate than would otherwise have been awarded on any sum to be paid to the claimant (para.4.6).

7.8 MORTGAGE PRE-ACTION PROTOCOL CHECKLIST

The 50th update of the CPR brought in changes to Part 55, Practice Direction 55A and the Mortgage Pre-Action Protocol, with effect from 1 October 2009. One of the changes was the addition of a new para.5.5 to Practice Direction 55A, which states that the claimant must bring two completed copies of Form N123 (the Mortgage Pre-Action Protocol checklist) to the hearing of the possession action. Practice Direction 4, which lists the forms required to be used under the CPR, is also amended to make reference to the new Form N123 (reproduced at **Appendix B1**).

The use of the Mortgage Pre-Action Protocol checklist came into effect on 1 October 2009 for all claims issued on or after that date, in order to provide a uniform format for the provision of information to demonstrate compliance with the Mortgage Pre-Action Protocol.

7.8.1 Completion of the checklist

The checklist must be completed by all claimants (lenders) or their representatives making a possession claim. The claimant or the claimant's representatives should be able to explain to the court the actions taken or not taken by the claimant, and the reason for issuing a possession claim (see the guidance attached to the Form N123).

Once the claimant and defendant (borrower) have been notified by the court of the date of the hearing, a checklist must be completed indicating the action taken by the claimant within the previous three months to reach an agreement with the defendant and to comply with the Protocol.

7.8.2 Use at the hearing

The claimant must present two copies of the checklist on the day of the hearing. No additional documents are necessary unless an issue arises. Claimants can copy the Courts and Tribunals Service form onto their own word-processing systems, but the form must not go beyond two sides in length.

7.8.3 Information to be provided to the court

Form N123 requires the following questions to be answered:

(1)   Is the possession claim within the scope of the Protocol?
(2)   Has the claimant provided the defendant with the information/notice in the Protocol at:

   (a)   para.5.1(1) (i.e. the regulatory information sheet or the National Home-lessness Advice Service booklet on mortgage arrears);
   (b)   para.5.1(2) (i.e. information concerning the amount of arrears); and
   (c)   para.5.7 (i.e. 15 business days' notice of an intention to start a posses-sion claim, unless the borrower remedies a breach in the agreement)?

(3)   Does the claimant have evidence that the defendant has made a claim for SMI, support under the Mortgage Rescue Scheme or mortgage payment protec-tion? If yes, the claimant must explain why possession proceedings are continuing.
(4)   Is there an unresolved complaint by the defendant to the FOS that could justify postponing the possession claim? If yes, the claimant must explain why proceedings are continuing.
(5)   The claimant must summarise the number and dates, in the three months prior to the date of the checklist, when he attempted to discuss with the defendant ways of repaying the arrears.
(6)   In the three months prior to the date of the checklist has the claimant rejected any proposals by the defendant to change the date or method of regular payments? If yes, did the claimant respond in accordance with the protocol? If no, the claimant must explain why.
(7)   Has the claimant rejected a proposal for repayment by the defendant in the three months prior to the date of the checklist? If yes, has the claimant responded in accordance with the Protocol? If no, the claimant must explain why.
(8)   Has the defendant indicated that the property will be or is being sold? If yes, the claimant must explain why possession proceedings are proceeding.

7.8.4 Signature of the checklist

The person signing the checklist must be authorised to do so and must sign a statement of truth. Only certain people, specified by Practice Direction 22, para.3 may sign a statement of truth (see **6.4.2**). A failure to sign the checklist properly would be grounds for an adviser to apply for an adjournment of a hearing, so that the error could be rectified.

7.8.5 Using the Protocol: a case study

A right-to-buy leaseholder remortgaged her flat for £120,000. She worked as a secretary on a renewable six-month contract, but found that her work dried up. As a result, she fell into mortgage arrears and fell behind in payments to other creditors. The lender sought an outright possession order when the mortgage arrears exceeded £6,000. The borrower had made sporadic payments, but the last full payment of the mortgage instalment was six months previously. She had repeatedly asked her lender over a period of several months for her repayment mortgage to be changed to an interest-only mortgage, which would have the effect of significantly reducing the monthly payments. She received no reply to her proposal.

By the time of the court hearing the borrower had secured a new six-month contract. Her cousin had also moved into the spare bedroom and was ready to contribute to the borrower's household expenses. At the hearing, the borrower's representative asked the lender's representative to explain what steps had been taken to comply with the Mortgage Pre-Action Protocol. In particular she asked about the discussion between the lender and the borrower, which para.5 of the Protocol encourages before proceedings are started.

The lender's representative produced a proforma sheet. Against the entry for changing the mortgage to interest only, it had been marked 'not applicable'. The lender's representative could provide the district judge with no information about the borrower's proposals.

The borrower's representative asked for an adjournment on the grounds that the discussion encouraged by para.5.2 of the Protocol did not appear to have taken place. In particular, para.7.1 of the Protocol states that any discussion between the lender and borrower may include options such as changing the type of the mortgage. The purpose of those discussions is to avoid court proceedings by the lender reaching an agreement with the borrower over paying the mortgage arrears.

It appeared that the lender had not complied with the Protocol and that non-compliance would be taken into account by the court when giving directions for the management of claims (Practice Direction – Pre-Action Conduct, para.4.1). Alternatively, the court could impose a stay on the proceedings until steps which ought to have been taken have been taken (para.4.6(1)). The adjournment was to enable the proposals to be considered properly and for the borrower to take debt advice in relation to the other monthly payments which she was making to creditors.

Although strongly opposed by the lender's representative, the district judge granted the adjournment for two months (on terms) stating that unless he did so there would be no opportunity for the discussion about changing the type of mortgage to take place, but that if the discussion did take place it may result in a substantial reduction in the monthly instalment, which the borrower could then afford, and that this may have an effect on the eventual order that the court might make in the case, i.e. the court may be persuaded to suspend any possession order made.

The district judge had intended to grant a much shorter adjournment, but he took into account the need for the borrower to take proper debt advice and he accepted that this was a legitimate reason to adjourn for two months, so that the court would have a complete picture at the next hearing.

A further case study involving the Mortgage Pre-Action Protocol will be found in **Appendix F3**.

7.8.6 Conclusion

Advisers need to be aware of the Mortgage Pre-Action Protocol and of the fact that non-compliance by lenders can make all the difference to whether borrowers save their homes or not.

CHAPTER 8

The court's powers

8.1 OVERVIEW

The jurisdiction of the courts to deny possession to lenders is found in a mix of common law rules and statutory provisions. Advisers are likely to come across three main types of legal charge:

1. the bulk will be first legal charges repayable by instalments where purchaser loans are secured on the property by way of mortgage. Some will be second or third charges, where loans have been taken out for the repair, improvement, alteration or enlargement of the property;
2. 'all monies charges'; for example, secure bank overdrafts, which are repayable on demand without there being any right to repay by instalments; and
3. 'regulated agreements' within the meaning of CCA 1974 (as amended by CCA 2006), which are secured by a legal charge on the property. Usually the documentation makes it clear if the loan falls within CCA 1974.

The court's powers in respect of each main type of legal charge vary.

8.2 COMMON LAW POSITION

As the law stood before 1970 the lender had an immediate right to possession and it was not in the power of the court to refuse it, subject only to the following exceptions:

- the application could be adjourned for a short time to give the borrower a chance of paying off the mortgage in full, or otherwise satisfying the lender (though an adjournment should not be granted if there is no reasonable prospect of this occurring); or
- adjournments which in the ordinary course of procedure may be desirable in circumstances such as temporary inability of a party to attend the hearing (for example, through illness).

These limited exceptions appear from the judgment of Russell J in *Birmingham Citizens Permanent Building Society* v. *Caunt* [1962] Ch 883. Subsequently, Parliament enacted the Administration of Justice Act (AJA) 1970, and then AJA

1973, because it was considered that the jurisdiction of the courts to deny lenders possession was too limited. However, the residual powers of court expressed in *Caunt* remain, in any case where the court has no jurisdiction under the 1970 and 1973 Acts to defer the order for possession.

8.3 INSTALMENT MORTGAGES

The court's additional powers are set out in the AJA 1970, s.36 (in Part IV of the Act), as amended by AJA 1973, s.8 (see **Appendices A1 and A2**).

8.3.1 Actions by mortgage lenders for possession

AJA 1970, s.36 gives the court additional powers in an action where a mortgage lender claims possession of a dwelling-house (which is not an action for foreclosure). The court's powers set out in s.36(2) are:

- to adjourn the proceedings;
- to stay or suspend execution of a judgment or possession order; or
- to postpone the date for delivery of possession

in each case, for such period or periods as the court thinks reasonable.

In *Nationwide Building Society* v. *Purvis* [1998] BPIR 625, the Court of Appeal held that a bankrupt borrower has a right to appear before the court to address it on what order should or should not be made under AJA 1970, s.36 and on what terms.

The court may exercise those powers where, according to s.36(1), the borrower is likely to be able within a reasonable time to pay any sums due under the mortgage or to remedy a default consisting of a breach of any other obligation arising under or by virtue of a mortgage.

The court's powers under s.36 end once an order for possession has been executed (*Cheltenham and Gloucester Building Society* v. *Obi* (1996) 28 HLR 22) so once the borrower has been evicted he will only be able to regain entry if he is able to set the possession order aside: see **Chapter 13**.

Amendment brought about by AJA 1973, s.8

The original wording of AJA 1970, s.36(1) caused a problem, because it required the borrower 'to pay any sums due under the mortgage'. The standard terms of most mortgages state that the whole capital sum becomes due and payable immediately if there is a default in payment of any single instalment.

The amendment brought in by AJA 1973, s.8(1) made it clear that a court may treat 'as due' under the mortgage only the unpaid instalments, rather than the whole capital sum of the mortgage.

Additional need to pay current instalments

A court is not to exercise the amended powers under AJA 1970, s.36 unless it appears to the judge not only that the borrower is likely within a reasonable period to pay the missed instalments with interest, but also that he is likely to be able by the end of that period to pay any of the current instalments that would fall due in the meantime (AJA 1973, s.8(2)).

8.3.2 Interpretation

A 'dwelling-house' is defined by AJA 1970 s.39(1) as including any building or part thereof which is used as a dwelling. By s.39(2) the fact that part of the premises comprised in a dwelling-house is used as a shop or office or for business, trade or professional purposes does not prevent the dwelling-house from being a 'dwelling-house' for the purposes of Part IV of AJA 1970.

The relevant time for determining whether land consists of or includes a dwelling-house is the time when the lender claims possession of the mortgaged property, not the date when the legal charge was entered into (*Royal Bank of Scotland* v. *Miller* [2001] EWCA Civ 344, [2001] 3 WLR 523). The statute therefore recognises that land may consist of or include a dwelling-house at one point in time and cease to do so at another.

8.3.3 Capital repayment and endowment mortgages

The court's powers under AJA 1970, s.36 make no distinction between capital repayment mortgages and interest-only endowment mortgages, and the powers apply equally to both so long as the mortgage is repayable by instalments (*Governor and Company of the Bank of Scotland* v. *Grimes* [1985] 1 QB 1179).

8.3.4 The court's power to impose conditions

When exercising its powers to adjourn proceedings, to stay or suspend execution or the judgment or to postpone the date for delivery of possession, the court may impose conditions with regard to the payment of any sum secured by the mortgage or the remedying of any default (AJA 1970, s.36(3)).

Typically, the court will adjourn proceedings either generally or to another date, or suspend a possession order, on terms that the borrower pays the current monthly instalment (CMI), plus a fixed amount per month towards the repayment of arrears which have accrued by the date of the hearing.

8.3.5 The period of any adjournment

In *Western Bank Ltd* v. *Schindler* [1977] Ch 1, Buckley LJ stated (at 14):

Under Section 36(2), the court can hold the matter in abeyance for a 'reasonable period'. … What would be reasonable must depend upon the circumstances of the case. This may involve, amongst other things, considering why the mortgagee is anxious to obtain possession and what degree of urgency may exist in relation to any particular aspect of the case. It might, perhaps, also involve consideration of whether the mortgagor is likely to be able to pay sums accruing due from time to time under the mortgage punctually as and when they should become due.

He added:

In a suitable case the specified period might even be the whole remaining prospective life of the mortgage. I would not myself dissent from the view that the court could, if it thought it reasonable to do so, grant an adjournment, suspension or postponement for an indefinite period (e.g. until further order) with liberty for either party to apply. If the discretion can be regarded as being as wide as this, as in my opinion it can, I see no reason why the court should not be able to decide what period is reasonable in any particular case.

Notwithstanding that in the same case Scarman LJ considered that AJA 1970, s.36(2) 'does not, in terms, confer a power to adjourn generally or *sine die*', in practice the courts adjourn possession claims generally, on specified terms, on a daily basis.

8.3.6   Definition of 'a reasonable period'

The powers in AJA 1970, s.36(2) are exercisable if it appears to the court that the borrower is likely to be able to pay any arrears accruing due under the mortgage, or to remedy other default 'within a reasonable period' (AJA 1970, s.36(1) (as amended)).

Where discharge of all arrears by periodic payments is proposed, *prima facie* 'a reasonable period' means the remaining term of the mortgage: see the leading case of *Cheltenham & Gloucester Building Society* v. *Norgan* [1996] 1 WLR 343, CA.

8.3.7   Considerations for establishing the 'reasonable period'

As part of his judgment in *Norgan* Evans LJ provided a practical summary which 'may be helpful in future cases'. He stated (at 357–8) that:

the following considerations are likely to be relevant when a 'reasonable period' has to be established for the purposes of section 36 of the Act of 1970:

(a)   How much can the borrower reasonably afford to pay, both now and in the future?
(b)   If the borrower has a temporary difficulty in meeting his obligations, how long is the difficulty likely to last?
(c)   What was the reason for the arrears which have accumulated?
(d)   How much remains of the original term?
(e)   What are relevant contractual terms, and what type of mortgage is it, i.e. when is the principal due to be repaid?
(f)   Is it a case where the court should exercise its power to disregard accelerated payment provisions (section 8 of the 1973 Act)?

(g)   Is it reasonable to expect the lender, in the circumstances of the particular case, to recoup the arrears of interest (1) over the whole of the original term, or (2) within a shorter period, or even (3) within a longer period, i.e. by extending the repayment period? Is it reasonable to expect the lender to capitalise the interest, or not?

(h)   Are there any reasons affecting the security which should influence the length of the period for payment?

These considerations are not exhaustive. It may be relevant to take into account additional factors, upon which the adviser may wish to take instructions and present to the court, such as:

- the wider circumstances of the family and the income of other family members;
- whether an order is likely to be made in any proceedings arising from matrimonial breakdown, that would allow any arrears to be paid off;
- whether the borrower is in receipt of SMI, or any other financial support from the government, or whether any application is outstanding or awaiting to be made.

8.3.8   Calculating the minimum conditions that a court may impose

In every case the adviser will calculate the 'minimum *Norgan* order', which represents the lowest amount of money required to be paid by monthly instalments in order to clear the arrears by the end of the mortgage term. To calculate the minimum *Norgan* order the adviser must:

- work out the number of months remaining on the mortgage; and
- divide the current mortgage arrears by that number.

The resulting figure is the minimum amount the borrower would have to pay to clear the arrears off over the remaining term of the mortgage, assuming that the current monthly instalments were also being paid.

While the court will take the minimum *Norgan* instalment payments as its starting point, in practice it will often order that the arrears are paid off over a shorter period (typically over 3, 5 or 10 years), so that the monthly payments towards arrears will be higher than the *Norgan* minimum.

8.3.9   Adequacy of any security

In *Norgan* there was 'ample security' for the lender's loan and that security was not at risk by giving the borrower a period of time in which to repay the arrears. However, the court is likely to be much more cautious in the exercise of its s.36 discretion, where the lender's security might be put at risk by any postponement, or where there is negative equity (i.e. where the proceeds of sale would be insufficient to clear off the mortgage loan secured on the property).

8.3.10 Period of postponement for the property to be sold

In certain circumstances the courts may order instalment payments towards the arrears which are lower than the minimum *Norgan* order, or dispense with instalment payments altogether, where there is sufficient evidence that the borrower will be able to sell the property within a reasonable period and pay off the mortgage debt in full.

However, the convenient starting point in *Norgan*, that arrears may be repaid over the remaining term of the mortgage, is only available to a borrower who can discharge the arrears by periodic payments. A borrower whose only prospect of repaying the entire mortgage loan and accruing interest is from the sale of the property will not benefit from the longer time span available as a result of *Norgan*.

In such a case the only general guidance is that the reasonableness of the period under s.36 is a matter for the court in the circumstances of the case: see *Royal Canada Trust Co. of Canada* v. *Markham* [1975] 1 WLR 1416, CA and *National & Provincial Building Society* v. *Lloyd* [1996] 1 All ER 630, CA.

In *Bristol & West Building Society* v. *Ellis* (1996) 73 P & CR 158 at 162, Auld LJ expressed the matter in this way:

> The critical matters are, of course, the adequacy of the property as a security for the debt and the length of the period necessary to achieve a sale. There should be evidence, or at least some informal material (see *Cheltenham & Gloucester Building Society v. Grant* [(1994) 26 HLR 703, CA]), before the court of the likelihood of a sale, the proceeds of which will discharge the debt and of the period within which such a sale is likely to be achieved. If the court is satisfied on both counts and that the necessary period for sale is reasonable, it should, if it decides to suspend the order for possession, identify the period in its order.

In *Bristol & West Building Society* v. *Ellis* the borrower offered to sell the property in about three to five years, when her children would have finished university education. The Court of Appeal allowed the building society's appeal because there was insufficient evidence before the judge that the property could be sold within the proposed timescale, or that it would achieve a sufficient price to discharge the mortgage.

In *National and Provincial Building Society* v. *Lloyd* [1996] 1 All ER 630, Neill LJ held that what was a reasonable period was 'a question for the court in the individual case'. He said (at 466–7) that:

> if there were … clear evidence that the completion of the sale of a property, perhaps by piecemeal disposal, could take place in six or nine months or even a year, I see no reason why a court could not come to the conclusion … that … the mortgagor [was] likely to be able within a reasonable period to pay any sums due under the mortgage.

However, in the circumstance of that case there was insufficient evidence to show that the arrears would be paid within a reasonable period. Much of it was 'a mere expression of hope'.

In *Target Home Loans Ltd* v. *Clothier* [1994] 1 All ER 439, CA, the court was willing to make a possession order to take effect in three months' time, to enable the borrowers to sell the property, in circumstances where they produced a letter from an estate agent indicating that a substantial offer for the house had been received. Nolan LJ stated (at 447):

> ... is there a prospect of an early sale? If so, is it better in the interests of all concerned for that to be effected by [the borrower] and his wife or by the mortgage company? If the view is that the prospects of an early sale for the mortgagees as well as for [the borrower] are best served by deferring an order for possession, then it seems to me that that is a solid reason for making such an order but the deferment should be short.

8.4   ALL MONIES CHARGES

All monies charges, which commonly secure loans and bank overdrafts payable on demand, are dealt with in detail in **Chapter 9**.

Under an all monies charge there is no right for payment to be deferred by instalments, although as a concession lenders will normally have agreed to accept instalment payments, so long as there are no arrears.

Where there is an all monies charge the court has no power under AJA 1973, s.8 to postpone the date of delivery for possession to enable any accrued arrears to be repaid: see *Habib Bank Ltd* v. *Tailor* [1982] 3 All ER 561, CA. However, the court's powers under AJA 1970, s.36 remain available where the charge is secured against a dwelling-house, so that the court can exercise its powers under s.36(2), if the whole of the loan can be repaid within a reasonable period. This is in addition to the 'adjournments which may be desirable in the ordinary course of procedure, for example due to the temporary inability of a party to attend court' referred to in *Birmingham Citizens Permanent Building Society* v. *Caunt* (see **8.2**).

There have also been cases where the courts have found that, notwithstanding the decision in *Habib Bank Ltd* v. *Tailor*, where there was a loan payable on demand but the agreement also contained a clause providing for deferred payment or payment by instalments, the borrower would still have the protection of AJA 1973, s.8: see *Bank of Scotland* v. *Grimes* [1985] 2 All ER 254 and *Royal Bank of Scotland* v. *Miller* [2001] EWCA Civ 344, [2001] 3 WLR 523 both dealt with in greater detail at **9.4.1** and **9.4.2**.

8.4.1   Correlation with the Consumer Credit Act 1974

Advisers should be aware that most personal loans will be covered by the provisions of CCA 1974. Where that is the case, the court's powers under CCA 1974 would still be available and will override the fact that the loan is secured under an all monies charge repayable on demand: see **8.5** and **Chapter 10**.

If an all monies charge secures a number of different debts, for example, a bank overdraft, an instalment mortgage and a regulated agreement covered by CCA

76

1974, each one of the underlying debts needs to be considered separately, to determine the appropriate powers of the court in any possession action brought by the lender. Even if the debts are secured under an all monies charge, AJA 1970, s.36 (as amended) and *Norgan* will still apply to the instalment mortgage because payment in respect of that debt is deferred, and the provisions of CCA 1974 will still apply to the regulated agreement.

8.5   REGULATED AGREEMENTS UNDER THE CONSUMER CREDIT ACT 1974

AJA 1970 does not apply to regulated consumer credit agreements. Instead, the adviser must look to the power of the court to make a 'time order' under CCA 1974, s.129.

The court may make a time order if it appears 'just to do so' (CCA 1974, s.129(1)). As the name suggests, the primary purpose of a time order is to extend the time available to a debtor to pay any sums owed under a regulated agreement or a security, or to remedy any breach of the regulated agreement.

The powers of the court are very wide. Unlike the powers under AJA 1970, s.36, the court is not restricted to extending the payment of any arrears to the end of the mortgage term, but in a suitable case can extend the time for payment to a date beyond the term.

A time order may be combined with an order under CCA 1974, s.135, which gives the court power to impose conditions or suspend operation of an order, or with an order under s.136, which gives the court power to amend any agreement or security, for example by reducing the rate of interest payable.

Fuller details of applications for time orders and the court's powers under the 'unfair relationships' provisions brought in by CCA 2006 are dealt with in **Chapter 10**.

CHAPTER 9

All monies charges

9.1 OVERVIEW

The distinctive feature of an 'all monies charge' or 'all accounts charge' is that all of the money owing to the lender (usually the bank) becomes due when payable and the lender makes a written demand.

A common example is a bank overdraft. The terms of the overdraft will state that the monies must be repaid in full when the bank makes a demand, and usually the demand will follow the borrower's failure to make payments of interest and/or capital.

The borrower's position may be more precarious under an all monies charge, but many of the protections afforded to borrowers under instalment mortgages (see **Chapter 8**) can still apply, depending upon the circumstances.

9.2 THE MOST BASIC PROTECTION

Once a written demand is made for the repayment of all monies due and payable to the lender, the borrower is afforded a reasonable time to access funds and pay the money owed (*Birmingham Citizens Permanent Building Society* v. *Caunt* [1962] Ch 883). This does not mean that the borrower is afforded time to try to raise the money necessary to repay the loan. It only means that where the funds are available, for example in a different account, the borrower should have sufficient time to obtain those funds and pay them to the lender.

In practice, this will only be of benefit to a borrower if the sum of money borrowed is modest. Where the monies loaned are substantial, it is unlikely that the borrower will have the funds available to make immediate repayment of the full amount.

9.3 MONIES SECURED ON A DWELLING-HOUSE

If the bank overdraft is secured on a dwelling-house and the lender makes a written demand for payment of the full amount, the borrower may still rely upon the protections in AJA 1970, s.36 (see **8.3.1**).

As advisers will recall, where monies are secured against a dwelling-house, but that upon default the whole of the mortgage becomes payable, AJA 1970, s.36 gives the court power to adjourn proceedings, stay or suspend execution of any possession order or postpone possession if it is satisfied that the whole of the mortgage debt can be repaid 'within a reasonable period' (*Habib Bank Ltd* v. *Tailor* [1982] 3 All ER 561, CA).

The court will look at all of the surrounding circumstances when deciding what is a reasonable period. Because the loan arose on a running account and became due and payable upon demand, there is no 'fixed term' to act as a starting point in any calculations by the court. In practice, the court will need evidence of an ability to pay the whole within a matter of weeks or months, rather than years.

The additional protection brought about by AJA 1973, s.8 (allowing the court to treat as due and payable only the arrears, rather than the whole principal sum) (see **8.3.1**) did not apply in *Habib* v. *Tailor*. This was because the court found no provision in the overdraft agreement permitting the borrower to defer payment of the principal sum. The court said that nothing became due and payable until the written demand was made by the lender. Thereafter, there was no agreement that the principal sum could be deferred – to the contrary, it had all to be paid immediately.

9.4 SITUATIONS WHERE AJA 1973, S.8 APPLIES

In certain circumstances the court will have a full range of powers to protect borrowers, even though the loan can be characterised as having been secured under an all monies charge (see **8.3.1** for a description of those powers).

9.4.1 All monies charge with endowment policy

In *Bank of Scotland* v. *Grimes* [1985] 2 All ER 254 the mortgage was evidenced by two documents: a mortgage deed which provided for the repayment of the whole of the principal sum upon written demand (the characteristic feature of an all monies charge) and an agreement that the borrower should only pay interest for the lifetime of the loan, repaying the capital after 25 years with the benefit of the proceeds of an endowment policy. The mortgage loan was secured on a dwelling-house.

The Court of Appeal held that whilst the mortgage deed clearly contained a clause requiring payment of the whole sum upon demand, the agreement which represented the mortgage offer clearly envisaged deferment of payment of the capital sum until the end of the 25-year term. There was no dispute that the court had powers under AJA 1970, s.36, because this was a mortgage in respect of a dwelling-house.

However, in this case, the court was able to go further: by taking the two agreements together it held that there was clearly provision for the deferment of payment of the principal sum. Therefore, the borrower had the benefit of the added protection afforded by AJA 1973, s.8 (which, as noted above, allows the court to treat as due and payable only the arrears, rather than the whole principal sum).

9.4.2 All monies charge with personal equity plans

In *Royal Bank of Scotland* v. *Miller* [2001] EWCA Civ 344, [2001] 3 WLR 523 the borrower had two accounts with her bank: a business current account and a loan account. The borrower took out a loan for the refurbishment of a nightclub, in premises which also comprised substantial living accommodation above the commercial premises. A clause of the loan agreement provided that the loan would be repayable 'from the maturity proceeds of personal equity plans in 10 years time'. The all monies charge secured on the premises was in respect not only of the commercial loan, but also in respect of the business overdraft on the current account.

When the borrower fell into financial difficulties, the bank made formal written demands for repayment of the full amounts of the overdraft and loan.

Although it was unclear whether the borrower had been living in the accommodation at the time that the commercial loan was taken out, she was living in that accommodation at the date of the bank's possession proceedings. The Court of Appeal held that since the premises included part of a dwelling-house, AJA 1970, s.36 applied. Reliance was made on s.39(1), which provides that a dwelling-house 'includes any building or part thereof which is used as a dwelling'.

The court also held that, notwithstanding the provision that all sums would become immediately due and payable following a demand, that there was still provision for deferment of the capital sum, for a period of 10 years, in the anticipation that the loan would be repaid from the maturity proceeds of personal equity plans. Accordingly, the court once again found that AJA 1973, s.8(1) applied to this case. The court followed *Grimes* (at **9.4.1**) and distinguished *Habib* (at **9.3**).

9.4.3 Emphasis on the social purpose of the legislation

The all monies charges in *Grimes* and *Miller* both provided for a deferment of the repayment of the capital loaned, which allowed the court to find that AJA 1973, s.8 applied. However, in both cases the Court of Appeal also made reference to the social purpose of the legislation.

In *Miller*, the court stated (at [27]) that:

> mortgagors of dwellinghouses are … given more favourable treatment than other mortgagors, no doubt because Parliament thought that it was socially desirable that mortgagors of dwellinghouses should have some degree of protection from being evicted from their homes.

The fact that, in *Miller*, the purpose of the loan and overdraft secured by the charge was purely of a business nature and that the loan was not advanced in order to acquire domestic property, did not affect the social purpose of protecting mortgagors of dwelling-houses and, since the borrower in this case lived in the residential part of the building, she was entitled to that protection.

9.5   INTERACTION WITH THE CONSUMER CREDIT ACT 1974

Advisers may come across the situation where the all monies charge secured on the dwelling-house is in respect of not only an overdraft on a current account, but also a loan agreement which is regulated under CCA 1974. Where that arises, the above provisions may continue to apply to the overdraft, but the adviser will need to refer to the powers of the court under CCA in respect of the regulated loan agreement: see **8.4.1** and **Chapter 10**.

9.6   TACTICAL CONSIDERATIONS

When faced with an all monies charge, the adviser will need to examine the documentation carefully and be aware that this may come in more than one document, for example, a mortgage deed and an agreement evidencing the offer and acceptance of the mortgage arrangement.

Problems advising a borrower in difficulty will only generally arise where there is a simple bank overdraft situation or where no dwelling-house is involved. Otherwise, with careful examination of the documentation and the surrounding circumstances, advisers may well be able to make use of the court's usual powers to assist mortgage borrowers.

9.7   OTHER POWERS OF THE COURT

9.7.1   Procedural adjournments

Regardless of the likely outcome of possession proceedings, advisers should remember that the court retains the power to adjourn proceedings 'which may be desirable in the ordinary course of procedure, for example due to the temporary inability of a party to attend court': *Birmingham Citizens Permanent Building Society* v. *Caunt* (see **8.2**). The most usual example will be inability to attend due to illness.

9.7.2   Satisfaction of judgments and orders for payment of money

Where a lender has obtained a money judgment against the borrower, by s.71 of the County Courts Act 1984, the court may order the money to be paid either:

- in one sum, whether forthwith or in such period as the court may fix (s.71(1)(a)); or
- by such instalments payable at such times as the court may fix (s.71(1)(b)).

Application of this power may give the borrower more time to repay the money owed. Section 71(2) allows the court to suspend or stay any judgment order for such time and on such terms as it thinks fit, where it appears that any party (the borrower) is unable from any cause to pay any sum recovered against him.

9.8 UNFAIR TERMS

When considering the terms of any mortgage deed or any other terms of a loan set out in a separate document, the adviser should bear in mind the provisions of the Unfair Terms in Consumer Contracts Regulations 1999, SI 1999/2083 (see **3.4**).

Advisers are reminded that any unfair terms will be void as against the borrower, and the regulations apply not only to those terms which create significant imbalance between the parties, but also those which are not drafted in plain, intelligible English.

9.9 LIMITATION

By s.15 of the Limitation Act 1980, there is a 12-year time limit for actions to recover land and by s.17 at the expiration of that period the title of the lender to the land 'shall be extinguished' (see **Appendix A6**).

The application of the Limitation Act 1980 to a lender's right of possession of a dwelling-house occupied by the borrowers under an all monies legal charge was considered by the Court of Appeal in *National Westminster Bank plc* v. *Ashe* [2008] EWCA Civ 55, [2008] 1 WLR 710 (see **21.6.4**).

Advisers should therefore check that the lender's claim is still 'live' in every case.

CHAPTER 10

Regulated agreements under the Consumer Credit Acts

10.1 OVERVIEW

Normally, it is usually straightforward to determine whether a loan agreement secured on property is a 'regulated agreement' under CCA 1974, as this fact is usually stated in the particulars of claim and on the face of the loan agreement itself. However, a working knowledge of the characteristics of regulated agreements is necessary for those cases where there is doubt, and to enforce the borrower's rights where the position is clear.

10.1.1 Relevant legislation

CCA 1974 is the major piece of legislation in the field of consumer protection. It has been amended by CCA 2006. Copies of relevant sections of CCA 1974, as amended, will be found in **Appendix A3**. Both are supplemented by numerous regulations, which contain detailed requirements in relation to advertising, disclosure of pre-contract information, the form and content of agreements, the requirement to provide copies to the borrower, calculation of charges for credit, the provision of post-contract information during lifetime of agreement and the service of notices.

Of particular importance are the Consumer Credit (Agreements) Regulations 1983, SI 1983/1553 (as amended in 2004) and the Consumer Credit (Agreements) Regulations 2010, SI 2010/1014, although, as indicated, there are many others.

10.1.2 Regulation by the Office of Fair Trading

Where they are secured on property, most regulated loan agreements will be second or third residential mortgages, which are currently regulated by the Office of Fair Trading (OFT). Such secured loans are often taken out by those people who may have difficulty in obtaining credit by other means. As defaulting on a second charge loan can lead to possession of the borrower's property, the product is considered to be high risk under the OFT's approach to regulation.

Following extensive consultation, the government published a financial regulation White Paper, *A new approach to financial regulation: a blueprint for reform* (Cm 8083, June 2011), which includes a draft Financial Services Bill, with a view to creating a new Financial Conduct Authority (FCA) to replace the Financial Services Authority (FSA) in the regulation of financial firms providing services to consumers. While it is also envisaged that the FCA will have responsibility for regulating the provision of consumer credit, that is subject to separate consultation. In due course this may lead to the transfer of responsibility for the regulation of consumer credit from the OFT to the FCA.

10.1.3   Range of protections

Where a loan is a regulated agreement, the provisions of the AJA 1970 and AJA 1973 (see **Chapter 8**) will not apply, but CCA 1974 provides a quite separate range of protections for borrowers. In particular, the court:

- may refuse to enforce agreements which are improperly executed, if it is just to do so (s.127);
- may make a time order under s.129;
- may suspend a possession order under s.135; and/or
- and, if it does so, may make a further order under s.136 to reduce or vary interest, or otherwise amend the agreement; and
- may make a finding that a relationship between a creditor and a debtor is 'unfair' with a range of consequent orders that can then be made affecting the agreement and the parties (ss.140A–140C, inserted by CCA 2006, ss.19–21).

Fuller details will be found later in this chapter.

10.2   THE DEFINITION OF REGULATED AGREEMENTS

Section 189(1) of CCA 1974 defines a 'regulated agreement' as 'a consumer credit agreement, or consumer hire agreement, other than an exempt agreement'. CCA 1974, s.8 provides that a consumer credit agreement is an agreement between an individual ('the debtor') and any other person ('the creditor') by which the creditor provides the debtor with credit of any amount, and it is not an 'exempt agreement'.

10.2.1   Amount of credit

Prior to 1 May 1998 agreements were excluded from regulation if the amount of credit exceeded £15,000; and before 6 April 2008 if the amount of credit exceeded £25,000. However, these financial limits were removed by CCA 2006.

In *Southern Pacific Mortgage Ltd* v. *Heath* [2009] EWCA Civ 1135, [2010] Ch 254, the defendant borrowed £28,000 secured against her home. Of that sum, £19,000 was used to pay off a pre-existing mortgage and £9,000 was paid to her as a cash loan. In possession proceedings by the lender, the borrower sought to say that each of the constituent parts of the loan fell below the £25,000 credit limit, which applied at that time, and so each was regulated by CCA 1974. The Court of Appeal disagreed, holding that the loan could only be drawn down as a whole, that it was not to be treated as two separate agreements but as 'a unitary agreement', and that because the amount of the credit provided exceeded £25,000, the agreement was not one regulated by CCA 1974.

10.2.2   Exempt agreements

The list of exempt agreements will be found in CCA 1974, ss.16, 16A, 16B and 16C. These include:

- loans provided for the purchase of land, or secured by mortgage on land, and made by local authorities, friendly societies, charities, building societies and banks (described as 'deposit-takers'), amongst others; and
- first charge mortgages of land regulated by the FSA, included within s.22 of and Sched.2 to the Financial Services and Markets Act 2000;
- lending to individuals of 'high net worth', in respect of whom a statement has been made that their income is not less than £150,000 per annum, or they have net assets the total value of not less than £500,000; and
- lending to businesses, wholly or predominantly for the purpose of the business, where the credit provided exceeds £25,000 and an appropriate declaration has been made for exemption.

The largest category of exempt agreements, which are not covered by CCA 1974, are first main mortgages for the purchase of the borrower's home. Any additional loans from the same lender, which may be used by the borrower, for example, to carry out works on the same property, will also be exempt.

10.3   CONSUMER CREDIT (AGREEMENTS) REGULATIONS

The detailed rules on the documentation of regulated consumer credit agreements, including modifying agreements, are set out in:

- the Consumer Credit (Agreements) Regulations 1983, SI 1983/1553, as amended by the Consumer Credit (Agreements) (Amendment) Regulations 2004, SI 2004/1482, for agreements before 1 February 2011; and
- the Consumer Credit (Agreements) Regulations 2010, SI 2010/1014 for certain agreements after 1 February 2011.

The regulated credit agreement must contain certain financial and other information. This must be set out in a specified order, with sub-headings, and shown together as a whole. The information must be of equal prominence, and easily legible.

The required information is set out in the Schedules to the regulations and includes:

- the nature of the agreement and the parties to it;
- key financial information (including the amount of credit or the credit limit, the duration of the agreement, the annual percentage rate, the total amount payable, and the amounts and timing of repayments);
- other financial information (including a description and cash price of goods or services, any advance payments, the total charge for credit, the rate of interest, how and when interest charges are calculated and applied, the order of allocation of payments, and variable rates and charges);
- key information (including default or other charges, any security provided by the borrower, and prescribed statements of the protection and remedies available to the borrower);
- statements of protection and remedies available to borrowers under CCA 1974; and
- a signature box and other form of consent, where applicable.

10.3.1 Signature and copies

Both the borrower and the lender must sign the agreement. A copy of the executed agreement must be given to the borrower, either when he signs it or within seven days. A further copy of the unexecuted agreement may also need to be provided. If the agreement is cancellable (because it was signed off trade premises), notice of cancellation rights must be included in the copy agreement, and must also generally be sent by post or email to the borrower within seven days.

10.3.2 Sanctions

If the above requirements are not met, or if the agreement has not been executed properly (see below), the lender may not be able to enforce the agreement against the borrower at all, or may not be able to enforce it unless the lender obtains an order from the court (see below).

Local authority trading standards services or the OFT can also take enforcement action against the lender, using powers in the Enterprise Act 2002, Part 8.

10.4 UNENFORCEABLE REGULATED AGREEMENTS

Regulated agreements, which have not been executed properly or which are not in the prescribed form complying with regulations, may not be enforceable against the borrower, who may seek a declaration to this effect, most commonly as a defence to the lender's possession action. Precedent defences will be found in **Appendices E9** and **E10**.

10.4.1 Improperly executed agreements

Section 61(1) of CCA 1974 states that a regulated agreement is not properly executed unless:

- a document in the prescribed form, containing all the prescribed terms and conforming to regulations is signed in the prescribed manner, both by the debtor (borrower) and by or on behalf of the creditor (lender); and
- the document embodies all the terms of the agreement, other than implied terms; and
- the document is, when presented or sent to the debtor (i.e. borrower) for signature, in such a state that all its terms are readily legible.

An improperly executed regulated agreement is enforceable against the borrower only by order of the court (CCA 1974, s.65).

Even then, the court's discretion to allow a regulated agreement to be enforced is limited by s.127(1) and (2), which provide that the court shall dismiss an application to enforce an improperly executed agreement if it considers it just to do so having regard to:

- prejudice caused to any person by the contravention in question, and the degree of culpability for it; and
- its power to reduce or discharge any sum payable by the debtor (borrower), so as to compensate him for prejudice suffered as a result of the contravention in question (s.127(2)); and
- its power to impose conditions or suspend operation of an order (s.135) or to vary the agreement (s.136).

10.4.2 Agreements made before 6 April 2007

While CCA 1974, s.127(1) and (2) give discretion to the court as to whether to allow enforcement of an improperly executed agreement, as originally enacted, CCA 1974, s.127(3) provided for an absolute bar to enforcement, if the regulated agreement did not contain the 'prescribed terms'.

Section 127(3) of the 1974 Act was repealed by CCA 2006, ss.15, 70 and Sched.4 and does not apply to agreements made after 6 April 2007. However, s.127(3) may still apply to agreements made before 6 April 2007 and, where an agreement is wholly unenforceable as a result, the lender would not be entitled to possession of the land on which the agreement was secured.

Before its repeal in respect of agreements made after 6 April 2007, CCA 1974, s.127(3) stated:

> The court shall not make an enforcement order under section 65(1) if section 61(1)(a) (signing of agreements) was not complied with unless a document (whether or not in the prescribed form and complying with regulations under section 60(1)) itself containing all the prescribed terms of the agreement was signed by the debtor or hirer (whether or not in the prescribed manner).

In *Wilson* v. *First County Trust* [2001] QB 407, a regulated agreement was unenforceable because the amount of credit was not correctly stated in it. In that case, the lender had agreed a loan of £5,000, to which a document fee of £250 was added. The agreement stated that 'the amount of the loan' was £5,250. However, the Court of Appeal held that the amount of the credit was only £5,000, as the £250 document fee was part of the charge for credit, not the credit loaned. Since the 'amount of the loan' was incorrectly stated as £5,250, the agreement was unenforceable because:

- it was not a properly executed regulated agreement, within the terms of CCA 1974, s.61(1);
- an order of the court was necessary to enforce the agreement, by s.65; but
- such enforcement was precluded by s.127(3), because the statement as to the total amount of credit was a 'prescribed term'.

The *Wilson* decision was approved by the Supreme Court in the subsequent case of *Southern Pacific Personal Loans* v. *Walker* [2010] UKSC 32, [2010] 1 WLR 1819, where a different outcome ensued, because the £875 'broker administration fee' in that case was not added to the total of credit loaned.

In addition to the repeal of s.127(3), the position for creditors (lenders) has been relaxed further in respect of new regulated agreements by the Consumer Credit (Agreements) Regulations 2010, SI 2010/1014, which came into force on 1 February 2011. These require documentation to specify the 'total amount of credit', which is defined as 'the credit limit or the total sums made available under a consumer credit agreement' (reg.1(3)).

10.5 PROCEEDINGS

By CCA 1974, s.141(1) any action by the creditor (i.e. by the lender) to enforce a regulated agreement must be brought in the county court. If proceedings are issued in the High Court, then 'it shall not be treated as improperly brought, but shall be transferred to the county court' (s.141(2)).

However, by the County Courts Act 1984, s.40(1), as substituted by the Courts and Legal Services Act 1990, s.2(1), the county court has power to strike out proceedings commenced in the High Court if satisfied that the claimant knew or ought to have known that they should have been brought in the county court: see *Barclays Bank plc* v. *Brooks* [1997] CCLR 60, QBD.

10.6 NOTICES BY LENDERS

Almost invariably, regulated agreements which are secured on property are for smaller sums of money, repayable over shorter periods of time and at a higher rate of interest than main first charge mortgages. When borrowers run into financial difficulties and find they cannot pay the monthly instalments, lenders must follow a set procedure before the institution of proceedings for possession and a money judgment.

10.6.1 Enforcing terms

During the currency of the regulated agreement the lender is not entitled to enforce a term of the agreement by demanding earlier payment of any sum or recovering possession of land, except by or after giving the borrower not less than seven days notice of his intention to do so (CCA 1974, s.76(1)).

10.6.2 Notice of arrears

By ss.86B and 86C, the creditor must serve notice of arrears in fixed-sum or running-account credit agreements.

10.6.3 Default notice for breach

Section 87 provides that a 'default notice' is necessary before the creditor can become entitled by reason of any breach of a regulated agreement to terminate it, to demand earlier payment of any sum, to recover possession of any goods or land or to enforce any security.

By s.88 the default notice must be in a prescribed form and it must specify:

- the nature of the alleged breach;
- the action required to remedy it (if possible) and the date before which that action is to be taken;
- if the breach is not capable of remedy, the amount of compensation which should be paid for the breach and the date before which it is to be paid.

The creditor must give the borrower 14 days to take action to remedy the breach before taking enforcement action.

10.6.4 Termination

The lender may not terminate a regulated agreement (in a case where there is no default), except by or after giving the borrower not less than seven days' notice of the termination (s.98(1)).

10.6.5 Scrutiny of notices

In practice, the terms of any notice served by the lender on the borrower should be scrutinised carefully and compared against the statutory requirements, because any proceedings which are commenced after service of an invalid notice will themselves be invalid and subject to striking out.

10.7 APPLICATION FOR A TIME ORDER

The main purpose of a time order is to give the debtor further time to pay the sums owed under the regulated agreement or any security. The court can make a time order if it is 'just to do so' (CCA 1974, s.129(1)). The court may exercise its discretion:

- on an application for an enforcement order (for example under s.65(1) in respect of an improperly executed agreement);
- on an application by the debtor following service of a default notice or a notice under s.76(1), 86B, 86C or 98(1); or
- in an action brought by the lender to enforce a regulated agreement or any security, or to recover possession of any goods or land to which a regulated agreement relates (s.129(1)).

This means that the debtor can take the initiative by applying for a time order either when a notice is served on him, or after the issue of possession proceedings.

However, the court is not limited only to making a time order upon direct application by the debtor. Section 129(1)(c) gives the court power to make a time order in possession proceedings brought by the creditor – whether the debtor has made an application, or not.

10.7.1 The court's powers under a time order

The court's powers are set out in CCA 1974, s.129(2). In essence, the court can fix new instalment payments 'payable at such times, as the court, having regard to the means of the debtor … and any surety, considers reasonable'. By reducing the amount of instalments under a regulated agreement, the court can effectively extend the period over which the agreement is to be repaid.

10.7.2 Judicial guidance on the making of time orders

The power to make a time order under s.129 is essentially a social provision to assist debtors who find themselves unable to repay loans through no fault of their own.

The leading case in relation to time orders is the Court of Appeal decision in *Southern and District Finance plc* v. *Barnes* [1996] 1 FCR 679. In that case the Court of Appeal gave the following guidance in relation to the granting of time orders under s.129:

- When a time order is applied for – or a possession order is sought of land to which a regulated agreement applies – the court must first consider whether it is 'just' to make a time order. That will involve consideration of all the circumstances of the case and of the position of the creditor (lender) as well as the debtor (borrower).
- When a time order is made, it should normally be made for a stipulated period on account of temporary financial difficulty. The time order should not be made

if the debtor (borrower) is unlikely to be able to resume repayment at least at the rate of the contractual instalments. In such circumstances 'it will be more equitable to allow the regulated agreement to be enforced'.

- The 'sum owed' in s.129(2)(a) means every sum owing to the creditor (lender), and where possession proceedings have been brought, that will normally comprise the total indebtedness. The court must consider what instalments would be reasonable, both as to amount and timing, having regard to the debtor's (borrower's) means.
- The court may include in a time order any amendment of the agreement, which it considers just to both parties and which is a consequence of a term of the order (a power contained in s.136, which is dealt with below).
- If a time order is made when the sum owed is the whole of the outstanding balance due under the loan, the order will inevitably alter the term of the loan, or the rate of interest, or both.
- If the court makes a time order, the court should suspend any possession order that it also makes, so long as the terms of the time order are complied with.

The aim of a time order is directed at rescheduling the whole of the indebtedness under the regulated agreement, i.e. the principal which has become payable as a result of the default, as well as arrears and current interest. However, when considering whether to make a time order the court should consider the interests of both the lender and the borrower. A time order should not be made where there has been a history of default, where an order which the debtor could afford would not meet the accruing interest and there is no realistic prospect of the debtor's financial position improving (*First National Bank plc* v. *Syed* [1991] 2 All ER 250, CA).

10.8   ADDITIONAL POWERS OF THE COURT WHEN MAKING A TIME ORDER

Where the court makes a time order under CCA 1974, s.129, the court may also impose conditions on the order or suspend the operation of the order, for example, by suspending a possession order on terms (see s.135). In addition, s.136 gives the court a wide power to reduce or vary instalment payments or the rate of interest, or otherwise amend this. The exercise of powers under ss.135 and 136 must be consequent upon the making of a time order under s.129. In addition, the court may only exercise these powers if it considers it 'just' to do so.

In *Southern and District Finance plc* v. *Barnes* (above), the Court of Appeal overturned an assistant recorder's decision to dismiss an application for a time order under s.129 and held that he was wrong to conclude that s.136 did not empower him to alter the rate of interest payable on the unpaid instalments. The court said (at 687):

It would have been a proper exercise of discretion, in order to mitigate the impact of the interest charged on the unpaid instalments, to reduce the monthly rate of interest from 1.952 per cent to 1 per cent during the period of suspension of the possession order.

In the linked case of *J & J Securities Ltd* v. *Ewart* (heard with *Barnes*) the Court of Appeal approved the decision of a deputy district judge making a time order under s.129 and making a consequential order under s.136 reducing the monthly payments from £190.80 to £150 and the interest rate from 2.31 per cent to 2 per cent.

In the second linked case, *Equity Home Loans Ltd* v. *Lewis* (also heard with *Barnes*) the Court of Appeal approved the decision of the circuit judge to suspend a possession order on terms that the defendant complied with a time order, which he also made under s.129. Having made the time order, the circuit judge then made a consequential order under s.136, first substituting lower monthly instalment payments for the existing contractual payments and then reducing the rate of interest from 2.72 per cent per month to nil. The Court of Appeal justified the latter, stating (at 689) that:

> Since otherwise throughout the extending period of the loan interest would have been payable on the arrears at the exorbitant rate prescribed, and that would have defeated the purpose of giving time.

In *Lewis* the original regulated agreement was for 15 years and the borrower had defaulted after three years. The circuit judge, having reduced the monthly instalment payments and the rate of interest, then rescheduled the instalments due under the agreement over a fresh period of 15 years. The Court of Appeal upheld that decision notwithstanding its guidance that when a time order is made 'it should normally be made for a stipulated period on account of temporary financial difficulty'.

In *Director General of Fair Trading* v. *First National Bank plc* [2001] UKHL 52, [2002] 1 AC 481, Lord Bingham of Cornhill, giving the first judgment of the House of Lords, gave further approval to the approach of the circuit judge in *Equity Home Loans Ltd* v. *Lewis*. Although he 'would in general agree that time orders extending over very long periods of time are usually better avoided', Lord Bingham accepted that 'the broad language of section 129 should be so construed as to permit the county court to make such order as seems to it just in all the circumstances' (at [28]).

Lord Bingham also approved the decision of the Court of Appeal upholding the judge's order that no additional interest should be payable beyond that which had already accrued. He emphasised (at [29]) that:

> provided the amendment [under s.136] is a consequence of a term of the time order [under s.129], the court should be ready to include in a time order ... any provision amending the agreement which it considers just to both parties.

10.9 APPLYING FOR A TIME ORDER

It will be seen from the above that the court's approach in possession proceedings concerning a regulated agreement may be to make a possession order, but suspend enforcement upon condition that the borrower complies with the terms of a time order made at the same time or subsequently.

There are two situations when an adviser may wish to consider making an application for a time order on behalf of a borrower under a regulated agreement. The first will be an application by the borrower as claimant immediately following the service of a default notice or a notice under CCA 1974, s.76(1), 86B, 86C or 98(1). The second will be as a defendant, by way of application in existing county court possession proceedings brought by the lender.

10.9.1 Consumer Credit Act procedure

A borrower does not need to wait for the lender to bring mortgage possession proceedings, following the service of a default notice. Practice Direction 7B (see **Appendix C4**) makes provision for a 'Consumer Credit Act procedure', which will include a claim by a debtor (i.e. borrower) for a time order under CCA 1974, s.129.

Practice Direction 7B does not apply to any claim for a time order if the claim relates to the recovery of land (para.3.2). However, it will apply in a situation between the service of a default notice and the issue of mortgage possession proceedings by the lender.

Procedure

Where a borrower wishes to apply for a time order, the first practical step is to send a letter before action to the lender with proposals which would otherwise be sought from the court. Only if the lender rejected the proposals or failed to respond would the borrower then apply to the court under CPR Part 7, as modified by Practice Direction 7B.

Particulars of claim

Paragraph 7.3 of Practice Direction 7B states that a claimant making an order for a time order must include certain information in the particulars of claim. The information required includes numerous details of the regulated agreement, details of the default or other notice served by the creditor giving rise to the claim for the time order, details of the unpaid balance due under the agreement, the amount of any arrears and instalment payments and the claimant's proposals for payment of any arrears and of future instalments, together with details of his means. A copy of the default or other notice must be attached to the particulars of claim.

The particulars of claim may take the form of a specially prepared, separate document verified by a statement of truth (as required by CPR Part 22). However, it may be more convenient for the adviser preparing the application to:

- incorporate the particulars into the reverse side of the claim form (Form N1); and attach to it –

- a completed notice of application for a time order (Form N440), since that form will contain all the information required by Practice Direction 7B, para.7.3 (see **Appendix C4**); and
- a completed defence form (mortgaged residential premises) (Form N11M), since that contains detailed questions about the borrower's means, referred to in Form N440.

All the above forms are freely available online on the Ministry of Justice website. Forms N11M and N440 are reproduced in **Appendices B5** and **B6** respectively.

Fees and remission

When making an application the borrower will also have to pay a fee, unless the borrower qualifies for remission of the fee: see Courts and Tribunals Service leaflet EX160A for details of the remission scheme. In general terms, borrowers will receive a full remission of the court fee if they are in receipt of one of the state benefits listed or if their gross annual income is below amounts specified in the leaflet. Borrowers will receive either a full or a part remission based on a sliding scale of monthly disposable income, also specified in the leaflet. An application form for a fee remission, Form EX160, is included within leaflet EX160A (available to download from the Ministry of Justice website).

Need for a witness statement

There is no requirement in the CCA procedure for a witness statement, though advisers will usually wish to prepare one on the borrower's behalf (see **10.9.2**).

The hearing

Where the CCA procedure applies, the court will fix a hearing date on the issue of the claim form, which must be served with the particulars of claim (in whatever form they have been prepared). Each party must be given at least 28 days' notice of the hearing date. Where a borrower is using the CCA procedure the defendant to the claim (the lender) is not required to serve an acknowledgement of service or to file a defence, although he may choose to do so.

At the hearing, the court may dispose of the claim or give directions as appropriate. If the court disposes of the claim, it may make a time order under s.129 if it considers it just to do so, impose any conditions, under s.135, and make any consequential variation of the agreement, instalments or interest, under s.136.

10.9.2 Application in proceedings

Often, the borrower will consider making an application for a time order within the mortgage possession proceedings brought by the lender. In such a case the CCA procedure in Practice Direction 7B does not apply (para.3.2). Instead, the position is governed by Practice Direction 55A, para.7.1. This states that:

> Any application by the defendant for a time order under section 129 of the Consumer Credit Act 1974 may be made:
>
> (1)   in his defence; or
> (2)   by application notice in the proceedings.

Where an application is made in the defence, it should contain a separate paragraph applying to the court for a time order under CCA 1974, s.129, with consequential variations of the agreement under s.136.

An application for a time order within proceedings is made on Form N440 (see above). The notice of application requires the borrower to give the same information about the regulated agreement, the unpaid balance and arrears as would appear in the particulars of claim under Practice Direction 7B (see above).

The borrower's proposals

Where the borrower is applying for time to pay, there is space for his proposals for payment to clear the arrears and future instalment payments.

There is no specific place for the borrower to apply for a consequential variation of the regulated agreement, for example by reducing the rate of interest or mitigating other terms in the agreement, but these might usefully be inserted in the section of the form for the debtor's proposals for remedying other breaches of the regulated agreement.

Schedule of financial circumstances

Form N440 allows the borrower to state at para.3 that 'I have answered the questions about my financial circumstances set out in the schedule to this application', but the form itself does not include a schedule. As indicated above, advisers may wish to complete Form N11M, a defence form (mortgaged residential premises), which includes several pages with questions about the borrower's financial circumstances, and includes specific questions as to whether the borrower wishes to apply for a time order and/or wants the court to consider whether or not the terms of the original loan agreement are fair (see **Appendix B5**).

Fees and remission

A fee is payable, unless the borrower qualifies for remission of the fee (see **10.9.1**).

Need for a witness statement

Although there is no requirement in the CPR for an application for a time order to be accompanied by a witness statement, advisers will usually wish to prepare one on the borrower's behalf. A witness statement gives the borrower an opportunity to amplify the arguments in favour of making a time order. In particular, the borrower will want to develop arguments why it will be 'just' as between the interests of the lender and the borrower to make a time order and any consequential orders under CCA 1974, s.136.

The borrower may also wish to address the points of guidance given by the Court of Appeal in *Southern and District Finance plc* v. *Barnes* (see **10.7.2**) to bolster the application. However, advisers are reminded of the potentially unhelpful comment by the court (at 686) that:

> When a time order is made, it should normally be made for a stipulated period on account of temporary financial difficulty. If, despite the giving of time, the debtor is unlikely to be able to resume repayment of the total indebtedness by at least the amount of the contractual instalments, no time order should be made. In such circumstances it will be more equitable to allow the regulated agreement to be enforced.

10.9.3 Applications at court

There may be circumstances, for example where the adviser is representing the borrower for the first time as part of a court duty scheme, where an application for a time order is being addressed for the first time. Courts generally are unwilling to deal with such an application at the first hearing, if for no other reason than that insufficient time has been allocated in a long list of similar cases.

Although strictly speaking s.129(1)(c) allows the court to make a time order there and then, without separate application by the debtor, it is usually advisable to seek an adjournment to a fixed date with directions for the filing of an application in Form N440, with a witness statement in support. Otherwise, the court is unlikely to have sufficient information before it to make a judgment that it is or is not 'just' to make a time order.

Further time is also needed to consider the precise terms of the regulated agreement and to formulate proposals perhaps with regard to the variation of instalments and interest rates under s.136, consequent upon the making of any time order under s.129.

10.10 EXTORTIONATE CREDIT BARGAINS

Under CCA 1974, ss.137–140, the court was given power to reopen a credit bargain that was extortionate 'so as to do justice between the parties'. These provisions have now been replaced by the unfair relationships provisions introduced by the CCA 2006 (see below), but they remain in force for regulated agreements completed before the new provisions took effect (i.e. before 6 April 2007 for new agreements and before 6 April 2008 for pre-existing agreements). An agreement is 'completed' if there is no longer any sum, which is or may become payable.

Since the vast majority of cases will now be dealt with under the unfair relationships provisions, this book will not deal with the previous extortionate credit bargains provisions any further.

10.11 UNFAIR RELATIONSHIPS

Paragraph 5 of Form N11M, the defence form (mortgaged residential premises), asks the borrower where the loan is a regulated consumer credit agreement: 'Do you want the court to consider whether or not the terms of your original loan agreement are fair?'

This is a reference to new powers given to the court under the 'unfair relationships' provisions introduced by CCA 2006, amending CCA 1974.

The unfair relationships provisions replace previous provisions relating to 'extortionate credit bargains', which were felt to have been inadequate to protect consumers.

The new rules came into force for all new non-FSA regulated agreements with individuals made on or after 6 April 2007. The new rules applied retrospectively to pre-existing agreements from 6 April 2008. Agreements which were completed before the new provisions took effect remained subject to the earlier extortionate credit bargain provisions (see above).

10.11.1 The unfair relationships provisions

The provisions relating to unfair relationships are set out in CCA 1974, ss.140A–140C of CCA 1974, as inserted by CCA 2006, ss.19–21 (see **Appendix A3**). Section 140A enables the court to make an order in connection with a credit agreement if it determines that the relationship between the creditor (lender) and the debtor (borrower) arising out of the agreement (or the agreement taken with any related agreement) is 'unfair'.

The court is specifically enjoined to 'have regard to all matters it thinks relevant', which means all aspects of the relationship between the lender and the borrower.

A relationship may be found to be unfair because of one or more of the following:

- any of the terms of the agreement or of any related agreement;
- the way in which the lender has exercised or enforced any of his rights under the agreement or any related agreement;
- any other thing done (or not done) by, or on behalf of, the lender (either before or after the making of the agreement or any related agreement) – this would include the lender's employees or agents, and may also include a broker or other intermediary, where that person is acting on behalf of the lender.

The court can look at the actions or omissions of any associates or former associates of the lender; a determination may still be made in relation to a relationship which has ended (s.140A(3) and (4)).

There is no credit limit on agreements that may be scrutinised under the unfair provisions. They apply equally to credit agreements which are regulated or not (s.140C(1)). The sole exception is where the agreement is 'exempt', because it is a regulated mortgage contract under the Financial Services and Markets Act 2000 (i.e. most first charge legal mortgages would not be covered by the unfair relationships provisions) (s.140A(5)).

10.11.2 Powers of the court

The powers available to the court are set out in CCA 1974, s.140B. Where the court determines that the relationship between the creditor and debtor is unfair, the court may make an order to do one or more of the following:

- require the lender, or any associate or former associate, to repay (in whole or in part) any sum paid by the borrower (or by a surety) by virtue of the credit agreement or any related agreement;
- require the lender, or any associate or former associate, to do or not to do (or to cease doing) anything specified in the order in connection with the agreement or any related agreement;
- reduce or discharge any sum payable by the borrower (or by a surety) by virtue of the agreement or any related agreement;
- direct the return to a surety of any property provided by him for the purpose of a security;
- otherwise set aside (in whole or in part) any duty imposed on the borrower (or on a surety) by virtue of the agreement or any related agreement;
- alter the terms of the agreement or any related agreement (for example, reduce the interest rate); and/or
- direct accounts to be taken between any person.

10.11.3 Time to make an application

An application for an order under s.140B may be made by the borrower (or by a surety) either as a stand-alone application or as part of court proceedings to enforce the agreement or any related agreement, or where the amount paid or payable under the agreement or any related agreement is relevant.

In the case of a stand-alone application, the procedures set out in Practice Direction 7B are to be followed (the 'CCA procedure'). These have been set out above in relation to an application for a time order after service of a default or other notice (see **10.9.1**). The stand-alone procedure requires a claim form and particulars of claim to be served on the lender at the same time and the court will fix a hearing date on the issue of the claim form. The CCA procedure is appropriate only where the claim does not relate to the recovery of land by the lender.

With regard to an application in the course of proceedings to which the borrower and lender are parties, the borrower may claim relief under CCA 1974, ss.140A–140D by asking the court to consider whether or not the terms of the original loan agreement are fair (in para.5 of Form N11M, the defence form (mortgaged residential premises)) and/or by filing a detailed defence and counterclaim for this purpose (see the precedent in **Appendix E10**).

In his defence and counterclaim the borrower or adviser should seek a determination that the relationship is unfair and specify the steps that the court should take in connection with the credit agreement, by reference to the court's powers in CCA 1974, s.140B (see **10.11.2** and **Appendix A3**).

10.11.4 Burden of proof

Section 140B(9) provides that where a borrower or surety alleges that the relationship is unfair to the borrower, it is for the lender to prove to the contrary. This means that the burden of proof is on the lender to show that the relationship is not unfair. However, in practice, at the hearing the borrower will want to rely upon a witness statement in support of his claim, exhibiting relevant documents.

10.11.5 Guidance by the Office of Fair Trading

The OFT has produced guidance on unfair relationships (*Unfair relationships – Enforcement action under Part 8 of the Enterprise Act 2002* (OFT854Rev, May 2008 (updated August 2011)), available via the OFT website at **www.oft.gov.uk**. The guidance covers the new unfair relationships provisions and regulatory enforcement action which the OFT may take under the Enterprise Act 2002, Part 8.

In its guidance the OFT invites comparison between the unfair relationships provisions in CCA with the test of fairness and reasonableness to be found in other legislation and guidance. For example, the OFT 'has no reason to suppose that the courts will give a meaning to the concept of unfairness in relationships arising from contract terms which is fundamentally different from that given in the context of UTCCRs' (OFT854Rev, para.3.16) where, in certain circumstances, contract terms can be found to be 'unfair'.

Comparisons are also drawn with the Consumer Protection from Unfair Trading Regulations 2008, SI 2008/1277, with OFT guidance in relation to non-status lending (OFT192), second charge lending (OFT1105), irresponsible lending (OFT1107), unfair terms (OFT311) and debt collection (OFT664) and with the rules, principles and guidance of the FSA.

Advisers assisting borrowers in relation to an application to the court that a relationship is unfair may wish to draw inspiration from these sources.

Terms which tend to show a relationship is unfair

The OFT guidance on unfair relationships gives many helpful examples of commercial practice and contractual terms, which may in appropriate circumstances tend to show that a relationship between a borrower and a lender is unfair. Such examples include:

- contractual terms which are 'unfair terms' under the Unfair Terms and Consumer Contracts Regulations (UTCCR) 1999, for example financial penalties which are disproportionate sanctions for breach of contract, terms which are not clearly expressed or in plain English and therefore difficult to understand (see **3.4**);
- excessive interest rates, which in the particular circumstances may be oppressive or exploitative of the individual borrower, even if they are in line with market rates;
- excessive costs to the borrower;
- a failure to disclose relevant information or to have provided false or misleading information, or information which is unclear or ambiguous and so may not have been readily comprehensible;
- excessive marketing;
- business practices in breach of the law;
- business practices not necessarily in breach of the law, but which might constitute irresponsible lending, or involve false or misleading statements, hiding important details in the small print or misrepresenting long-term implications of loan agreements.

In addition to publishing guidance on unfair relationships and other aspects of consumer protection, the OFT seeks to obtain details of court judgments in individual cases under CCA 1974, s.140A, particularly where these involve a finding of an unfair relationship. A list of the relevant judgments of which the OFT is aware can be found on the OFT website, together with case summaries.

An example of such a case is *Barons Finance Ltd* v. *Olubisi* (unreported, Mayor's and City of London Court, 26 April 2010, Claim No. 8PB08963 (OFT unfair relationships cases, Case 19)). In that case, a district judge made a possession order against the borrower for arrears that had arisen in respect of a secured loan agreement for only £2,950, but repayable at an interest rate of 3.5 per cent per month. The borrower appealed claiming that the agreement had not been properly executed under CCA 1974, that the interest rate was 'usuriously high' and that the lender had exploited the borrower's vulnerability and lack of understanding.

On appeal, the judge found that the agreement was not properly executed and that there had been flagrant breaches of CCA 1974 and the Consumer Credit (Agreements) Regulations 1983. The judge also had no doubt that there was an unfair relationship between the parties, within the meaning of CCA 1974, s.140A. As well as setting aside the possession order, he also made an order under s.140B that the outstanding balance be paid over five years with an interest rate fixed at 8 per cent per annum and with no additional fees to be payable.

10.12 ALTERNATIVE DISPUTE RESOLUTION

In addition to an application to the court for an order against the lender, the borrower may also seek redress outside the court. The borrower may make a complaint to the lender or (having done so) may seek resolution of the dispute by approaching the Financial Ombudsman Service (FOS), which will determine disputes according to what is fair and reasonable (see **Chapter 23**).

If the borrower intends to pursue a complaint to the FOS, the court can be asked to adjourn possession proceedings to allow this to take place. CPR rule 26.4(2)(b) states that where the court, of its own initiative, considers that a stay of the proceedings would be appropriate, while the parties try to settle the case by alternative dispute resolution or other means, 'the court will direct that the proceedings ... be stayed for one month, or for such specified period as it considers appropriate'.

Where the borrower has already complained to the FOS before the start of possession proceedings, para.8 of the Mortgage Pre-Action Protocol (see **7.5** and **Appendix C5**) states that the lender should consider whether to postpone the start of the possession claim. Where a lender does not intend to await the decision of the FOS, by para.8.2 of the Protocol, it should give notice to the borrower with reasons that it intends to start a possession claim at least five business days before doing so. A failure on the part of the lender to comply with these provisions could be grounds in themselves to invite the court to adjourn or stay proceedings pending the outcome of the complaint to the FOS.

10.13 UNFAIR TERMS

All standard mortgage terms may fall to be considered under UTCCR 1999. These are dealt with at **3.4**, but they should be considered by the adviser when considering the terms of regulated loan agreements. As a brief reminder, an unfair term is not binding on a borrower. A term may be unfair if it is not in plain, intelligible English.

Otherwise, '[a] contractual term which has not been individually negotiated shall be regarded as unfair if, contrary to the requirement of good faith, it causes a significant imbalance in the parties' rights and obligations arising under the contract, to the detriment of the consumer' (UTCCR 1999, reg.5).

There have been several decided cases which have applied UTCCR 1999 to the calculation of interest rates and redemption terms and conditions.

10.14 CONCLUSION

Regulated loan agreements tend to be on less favourable terms and at higher rates of interest than first main mortgages. Defaulting on a second or third charge loan can lead to the repossession of the borrower's home. It is for this reason that CCA 1974 (as amended) provides a wide range of protections for borrowers, to add to the adviser's armoury.

CHAPTER 11

Duty advice schemes

11.1 INTRODUCTION

The Legal Services Commission (LSC), which runs the legal aid system in England and Wales, funds numerous emergency schemes so that anyone in danger of eviction or having property repossessed can receive free legal advice and representation on the day of the hearing, regardless of their financial circumstances. Approximately 125 county courts with over 300 possession cases listed per year have a 'Housing Possession Court Duty Scheme' (HPCDS) funded by the LSC. Approximately 50 county courts with fewer numbers of possession cases each year have an HPCDS funded by the Department for Communities and Local Government, often in conjunction with local authorities, or have other local funding, or run pro bono or voluntary schemes.

The first LSC-funded scheme ran in 2005. It was estimated that the temporary accommodation costs for families accepted as homeless can run as high as £16,000 a year; whereas the cost of representing someone under the HPCDS and helping them to keep their home averages under £100 (LSC Press Release, 7 August 2008).

11.2 LSC RULES GOVERNING THE HPCDS

The rules governing how an HPCDS should be delivered are set out in section 10 of the 2010 Standard Civil Contract Specification (paras.10.31–10.70). The LSC contracts with a single organisation to provide the service. The organisation must employ a housing supervisor to oversee the scheme, a requirement which cannot be delegated. The organisation may delegate provision of the service to agents, who will generally be experienced housing advisers and/or solicitors in local advice centres and firms. The appropriate adviser must be a case worker who conducts a minimum of 12 hours' housing case work per week.

11.2.1 People who can use the scheme

The scheme is available to any person ('the client') (regardless of means) whose home is at immediate risk because of possession proceedings (para.10.52). This means that the HPCDS does not cover any person facing possession proceedings in respect of business premises only or buy-to-let properties in which they do not live.

The service is free to the client, regardless of whether or not the client would otherwise qualify for legal aid (although the duty adviser must carry out a means test of the client and assess financial eligibility for legal aid, purely for statistical purposes).

11.2.2 Scope of the scheme

The HPCDS covers possession proceedings brought by:

- mortgage lenders or private, public or other social landlords;
- applications to stay/suspend execution of warrants of possession; and
- clients with charging orders relating to property, whereby the clients are at immediate risk of losing their home through a forced sale (i.e. not when the charging order is put in place).

11.2.3 Services covered by the HPCDS

For clients within the scope of the scheme, the following services must be provided:

- face-to-face advice to the client on the day, prior to the hearing;
- advocacy for the relevant proceedings on the day of the hearing;
- face-to-face advice to the client on the day, after the hearing, explaining the outcome and the options available to the client;
- on the day of the hearing assisting clients to liaise with third parties, for example negotiating payments with lenders or landlords, or assisting clients with payment plans, if appropriate in the circumstances;
- referrals to other providers to take on follow-up work, where advisers are unable to take on work themselves, or to other organisations where the client may not be eligible for legal aid; and
- sending a letter to each client explaining the outcome of the hearing, the options that are available and the adviser's follow-up advice (see the precedent post-hearing letter to a borrower in **Appendix E11**).

The adviser must complete a standard matter report form in respect of each client seen and complete a proxy legal aid means test form, both provided by the LSC. The adviser must keep a central record of clients seen under the scheme.

11.2.4 Payment

The HPCDS is 'controlled work', in the same way as Legal Help or Help at Court. A fixed rate is payable per client seen and this covers all work for a client under the scheme (including, for example, advice, representation, advice in writing) so that no additional payments will be made. There are no additional payments for travel or waiting. After each hearing the adviser must report work done separately from reporting other controlled work. Payment will be monthly in arrears for work done and will be made separately from the standard monthly payment for other controlled work.

If a client seeks advice outside the terms of the scheme then, subject to any means or merit tests, the adviser should consider whether it is more appropriate in the circumstances to assist the client using other forms of legal aid instead, such as Legal Help, Help at Court or Legal Representation. The adviser will be entitled to claim payment for assisting that client in accordance with their organisation's contract, but will not be entitled to claim any fee under the HPCDS (see also **15.4**).

If the adviser's organisation provides services at court under the HPCDS, and within six months of doing so, subsequently opens a new housing matter start in relation to the same case, then the adviser cannot claim any payment for providing the services at court. However, advisers may include time spent under the HPCDS within their claim for the Legal Help matter start.

11.3   STRUCTURE OF AN HPCDS

Where an organisation has successfully bid for a contract to run an HPCDS and is sufficiently large, it may supply all of the appropriate advisers at court, without the need to delegate to experienced advisers in outside agencies. Otherwise, the organisation will maintain a rota of outside organisations and solicitors' firms who provide services at court on possession day. In either case, the organisation will ensure that there are effective systems of supervision in place.

The organisation will liaise with the court, most usually with the listing officer or court manager and obtain details of the housing possession lists on a monthly basis. Advisers will be allocated either to a morning or afternoon period when the court is in session. Having been advised of their session, advisers will normally attend court soon after the court opens for business or at least 45 minutes before the session begins.

11.3.1   Liaison with the court

The LSC funding criteria for an HPCDS include a requirement that the court must be willing to accommodate a scheme. This means that the court will give it space (within the limits of the court building), block-list the possession hearings in reasonable length sessions and support the scheme, for example by requiring ushers to signpost people to the scheme.

The organisation running the HPCDS should liaise with the court manager to make these arrangements. Where possible, one or more consultation rooms should be reserved for the duty adviser and/or a table should be provided in the main waiting area. At least two copies of each relevant housing possession list should be provided to the duty adviser for each session covered.

Court staff should be told about the presence of duty advisers. It should be an active part of their job to ascertain from defendants whether they need advice under the duty scheme in advance of their hearing. Appropriate cases should be noted on the possession list and held back to give advisers time to take instructions, liaise with the parties and prepare representations to the court later in the day.

11.3.2   Organising the duty adviser's time

Where possible, duty advisers should be assisted by 'runners', who may be junior members of staff, trainee solicitors or law students. Arrangements may be made for local firms, colleges or universities to provide people who are willing to assist without remuneration in return for court experience. Runners are invaluable for completing the standard forms prescribed by the LSC, liaising with ushers and third parties, copying documents and, in a busy session, beginning to take instructions.

The duty adviser should make use of a pre-printed checklist (see **Appendix E1**), which will be used to collect some or all of the following useful information:

Documents

- Check documentary evidence: can any defence or procedural defects be identified from the face of the documents?
- Check compliance with the Mortgage Pre-Action Protocol (see **Chapter 7** and **Appendix C5**) – in particular letters that may have been sent by the lender to the borrower.
- Check the sufficiency of any schedule of mortgage arrears and confirm with the borrower whether there are any additional payments made by the borrower since, which would reduce the arrears. Ask the borrower whether there are any receipts for such payments (though these are unlikely where payment has been made over the telephone using a credit or debit card).

The property

- Who lives in the property and will be affected by any possession order?
- Is it the borrower's home or is it a buy-to-let property (which would not be covered by the scheme)?
- What is the current estimated value of the property (information which will be necessary to calculate the likely level of equity in the property)?
- Are there any current proposals to remortgage or sell the property? If so, how far advanced are the procedures and does the borrower have any documentary evidence of them at court?

Mortgage/arrears

- Is this a first, second or subsequent charge?
- What is the date and original amount of the mortgage?
- What is the remaining term of the mortgage?
- Is the level of arrears admitted and what is the reason for those arrears?
- How much is required to discharge the mortgage now?
- Is this a mortgage payable by instalments, an all monies charge or a secured loan regulated under the CCA?

The borrower's offer

- In the case of an instalment mortgage what is the minimum *Norgan* offer (i.e. the minimum monthly payment spread over the remaining term of the mortgage), which would clear the arrears that have arisen (see **Chapter 8**)?
- Can the borrower offer regular payments to the court which exceed the minimum *Norgan* offer, to increase the attractiveness of any proposal to be made to the court?
- What recent payments have been made and what is the source of those payments?
- What changes have been made (or will be made) to the borrower's personal circumstances or employment to demonstrate to the court that past problems are over (or will be soon) and that the borrower can not only pay current mortgage instalments, but can also pay a regular monthly sum towards the arrears?
- What is the offer being put forward?
- Does the borrower have the ability to pay either under his own resources, if working, or with the benefit of SMI (if on benefits), or with contributions from family and friends?
- Has the borrower completed the defence form and statement of means?
- How much equity is there in the property and, in particular, is there proper security for the lender, if the court chooses to exercise its powers under AJA 1970, s.36 (as amended) to adjourn, stay, suspend or postpone possession, or in the case of a regulated agreement under CCA 1974 s.129?

(This information will also be useful when proposing a time order under CCA 1974, s.129, although the court would have power to extend the period of payment in an appropriate case beyond the term of the mortgage.)

The order being sought by the adviser

- Are there grounds to seek to strike out the proceedings or, more likely, adjourn them?
- Are directions needed for further evidence to be filed (either by the lender or the borrower) or for a defence to be filed and served?

- In the case of a regulated agreement, should an adjournment be sought in order to submit an application for a time order?
- In the case of any adjournment, can the borrower make a proposal for interim payments towards the current monthly instalment and/or arrears while the case progresses?

11.4 FOCUSING ON OUTCOMES

Time is often limited when acting as a duty adviser in a county court possession list. It is usually necessary to act at speed to read and absorb numerous documents, take instructions from the borrower and formulate a plan of action. Subject to receiving the borrower's instructions, wherever possible the duty adviser should seek an adjournment of the first instance hearing and avoid the making of a possession order.

The adviser should advise the borrower about the possible outcomes of the possession hearing and the merits of seeking an adjournment. If the borrower gives instructions that an adjournment should be sought, the next step is for the adviser to seek the agreement of the lender's representative. It is particularly important not to let the borrower be pressurised into feeling that he has to reach a deal (such as a suspended possession order) with the lender's representative, without allowing time for other options (or maybe just better terms) to be explored.

While it will not always be possible to agree an adjournment outside court, very often information can be gleaned from the documents and from the borrower to demonstrate to the judge that, with time and proper advice, the borrower's position can be significantly improved before the court makes a final decision.

11.4.1 Emphasising change

The key tactic is to tell the court about the borrower's troubled background resulting in arrears and to contrast that with any change at all since then, and with the promise of further change to come.

11.4.2 Use of technical defects

The adviser should not hesitate to make use of any technical defect in the documentation or the proceedings in order to obtain an adjournment. The proceedings concern the borrower's home and the court must be certain that the documents and procedures are in order before it makes a determination in any particular case.

11.4.3 Seeking an adjournment

Wherever possible the desired outcome is to persuade the court to exercise its powers to adjourn the proceedings or, where this proves not to be possible, to stay or suspend any order for possession or postpone the date of execution of any possession order. In the case of a regulated agreement a short adjournment should be sought to enable an application for a time order to be made, with a witness statement in support. For case studies relating to different types of adjournment application, see **7.8.5** and **Appendices F1, F2** and **F3**.

11.4.4 Outright possession orders

In some cases, it will not prove possible to secure an adjournment of the initial possession hearing or even a suspension of any order, but the court will make an outright possession order. The issues that arise are dealt with in **Chapter 13**.

Possession orders are usually expressed to take effect 'forthwith' or in 14 or 28 days from the date of the hearing. In a case of exceptional hardship, it may be possible to persuade the court to extend the postponement. If borrowers are likely to be able to sell the property within a reasonable time (and have evidence of their ability to do so), an extension of two or three months might be appropriate.

Advisers may wish to consider applying for permission to appeal, preferably at the hearing itself from the judge making the order or later in the Appellant's Notice. Time limits apply (see **13.5.3**).

Of course, the borrower will be at risk of losing his home as a result of any outright possession order that is made against him. It will therefore be appropriate to advise him about his rights to housing advice and assistance and/or to rehousing by the local authority. For a summary of the law relating to homelessness, see **Appendix G**.

11.4.5 Costs of proceedings

Regardless of the outcome of any hearing, the lender is likely to seek to recover its costs of the proceedings, either by way of an express order for costs from the court (which may be summarily assessed in a given amount) or through the contractual provisions of the mortgage deed. In some instances, there may be scope for borrowers to challenge the level of costs that they are liable to pay and this issue is dealt with more fully at **12.17**.

Where the lender has acted in an unreasonable way, for example, by failing to comply with the Mortgage Pre-Action Protocol or by attending court with incomplete documentation resulting in an adjournment, the adviser may wish to ask the court to make an order that the lender's costs 'should not be added to the security' or, failing that, that there should be an assessment of those costs by the court pursuant to CPR rule 48.3. Again, see **12.17.1**.

CHAPTER 12

The possession hearing

12.1 INTRODUCTION

The previous chapters have dealt with the different types of mortgage, the law relating to them and various procedural requirements that lenders have to comply with before and after the issue of proceedings. This chapter will focus on the possession hearing itself and will give some pointers to how to maximise the chances of a favourable exercise of judicial discretion for the benefit of the borrower.

Where advisers have the chance to consider the proceedings in the office, they have an invaluable chance to scrutinise the papers, to identify mistakes made by lenders and by the court and to prepare the borrower's case.

12.2 THE ISSUE OF PROCEEDINGS

In possession claims the court will fix a date for the hearing when it issues the claim form (CPR rule 55.5(1)). The hearing date will be not less than 28 days from the date of issue of the claim form, although the standard period between the issue of the claim form and the hearing will be not more than eight weeks (CPR rule 55.5(3)).

The defendant must be served with the claim form and particulars of claim not less than 21 days before the hearing date (CPR 55.5(3)(c)). Non-compliance with this rule may justify an application by the borrower for an adjournment and re-service of the notice of hearing and, in practice, the court will usually grant this.

However, advisers should be aware that CPR rule 3.1(2)(a) provides that the court may extend or shorten the time for compliance with any rule.

12.3 ESSENTIAL INFORMATION TO OBTAIN FROM THE BORROWER

There is a list of essential information to obtain from the borrower at **Appendix E1**.

In addition to using a checklist, the adviser will find it useful to complete Form N11M, the defence form (mortgaged residential premises) (see **Appendix B5**).

12.4 PROCEDURAL REQUIREMENTS THE LENDER MUST SATISFY

The procedural requirements that lenders must satisfy have been dealt with in **Chapter 6**. Court rules set out strict requirements for possession hearings and in most cases the court will be keen to ensure that they have been followed. Some of the most common procedural defects are at **6.5**.

12.5 KEY COURT FORMS

It may assist advisers to download copies of the key court forms used in mortgage possession proceedings from the Ministry of Justice website (**www.justice.gov. uk**).

The claim form and particulars of claim will enable the adviser to check the documents utilised by lenders and their solicitors, which are often produced on their own computer systems. Where inconsistencies occur, or the lender has used an out-of-date format and as a result omitted required information, borrowers can use these errors to their advantage, either to adjourn or in a serious case to dismiss a claim.

The key court forms, which are reproduced in **Appendix B**, are:

- Form N5 – claim form for possession of property;
- Form N120 – particulars of claim for possession (mortgaged residential premises);
- Form N7 – notes for defendant (mortgaged residential premises);
- Form N11M – defence form (mortgaged residential premises).

12.6 PROBLEMS WITH POSSESSION CLAIM ONLINE

Many lenders make use of the bulk-issuing facilities provided by Possession Claim Online (PCOL). The common problems that arise are set out at **6.5.2** and case studies relating to such problems are in **Appendix F1**.

12.6.1 The schedule of arrears

The requirements for a schedule of arrears are at **6.4.7** and common deficiencies at **6.5.3**.

Any failure to comply with Practice Direction 55A or Practice Direction 55B may justify an application to dismiss the possession claim, although often the court will adjourn to give the lender time to rectify the mistake. The appropriate step is for the lender to file and serve a full statement of account.

12.7 THE DEFENDANT'S RESPONSE

12.7.1 Acknowledgement of service

An acknowledgement of service is not required from the defendant and CPR Part 10 (which relates to acknowledgement of service) does not apply to possession claims (CPR rule 55.7(1)).

12.7.2 Defence

However, provisions of CPR Part 15 (defence and reply) do apply to possession claims. In particular, CPR rule 15.2 states that a defendant who wishes to defend all or part of a claim must file a defence. The general rule is that the period for filing a defence is 14 days after service of the particulars of claim (CPR rule 15.4).

Where the defendant does not file a defence within the time specified in CPR rule 15.4, he may still take part in any hearing, but the court may take his failure to do so into account when deciding what order to make about costs (CPR rule 55.7(3)).

The provisions of CPR Part 12 (default judgment) do not apply to possession claims under CPR Part 55 (CPR rule 55.7(4)).

Substantive defences are dealt with in **Chapter 3**.

Use of Form N11M

The defence to a mortgage possession claim must be in Form N11M, the defence form (mortgage residential premises) (see Practice Direction 55A, para.1.5). The current version of the form is dated April 2006 (see **Appendix B5**).

Form N11M is a six-page document which contains numerous questions about the mortgage and arrears, the borrower's income and expenses and ability to pay. As such it provides the adviser with a useful checklist of relevant matters.

Question 10 of the form asks how much the borrower can afford to pay in addition to the current instalments. Advisers will find assistance in formulating an appropriate offer to the court at **8.3.8**.

Question 27 of the form asks the borrower to give details of any events or circumstances which have led to his being in arrears with the mortgage, suggesting divorce, separation, redundancy, bereavement, illness, bankruptcy as examples. This is the space to emphasise to the court:

- the recent payments that the borrower has made;
- the changes in the borrower's circumstances that have been made (or will be made) to demonstrate to the court that past problems are over and the borrower not only can pay current mortgage instalments, but a regular monthly sum towards the arrears;
- the offer being put forward on the borrower's behalf;
- the borrower's ability to pay, either using his own resources if working, or with the benefit of SMI, or with contributions from family and friends;

- the amount of equity in the property, emphasising in particular (if it is the case) that there is ample security for the lender, should the court exercise its power to adjourn the hearing or stay, suspend or postpone possession.

Since the provisions of Practice Direction 55A, para.1.5 are mandatory as to the use of Form N11M, advisers should use it in every case. However, in practice, and particularly where there is a substantive defence to the mortgage action (see **Chapter 3**) a standard defence drafted by the borrower's representative is used. Best practice would be to attach one to the other, so that the lender is not able to take any technical point about non-compliance with Practice Direction 55A. Precedent defences will be found in **Appendix E**.

12.8   NOTIFICATION OF THE DATE OF THE HEARING

In possession claims relating to mortgaged residential property CPR rule 55.10 lays down strict requirements for the claimant to give notice of the hearing. Within five days of receiving notification of the date of the hearing by the court, the claimant must send a notice to:

- the property, addressed to 'the tenant or the occupier';
- the housing department of the local authority within which the property is located; and
- any registered proprietor (other than the claimant) of a registered charge over the property.

The notice to the tenant or the occupier of the property must state that a possession claim for the property has started, show the name and address of the claimant, the defendant and the court which issued the claim form, and give details of the hearing (CPR rule 55.10(3)). The notice to the local authority housing department must provide this information and must also state, as one would expect, the full address of the property (CPR rule 55.10(3A)).

There is express provision in CPR rule 55.10(4) that the claimant must produce at the hearing:

- a copy of the above notices; and
- evidence that they have been sent. This will usually be in the form of copy letters from the claimant's file or the file of their legal representatives, which should be exhibited to the witness statement verified by statement of truth.

Failure to give notice in accordance with the rules is likely to result in the adjournment of the hearing (see case study 3 in **Appendix F1**).

An unauthorised tenant of residential property which is subject to a mortgage possession action by a lender may apply to the court for the order for possession to be suspended (CPR rule 55.10(4A)). The position of tenants of borrowers is dealt with in **Chapter 24**.

12.9 THE HEARING

At the hearing fixed in accordance with CPR rule 55.5(1) or at any adjournment of that hearing, the court may under CPR rule 55.8(1):

- decide the claim; or
- give case management directions.

Where the claim is genuinely disputed on grounds which appear to the court to be substantial, the case management directions will include the allocation of the claim to a track or directions to enable it to be allocated (CPR rule 55.8(2)). The substantial dispute might by a defence to the claim or a material dispute as to the facts or the amounts claimed.

In such a case, the court will often give directions for the filing of a defence and, if appropriate, a reply by the lender, together with a date for the filing of allocation questionnaires. Alternatively, it is quite common for the court to fix a subsequent hearing date, sometimes before the same judge, when the court itself will consider the merits of the case put forward by the defendant.

12.10 EVIDENCE AT THE HEARING

12.10.1 Evidence in writing

Any fact that needs to be proved by the evidence of witnesses at a hearing may be proved by evidence in writing (CPR rule 55.8(3)). Usually this will be in the form of a witness statement prepared by the claimant. By CPR rule 55.8(4) all witness statements must be filed and served at least two days before the hearing.

Further details about the giving of evidence at the hearing appear in Practice Direction 55A (see **Appendix C2**). Each party should wherever possible include all the evidence he wishes to present in his statement of case, verified by a statement of truth (Practice Direction 55A, para.5.1). The rules relating to who may sign a statement of truth in Practice Direction 22 are dealt with at **6.4.2**.

If relevant, the claimant's evidence should include the amount of any mortgage arrears and interest on those arrears (Practice Direction 55A, para.5.2). These amounts should, if possible, be up to date to the date of the hearing (if necessary by specifying a daily rate of arrears and interest). However, CPR rule 55.8(4) does not prevent such evidence being brought up to date orally or in writing on the day of the hearing, if necessary.

12.10.2 Oral evidence

The combined effects of CPR rule 55.8 and Practice Direction 55A, paras.5.1 and 5.2 mean that oral evidence can be given at the hearing, and this is particularly important for borrowers who attend court and wish to defend the possession claim without having obtained prior legal advice.

This was confirmed by Nourse LJ in *Cheltenham & Gloucester Building Society v Grant* (1994) 26 HLR 703, CA, who stated (at 707):

> It is not the function of this court to lay down rigid rules as to how busy district and county court judges should satisfy themselves of what they have to be satisfied for the purposes of sections 36 and 8. It must be possible for them to act without evidence, especially where, as here, the mortgagor is present in court and available to be questioned and no objection to the reception of informal material is made by the mortgagee. Clearly, it will sometimes be prudent for the mortgagor to put in an affidavit before the hearing.

12.11 THE CLAIMANT'S WITNESS STATEMENT

At the hearing the court will expect to see a signed witness statement from the lender, which should have been served on the borrower, giving evidence:

- of up-to-date figures for arrears, balance owing, monthly instalment and last payment by the defendant (with the proviso that these can be updated orally at the hearing);
- of having, within five days of receiving notification of the date of the hearing by the court, served the notice to 'the tenant or the occupier' of the property and to the housing department of the local authority within which the property is located, giving details of the claim and hearing (with copies of such notices) (CPR rule 55.10). The service of this notice is a mandatory requirement and a failure to comply precisely with it should at least result in the adjournment of the case for 28 days;
- if a Class F land charge, a notice under the Family Law Act 1996 or a notice or caution under the Matrimonial Homes Act 1983 has been registered against the owner or against the property, of evidence that notice of the claim and hearing has been given to the person who has registered that charge, notice or caution;
- if the mortgage is a regulated consumer credit agreement, of service of the default notice;
- if the claim has been issued using PCOL, a statement verifying that the lender has complied with the requirements of Practice Direction 55B, paras.6.3A, 6.3B and 6.3C (which relate to the provision of schedules of arrears both before and after the issue of an online possession claim) (see **Appendix C3**); and
- if the claimant is not the registered charge holder on the land register, of the transfer of the mortgage to the claimant or of the original lender's change of name, as appropriate.

If a witness statement is not served or is incomplete, the adviser should bring this to the attention of the court. In busy hearings, judges sometimes do not look at the contents of witness statements very closely, but look in more detail at the documents handed in by the lender's representative, and rely on updating evidence given orally.

12.12 DOCUMENTS TO BE HANDED TO THE COURT

The judge will expect to see the following documents at the hearing:

- two copies of Form N123 (Mortgage Pre-Action Protocol checklist) (see **Appendix B1**), properly completed and signed by an authorised person of sufficient seniority (Practice Direction 22 (see **6.4.2**));
- an official copy of the land register entry for the property concerned;
- an official copy of the legal charge;
- an official search certificate for notices required by the Family Law Act 1996, s.56;
- the mortgage terms and conditions, although often these are not available at the hearing and their absence is not critical, unless the defendant raises a substantive issue in relation to the terms and conditions. An example of this might be where a dispute arises as to whether or not the mortgage terms prohibit lodgers, which the borrower has taken into his home to help meet the mortgage payments. In such a case the court may adjourn the hearing for the lender to produce the mortgage terms and conditions, if they are not available at the original hearing (see case study 2 in **Appendix F1**);
- the regulated consumer credit agreement (in the case of agreements falling within the provisions of CCA 1974); and
- a copy of the default notice, which must have been served on the borrower prior to the issue of proceedings (see **10.6.3**).

Where the claimant rather than the court has served the claim form and particulars of claim, the claimant must produce at the hearing a certificate of service of those documents (CPR rule 55.8(6)). The requirement, under CPR rule 6.17(2)(a), for a certificate of service to be filed within 21 days of the particulars of claim, does not apply to possession proceedings under CPR Part 55.

12.12.1 Documentary and procedural deficiencies

In any of the above cases, the lack of such documentary evidence or its insufficiency in any respect may result in the hearing being adjourned. Alternatively, in the case of serious default, such as the failure to serve a default notice in respect of a regulated consumer credit agreement, a strong argument may be made that the claim should be dismissed.

Advisers should make use of any procedural deficiencies, regardless of whether or not prejudice to the borrower can be shown. The court is usually strict in ensuring that the court procedures are adhered to and that inadequacies in court documents are resolved. Although in a serious case the court may be persuaded to dismiss possession proceedings due to deficiencies, it is more likely that they will justify an adjournment (see case studies in **Appendix F**).

12.13 THE BORROWER'S EVIDENCE

Although a defendant can give oral evidence at the hearing (see **12.10.2**), ideally the borrower will have completed and filed a defence in Form N11M (see **Appendix B5**), which will contain much of the relevant information required by the court in deciding how to deal with the claim. A witness statement is not strictly necessary, but the adviser may wish to prepare one to set out for the court:

- a brief history of the past problems;
- any change in the borrower's circumstances, which has occurred (or which will occur soon) to enable the borrower to remedy the default; and
- the offer which the borrower makes to the court in relation to payment of mortgage arrears.

The witness statement could usefully include details of the property, its occupants, the borrower's financial circumstances, the value of the property concerned and any equity.

Judges usually ask for documentary evidence of payments that the borrower has made, income that he receives from work, a valuation of the property and, where the borrower is trying to sell the property, evidence of the sale transaction. The better the documentary evidence, the more convincing will be the mortgage borrower's case.

If relevant, the borrower should give evidence of the amount of any outstanding payments relevant to the mortgage arrears, such as SMI; the status of any claims for benefit about which a decision has not yet been made, and any applications to appeal or review a benefit decision which has not yet concluded (Practice Direction 55A, para.53). Such information might be inserted into the Form N11M defence.

12.14 WHAT THE COURT CAN AND CANNOT ORDER

12.14.1 Directions

If the claim is genuinely disputed on grounds which appear substantial, directions will include allocation to track or directions to enable it to be allocated (CPR rule 55.8(2)). An obvious example would be a direction that a defence is filed by a certain date.

12.14.2 The court's powers

Detailed descriptions of the court's powers will be found at **8.3.1** (for instalment mortgages), at **9.2** to **9.4** (for all monies charges) and at **10.1.3** (for consumer credit agreements). However, in summary, there are several orders which the court might make (AJA 1970, s.36, as amended):

- an adjournment to another date for the lender and/or borrower to provide further evidence or, for example for the borrower to make a lump sum payment. If the adjournment is the result of the lender's failure to comply with the rules, the court may make an order that it cannot add the costs of that hearing to its security;
- a suspended possession order on terms that the borrower pays the current monthly instalment (CMI) and a regular amount towards arrears. The dates for payments should be structured to fit in with the borrower's circumstances. If initial payments are very low, the court may order that there should be a review hearing after a fixed period;
- an outright possession order forthwith or after a set number of days (usually in multiples of 14), particularly if the borrower can show exceptional hardship. The period may be longer still, if there is evidence of a realistic prospect of the property being sold (see **8.3.10**);
- a general adjournment with permission to restore, if there are no arrears or less than two months' arrears (see **8.3.5**). The adviser should also seek an order that the claim is to stand struck out, if not restored within a fixed period, such as 12 months; or
- in the case of a regulated consumer credit agreement, the court may make a time order under CCA 1974, s.129. An adjournment to another date will be required, with more time allotted for the hearing.

12.14.3 Approach to be taken by the adviser

If there is any prospect that the borrower's situation will improve or that more or better information will emerge over time, the adviser should seek an adjournment.

However, if there is no prospect of improvement even with an adjournment (which, it is submitted, should rarely be the case), the adviser might accept that the judge is likely to be considering an alternative disposal of the claim, i.e. a possession order of some kind. In this case, the adviser will strive to have any possession order suspended on terms that the borrower can meet.

If a case is truly hopeless, it may be best for the borrower that an outright possession order is made at the first hearing, rather than prolong his agony and add to his financial burdens by increasing the arrears and the lender's costs, which will be added to the security. Such hopeless cases exist, but are rare. Even then, it is submitted that the adviser should not actively agree to the making of an outright order but rather, having tested the evidence before and during the hearing, it would be better to say nothing and leave the decision in the hands of the court.

Ultimately, it may depend on what the borrower's instructions are. He may take the view that any adjournment is for the best, regardless of the additional arrears and costs that will occur. If so, the adviser can legitimately argue for an adjournment or a suspension of the order.

12.15 TIME ALLOCATED FOR THE HEARING

In a busy county court list, it is likely that the claim against the borrower will have been scheduled with many other, similar cases and that only five minutes will have been allocated to the hearing. In a straightforward case where the evidence is in order, that may be sufficient time for the court to dispose of the lender's claim and many possession orders will be made at first hearings.

However, where borrowers or their advisers are in a position to raise questions about proper compliance with any aspect of the court procedure or the lender's evidence, or where further time is needed for borrowers to give instructions, take advice or arrange their affairs, the courts are often willing to grant an adjournment, rather than take up substantial amounts of time in an otherwise busy possession list.

12.15.1 Attempting to agree an adjournment

The request for an adjournment should be made to the lender's representative outside court before the hearing begins. If the lender's representative agrees, the court will invariably adjourn the possession claim to another date.

12.15.2 Applying to the court for an adjournment

If the lender rejects the request for an adjournment, then the application must be made to the court at the start of the possession hearing.

Inherent jurisdiction to adjourn proceedings

The court has an inherent jurisdiction to grant adjournments 'which in the ordinary course of procedure may be desirable in circumstances such as temporary inability of a party to attend, and so forth': Russell J, in *Birmingham Citizens Permanent Building Society* v. *Caunt* [1962] Ch 883 at 912.

Civil Procedure Rules

More specifically, courts have the power to adjourn any hearing pursuant to their general case management powers under CPR rule 3.1(2)(b). The court will take into account:

- the timing of the request;
- whether the mortgage borrower has previously sought advice and, if not, why not;
- the general merits of the borrower's case in the light of the level of arrears;
- the borrower's personal circumstances and likely ability to pay the CMI and/or arrears (particularly until the next hearing);
- what the borrower hopes to achieve in the time that would be provided by an adjournment; and

- what the risk may be to the lender of granting an adjournment, which usually entails an assessment of the likely equity in the property.

If a good case can be made out, the court should grant the adjournment application but, of course, there is no guarantee. Therefore, advisers must be prepared to make the best offer in relation to the arrears that the mortgage borrower can realistically make, in case the adjournment is refused and the court proceeds to deal with the claim for possession.

12.16 IMPROVING THE CHANCES OF A FAVOURABLE EXERCISE OF JUDICIAL DISCRETION

There are three essential steps that the borrower can take to improve his chance of obtaining a favourable exercise of judicial discretion (whether it be an adjournment or the suspension of a possession order). The borrower must if at all possible:

- come to the hearing (because, in the absence of the borrower, the court will have no evidence on which to exercise its discretion);
- bring documentary evidence to the hearing (to confirm what he says); and
- make a reasonable offer of payment.

It is for the court to decide what constitutes a reasonable offer of payment, not for the lender. The court will not necessarily follow what the lender and borrower have agreed before the hearing, but will want to be satisfied that the proposals are affordable.

12.16.1 Emphasising the human angle

Some judges claim not to be interested in 'why' the mortgage arrears arose, but this is one of the considerations that the Court of Appeal in *Cheltenham & Gloucester Building Society* v. *Norgan* [1996] 1 WLR 343 said are likely to be relevant in establishing the relevant period for the repayment of those arrears (see **8.3.7**).

Wherever possible, therefore, the adviser should obtain information from the borrower about their personal circumstances and let the judge hear it. The human angle to a possession claim can easily be lost amongst the long list of cases that the judge will be dealing with each day. In particular, the adviser should try to contrast the borrower's past problems, with future solutions.

12.16.2 Using the Mortgage Pre-Action Protocol

In the hearing advisers should also test the evidence by asking:

- to see Form N123 in order to check that it has been properly completed;
- whether the lender has provided all the information required under the Protocol;

- whether the lender answered any reasonable requests that the borrower may have made, for example to change the date or method of payment or the type of mortgage and, if so, whether the lender has given reasons for its decision (especially for any refusal);

If there are any non-compliances, the adviser should ask the court for an adjournment (see case studies at **7.8.5** and **Appendix F3**).

12.16.3 Prior agreements

Even if a borrower has previously agreed to an arrears repayment regime before the hearing, the court will often interfere (and usually reduce) the monthly payments towards arrears, if the amounts agreed appear to be unrealistic.

12.16.4 Review hearings

Where the future is uncertain, the court can sometimes be persuaded to adjourn for a fixed period, or make a possession order suspended on terms as a temporary measure, and then order a review in 6 to 12 months' time. If a review hearing is arranged the borrower needs to make use of the time made available to improve their circumstances (see **Chapter 19**).

Where the borrower needs time to sell his property, but an adjournment or a suspended order is not appropriate, the courts prefer to an outright possession order postponed to a future date (for example, in two or three months' time). It is then open to the borrower to make a subsequent application to the court to vary the possession order, to postpone it further, if the sale has progressed.

12.16.5 Changing contractual terms

Unless a term is 'unfair', see **3.4**, the courts cannot interfere with the contractual terms of the mortgage deed, for example the instalment payment dates. However, the court will sometimes adjust payment dates under suspended possession orders, if there are good reasons (for example, where the borrower is now paid on a different day of the month).

12.16.6 All monies charges

The court's powers will be more limited where the charge is repayable on demand, with no right to pay by instalments. However, advisers should check the terms of the agreement for hidden clauses permitting instalment payments (which may have the effect of enhancing the court's powers) (see **9.4**) and for any unfair terms (see **9.8**).

If the borrower is likely to be able to repay the entire debt over a reasonable period, that will give grounds for an adjournment.

12.16.7 Regulated agreements

If the claim is in respect of a regulated consumer credit agreement under CCA 1974, the adviser should check that it has been properly executed and is in the prescribed form, because if not, it will be enforceable only by way of a court order (**10.4**).

The receipt of a default notice by a borrower entitles the borrower to apply to the court for a time order (CCA 1974, s.129), by means of which the court can reschedule payment of money owed under the agreement (over any length of time). Where the adviser considers that a time order may be appropriate, he should ask for an adjournment for an application to be made (on Form N440) and for witness statement in support to be filed, with a skeleton argument (see **10.9**).

12.17 COSTS OF THE PROCEEDINGS

The general rule is that the unsuccessful party in litigation will be ordered to pay the costs of the successful party, though the court may make a different order (CPR rule 44.3(2)).

In mortgage possession proceedings, the lender will usually be the successful party, since the default of the borrower in making payments under the mortgage deed will have caused the proceedings to be issued in the first place. The lender is likely to seek to recover its costs of the proceedings, either by way of an express order for costs from the court (which may be summarily assessed in a given amount) or through the contractual provisions of the mortgage deed.

Not every mortgage deed includes an express contractual provision for the recovery of the lender's costs from the borrower. *Helden* v. *Strathmore Ltd* [2011] EWCA Civ 452 was such a case, where the Court of Appeal overturned the decision of the first instance judge awarding the lender its costs of the proceedings on an indemnity basis, and substituted an order that the borrower pay 60 per cent of the lender's costs, but on the standard basis.

However, the great majority of mortgages do contractually provide for the lender to recover its costs of enforcing the mortgage on an indemnity basis. As a result, it is very common for the lender not to seek an order for costs from the court, on the basis that it will charge them to the borrower anyway, by adding them to the security, i.e. by adding them to the total amount loaned and secured on the property. It is often difficult for the borrower to challenge the lender's legal costs, but he may do so where the lender has acted unreasonably or where the amount of the costs is unreasonable.

In an appropriate case, it may also be possible to challenge the express contractual provision for the recovery of costs as an 'unfair term' under UTCCR 1999, in which case it will not be binding on the borrower (see **3.4**).

12.17.1 Challenging unreasonable costs

The leading case on costs in mortgage possession proceedings is *Gomba Holdings (UK) Ltd* v. *Minories Finance Ltd (No. 2)* [1993] Ch 171, CA. In that case, the court held that the lender was contractually entitled to payment of its costs on an indemnity basis. However, the court still had discretion to assess those costs and the lender was not entitled to 'any costs that had not been reasonably incurred or were unreasonable in amount'.

The principles set out in *Gomba Holdings* are now reflected in CPR rule 48.3 and Practice Direction 48, para.50. Unhelpfully for the borrower, where costs are payable pursuant to a contract, such as a mortgage deed, there is a presumption that those costs have been reasonably incurred and are reasonable in amount (CPR rule 48.3). Further, the court is not required to make an assessment of such costs, nor is the lender required to apply to the court for an order for those costs that it has a contractual right to recover out of the mortgage funds (Practice Direction 48, para.50.2).

12.17.2 Borrower's application for an account

However, by Practice Direction 48, para.50.4:

- the borrower may make an application for the court to direct that an account of the lender's costs be taken (which the court may order under CPR rule 25.1(1)(a));
- the borrower may then dispute an amount in the lender's account on the basis that it has been unreasonably incurred or is unreasonable in amount; and
- where the borrower disputes an amount, the court may make an order that the disputed costs are assessed under CPR rule 48.3.

Where the lender has acted in an unreasonable way, for example, by failing to comply with the Mortgage Pre-Action Protocol or by attending court with incomplete documentation resulting in an adjournment, the adviser may wish to take a short cut, by asking the court to make an order that the lender's costs 'should not be added to the security'. Failing that, the borrower could ask for an account of the lender's costs with a view to an assessment of those costs by the court pursuant to CPR rule 48.3.

12.17.3 Challenging the costs of the lender's solicitors

Another approach is for the borrower to ask the court to direct that an account be taken of the costs of the lender's solicitor, either under CPR rule 25.1(1)(a) or under the Solicitors Act (SA) 1974, ss.70 and 71. That should be done either at the hearing, or within one month of the delivery of the bill (SA 1974, s.70(1)). Application may be made after this time, but the court will not then be bound to carry out the assessment, and after 12 months it will only do so 'in special circumstances' (SA 1974, s.70(2) and (3)).

The application will have to be made in the High Court, unless the work related to proceedings in the county court and the bill does not exceed £5,000 (SA 1974, s.69(3)).

12.17.4 Possession orders, appeals and warrants

Possession orders and appeals are dealt with in **Chapter 13**. Warrants for possession are dealt with in **Chapter 14**.

CHAPTER 13

Possession orders and appeals

13.1 SUSPENDED POSSESSION ORDERS

Any possession order is a step nearer to eviction. A suspended possession order reflects the view of the court that the borrower's default is sufficiently serious to entitle the lender to possession, but the borrower's circumstances are such that it appears he is likely to be able within a reasonable period to pay off the arrears, together with the current monthly instalments.

So long as the borrower keeps to the terms imposed by the court, the lender is unlikely to take further action to evict the borrower. However, should the borrower breach the term of the suspension, even, for example, by delaying a monthly payment by a day, the lender will be entitled to apply for a warrant of eviction.

In practice, lenders do not take such action for minor breaches of the court order, particularly where the borrower has kept in contact with the lender, explained any temporary difficulty and put things right within a reasonable period. The problems arise when the borrower is not able to remedy the default.

Should the lender apply for a warrant of eviction, the borrower is advised to apply for a stay of eviction and a variation of the suspended order. Fuller details will be found in **Chapter 14**.

13.2 OUTRIGHT POSSESSION ORDERS

Sometimes it may not be possible to prevent an outright order being made. Although lenders will often seek an immediate possession order (i.e. enforceable 'forthwith'), courts will typically order possession to take effect in 14 or 28 days. There may even be circumstances in which the court may be persuaded to postpone the giving of possession for a longer period, for example if there is a realistic possibility that the property will be sold in a reasonable period.

13.2.1 Options

At this stage the options open to the borrower are:

- to apply to set aside the possession order;

- to apply to suspend the outright order; or
- to appeal against the possession order.

These options are explored in detail below. Where they prove successful, they will enable the borrower to remain in his home. However, if the borrower decides not to take one of these options or if they prove unsuccessful, the adviser will need to advise him about his rights to housing advice and assistance and/or to rehousing by the local authority. For a summary of the law relating to homelessness, see **Appendix G**.

13.3 SETTING ASIDE THE POSSESSION ORDER

There may be grounds to apply to set aside the possession order if the borrower did not attend the hearing, for example due to illness, or if the borrower did not receive a copy of the summons. There are two competing provisions of the CPR, which have potential application to such a situation:

- the court's general power under CPR rule 3.1(2)(m) to 'take any other step or make any other order for the purpose of managing the case and furthering the overriding objective'; and
- the specific provision in CPR rule 39.3(3) that where a party does not attend a trial and the court gives judgment or makes an order against him, the party who failed to attend may apply for the judgment or order to be set aside. Such an application must be supported by evidence.

Of the two, CPR rule 39.3 is more problematic for the borrower, since CPR rule 39.3(5) goes on to say that where an application is made to set aside an order under the above provision, the court may grant the application only if the applicant:

- acted promptly when he found out the court had exercised its discretion to strike out or to enter judgment or to make order against him;
- had a good reason for not attending the trial; and
- had a reasonable prospect of success at the trial.

Fortunately for borrowers, it was held in the case of *Forcelux Ltd* v. *Binnie* [2009] EWCA Civ 854, [2010] CP Rep 7 (a landlord and tenant case) that the first hearing of a possession claim under CPR rule 55.8 is not considered to be 'a trial'. Therefore, CPR rule 39.3 does not apply, since it expressly relates to the situation where a party does not attend 'a trial'.

While *Forcelux* allowed a party to set aside a possession order under CPR rule 3.1(2)(m), the court also stated that the factors set out in CPR rule 39.3 should still be 'taken into account' in the exercise of the CPR rule 3.1(2)(m) discretion.

The matter was considered again in the more recent case of *London Borough of Hackney* v. *Findlay* [2011] EWCA Civ 8, [2011] NPC 7. In that case the Court of Appeal said that 'in the absence of some unusual and highly compelling factor as in *Forcelux* [which involved the forfeiture of a lease on the basis of non-payment of a small amount of ground rent] a court that is asked to set aside a possession order under CPR 3.1 should in general apply the requirements of CPR 39.3(5) by analogy' (at [24]).

The effect of these cases is that in any application by a borrower to set aside an outright possession order the factors set out in CPR rule 39.3(5) will be relevant to the CPR rule 3.1 discretion, although they are still not absolute requirements. Even so, advisers should address those factors in any application that is made. A precedent application to set aside a possession order, a draft order and a sample witness statement in support will be found in **Appendices E3, E4** and **E5**.

13.3.1   Inter-relation with CPR Part 52 (appeals)

In *Bank of Scotland* v. *Pereira* [2011] EWCA Civ 241, [2011] 11 EG 102 (CS), the defendant in mortgage possession proceedings knew about the hearing, requested an adjournment, but did not attend. Orders were made in her absence for possession and a money judgment. Two years later she applied to set aside parts of the order. Her application under CPR rule 39.3 was refused.

In dismissing her appeal, the Court of Appeal considered the criteria to be applied when hearing applications to set aside judgment under CPR rule 39.3 and the inter-relationship between CPR rule 39.3 and appeals under CPR Part 52. Lord Neuberger MR expounded six detailed points of guidance which 'would apply in the great majority of cases', the first two which were:

- where the defendant is seeking a new trial on the ground that she did not attend the trial, then, even though she may have other possible grounds of appeal, she should normally proceed under CPR rule 39.3;
- if the defendant concludes that she cannot establish that she had a good reason for not attending the trial and/or that she made her CPR rule 39.3 application promptly, she can nonetheless seek to appeal against the trial judge's decision in the same way as any other defendant under CPR Part 52.

Lord Neuberger MR also stated that the court should wherever possible scrutinise applications under CPR rule 39.3 and deal with them on the basis of written evidence (at [52]).

13.4   APPLYING TO SUSPEND THE OUTRIGHT ORDER

If there has been a change of circumstances an application can be made on Form N244 to suspend the outright order. This is in effect a variation of the order that has been made and a request for the court to reconsider its discretion under AJA 1970, s.36, as amended. In order for such an application to succeed there would have to be a significant change in circumstances.

Appropriate circumstances for making an application to vary might include where the borrower finds well-paid work immediately following the making of an outright possession order.

Sometimes judges will also give an indication that an application to vary an outright order may be made where the borrower is in the process of selling the property but, at the date of the hearing, there has been insufficient progress to justify a suspended order. In those circumstances the judge may well make an outright possession order, while postponing the date for giving that possession by two or three months. If there has been significant progress, such as the exchange of contracts, an application to vary or to suspend the outright order may be appropriate. The precedents in **Appendices E6, E7** and **E8** (relating to an application to suspend a warrant of eviction) might be adapted for this purpose.

13.5 APPEALS

The court rules about appeals will be found in CPR Part 52 and Practice Direction 52.

13.5.1 Permission to appeal

An application for permission to appeal should be made orally at the hearing at which the decision to be appealed against is made. Where no application for permission to appeal is made at the hearing, or the lower court refuses permission to appeal, an application for permission to appeal may be made to the appeal court in accordance with CPR rule 52.3(2) and (3).

Permission to appeal will only be given where the court considers that the appeal would have a real prospect of success or there is some other compelling reason why the appeal should be heard.

13.5.2 Routes of appeal

An appeal against a possession order made by a district judge is to the circuit judge in the county court. An appeal from a possession order made by a circuit judge lies to a single judge of the High Court.

13.5.3 Time for appeal

The borrower must file an appellant's notice in Form N161 at the appeal court usually within 21 days after the date of the decision being appealed against (CPR rule 52.4(2)). Unless a separate application for permission has been made to the appeal court, a request for permission from the appeal court must be requested in the appellant's notice.

13.5.4 Application for a stay of execution

The lodging of an appeal itself does not operate as a stay of the possession order (CPR rule 52.7). Therefore, when applying for permission to appeal, either to the lower court or to the appeal court, an application should be made at the same time to stay execution of the possession order pending the outcome of the appeal.

If necessary, the application for a stay of execution should be repeated in the appellant's notice.

13.5.5 Respondent to an appeal

By CPR rule 52.4 an appellant's notice must be served on each respondent as soon as practicable and, in any event, not later than seven days after it is filed. This will usually happen where a respondent wishes to ask the appeal court to uphold the order of the lower court for reasons different from, or additional to, those given by the lower court. A respondent's notice may also be filed if the appeal is successful and the respondent seeks permission to appeal from the appeal court.

As with an appellant's notice, the respondent's notice must be served on the appellant as soon practicable and, in any event, not later than seven days after it is filed.

13.5.6 Extending time for appeal

By CPR rule 52.6 an application to vary the time limit for filing an appeal notice must be made to the appeal court. The parties themselves may not agree to extend that time.

The court may extend or shorten the time for compliance with any rule, practice direction or court order, even if an application for extension is made after the time for compliance has expired (CPR rule 3.1(2)(a)).

Further guidance is given in paras.5.2–5.4 of Practice Direction 52. Where the time for filing an appellant's notice has expired, the appellant may still file a notice, but must include in it an application for extension of time. The appellant's notice should state the reason for the delay and the steps taken prior to the application being made.

Where the appellant's notice includes an application for an extension of time, the respondent has the right to be heard on that application. Therefore, the appellant must serve a copy of the appeal bundle (see below) although a respondent who unreasonably opposes an extension of time runs the risk of being ordered to pay the appellant's costs of that application.

13.5.7 Fees

A fee is payable on the lodging of an appellant's notice unless the appellant seeks and qualifies for a waiver using Form EX160 (for example, if he is in receipt of certain state benefits). Details of the current court fee can be found in Form EX50, obtainable online from the Ministry of Justice website (**www.justice.gov.uk**).

13.5.8 Documents to accompany an appellant's notice

Practice Direction 52, paras.5.6 and 5.6A list the documents that must accompany an appellant's notice. These are also listed in the Form N161 as a checklist. The simplest way of collating documents that are required is by using a ring binder with the Form N161 checklist as a front sheet.

Form N161 provides space at the end to list those documents that are not available in time, with the reasons why they are not supplied and the date when they will be supplied. Therefore, there is no reason to delay filing an appellant's notice or to miss the 21-day time limit simply due to the fact that certain documents are not yet available.

The appellant's notice must be accompanied by the following documents, together with an appeal bundle (which is dealt with below):

- two additional copies of the appellant's notice for the appeal court;
- one copy of the appellant's notice for each of the respondents;
- one copy of the appellant's skeleton argument (unless it is included in the appellant's notice itself) – see below for other provisions relation skeleton arguments;
- a sealed copy of the order being appealed;
- a copy of any order giving or refusing permission to appeal, together with a copy of the judge's reason for allowing or refusing permission to appeal;
- any witness statements or affidavits in support of any application included in the appellant's notice (for example, applications requesting permission to appeal, extending time to appeal or seeking a stay of execution of the possession order); and
- a copy of the order allocating a case to a track (if any).

13.5.9 The appeal bundle

In addition to the appellant's notice and the documents which must accompany it, the appellant must prepare and file two copies of the appeal bundle. Where the appellant is applying for permission to appeal in his appellant's notice, while he must serve on the respondent his appellant's notice and skeleton argument, he need not serve a copy of the appeal bundle at that stage, unless the court directs otherwise. However, where permission to appeal has already been given by the lower court, the appellant must serve the appeal bundle on the respondent with the appellant's notice.

The appeal bundle should contain:

- a sealed copy of the appellant's notice;
- a sealed copy of the order being appealed;

- a copy of any order giving or refusing permission to appeal, together with a copy of the judge's reasons for allowing or refusing permission for the appeal;
- any affidavit or witness statement filed in support of any application included in the appellant's notice;
- a copy of the skeleton argument;
- a transcript or note of judgment and a transcript of evidence which is directly relevant to any question of issue on the appeal;
- the claim form and statements of case;
- any application notice or case management documentation relevant to the subject of the appeal; and
- any other documents which the appellant reasonably considers necessary to enable the appeal court to reach its decision on the hearing of the application for the appeal.

Where the appellant is represented, the appeal bundle must contain a certificate signed by the appellant's solicitor, counsel or other representative to the effect that he has read and understood para.5.6A(2) of Practice Direction 52 (which requires documents extraneous to the issues to be excluded) and that the composition of the appeal bundle complies with it.

Where it is not possible to file all of the above documents, the appellant must indicate which documents have not yet been filed and the reasons why they are not currently available. There is space for this at the end of Form N161. The appellant must then provide a reasonable estimate of when the missing document or documents can be filed and file them as soon as reasonably practicable.

13.5.10   Skeleton arguments

Paragraphs 5.9 and 5.10 of Practice Direction 52 relate to the preparation and filing of skeleton arguments. The purpose of a skeleton argument is to define and confine the areas of controversy.

The skeleton argument must accompany the appellant's notice or may be included within the notice. Where it is impracticable for the appellant's skeleton argument to accompany the appellant's notice, it must be filed and served on all the respondents within 14 days of filing the notice. Whilst an appellant who is not represented does not need to file a skeleton argument, the court rules encourage him to do so, since it will be helpful to the court.

The skeleton argument must contain a numbered list of the points which the party wishes to make. Reference must be made to any document on which the party wishes to rely. The skeleton argument should also make reference to relevant law and cite relevant authorities. In the case of each authority cited, the skeleton argument must state the proposition of law that the authority demonstrates and the parts of the authority (identified by page or paragraph references) that support the proposition.

13.5.11 Suitable record of the judgment

Many, if not most, possession hearings in the county court will have been recorded. Where the judgment to be appealed has been officially recorded by the court, an approved transcript of that record should accompany the appellant's notice. In reality, a transcript of the record will take many weeks to obtain. Application is made to the court on Form EX107. Information about the companies providing transcriptions services and the maximum prices for transcripts from authorised bodies are found in Form EX107 Info. Both are obtainable online from the Ministry of Justice website (**www.justice.gov.uk**).

13.5.12 Transcripts at public expense

Where the appellant is unrepresented or representation is being provided free of charge (not funded by the Community Legal Service), the lower court or the appeal court may certify that the cost of obtaining one official transcript should be borne at public expense, where it is satisfied that the appellant is in such poor financial circumstances that the cost of a transcript would be an excessive burden.

In effect, this is an application for a waiver of the fees that would be incurred in obtaining a transcript. The appellant must complete Form EX105 for this purpose. The court must also be satisfied that there are reasonable grounds for appeal.

Wherever possible a request for a transcript at public expense (using Form EX105) should be made to the lower court when asking for permission to appeal. It may be that the court will postpone consideration of that request until a Form EX105 has been completed and submitted to the court.

13.5.13 Alternatives to a transcript

Where there is no officially recorded judgment alternative documents will be acceptable as listed in para.5.12 of Practice Direction 52. These include:

- where the judgment was made in writing, a copy of that judgment endorsed with the judge's signature;
- a note of judgment agreed between the parties' advocates, which should be submitted for approval to the judge whose decision is being appealed (or if agreement cannot be reached, then copies of both versions should be submitted to the judge). For the purpose of an application for permission to appeal the note need not be approved by the respondent or the lower court judge;
- advocates' notes of judgment where the appellant is unrepresented.

13.5.14 Transcripts or notes of evidence

Where the evidence is relevant in an appeal an official transcript of the relevant evidence must be obtained (over and above the record of the judgment). Transcripts

132

or notes of evidence are generally not needed for the purpose of determining an application for permission to appeal.

If evidence relevant to the appeal was not officially recorded, a typed version of the judge's notes of evidence must be obtained.

13.5.15 Permission hearings

Where the lower court has refused permission to appeal, the application for permission to appeal in the appellant's notice may be considered by the appeal court without a hearing. If permission is granted, the parties will be notified of that decision. If the appeal court gives permission to appeal, the appeal bundle must be served on each of the respondents within seven days of receiving the order giving permission to appeal.

If permission is refused without a hearing, the appellant may file a request for the decision to be reconsidered at an oral hearing. Such a request must be filed at the appeal court within seven days after service of the notice that permission has been refused. A copy of the request must be served by the appellant on the respondent at the same time. The oral hearing may be before the same judge.

Where a request has been made for the decision to be reconsidered at an oral hearing, the appellant's advocate (where the appellant is represented) must in a brief written statement:

- inform the court and the respondent of the points which he proposes to raise at the hearing;
- set out his reasons why permission should be granted, notwithstanding the reasons given for the refusal of permission; and
- confirm, where applicable, that the Legal Services Commission has been notified of the reason why the appeal court refused permission without a hearing.

13.5.16 Hearing of appeals

Every appeal will be limited to a review of the decision of the lower court unless the court considers that, in the circumstances of an individual appeal, it would be in the interests of justice to hold a rehearing (CPR rule 52.11).

In either case, the appeal court will only allow an appeal where the decision of the lower court was:

- wrong; or
- unjust because of a serious procedural or other irregularity in the proceedings in the lower court.

Generally, the appeal court will not receive oral evidence or evidence which was not before the lower court, unless the appeal court orders otherwise. In addition, at the hearing of the appeal, a party may not rely on a matter not contained in his appeal notice unless the appeal court gives permission.

Rehearings in practice

In practice, consideration of the application for permission to appeal and the substantive appeal are often dealt with at the same time. Although not usually a rehearing, the time spent by the appeal court on the matter will often be similar to or greater than the time spent by the lower court so that, effectively, the appellant achieves a rehearing of their case.

New evidence

A strict application of the rules would prevent new evidence being admitted, but the advisers will always seek to emphasise advantageous changes in circumstances since the original hearing and, in practice, the appeal court will usually take these into account when reaching its decision.

A well-constructed appeal will therefore result in a thorough review of the appellant's case by a more senior judge.

13.5.17 Disposing of applications of appeal by consent

While an appeal is pending, the advisers should negotiate with the respondent (lender) to see if agreement can be reached with regard to the disposal of the appeal.

While the appeal court will not normally make an order allowing an appeal unless satisfied that the decision of the lower court was wrong, the appeal court may set aside or vary the order of the lower court with consent and without determining the merits of the appeal, if it is satisfied that there are good and sufficient reasons for doing so.

Where the appeal court is requested by all parties to allow an application or an appeal, the court may consider the request on the papers. It is a requirement of the rules that the request should state that none of the parties is a child or protected party and that the application or appeal is not from a decision of the Court of Protection. The request should also set out the relevant history of the proceedings and the matters relied upon as justifying the proposed order. A draft order should accompany the request.

13.5.18 Second appeals

Permission is required from the Court of Appeal for any appeal to that court from a decision of a county court or the High Court, which was itself made on appeal. The Court of Appeal will not give permission unless it considers that:

- the appeal would raise an important point of principle or practice; or
- there is some other compelling reason for the Court of Appeal to hear it.

Special provisions apply regarding the filing of documents, the preparation of bundles and the listing of hearings before the Court of Appeal, which will be found in Practice Direction 52, para.15. These are not dealt with in this book.

CHAPTER 14

Applications to stay warrants for possession

14.1 OVERVIEW

The lender will seek to enforce a possession order in two circumstances:

- where an outright possession order has been made by the court and the date for giving possession has passed; and
- where a suspended possession order has been made, but the borrower has breached the terms of the suspension.

14.2 ENFORCEMENT BY THE COURT

In either case the lender can only enforce the order for possession through the courts, i.e. by requesting the attendance of the county court bailiff to attend the property and evict the occupants (or, unusually, by registering the possession order in the High Court and instructing High Court enforcement officers, formerly known as sheriffs).

14.2.1 Time for issue and duration

If six years have elapsed since the possession order was made, it cannot be enforced without the permission of the court (CPR Sched.2; CCR Order 26, rule 5). Once issued, the warrant is valid for 12 months, but may be renewed from time to time (CCR Order 26, rule 6).

14.2.2 Procedure for issue

The lender completes Form N325, a request for warrant of possession of land. That must certify that:

- the defendant has not vacated the land as ordered and/or that the whole or part of any instalments due under the judgment or order have not been paid;

- 14 days' notice has been given to the occupier or tenant that an application has been made to the court for a warrant of possession of the property pursuant to the Mortgage Repossessions (Protection of Tenants etc) Act 2010, s.2(2) and the Dwelling-houses (Execution of Possession Orders by Mortgagees) Regulations 2010, SI 2010/1809 (both reproduced in **Appendices A8** and **A9**); and
- the form must also indicate accurately the date of possession under the judgment or order.

Upon receipt of the request, the court bailiff will fix the date and time of an appointment to enforce the possession order. A letter is usually sent to the borrower giving 7 to 14 days' notice of that appointment (but this is not a requirement in the High Court).

14.3 APPLICATION TO SUSPEND THE WARRANT

The first step for an adviser is to check whether the conditions for the grant of a bailiff's warrant of possession have been met, see **14.1** and **14.2**.

If any of the conditions are not satisfied, the lender should be invited to withdraw the bailiff's warrant. If the lender agrees, this must be confirmed in writing both to the court and to the borrower and the borrower's adviser. If the lender is unwilling to withdraw the warrant, the fact that the conditions have not been satisfied will significantly strengthen an application to suspend the warrant.

14.3.1 Application form

Application for suspension of a warrant is made on Form N245, available online on the Ministry of Justice website (**www.justice.gov.uk**). The form provides space to enable the borrower to apply for a suspension of the warrant and/or a reduction in the instalment order on the grounds that the borrower cannot pay the amount ordered by the court. The bulk of the two-page application form is a financial means questionnaire. Space is also provided for an offer to be made by the borrower.

In practice, it is common for Form N245 to be combined with the standard application notice Form N244, since this allows greater detail to be given about the order that the court is asked to make and the grounds for the application. Although there is space on the reverse of Form N244 to provide information in support of the application, very often a witness statement will be appropriate where there is a great deal of information to convey to the court. A precedent application to suspend a warrant of eviction, a draft order and a sample witness statement in support will be found in **Appendices E6, E7** and **E8**.

14.3.2 Fees and remission

A fee is payable (see Form EX50) unless the borrower qualifies for a fee remission, see details in Form EX160A ('Court fees do you have to pay them?') and the application for a fee remission at the end of that booklet.

In the case of an emergency application for a stay, it is possible to provide the court with an undertaking to apply for remission of a court fee or to pay a court fee at a later date, by completing Form EX160B.

14.3.3 Time for an application to suspend

An application for a stay of execution should be made at the earliest opportunity. However, it is never too late to apply for a stay prior to the eviction, even if the application is made on the day before, or even the morning of the eviction itself.

Where an application is made at the last minute, steps should be taken to ensure that the court bailiffs are advised of the application and that a hold is placed on the eviction until such time as the application is heard

14.3.4 Possession Claim Online

Where proceedings were brought using Possession Claim Online (PCOL), the borrower can apply online for a stay of execution so long as it is not less than five days before the eviction is due to take place. Further details about an application to suspend a warrant of possession under PCOL will be found in Practice Direction 55B, para.13 (see **Appendix C3**).

14.3.5 Evidence in support

The application and/or witness statement should provide evidence as to why the borrower has not adhered to the terms of a suspended possession order, and to show that the borrower will be able to make payments in the future, either those originally ordered by the court or other payments which the borrower now proposes by way of variation of the suspended order. In short, the borrower should explain:

- what the problem was;
- how that problem has been resolved; and
- the new offer is being placed before the court.

The borrower should provide as much evidence as possible of any recent change in circumstances and generally to support the contention that the proposed payments will be met in the future. It is helpful to provide documentary evidence of payments that have been made since the possession order. This is because lenders' agents are often not provided with such information and the court will be interested to know what efforts have been made by the borrower to date.

14.4 HEARING OF THE APPLICATION

Applications to suspend a warrant of possession are usually listed by the county court at 9.30 or 10 am each morning, though occasionally they may be heard at 2 pm. In the vast majority of cases, they will be heard by a district judge.

The adviser's task is to find and present to the judge something upon which discretion may be exercised. It is often helpful to calculate payments that have fallen due since the making of the original possession order and compare that figure with payments actually met (regardless of whether these are contractual payments or payments made under the terms of the suspended order). District judges are often impressed by serious attempts by the borrower to pay over time, even if the payments fall short of the amount previously ordered by the court.

Advisers should emphasise the effects of any eviction, especially with regard to the health and well-being of the borrower and the effect on any children living at the property. In all cases, it is beneficial to emphasise any change in circumstances since the suspended possession was made or since the default occurred.

14.4.1 The court's powers

The court's powers on an application to suspend a warrant for possession are the same as those available on the making of the possession order itself.

Where AJA 1970, s.36 applies (see **Chapters 8** and **9**), the court has power to adjourn the proceedings, stay or suspend execution of the possession order, or postpone the date for delivery of possession, for such period or periods as the court thinks reasonable. The court also has power to vary or revoke any condition that it has previously imposed by virtue of AJA 1970, s.36 (see AJA 1970, s.36(4)).

Where CCA 1974 applies (see **Chapter 10**) the court has power to make the operation of any term of the order conditional on the doing of specified acts by any party to the proceedings or to suspend the operation of any term of the order for a period of time or subject to conditions (see CCA 1974, s.135).

These powers are in addition to the court's general powers of management. In particular, CPR rule 3.1(2)(f) permits the court to stay the whole or part of any proceedings or judgment either generally or until a specified date or event and CPR rule 3.1(2)(m) to take any other step or make any other order for the purpose of managing the case and furthering the overriding objective.

By CPR rule 3.1(7), '[t]he power of the court under these Rules to make an order includes the power to vary or revoke the order'. However, it should be noted that the power of the court to revoke an order is likely to be used sparingly, since an appeal would be the normal procedure.

14.5   SEEKING A SUSPENSION OF A WARRANT IN ORDER TO SELL THE PROPERTY

The court may suspend execution of a warrant for possession, if there is evidence that a sale may be effected within a reasonable period of time. However, there are several cases where the courts have declined to do so, where the evidence has been insufficient. See, for example, *Bristol & West Building Society* v. *Ellis* [1996] EWCA Civ 1294, (1996) 73 P & CR 158; and *National and Provincial Building Society* v. *Lloyd* [1996] 1 All ER 630. See **8.3.10** for more detail.

In *Cheltenham & Gloucester Building Society* v. *Krausz* [1997] 1 WLR 1558, the borrowers were in negative equity (i.e. the value of their home was less than the amount owed to the lender). The borrowers sought to suspend a warrant of possession, to prevent their eviction while they applied to the court for an order for sale under LPA 1925, s.91. The Court of Appeal held that the county court had no jurisdiction to suspend the warrant to enable the borrowers to apply to the High Court for the order for sale.

However, in *Cheltenham & Gloucester plc* v. *Booker* (1997) 29 HLR 634, the court's powers under AJA 1970, s.36 were not available, because the court could not be satisfied that the borrowers would be able to pay off the arrears within a reasonable period. The Court of Appeal held that the county court did have a residual jurisdiction to suspend a warrant to enable the borrowers to remain in the property while the lender sold it.

14.6   AFTER THE WARRANT FOR POSSESSION HAS BEEN EXECUTED

Once the court bailiff has executed a warrant for possession and evicted the borrower, the court's statutory powers under AJA 1970, s.36 are exhausted: see *Cheltenham and Gloucester Building Society* v. *Obi* (1994) 28 HLR 22.

14.6.1   Setting aside the possession order

However, it may still be possible to apply to the court to set aside the possession order itself since, if such an application were successful, the warrant for possession would also be set aside, and with it the eviction (see *Governors of Peabody Donation Fund* v. *Hay* (1987) 19 HLR 145 (a landlord and tenant case)).

A possession order may be set aside by the court exercising its case management powers under CPR rule 3.1(2)(m) and (7). For a discussion of the procedures and the competing provisions in CPR rule 39.3(5), see **13.3**.

14.6.2   Setting aside the warrant for possession

Another approach may be to apply to the court to set aside the warrant for possession itself on grounds of fraud, oppression or abuse of process by the lender

(*Leicester City Council* v. *Aldwinckle* (1992) 24 HLR 40 (a landlord and tenant case); *Cheltenham and Gloucester Building Society* v. *Obi* (1994) 28 HLR 22).

These grounds may be difficult to establish but, for example, a failure by the lender to follow its own mortgage arrears procedures may amount to abuse of process.

14.6.3   Right to redeem

Even after the warrant has been executed the borrower retains the right – up to the moment of sale by the lender – to redeem the mortgage and upon such redemption both the lender's right to possession and right of sale cease to exist, so that the borrower may lawfully re-enter the property.

14.6.4   Homelessness rights

If it is not possible to set aside either the possession order or the warrant for possession, borrowers will need advice about any rights that they and their families may have to be rehoused under the homelessness legislation, which is outside the ambit of this book. For a summary of the law relating to homelessness, see **Appendix G**.

CHAPTER 15

Funding

15.1 SOURCES OF FREE ADVICE

There are many sources of free legal advice for mortgage borrowers in financial difficulties.

Community Legal Advice is a free and confidential advice service in England and Wales paid for by legal aid. Initial telephone advice can be given to borrowers living on a low income or benefits by calling the help line on 0845 345 4345 (Monday to Friday 9 am to 8 pm, Saturday 9 am to 12.30 pm). Callers will be asked a number of questions about their finances to see if they are eligible for legal aid, together with a number of questions about their problem, to find out what help is needed.

Shelter England is a charity working to alleviate the distress caused by homelessness and bad housing. Free advice can be obtained from the website at **http://England.shelter.org.uk**. Alternatively, Shelter can answer queries by email or borrowers may make use of their free, national telephone housing advice line, staffed by trained housing advisers, on 0808 800 4444 (Monday to Friday 8 am to 8 pm; Saturday to Sunday 8 am to 5 pm).

Further web-based advice can be obtained from Citizens Advice (**www.adviceguide.org.uk**), the National Debtline (**www.nationaldebtline.co.uk**) and the Money Advice Service (**www.moneyadviceservice.org.uk**).

In addition, certain other charities and local authorities will fund pre-mortgage advice schemes in their areas, primarily through local advice centres and Law Centres.

However, the above sources of free advice will not necessarily cover the casework that may be needed in order to deal with negotiations with the lender or representation in mortgage possession proceedings before the court.

15.2 ELIGIBILITY FOR LEGAL AID

Legal aid is currently administered by the Legal Services Commission (LSC), an executive non-departmental public body created to develop and administer the Community Legal Service (CLS) and the Criminal Defence Service.

At its simplest, advice and assistance can be given to mortgage borrowers through the Legal Help scheme. Representation at court may be provided in simple cases, for example, where the probable outcome is a suspended possession order and there is no defence, to help the borrower with the terms of a suspended order, to dispute the amount of the arrears or to suspend a possession warrant, through an extension of the Legal Help scheme known as Help at Court (see para.19.3 of Volume 3C (Funding Code Guidance) of the LSC Manual). In more complex cases, for example, where there is a substantive defence such as fraud, duress or undue influence or a substantive counterclaim, a higher form of legal aid known as Legal Representation may be available (see para.19.7.16 of Volume 3C).

There are provisions in the Legal Aid, Sentencing and Punishment of Offenders Bill, presented to Parliament on 21 June 2011 (see **15.5**), to abolish the LSC and transfer LSC functions to an Executive Agency of the Ministry of Justice (on or after 1 October 2012).

15.2.1 Assessment of income and capital

In all cases an assessment has to be carried out of the borrower's income and capital. In the case of Legal Help and Help at Court that assessment will be carried out by the adviser. In the case of Legal Representation this assessment is carried out by the LSC.

The CLS provides an online 'civil legal aid eligibility calculator', which is designed for LSC service providers (i.e. solicitors and other advisers). It can be found via the CLS website (**www.legalservices.gov.uk/civil.asp**). The online tool helps work out eligibility for those levels of Legal Help where the provider is responsible for means assessment.

Members of the public should use the alternative legal aid calculator on the Ministry of Justice website: **http://legalaidcalculator.justice.gov.uk/calculators/ eligiCalc**.

The online legal aid calculators are not a replacement for the detailed financial eligibility guidance in Volume 2E (Financial Eligibility) of the LSC Manual (which is dealt with below). There is a link ('For more information') to Volume 2E on the first web page of CLS eligibility calculator and extracts are reproduced at **Appendix D1**.

Assessment of capital

The main problem for homeowners may be the amount of their capital, i.e. the value of their property to be taken into account in the assessment.

15.2.2 Borrowers who are 'passported' to financial eligibility

In the case of Legal Help and Help at Court, those in receipt of income support, income-based jobseeker's allowance, income-based employment and support allowance or guarantee credit qualify for legal aid automatically regardless of the level of their capital. These benefits act as a 'passport' to financial eligibility for all levels of legal aid. This means that, currently, the adviser does not need to be concerned with capital limits and/or the value of the borrower's home.

However, there are proposals to remove 'passporting' and instead apply the same capital eligibility rules to applicants in receipt of benefits, as apply to other applicants for legal aid (see **15.5**).

15.2.3 Borrowers who are not 'passported' to financial eligibility

At all times, the borrower's income and capital must be aggregated with those of their spouse or partner (including a person of the same sex) with whom the borrower lives as a couple. This definition includes a spouse or partner with whom the borrower concerned is physically separated (for example, due to different job locations or the fact that one of the parties is in prison, hospital, residential care), but they are not 'living separate and apart' due to the breakdown of the relationship.

Further details are found in para.4.2 of Volume 2E (Financial Eligibility) of the LSC Manual (see **Appendix D1**).

Contributions towards legal aid

Calculations must be made for the borrower's gross income and disposable income (with allowable deductions), as well as the borrower's disposable capital. In certain circumstances where disposable income and/or capital are at a certain level within the legal aid limits, the borrower may be called upon to make a financial contribution towards legal aid.

Capital disregards

Assuming that the borrower's income is within legal aid limits (for which see Volume 2E (Financial Eligibility) of the LSC Manual), the capital disregard is £8,000 as at 11 April 2011. There are additional capital disregards on assessments where either the borrower (or their spouse/partner with whom their resources are to be aggregated) is aged 60 years or over at the date of computation, and their disposable income is less than £315 per month. The additional capital disregards range from £10,000 to £100,000 (LSC Manual, Volume 2E (Financial Eligibility), para.7.5).

Capital arising from the borrower's home

For Legal Help and Help at Court, when calculating the borrower's disposable capital, the whole amount or value of the subject matter of dispute (SMOD) (usually the borrower's home) is disregarded when calculating capital.

Different rules apply to Legal Representation, where the SMOD disregard is limited to £100,000 (reg.32A of the Community Legal Service (Financial) Regulations 2000, SI 2000/516 as amended by the Community Legal Service (Financial) (Amendment) Regulations 2005, SI 2005/589). However, when assessing the level of a borrower's capital, the legal aid rules also allow the adviser/LSC to disregard the first £100,000 of net equity of the borrower's main or only dwelling in which the borrower resides. 'Net equity' is defined as the market value of the property less an allowance for the mortgage, up to a maximum of £100,000.

Details of how to calculate the value of a property for legal aid purposes are set out in paras.7.3 and 7.4 of Volume 2E (Financial Eligibility) of the LSC Manual (para.7.4 is reproduced at **Appendix D1**). In short, to calculate the capital arising from the borrower's home:

- the dwelling should be valued at the amount for which it could be sold on the open market;
- deduct 3 per cent from the current market value to reflect the notional sale costs, to give the net market value;
- deduct either (i) the outstanding mortgage or (ii) £100,000, whichever is the lower, to give the net equity;
- the whole of the net equity is to be taken into account for the next calculation if the borrower's share falls to be aggregated under the legal aid rules with the capital of their spouse or partner; otherwise the net equity figure is multiplied by the borrower's percentage share of the property (where, for example, the borrower has separated and is living apart from their spouse or partner or where, for example, the property was purchased with a friend or other relative) to give the borrower's share of the net equity;
- if the property is the SMOD (for example, it is subject to mortgage possession proceedings), the first £100,000 of the borrower's share of the net equity is disregarded;
- if the property is the borrower's main dwelling, then a further £100,000 of the borrower's share of the net equity is disregarded and the remainder (if any) of the borrower's share is brought to account as capital. In all other cases the borrower's share of the net equity (for example, in a second property that the borrower owns) is brought to account as capital in full.

Paragraphs 7.3 and 7.4 of Volume 2E (Financial Eligibility) of the LSC Manual give some worked examples in different situations that may apply. Further details and worked examples will be found in Volume 3D (Guide to Assessing Financial Eligibility) of the LSC Manual at para.6.4 (3D-040).

The following example is adapted from the LSC Manual.

Example: The lender seeks possession of a house which is the borrower's main dwelling

The house value is £315,000. The mortgage outstanding is £150,000. In order to calculate the capital to take into account for the purposes of Legal Representation: deduct 3 per cent from the house value to obtain the net market value; then deduct the £100,000 mortgage allowance only from the net market value, as this is lower than the mortgage outstanding; then deduct the £100,000 SMOD disregard; finally, deduct the £100,000 equity disregard. The remainder will be treated as capital, i.e.:

House value	£315,000
Less 3 per cent	-£9,450
Net value	**£305,550**
Less mortgage allowance	-£100,000
Less SMOD disregard	-£100,000
Less equity disregard	-£100,000
Capital	**£5,550**

The borrower is therefore eligible under this example (as the capital arising from the house is less than the current £8,000 capital limit for legal aid).

15.3   RECEIVING PAYMENT FOR WORK CARRIED OUT

Unless advisers are covered by direct funding arrangements, for example, by local authorities or a charity, they will be concerned to ensure that payment is received for the work carried out advising and/or representing borrowers.

15.3.1   Borrowers who are eligible for legal aid

Legal Help/Help at Court

The adviser can claim the current standard fixed fee for a housing case for each eligible borrower advised. If the matter is complex and the exceptional case costs threshold is reached (i.e. where the costs on hourly rates are three times the standard fee), the adviser will then be able to make a claim to the LSC for work at hourly rates.

Help at Court may be appropriate where the mortgage arrears are not in dispute, it is unlikely that an immediate order for possession would be made and, in the absence of a defence to the proceedings, the only issue appears to be the terms on which a suspended order would be made: see the LSC Manual, para.19.3 (3C-158).

Legal Representation

Advisers will claim for all of their work at LSC prescribed rates unless (probably in a wholly exceptional case) party costs are recovered from a lender.

15.3.2 Borrowers who are not eligible for legal aid

There are several possibilities for recovering payment where borrowers are not eligible for legal aid:

- where the borrower has pre-existing legal expenses insurance that would cover their legal costs (for example, a free-standing insurance policy or one attached to a buildings or household contents policy);
- many borrowers are willing to pay for fixed fee advice (at Legal Help or Legal Representation prescribed rates);
- to charge the borrower for hourly paid advice (at Legal Help or Legal Representation prescribed rates);
- to charge the borrower at some other fixed fee or hourly paid rate (although borrowers who need to seek legal advice are likely to have limited disposable income); or
- to refer the borrower to an organisation with local authority or other funding, which allows work to be carried out for borrowers who are not eligible for legal aid.

15.3.3 The statutory charge

Where a borrower gains or keeps money or property with the help of legal aid in a civil case, he may have to repay all or some of his legal costs to the LSC out of that money or property (if costs are not recovered from the lender, as is often the case). In this situation, legal aid can act as a loan. This is called the 'statutory charge'.

In certain circumstances the legal aid statutory charge allows the LSC to recoup legal aid expenditure from the borrower.

The statutory charge does not apply to advice and assistance given under the Legal Help/Help at Court schemes. However, if acting under Legal Representation, the statutory charge will bite on any property (such as the flat or house involved in the mortgage possession proceedings), which is recovered or preserved; so the borrower will end up paying for the adviser's work in any event.

Deferring enforcement of the statutory charge

The LSC may defer enforcing the statutory charge (i.e. postpone repayment until the property is sold) if:

- the property subject to the charge is the home of the borrower or their dependants; and

- the LSC is satisfied that the home will provide security for the charge; and
- the charge is registered against the property concerned.

Borrowers will need to understand that interest will accrue on the registered charge until payment is made to the LSC. Fuller details relating to the statutory charge will be found in the LSC Manual, Volume 1D, para.1D-005, 'The Statutory Charge'.

15.4   HOUSING POSSESSION COURT DUTY SCHEMES

Duty advice schemes have been a feature of county court possession days for more than 20 years. The schemes arrange for borrowers and tenants attending court for a possession hearing, and whose home is at immediate risk, to be advised and/or represented by solicitor or adviser. Fuller details of the LSC Housing Possession Court Duty Scheme (HPCDS) will be found at **11.1**.

15.4.1   Payment to the adviser

Where an adviser represents a mortgage borrower at court as part of the HPCDS, payment to the adviser is made by way of a fixed fee per borrower seen. There is no additional fee for travelling and waiting and the fee includes the cost of writing a letter of advice after the hearing. Payment is strictly conditional upon submission of a fully completed session monitoring form for each client.

15.4.2   Interaction with Legal Help

However, advisers should be aware that where a client seeks advice outside the terms of the HPCDS, if Legal Help is given, the adviser will not also be entitled to claim any fee for later assisting that client under the HPCDS.

If a mortgage borrower is represented at court under the HPCDS and, within six months of doing so, the adviser subsequently opens a new housing matter start in relation to the same case (to advise further under Legal Help), the adviser cannot claim any payment for providing the service at court. The costs of providing the service at court will be included in the housing matter start (Legal Help) fixed fee.

15.5   FUTURE FUNDING PROPOSALS

On 15 November 2010 the Ministry of Justice published its Consultation Paper *Proposals for the reform of legal aid in England and Wales*. On 21 June 2011 the government published its response to the consultation, which set out its finalised proposals for reform, together with a draft Bill which implements many of these proposals.

The Legal Aid, Sentencing and Punishment of Offenders Bill 2010 was presented to Parliament on 21 June 2011 and, at the time of writing, it is making its passage through Committee and other stages. It may come into force by the time this book goes to press.

The Bill covers a wide range of issues. It comprises four Parts and 16 Schedules, of which Part 1 and Sched.1, which make provisions on legal aid, are relevant to this book.

15.5.1 Key areas of the Bill

In its current form and subject to future amendment, the Bill:

- reverses the position under the Access to Justice Act 1999, whereby civil legal aid is available for any matter not specifically excluded, takes some types of case out of scope for legal aid funding and provides that cases would not be eligible for funding unless of a type specified in the Bill;
- retains within the scope of legal aid 'civil legal services provided to an individual in relation to (a) court orders for sale or possession of the individual's home, or (b) the eviction from the individual's home of the individual or others';
- abolishes the Legal Services Commission;
- makes provision for new regulations to be made in relation to the assessment of an individual's financial resources, and the making and withdrawal of determinations about eligibility for legal aid; and
- provides for the delivery of civil legal aid services by arranging for the services to be provided by telephone or by other electronic means.

Since many of the future legal aid changes will be made by regulation, it is difficult to predict precisely what form they will take. The best guide however is the government's response to the consultation published on 21 June 2011, which so far as they are relevant to this chapter, proposed to introduce the following reforms to financial eligibility in civil proceedings:

- to apply the same capital eligibility rules to applicants in receipt of 'passporting' benefits as other applicants for legal aid;
- to retain the 'subject matter of the dispute disregard' and to cap it at £100,000 for all levels of service; and
- to increase the levels of income-based contributions to a maximum of approximately 30 per cent of monthly disposable income;

Advisers will need to reconsider the contents of this chapter in the light of the final Bill which receives Royal Assent and any regulations made under the resulting Act.

CHAPTER 16

How lenders seek to bypass the court's powers

Much of this book is taken up with the powers of the court to prevent or delay a lender obtaining possession of a property. However, in certain circumstances lenders are able to bypass the protections afforded to borrowers in AJA 1970, s.36.

16.1 OPTIONS AVAILABLE TO LENDERS

Where a borrower is in mortgage arrears, the lender has several options available to it. These will be found either within the express terms of the mortgage deed or, as will be seen, pursuant to the Law of Property Act (LPA) 1925, s.101. A lender may:

- bring a money claim;
- apply for possession;
- apply for foreclosure;
- appoint a receiver; or
- exercise a power of sale.

This section is particularly concerned with lenders appointing receivers and/or exercising powers of sale. Where the mortgage deed contains such powers, advisers will wish to consider any conditions which may be attached to the powers, which may not be available unless the conditions have been fulfilled.

16.2 LAW OF PROPERTY ACT 1925, S.101

Provided that they are not expressly excluded by the mortgage deed, LPA 1925, s.101 contains powers incident to the interest of the lender in the secured property. The key provision reads as follows:

> (1) A mortgagee, where the mortgage is made by deed, shall, by virtue of this Act, have the following powers, to the like extent as if they had been in terms conferred by the mortgage deed, but not further (namely):
>
> > (i) A power, when the mortgage money has become due, to sell or to concur with any other person in selling, the mortgaged property, or any part thereof,

> either subject to prior charges or not, and either together or in lots, by public auction or by private contract, subject to such conditions respecting title, or evidence of title, or other matter, as the mortgagee thinks fit, with power to vary any contract for sale, and to buy in at an auction, or to rescind any contract for sale, and to re-sell, without being answerable to any loss occasioned thereby; and …
>
> (iii) A power, when the mortgage money has become due, to appoint a receiver of the income of the mortgaged property, or any part thereof; or, if the mortgaged property consists of an interest in income, or of a rentcharge or an annual or other periodical sum, a receiver of that property or any part thereof …

These powers may be varied or extended by the mortgage deed (LPA 1925, s.101(3)).

The powers are very wide ranging and are effective to enable the lender either to sell the mortgaged property or to appoint a receiver of the income of the mortgaged property, without first obtaining a court order.

By exercising these powers the lender can effectively bypass the protections afforded to borrowers under AJA 1970, s.36. However, as will be seen, lenders are unlikely to rely on these powers where mortgages are secured against owner-occupied residential properties.

16.3 LENDER'S POWER OF SALE

The lender's power of sale was considered by the Court of Appeal in *Ropaigealach v. Barclays Bank plc* [2000] 1 QB 263. In that case the legal charge contained a covenant by Mr and Mrs Ropaigealach that they would, on demand in writing, pay to the bank all monies which should from time to time be owing by them to the bank. Clause 5 provided that, as between the bank and the purchaser from the bank, the statutory power of sale under LPA 1925, s.101 should arise on and be exercisable at any time after the execution of the legal charge, but that, as between the bank and the borrower, the bank should not exercise its power of sale until payment of the monies secured by the legal charge had been demanded.

Following a valid demand for repayment of the mortgage monies, the bank sold the property by auction, in exercise of the power of sale in s.101 and in the legal mortgage. The net proceeds of sale were used to reduce the liabilities of Mr and Mrs Ropaigealach to the bank.

When they learned of the sale Mr and Mrs Ropaigealach issued proceedings to challenge the sale of the property by the bank without first obtaining a court order. The appeal raised a point of general importance as to the effect (if any) of AJA 1970, s.36, in a case where the lender had taken possession of the mortgaged property by peaceable entry and sold it by auction without first having sought and obtained the order of the appropriate court.

The court reviewed the history and purpose of AJA 1970, s.36, which highlighted the apparently anomalous position that borrowers were protected by s.36 where lenders brought court proceedings, but not where they exercise a power of sale in the mortgage deed or pursuant to LPA 1925, s.101. In conclusion, Chadwick LJ stated at [41]:

> I find it impossible to be satisfied that Parliament must have intended, when enacting section 36 of the Act of 1970, that the mortgagee's common law right to take possession by virtue of his estate should only be exercisable with the assistance of the court.

As a result, the protections of s.36 had no application where a lender sought to exercise the power of sale, or any other power, by virtue of the mortgage deed or LPA 1925, s.101.

16.4   APPOINTMENT OF RECEIVERS

The decision in *Ropaigealach* (above) was referred to and considered by Briggs J in the more recent case of *Horsham Properties Group Ltd* v. *Clark* [2008] EWHC 2327 (Ch), [2009] 1 WLR 1255.

That case involved two defendants, Mr Clark and Ms Beech, who obtained a mortgage from the third party, GMAC RFC Ltd. When the defendants fell into arrears with payments due under the mortgage, GMAC appointed receivers pursuant to a power contained both in LPA 1925, s.101(1)(iii) and clause 12 of the mortgage conditions, to which the mortgage was subject.

The receivers then sold the property at auction, relying upon their power to do so conferred by clause 12 of the mortgage conditions. The purchaser was Coastal Estates Ltd. The receivers transferred the property to that company as agents for GMAC, pursuant to its powers of sale, conferred both by the mortgage and by s.101. On the same day Coastal Estates Ltd transferred the property to Horsham Properties Group Ltd, which became the registered proprietor of the property in succession to the defendants.

Horsham Properties Group then issued proceedings for possession of the property, claiming that the defendants were 'trespassing' in the property on the basis that all their rights in relation to the property had been overreached by the receiver's sale to Coastal Estates.

Ms Beech, the second defendant, disputed the possession claim by Horsham Properties Group arguing that:

(i)   LPA 1925, s.101 should be construed as requiring a mortgagee first to obtain a court order for possession or to make an application for an order permitting sale, and giving the court on such an application a discretion similar to that conferred by AJA 1970, s.36; or

(ii)   s.36 should be construed so as to confer on the court the discretionary powers to adjourn or suspend the making of a possession order where the application was made, not by the mortgagee, but by the mortgagee's purchaser; or

(iii) alternatively, if the statutory framework cannot be so construed, Ms Beech sought a declaration of incompatibility in relation to s.101, because it infringed Article 1 of the First Protocol to the European Convention on Human Rights, because she was deprived of her possessions, namely of her property.

Briggs J decided that he was bound by the decision of the Court of Appeal in *Ropaigealach* (above) and found that Horsham Properties Group was entitled to possession of the property as against Ms Beech. His findings included:

- By the express terms of the mortgage Ms Beech's rights in relation to the property were all made subject to being overridden by a sale of the property by GMAC, or by receivers appointed by GMAC, at any time after a default in paying sums due under the mortgage.
- LPA 1925, s.101 serves to *implement* rather than override the private bargain between the mortgagor and the mortgagee.
- Ms Beech's interest in the mortgaged property was her share in the equity of redemption. Although her share in the equity of redemption was a 'possession' within the meaning of Article 1, it was overridden once the mortgagee contracts to sell the mortgaged property in exercise of the statutory power of sale, or when a receiver, duly appointed under the mortgage contracts to sell the mortgaged property, and that she had lost her share in the equity of redemption when the receivers contracted to sell to Coastal Estates pursuant to their powers contained in the mortgage.
- '[A]ny deprivation of possession constituted by the exercise by a mortgagee of its powers under section 101 of the Law of Property Act after a relevant default by the mortgagor is justified in the public interest ... [because] it reflects the bargain habitually drawn between mortgagors and mortgagees for nearly 200 years, in which the ability of the mortgagee to sell the property offered as a security without having to go to court has been identified as a central and essential aspect of the security necessarily to be provided if substantial property based secured lending is to be available at affordable rates of interest. That it is in the public interest that property buyers and owners should be able to obtain lending for that purpose can hardly be open to doubt ...' (at [44]).
- The court was bound by the decision of the Court of Appeal in *Ropaigealach* (above) that the court's powers under AJA 1970, s.36 to stay or adjourn proceedings for possession were triggered only where the mortgagee considered it necessary or appropriate to go to court in the first place.
- The overall result was that the borrowers were unable to ask the court to exercise its powers to protect them under AJA 1970, s.36 in the possession proceedings brought by Horsham Properties Group, as purchasers from the mortgagee.

16.4.1 Powers of receivers

Advisers should note that while LPA 1925, s.101(1)(iii) confers on a mortgagee a statutory power to appoint receivers, such receivers are given no statutory power of sale. In the *Horsham Properties Group* case the power of sale arose from the mortgage deed. Advisers will therefore wish to examine the mortgage deed carefully when advising borrowers faced with similar circumstances.

Likewise, advisers should seek to obtain a copy of the deed of appointment of the receivers made under the mortgage and/or by statute to establish whether the deed has been properly executed, whether the appointment has been validly made, the powers which have been granted to the receivers and whether there are any conditions to be fulfilled or any limitations on such powers.

16.4.2   Response by the Council of Mortgage Lenders

The decision in *Horsham Properties Group* generated considerable concern. It appeared to give the green light to lenders to sell mortgaged properties without first obtaining a court order and enable subsequent purchasers to regain possession against borrowers without the court being able to exercise any discretion to suspend, stay or postpone possession under AJA 1970, s.36.

In response to such concern the Council of Mortgage Lenders (CML), which represents nearly all mortgagees of residential property, issued a voluntary statement on s.101 of LPA 1925 (last updated on 10 August 2011). The full wording of the statement (and any revisions) can be found at **www.cml.org.uk/cml/policy/ issues/4707**. This says of the *Horsham Properties Group* case that 'although not clear from some of the reports the loan to the borrower was a buy to let loan'. It goes on to say that:

> It is the case that a lender (or a receiver appointed by a lender) could in theory sell an occupied residential property without a court order to a third party. However for residential properties this would only occur in exceptional circumstances.

By publication of the statement, CML members have on a voluntary basis confirmed that:

> In respect of mortgages secured against owner occupied residential properties CML members will not seek to sell a mortgaged property when the borrower is in default without first obtaining a court order for possession. In addition, CML members will not appoint a receiver to sell a residential property without first obtaining a court order for possession.

The voluntary agreement only extends to a property which is the borrower's home. Expressly, it does not apply to commercial transactions, which would include buy-to-let loans, business loans secured against a residential property or bridging loans; nor does it apply to vacant or abandoned properties, cases of fraud or in exceptional cases where the borrower has given his full informed consent.

16.5   ATTEMPTS AT LEGISLATIVE REFORM

On 3 February 2009 Andrew Dismore MP introduced to Parliament the Home Repossession (Protection) Bill as a Private Member's Bill. The purpose was to amend LPA 1925 to require a mortgagee to obtain the court's permission before exercising the power of sale, where the mortgaged land consists of or includes a dwelling-house, and other purposes. The Bill was on the order paper for a second reading debate on 16 October 2009, but there was an objection and eventually it was dropped by its sponsor.

16.5.1   Government consultation

On 29 December 2009 the government published a Consultation Paper CP55/09 entitled *Mortgages: power of sale and residential property*.

The Consultation Paper sought views on a proposal to require mortgage lenders to obtain a court order or the consent of the borrower before repossessing and selling residential owner-occupied homes. The proposed changes would ensure that borrowers could access the protections offered by the court, mainly under AJA 1970, s.36. The consultation followed on directly from the concerns expressed after the High Court ruling in *Horsham Properties Group*. The consultation ended on 28 March 2010, shortly before the change of government following the general election on 6 May 2010. At the time of writing, the government has not published its response to the Consultation Paper.

Advisers should be alert for future changes in the law which may restrict lenders' powers and therefore enhance borrowers' protections in this area.

CHAPTER 17

Human rights

17.1 OVERVIEW

In recent years human rights have played an increasingly important role in housing law generally and in the field of possession proceedings specifically. A number of fundamental rights and freedoms set out in the European Convention on Human Rights (ECHR) have potential relevance to mortgage possession proceedings:

- Article 6 (right to a fair trial);
- Article 8 (right to respect for private and family life and home); and
- Article 1 of the First Protocol (protection of property).

These are collectively known as 'Convention rights'. The Human Rights Act (HRA) 1998 was enacted to make it easier for people to give effect to the rights and freedoms of the ECHR in domestic courts. The result is that human rights arguments can now be raised in courts of first instance – in particular the county courts – and where appropriate domestic judges can apply human rights principles to domestic law. Copies of relevant sections of HRA 1998 and of the above Convention rights will be found in **Appendix A4**.

17.2 APPLICATION OF CONVENTION RIGHTS

HRA 1998 applies Convention rights to domestic law in three main ways:

- by requiring, so far as it is possible to do so, primary legislation and subordinate legislation to be read and given effect to in a way which is compatible with Convention rights (s.3(1));
- primary legislation can be subject to a declaration of incompatibility by the High Court, Court of Appeal or Supreme Court (s.4(2)); and
- it is unlawful for a public authority to act in a way which is incompatible with a Convention right (s.6(1)).

The first and third points above are likely to be most relevant for mortgage possession proceedings.

17.2.1 Definition of a public authority

A 'public authority' is defined in HRA 1998, s.6(3) as including:

- a court or tribunal; and
- any person certain of whose functions are functions of a public nature.

17.2.2 Proceedings to enforce HRA 1998

A person who claims that a public authority has acted (or proposes to act) in a way which is made unlawful by HRA 1998, s.6(1) may:

- bring proceedings against the authority under HRA 1998 in the appropriate court or tribunal; or
- rely on the Convention right or rights concerned in any legal proceedings,

but only if he is (or would be) a victim of the unlawful act (HRA 1998, s.7(1)).

17.2.3 Judicial remedies

Where the court finds that an act of a public authority is unlawful, then by HRA 1998, s.8(1) 'it may grant such relief or remedy, or make such order, within its powers as it considers just and appropriate'.

What those remedies may constitute in the context of the mortgage possession proceedings is dealt with below, but may include granting an extended period of possession, suspending a possession order, or refusing it altogether.

17.3 RAISING CONVENTION RIGHTS AS A DEFENCE

Where a claimant in possession proceedings is a public authority, for example a local authority or a social landlord exercising public housing functions (see *R (on the application of Weaver)* v. *London & Quadrant Housing Trust* [2009] EWCA Civ 587, [2009] 4 All ER 865), it is easy enough to see how HRA 1998 may be pleaded by a defendant occupier. The defendant will file a defence to say that one or more Convention rights is 'engaged' by the claimant's actions, but that the claimant has acted in a way which is incompatible with a Convention right within the meaning of s.6(1), and to seek appropriate relief or an appropriate remedy from the court under s.8(1).

Where the claimant is not a public authority (for example a private bank or building society bringing mortgage possession proceedings) the position is less clear, although assistance may be found elsewhere in HRA 1998 and in recent case law.

17.4 THE COURT'S DUTIES AS A PUBLIC AUTHORITY

As a public authority itself, the court is bound by HRA 1998, s.6(1) not to act in a way which is incompatible with Convention rights.

Where it is the court itself that (as a public authority) has acted in a way which is incompatible with Convention rights, proceedings against the court in respect of its judicial act may be brought only by exercising a right of appeal (HRA 1998, s.9(1)) or by judicial review proceedings (HRA 1998, s.9(2)).

In mortgage possession proceedings the emphasis is therefore likely to be not on the actions of the claimant, but rather on the actions of the court within those proceedings.

Human rights arguments can be raised at first instance (i.e. at the possession hearing), but any alleged unlawful act by the court under s.7(1) can only be pursued by way of an appeal under s.9(1) (or as stated by way of judicial review under s.9(2)).

17.5 THE RELEVANT CONVENTION RIGHTS

The text of the rights and freedoms of the ECHR are found in Sched.1 to HRA 1998 (see **Appendix A4**).

17.5.1 Article 6 – right to a fair trial

Article 6 reads:

> In the determination of his civil rights and obligations ... everyone is entitled to a fair and public hearing within a reasonable time by an independent and impartial tribunal established by law ...

This fundamental right applies to every determination of a person's civil rights and obligations, regardless whether the claimant is a public authority, or a private person or body. Therefore, the Article 6 right imposes a duty squarely on the courts' shoulders.

Article 6 creates no substantive civil rights, but merely guarantees the procedural right to have a claim in respect of civil rights and obligations adjudicated by an independent tribunal. Any failure by a court to accord a borrower a fair trial would provide grounds for an appeal.

Equality of arms

One additional element to the rights under Article 6 is that the court has a duty to ensure that there is 'equality of arms' between the parties. This duty was described in the decision of the European Court of Human Rights (ECtHR) in *Niderost-Huber*

158

v. *Switzerland* (App. No. 18990/91) (1998) 25 EHRR 709 and it was restated by the ECtHR 10 years later in *SH* v. *Finland* (App. No. 28301/03) [2008] ECHR 741 at [33]:

> One of the elements of the broader concept of a fair trial is the principle of equality of arms, which requires each party to be given a reasonable opportunity to present his or her case under conditions that do not place him or her at a substantial disadvantage vis-à-vis his opponent

This principle will be of importance when only the lender is legally represented in possession proceedings. The court must ensure that the borrower is not procedurally disadvantaged. As stated in *SH* v. *Finland*:

> That right means, in principle, the opportunity for the parties to a trial to have knowledge of and comment on all evidence adduced or observations filed, with a view to influencing the court's decision ... (at [33])

A failure to ensure that there is equality of arms, could lead to an appeal against the court's decision.

This principle may become more important, if public funding (legal aid) becomes more restricted in the future, so that a borrower's opportunities to obtain legal advice about the proceedings and to be represented at court are reduced.

17.5.2 Article 8 – right to respect for the home

Insofar as it is relevant to mortgage possession proceedings, Article 8 states:

(1) everyone has the right to respect for ... his home ...
(2) there shall be no interference by a public authority with the exercise of this right except such as is in accordance with the law and is necessary in a democratic society in the interests of national security, public safety or the economic well-being of the country ... or for the protection of the rights and freedoms of others.

So long as the property concerned is a person's home, the issue of any possession proceedings will engage Article 8(1); that is, the right to respect for a home falls to be considered by the court at all stages of the possession claim, if not also by the lender.

Since the making of a possession order would constitute a potential interference by a public authority (i.e. by the court) with the exercise of that right, the test for the court is whether it is in accordance with the law and is *necessary* as set out above.

In the context of mortgage possession proceedings the 'rights and freedoms of others' may include the rights of the lender arising from the bargain struck with the borrower when monies were loaned on security of the property.

European case law

The portents of early case law were not good for borrowers, but as will be seen at **17.6**, these will now have to be revisited. The most often-quoted case dealing with the balance to be struck between a borrower's Convention rights and a lender's rights is *Wood* v. *United Kingdom* (App. No. 32540/96) [1997] ECHR 200, (1997) EHRR CD69. This was an old case which pre-dated the coming into force of HRA 1998. It involved the repossession of the applicant's house by a lender after she had defaulted on her mortgage payments. It is not a full decision of the ECtHR, but a decision ruling against the admissibility of a complaint under the ECHR. As such, it carries less weight.

In *Wood*, the Commission accepted that repossession by a lender might constitute interference with the applicant's home, but stated:

> this was in accordance with the terms of the loan and the domestic law and was necessary for the protection of rights and freedoms of others, namely the lender.

Accordingly, the application was 'manifestly ill-founded'.

Domestic case law

Human rights arguments were considered in the much more recent case of *Horsham Properties Group Ltd* v. *Clark* [2008] EWHC 2327 (Ch), [2009] 1 WLR 1255. This case involved a mortgage where the borrowers contested a mortgage lender's power of sale and right to appoint a receiver under LPA 1925, s.101 (see **16.2** and **16.4**). In that case Briggs J held (at [49]) *obiter* that:

> As for Article 8, it is equally well established, for example by *Harrow LBC v Qazi* ... that although the loss of the right to possession of a dwelling house does not automatically lead that house to cease to be the former owner's home, Article 8 was not intended to interfere with the legal rights of the person entitled to possession against the occupier such that, if a claimant had an unqualified right to possession (as in the present case), there is nothing in Article 8 to prevent the enforcement of that right.

As will be seen, both the above cases and indeed consideration of Article 8 may need to be revised in the light of the recent decision in *Manchester City Council* v. *Pinnock* (see below).

17.5.3 Article 1 of the First Protocol – right to possessions

Both of the above cases of *Wood* v. *United Kingdom* and *Horsham Properties Group Ltd* v. *Clark* also included claims that there had been a breach of Article 1 of the First Protocol to the ECHR, which states:

> Every natural or legal person is entitled to peaceful enjoyment of his possessions. No one shall be deprived of his possessions except in the public interest and subject to the conditions provided for by law ...

In *Wood* v. *United Kingdom* (above) the Commission, when rejecting the applicant's complaint, stated that 'to the extent that the applicant is deprived of her possessions by the repossession, the Commission considers that this deprivation is in the public interest, that is the public interest in ensuring payment of contractual debts, and is also in accordance with the rules provided for by law'.

The main focus of *Horsham Properties Group Ltd* v. *Clark* (above) was an alleged infringement of Article 1 of the First Protocol, although it was combined with dependent arguments under Articles 6 and 8. The borrower claimed that her loss of rights as a co-owner amounted to being deprived of a possession of hers within the meaning of Article 1 of the First Protocol.

Briggs J preferred to describe that as the loss of the borrower's share in the equity of redemption (being the right to pay off the loan and free the property from the security granted by the mortgage).

He had 'no difficulty' in concluding that her share in the equity of redemption was a 'possession' for the purpose of Article 1 of the First Protocol. However, he went on to find that the borrower had lost her equity of redemption by virtue of the exercise of powers conferred by contract in the mortgage deed, rather than any state intervention (in the form of powers contained in LPA 1925, s.101), so that there had been 'no relevant deprivation of possessions' within the meaning of Article 1 of the First Protocol.

Briggs J went on to consider the issue of supposed deprivation of possessions further, in case a higher court took a different view. He said (at [44]) *obiter*:

> In my judgment, any deprivation of possession constituted by the exercise by a mortgagee of its powers under section 101 of the Law of Property Act after a relevant default by the mortgagor is justified in the public interest, and requires no case-by-case exercise of a proportionality discretion by the court, for the following reasons. First, it reflects the bargain habitually drawn between mortgagors and mortgagees for nearly 200 years, in which the ability of a mortgagee to sell the property offered as a security without having to go to court has been identified as a central and essential aspect of the security necessarily to be provided if substantial property based secured lending is to be available at affordable rates of interest. That it is in the public interest that property buyers and owners should be able to obtain lending for that purpose can hardly be open to doubt, even if the loan-to-value ratios at which it has recently become possible have now become a matter of controversy.

17.6 *MANCHESTER CITY COUNCIL* V. *PINNOCK*

The Supreme Court judgment in *Manchester City Council* v. *Pinnock* [2010] UKSC 45, [2010] 3 WLR 1441 dealt with possession proceedings brought by local authorities against certain kinds of tenants, but its decision is likely to have much more far-reaching consequences for English law and for possession proceedings generally. The Supreme Court subsequently provided further guidance on the scope of any Article 8 defence in *Hounslow London Borough Council* v. *Powell* [2011] UKSC 8, [2011] 2 WLR 287 (another landlord and tenant case).

17.6.1 Need to assess proportionality

The key quote from the *Manchester City Council* v. *Pinnock* decision appears at [49] of the judgment delivered by Lord Neuberger:

> Therefore, if our law is to be compatible with article 8, where a court is asked to make an order for possession of a person's home at the suit of a local authority, the court must have the power to assess the proportionality of making the order, and, in making that assessment, to resolve any relevant dispute of fact.

The court elaborates further at [52]:

> The question is always whether the eviction is a proportionate means of achieving a legitimate aim.

The judgment applies not only to local authority landlords, but also to other social landlords to the extent that they are public authorities under HRA 1998 (at [3]).

Private landowners

The position regarding a private landowner seeking a possession was expressly left open by the court. Lord Neuberger stated (at [50]):

> ... nothing which we say is intended to bear on cases where the person seeking the order for possession is a private landowner. Conflicting views have been expressed both domestically and in Strasbourg on that situation. In *Harrow v Qazi* [2004] 1 AC 983 the views of Lord Bingham and Lord Steyn, at paras 23 and 26, can be contrasted with the view of Lord Hope, at para 52. In *Belchikova v Russia* (App no 2408/06, 25 March 2010), the application was held to be inadmissible, but the EurCtHR (First Section) seems to have considered that article 8 was relevant, even when the person seeking possession was a private sector landowner. Presumably, this was on the basis that the court making the order was itself a public authority. But it is not clear whether the point was in contention. In the rather older admissibility decision of *Di Palma v United Kingdom* (App no 11949/86) (1986) 10 EHRR 149, 155–156, the Commission seems to have taken a different view, but the point was only very briefly discussed. No doubt, in such cases article 1 of the First Protocol to the Convention will have a part to play, but it is preferable for this Court to express no view on the issue until it arises and has to be determined.

The question must therefore also arise as to what extent a borrower can raise proportionality as a defence in mortgage possession cases brought by a private mortgagee.

If a private mortgage lender has a quasi-public function (for example a lender so closely linked to a local housing authority in a right-to-buy situation that they are functional public authorities) the position will be clearer, because the lender will be more akin to a local authority referred to in *Pinnock*. If not, the borrower can still rely upon the court's duty as a public authority when making a possession order. It is for the court to strike a balance between the lender's right to possession and the borrower's fundamental Convention rights.

To this extent, the previous decisions in *Wood* v. *United Kingdom* (above) and *Horsham Properties Group* v. *Clark* (above) need to be reconsidered in the light of the decision in *Pinnock*.

17.6.2 Raising proportionality as a defence

In the *Pinnock* judgment, the Supreme Court sets out a number of general points about raising Article 8 proportionality arguments in a defence (at [60] onwards):

- Article 8 comes into play only where a person's 'home' is under threat. (This might exclude properties purchased under a buy-to-let mortgage, with the express intention of letting to tenants, rather than using the property as the borrower's home.)
- It is for the residential occupier to raise the Article 8 argument in proceedings (which in most cases will be the county court in which the mortgage possession claim is brought).
- The court should initially consider any Article 8 point summarily. A possession may result, unless the Article 8 defence has a real prospect of success.
- If domestic law justifies an outright order of possession, the effect of Article 8 may be to justify granting an extended period for possession, suspending the order for possession or even refusing an order altogether.
- The conclusion that the court must have the ability to assess the proportionality of making a possession order in respect of a person's home may require certain statutory and procedural provisions to be revisited. In the *Pinnock* case reference was made to s.89 of the Housing Act 1980 and to some of the provisions of CPR Part 55, but equally it may be argued that AJA 1970, s.36 (as amended) or even provisions of the CCA may fall to be reconsidered. However, in *Hounslow London Borough Council* v. *Powell* (above), the Supreme Court held that it was impermissible to apply HRA 1998, s.3(1) to read s.89 of the 1980 Act as enabling a court to postpone a possession order for more than the statutory maximum of six weeks in that section (see *Hounslow London Borough Council* v. *Powell* at [57]–[64]).
- Proportionality is more likely to be a relevant issue in respect of occupants who are vulnerable as a result of mental illness, physical or learning disability, poor health or frailty. (Although this was said in the context of social rented housing, in an appropriate case the same principle may be transported to mortgage possession proceedings.)

In any event, it must be remembered that regardless of the nature of the lender or its interests in relation to the property, as a public authority, it is for the court to ensure that it does not act in a way that is incompatible with a Convention right.

Issues that might be raised

Issues which may weigh against lenders include:

- Are there any reasonable alternatives to possession?
- If so, is immediate possession and/or eviction proportionate?
- Are there any substantial weaknesses in the lender's case?
- Has there been any improper behaviour on the part of the lender or any lack of fairness in its procedures (whether, for example, in breach of MCOB 13 or the Mortgage Pre-Action Protocol)?
- Is there any cogent evidence of vulnerability on the part of the borrower?

A borrower raising human rights arguments at first instance in the county court may well not succeed; however, such arguments may be renewed upon appeal.

17.7 CONCLUSION

Following the Supreme Court decision in *Pinnock*, domestic law is clearly moving to a greater scrutiny of the proportionality of possession proceedings of all types. Older cases, which may appear unfavourable to mortgage borrowers, need to be reconsidered in the light of *Pinnock* and advisers should be bold in questioning and challenging such cases.

Whether or not a HRA 1998 defence can be sustained, the exploration of proportionality issues may reveal defects in the lender's approach to possession, which can be utilised to the borrower's benefit. Raising these issues may also give borrowers much needed time, in which to improve their circumstances, to negotiate with the lender and to explore alternative options rather than the loss of a home.

CHAPTER 18

Shared ownership schemes

Shared ownerships schemes require a number of different considerations, where possession proceedings are brought against borrowers due to arrears.

18.1 TYPES OF SHARED OWNERSHIP SCHEME

There are many differing forms of shared ownership scheme. Fuller details of the various schemes can be found in the document 'Shared Ownership: Joint Guidance for England' prepared by the Homes and Communities Agency (HCA) in collaboration with the Council of Mortgage Lenders and National Housing Federation. The guidance was most recently updated in June 2011 and a copy can be downloaded from the websites of each of the organisations concerned.

While some of the schemes are not relevant to a book about mortgage possession proceedings, advisers may come across the following common arrangements:

- HomeBuy Direct, where the borrower is offered an equity loan towards part of the purchase price of a new-build home on selected developments. 'HomeBuy' may also be known as 'First Steps' and 'First Buy';
- Shared Ownership/New Build HomeBuy, where the borrower will buy a share of a brand new home and will rent the remaining share; and
- Social HomeBuy, where some existing tenants of local authorities or housing associations (now called 'private registered providers') are given the opportunity to buy a share in their rented home.

18.1.1 HomeBuy Direct

The HomeBuy Direct Equity Loan Scheme is available to people who rent council or housing association properties or first-time buyers who meet certain criteria. Application is made to a 'HomeBuy agent', which is one of a number of designated housing associations.

Homeowners buy their home with at least 70 per cent of the cost met by a commercial mortgage and their own savings (a deposit). The remaining cost of the home, up to 30 per cent, is paid for by the government and the house builder through an equity loan. The legal title of the property is wholly owned by the purchaser (whether it be the freehold of a house or a leasehold of a flat). There are no payments on the equity loan for the first five years, but fees apply thereafter.

At a later date homeowners can buy additional shares of the equity in their home, by paying back all or part of the equity loan early. This process is known as 'staircasing'. Homeowners can increase their share of equity or 'staircase' until they own 100 per cent of the equity.

If the homeowner wishes to sell the property, any remaining equity loan is repaid as a percentage of the market value at the time of sale.

18.1.2   Shared Ownership/New Build HomeBuy

The Shared Ownership Scheme is also administered by housing association Home-Buy agents with similar criteria. The purchaser buys shares worth between 25 and 75 per cent of the property's market value and then pays a subsidised rent on the remaining share. Unlike the HomeBuy Direct Scheme, the freehold title is retained by the housing association concerned, and the purchaser buys a long lease of the property, usually for a fixed period of 99 years.

The purchaser becomes a long leaseholder of the property. As owner of the lease, the purchaser will have the usual rights and obligations of a leaseholder and is likely to be liable to pay a service charge each year.

The purchaser may need to raise a mortgage to purchase their share of the property's market value and/or pay a deposit. The purchaser can then buy additional shares at a later date until they own 100 per cent, also called 'staircasing', at which point the freehold will be transferred to the borrower.

If the owner wishes to sell the property, the owner's share is marketed for sale by the housing association to allow other people in housing need to benefit from low-cost home ownership. The property is resold at the market value of the property at the time of sale.

18.1.3   Social HomeBuy

Under this scheme existing tenants can purchase a minimum initial share of 25 per cent of their home. The remaining unowned equity is retained by the landlord, which charges the purchaser an affordable rent on the unowned equity.

As with the other schemes, the purchaser can buy additional shares at a later date until they own 100 per cent. If the purchaser's share in the property is increased, the rent on the unowned equity is recalculated and reduced proportionately.

The purchaser may benefit from a right to acquire discount not only in relation to the initial share purchase, but also upon staircasing.

18.2   STAIRCASING

Having purchased an initial percentage share of the property concerned, the purchaser can vary the share by 'staircasing'.

18.2.1   Upwards staircasing

Generally, staircasing will be upwards, i.e. it will increase the share owned by the purchaser. Most schemes give a right for upward staircasing up to 100 per cent, at which point, in the case of a leasehold property, there is provision for the freehold to be transferred to the purchaser.

There is no right to staircase down, i.e. to reduce the share that the purchaser owns. However, this is allowed in exceptional circumstances, for example as a result of mortgage difficulties or where other alternatives to repossession have been explored. It is usually at the discretion of the housing association.

In certain circumstances staircasing is restricted to 75 per cent of the property, for example in shared ownership schemes for the elderly.

In a shared ownership scheme the staircase provision will be contained in model leases used by the housing associations. Staircasing must be done in minimum 10 per cent tranches/shares. For houses in which the housing association owns the freehold, the leases will imply that there should be a three-month delay from completion of final staircasing to the transfer of the freehold. For leasehold flats, various clauses fall away when the leaseholder reaches 100 per cent and the lease comes to resemble a standard long lease.

Former landlord's right of first refusal

There will be a standard clause or covenant inserted in all conveyances so that, during the period of 21 years from the date of staircasing to full ownership, the purchaser or any successor-in-title must make an offer of first refusal to the former landlord on resale.

18.2.2   Downward (or reverse) staircasing ('flexible tenure')

There is no reference to downward staircasing in the model shared ownership lease, but it will be offered solely at the discretion of the housing association concerned.

Downward staircasing involves the repurchase of equity by a housing association from a shared owner in difficulty, but not necessarily in arrears, with their mortgage repayments. Downward staircasing is only available where the shared owner currently owns less than 100 per cent of the property. The HCA guidance describes downward staircasing as a 'safety-net' to enable a shared owner to remain in their home, despite changes in their financial circumstances and is an 'option of last resort' where the leaseholder has got into or is about to get into mortgage arrears and is at risk of losing their home.

Downward staircasing should be to a level that the owner can afford and sustain, and may mean in some instances that the owner relinquishes ownership and becomes a tenant.

Equity repurchase

Equity repurchase will usually involve the payment of money direct to the shared owner's mortgage lender who has a first charge over the property. It can include repurchasing sufficient equity to clear the mortgage, pay off the arrears of interest and principal on the mortgage, and reduce payment to nil. If the option of full repurchase is taken, the leaseholder will become an assured tenant of the housing association. However, once the property has been staircased to 100 per cent or has been taken into possession by the lender, flexible tenure ceases to be an option.

18.3 SHARED OWNERSHIP LEASES

The HCA and other stakeholders, including lenders, have prepared a standard model shared ownership lease for use by landlords. This is to ensure that the leases are acceptable to lenders, so that the purchaser is able to obtain a mortgage to buy an initial share.

18.3.1 Standard clauses

The model lease contains standard clauses, some of which are fundamental requirements. In particular:

- although initially the property is not owned outright, the leaseholder will be obliged to pay 100 per cent of the outgoings relating to the property and to keep it in good and substantial repair and condition;
- the lease also contains other 'standard' obligations including, if applicable, the need to pay service charges and seek the landlord's consent before making alterations;
- the lease contains a rent review clause;
- any assignment or transfer of the lease before the leaseholder has staircased to 100 per cent must have the landlord's consent, but the leaseholder is not permitted to sub-let or part with possession of the property in any other way until they staircase to 100 per cent ownership of the property;
- the landlord has a right of first refusal on any sale and purchase of the lease within 21 years from the date that the leaseholder staircases to 100 per cent; and
- if the leaseholder fails to pay the rent reserved in the lease and/or observe and perform their obligations in the lease, the landlord may be entitled to terminate the lease. If that happens, the leaseholder will lose any shares in the property which they had acquired – see below.

18.3.2 Mortgagee protection provisions

In addition to the above clauses, the model lease contains one further standard clause of relevance to mortgage borrowers, namely a clause by which the landlord agrees that if the leaseholder (borrower) defaults on their mortgage payments, the landlord will compensate the lender for some part of any loss incurred, if the proceeds from the sale of the leaseholder's (borrower's) share of the property are insufficient.

For this reason, the lender will need to obtain the consent of the landlord to the terms of the borrower's mortgage.

These mortgagee protection provisions enable borrowers to dispense with any requirement to take out mortgage payment protection or indemnity insurance and they are aimed at encouraging the banks and building societies to lend to shared owners. Although lenders are protected through these provisions, borrowers may find themselves liable to landlords for any mortgage debt paid through these provisions.

By signing the lease, the tenant/borrower will authorise the landlord and lender to exchange personal information, including details of any arrears and loans secured against the property.

18.4   DEALING WITH MORTGAGE ARREARS

In a HomeBuy Direct Equity Loan Scheme, mortgage arrears may be dealt with in the normal way. However, in a Shared Ownership Scheme, the position is complicated by the tenant/borrower having to pay mortgage instalments to the lender in respect of the owned share and rent and/or service charges to the landlord for the remaining unowned share.

The tenant/borrower is therefore potentially at risk of possession proceedings from either the mortgage lender if there are mortgage arrears or the landlord if there are rent or service charge arrears.

18.4.1   Options available to the tenant/borrower

If there are mortgage arrears, the lender can bring mortgage possession proceedings in the county court. The borrower would have a number of options if this happens:

- The tenant/borrower will have the full protection of AJA, so the court has the full power to adjourn, stay or suspend execution, or postpone the date for delivery of possession, if the tenant/borrower can show that the mortgage arrears are likely to be paid off within a 'reasonable period' (see **8.3.6**).
- The tenant/borrower can ask the landlord to buy back a share of the lease, thereby reducing the share that they own. This would have the effect of reducing the monthly mortgage repayments and increasing the level of rent, but overall there would be less for the tenant/borrower to pay. 'Reverse' or

'downward' staircasing or 'flexible tenure', as this is known, not only requires the agreement of the landlord, but usually also requires the consent of the lender under a provision in the lease. If necessary, downward staircasing can involve the leaseholder becoming a full tenant once again, so that the whole mortgage is repaid.

- The tenant/borrower can try to sell the lease, which will involve the cooperation of the landlord, which has a right of first refusal. The sale will usually be to someone on the landlord's waiting list who is willing to buy the tenant/borrower's share of the lease, and become the leaseholder of the property. If the landlord declines to buy back a share of the lease and if an outright possession order is made, the mortgage lender may then seek to evict the borrower by applying for a bailiff's warrant in the normal way. Once the lender is in possession, it will then assign the lease to a new owner, staircase up to a full 100 per cent of the value of the property (to sell the lease on the open market) or sell the share back to the landlord (depending upon the terms of the lease).

18.5   DEALING WITH RENT AND/OR SERVICE CHARGE ARREARS

It may be, of course, that the tenant/borrower's problem lies with arrears of rent and/or service charges in respect of the unowned share of the property. If so, the landlord can bring possession proceedings in the normal way, seeking a possession order against the tenant.

As the lease granted by the landlord is likely to be an assured tenancy, all of the usual grounds for possession are available to the landlord. Equally, all of the usual defences including counterclaims and a right to set off, for example, for disrepair would be available to the tenant/borrower.

18.5.1   Leasehold Valuation Tribunal

Where there is a dispute about the payability or reasonableness of the service charges, the tenant/borrower can seek a determination from the Leasehold Valuation Tribunal (LVT) (Landlord and Tenant Act 1985, ss.19 and 27A). This can be done either by direct application to the LVT or by asking the county court to stay the possession proceedings and to transfer the service charge dispute to the tribunal for determination (Commonhold and Leasehold Reform Act 2002, Sched.12, para.3).

The LVT offers substantial expertise in residential property matters. Its procedures are less formal than the county court and it is a 'no-costs' jurisdiction, i.e. there is no power to award costs against the loser, apart from limited powers in the case of, for example, unreasonable conduct. However, the LVT has no jurisdiction over ground rents.

18.5.2   Notice to the lender

The landlord should give the mortgage lender not less than 28 days' notice of its intention to commence possession proceedings, especially where mandatory Ground 8 is used (see Housing Act (HA) 1988, Sched.2). The landlord will usually be obliged to give the lender an undertaking to this effect at the time that the lease is granted.

This 28-day period gives the lender an opportunity to pay off the rent arrears (and add them to the capital of the mortgage) and thereby protect its security, but is not obliged to do so. The risk for the lender is that if the court orders repossession in proceedings brought by the landlord for rent arrears, and the lease is forfeit and disappears, the security for the mortgage would also disappear. However, the mortgagee protection provisions in the lease may require the landlord to cover some of the mortgage debt, although the tenant/borrower will become liable to pay the landlord back.

18.6   NATURE OF THE TENANT'S INTEREST IN THE FREEHOLD

The case of *Richardson* v. *Midland Heart Ltd* (unreported, Birmingham Civil Justice Centre (ChD), 12 November 2007; *Legal Action*, September 2008, p.23) illustrates the potentially dire financial consequences for shared owners if they fall into rent arrears.

In 1995 Ms Richardson paid a premium of £29,500 for a 50 per cent shared ownership lease. Although the lease contained staircasing provisions, which would permit her to acquire further shares up to 100 per cent and then the freehold, Ms Richardson did not make use of them. The lease reserved an annual rent of £1,456 with indexed increases.

In 2003 Ms Richardson's husband was sent to prison and she had to leave the property because of threats from her husband's associates. Rent arrears grew and Ms Richardson decided to sell the property. Her landlord, Midland Heart, agreed to a sale and valued the property at £151,000.

When the property failed to sell, they issued proceedings for possession under Ground 8 (HA 1988, Sched.2). At the time of the possession hearing there was no mortgage on the property. In January 2006, an outright possession order was made against Ms Richardson on the basis that she was an assured tenant. In December 2006 Ms Richardson brought proceedings for declaration as to the extent of her interest in the property (as a shared owner) and an order for sale or an account for 50 per cent of the proceeds of sale.

The court held that the premium paid by Ms Richardson in 1995 when she entered into the shared ownership lease had not bought her a half share of the property. The relationship between Ms Richardson and Midland Heart was simply that of landlord and tenant, with an option to obtain the freehold by staircasing, which was not exercised. The court rejected the argument that the freehold was held on trust by the housing association for itself and Ms Richardson.

Although there was a suggestion that Midland Heart was willing to make an 'ex gratia payment' of the amount Ms Richardson had paid into the property in 1995, there was no obligation to do so. It is understood that Ms Richardson lodged, but then withdrew, an appeal to the Court of Appeal, apparently following the withdrawal of public funding.

In this case there was no mortgage provider which could have paid off the rent arrears. The case is clear illustration of the precarious position of tenants when they buy into shared ownership arrangements, because of the lack of clarity as to what interest (if any) they are purchasing by paying a premium for a share of the premises.

18.6.1 Human rights arguments

Human rights are dealt with in **Chapter 17**.

When exercising functions of a public nature housing associations/private registered providers are to be treated as 'public authorities' for the purposes of HRA 1998 and are susceptible to judicial review: see *R (on the application of Weaver)* v. *London & Quadrant Housing Trust* [2009] EWCA Civ 587, [2009] 4 All ER 865.

Where possession proceedings are brought against a shared owner by a housing association/private registered provider, it is likely that Article 8 (right to a home) and Article 1 of the First Protocol (no one shall be deprived of his possessions) will be engaged.

These, and traditional judicial review grounds, may allow a defence to be brought in the county court, challenging the proportionality and necessity of any possession order, particularly where the potential financial loss to the shared owner and the potential windfall to the housing association are likely to be huge.

The Supreme Court decision in *Manchester City Council* v. *Pinnock* [2010] UKSC 45, [2010] 3 WLR 1441, where it was held that the court must have the ability to assess the proportionality of making a possession order in respect of a person's home, is also likely to be important (see **17.6**). This is especially so, in circumstances where the shared owner is likely to lose significant sums of money as a result of a possession order, as occurred in *Richardson* v. *Midland Heart* (above).

CHAPTER 19

Maximising income and reducing outgoings

19.1 INTRODUCTION

Mortgage borrowers run into financial problems for a variety of reasons. These will often have to do with the loss of a job or reduced working hours, ill health or family bereavement. While advisers may be able to do little about these life events, they can help mitigate the financial consequences that arise, through a variety of strategies for maximising the borrower's income and reducing their outgoings.

19.2 NEED TO PREPARE A BUDGET

The usual starting point is to prepare a budget of the borrower's existing income and outgoings. There are several online budgeting resources. For example there is a printable budget sheet at **www.adviceguide.org.uk**. There is also an online budget planner at **http://yourmoney.moneyadviceservice.org.uk**.

Alternatively, advisers may simply complete the Courts and Tribunals Service Form N11M, the defence form (mortgaged residential premises), which is downloadable from the Ministry of Justice website (**www.justice.gov.uk**) and is reproduced in **Appendix B5**. This six-page form includes questions about the borrower's income, savings, regular expenses and priority debts.

A completed budget allows the adviser to see the extent of a borrower's disposable income, if any. It also identifies those areas of income which are wanting and those expenses which are unnecessarily onerous.

19.3 SPEAKING TO THE LENDER

In all cases where the borrower has run into difficulties paying their mortgage loan, it is advisable to make early contact with the lender. The budgetary exercise described above may have identified disposable income which will allow the borrower to make an immediate proposal to the lender, not only to pay the current monthly instalment of the loan, but also to start to repay arrears. However, more typically, the budget throws up the standard problem faced by borrowers that they have insufficient disposable income to meet their contractual obligations to their lender.

Lenders are often at pains to emphasise their desire to engage in discussions with their borrowers who fall into mortgage payment difficulties. It is usually the case that lenders prefer to try to reach an arrangement to pay with the borrower who is in arrears, although lenders often complain that this is difficult where the borrower fails to make contact or fails to respond to communications from the lender.

Particularly in a period of economic stagnation, lenders may well prefer to come to some arrangement with the borrower in difficulty, rather than incur the expense and uncertainty of repossession and sale. It is for this reason that advisers should encourage borrowers to make early contact with their lenders to minimise the impact of any arrears which may have accrued.

In any event, regulatory rules, the rules of court and/or the effect of statute may all exert influence or compel lenders to engage with borrowers in difficulty, before taking enforcement action.

19.3.1 FSA regulatory rules

Of particular note are the rules contained in the FSA Handbook, which relate to first charge owner occupier loans, the 'Mortgage and Home Finance: Conduct of Business sourcebook' (MCOB). These rules are dealt with in detail in **Chapter 5**. In short, the rules relate to first charge owner-occupier loans granted since 31 October 2004, although most lenders treat similar loans before this date in the same way. The FSA rules require lenders to treat customers fairly.

Volume 13 of MCOB (see **Chapter 5**) requires that lenders have a policy and procedures in place for dealing with customers in arrears. These include requiring a lender:

- to adopt a reasonable approach to the time during which the payment shortfall should be repaid;
- to establish, where feasible, a payment plan which is practicable in terms of the borrower's circumstances;
- to repossess the property only where all other reasonable attempts to resolve the position have failed.

19.3.2 Mortgage Pre-Action Protocol

The Mortgage Pre-Action Protocol for mortgage possession proceedings, which is dealt with in detail in **Chapter 7** and reproduced in **Appendix C5**, covers nearly all home loans and aims to encourage pre-action contact between lenders and borrowers. The Protocol sets out the steps which the parties should take if borrowers fall into arrears. These include:

- providing information about the arrears and discussing the borrower's circumstances and any proposals;
- considering reasonable requests to change the date or method of payment;
- discussing the possibility of extending the term of the mortgage, changing the type of the mortgage, deferring the payment of interest or capitalising the arrears; and
- postponing the start of proceedings where the borrower has made applications for financial support, is marketing the property for sale or has a genuine complaint, which has been lodged with the Financial Ombudsman Service.

19.3.3 Regulated agreements

In the case of second charge loans, which are often regulated according to CCA 1974, several provisions of that Act set out requirements that must be followed by lenders where borrowers fall into arrears (see **Chapter 10**). These include:

- setting out requirements in relation to arrears notices (ss.86B–86F);
- requiring the issue of a default notice before recovery action can commence (s.87); and
- giving the courts the right to grant time orders (s.129) and to suspend an enforcement order or to vary the terms of an agreement in the interests of a borrower in default (ss.135 and 136).

19.4 MAXIMISING INCOME

While lenders can provide assistance to borrowers to maximise their income and/or reduce their outgoings, in the first instance it may be down to the adviser to propose practical steps to be taken by the borrower.

19.4.1 State benefits and financial support

A full guide to the benefits system with a list of all the benefits that might be claimed can be found on the government's Directgov public services information website (**www.direct.gov.uk**). State benefits are available for a variety of personal situations including:

- unemployment;
- sickness or injury;
- disability;
- expecting or bringing up children;
- being in retirement and/or caring for someone;
- bereavement; and
- being on a low income.

The Directgov website also includes a helpful 'benefits adviser service' which enables borrowers to answer questions anonymously online about their savings, income and outgoings. The online benefits adviser will say which benefits a borrower may be entitled to receive, provide an estimate of the benefits, tax credits or pension that may be available and prepare estimates if the borrower's situation changes.

Borrowers should claim any benefits to which they are entitled without delay or they may risk losing money to which they would otherwise be entitled. Many benefits can be back-dated for up to three months, although in some cases there is a necessity to show reasons why there was a delay in claiming. Some benefits are more generous, but other benefits prevent any back-dating claims to be made at all.

The safest approach is to make an immediate claim for any benefit that appears to be applicable to the borrower, even if they have not yet provided all of the information necessary to process the claim. That can follow later.

In appropriate circumstances borrowers can request that earlier decisions are reconsidered or changed, for example if an earlier benefit claim had been refused, or they can appeal, as a way of obtaining arrears of benefits. However, the procedures involved are beyond the ambit of this book.

19.4.2 Support for Mortgage Interest

If borrowers are eligible for certain income-related benefits, they may also qualify for help towards the mortgage interest payments, called Support for Mortgage Interest (SMI).

Borrowers may qualify for SMI if they receive:

- income support;
- income-based jobseeker's allowance;
- income-related employment and support allowance; or
- pension credit.

SMI only covers mortgage interest payments for a mortgage or loan used to buy or improve the borrower's home. It is normally paid directly to the lender. However, it does not include:

- the capital sum borrowed (only interest on the mortgage is paid);
- anything towards the borrower's insurance policies (for example endowment policies linked to an interest only mortgage); or
- mortgage arrears.

How SMI is calculated

SMI contributes towards the interest borrowers pay on their mortgages. Although the interest rates for any given loan will vary from lender to lender, from 1 October 2010 SMI is calculated using a standard interest rate equivalent to the Bank of

England's published monthly average mortgage interest rate. That stands at 3.63 per cent (as at June 2011), but it is of course subject to change.

The use of a standard interest rate has two consequences. The first is that for many borrowers SMI contributions will be lower than the actual interest payments that borrowers are required to pay. This will generate a shortfall which borrowers will have to meet from other resources.

The second consequence is that some borrowers may have interest rates that are lower than the standard rate used to calculate SMI payments. They would receive more SMI than required to meet the contractual payments due to the lender, but the surplus can only be credited to the mortgage account.

The Social Security (Claims and Payments) Amendment Regulations 2010, SI 2010/796 provide that where the sum paid to a lender exceeds the borrower's actual liability in respect of the mortgage interest payable, the excess shall be applied by that lender first towards the discharge of arrears of mortgage interest and, secondly, towards the discharge of the principal sum, or any other sum payable by the borrower to that lender in respect of that loan.

19.4.3 Rules applicable to SMI since 5 January 2009

Prior to 5 January 2009 different rules applied to the payment of SMI. Borrowers who received SMI before this date will continue to receive the same level of help. However, new rules apply from 5 January 2009. Since then:

- SMI can be paid in respect of interest on up to the first £200,000 of the mortgage (this was previously £100,000);
- borrowers of working age will have to wait 13 weeks from the date of claim before SMI will be paid to the lender (this waiting period was previously 39 or 26 weeks, depending on the borrower's circumstances);
- if the borrower is receiving income-based jobseeker's allowance, SMI will be paid for a period of up to two years only (but there is no such limit for borrowers receiving income support, income-related employment and support allowance or pension credit).

If borrowers are claiming pension credit, there is no waiting period before they receive help with the mortgage interest payments, but the SMI will only contribute to mortgage interest on up to the first £100,000 of the mortgage.

However, for a borrower who is receiving one of the other eligible benefits, where they are entitled to mortgage interest payments on up to £200,000 of their mortgage, if within 12 weeks of the end of their claim, they then move on to pension credit, the £200,000 limit will still apply.

19.4.4 Interaction with the Mortgage Pre-Action Protocol

Paragraph 6.1 of the Mortgage Pre-Action Protocol states that a lender should consider not starting a possession claim for mortgage arrears where the borrower can demonstrate to the lender that the borrower has submitted a claim to the Department for Work and Pensions (DWP) for SMI and has provided all the evidence required to process a claim. In addition, the borrower must demonstrate a reasonable expectation of eligibility for payment from the DWP and an ability to pay any part of the mortgage instalment not covered by a claim to the DWP (see **7.5** and **Appendix C5**).

Advisers may seek an adjournment of a possession hearing on grounds that the borrower has submitted (or is about to submit) a claim for SMI. See case studies 4 and 5 in **Appendix F2**.

19.4.5 Mortgage interest run on

In certain circumstances a borrower may be eligible for mortgage interest run on. This is an extra four weeks' contribution towards the borrower's housing costs, i.e. the mortgage interest payments, if the borrower (or their partner or civil partner) has stopped receiving certain other benefits, because one of them is returning to work full-time, working more hours or earning more money. The eligible benefits are income support, income-based jobseeker's allowance or income-related employment and support allowance. Conditions apply, namely:

- the person has been claiming the eligible benefit continuously for at least 26 weeks; and
- they expect the work to last for five weeks or more; and
- they have been entitled to help with their mortgage interest payments before the work started, and will still have to make those payments after work starts.

Payments will be paid directly to the borrower instead of being paid direct to the mortgage lender.

19.4.6 Increasing hours/part-time work

For those borrowers who are in work, the benefits of increasing their hours and therefore their income may seem obvious. However, it is worth canvassing this as a possibility since advisers will often be surprised how this simple step is often overlooked by borrowers under financial stress.

Where borrowers are unlikely to be able to increase their hours at work, they may be willing to consider finding a second part-time job to supplement their income.

A borrower who is working less than 16 hours a week may also be eligible for income support and SMI. Where a borrower comes off income support, income-based jobseeker's allowance or income-related employment and support allowance, because they are about to return to work, work more hours or earn more money, they may be able to claim mortgage interest run on, see above.

19.4.7 Contributions from other members of the family

In the short term, borrowers may need to seek financial support from friends and family. Usually, this will be in the form of short-term support or one-off payments. Such financial help can give borrowers 'a breathing space' while other arrangements are made to meet mortgage payment commitments. This sort of help is only likely to turn into a longer term, regular help, if evidence can be provided by the borrower of other steps that have been taken to meet the mortgage commitments, in particular arrangements that are made with the agreement of the lender and/or a valid claim for SMI.

19.4.8 Tenants and lodgers

Very often mortgage deeds will prohibit any use of the dwelling other than as the principal or main home of the borrower. Sub-letting and creating tenancies will also be prohibited although, occasionally, these will be allowed with the lender's prior written consent.

Where there is such a prohibition, advisers will not be in a position to propose that a borrower sub-lets or creates a tenancy, because that would induce a breach of the mortgage deed. However, if a suitable tenant can be found, it may be worthwhile approaching the lender with a proposal as to the grant of a short-term tenancy.

Where the tenancy is of part of the dwelling in which the borrower still resides as their only or principal home, the tenancy will not be the usual assured shorthold tenancy, by reason of the resident landlord exemption (HA 1988, Sched. 1, para. 10). The resulting tenancy is likely to be a bare contractual tenancy which, if anything, has rather less security of tenure than an assured shorthold tenancy.

The position with regard to lodgers may be different under the mortgage deed. Lodgers, or paying guests, are mere licensees of the rooms that they occupy. As they acquire no proprietary interest in the dwelling or any part of it, their occupation is merely personal to themselves and they acquire no lasting security of tenure.

Some mortgage deeds are silent with regard to the position of lodgers or paying guests. A prohibition against sub-letting, the creation of a tenancy of part, or parting with possession of the whole or part of the dwelling should not prevent the borrower taking in a lodger or paying guest to occupy an empty room in his home.

Careful examination of the mortgage deed is necessary in every case. If the borrower has one or more spare bedrooms and is willing to rent them out in order to increase their income, such a proposal might be put to the lender.

19.4.9 Tax treatment of rental income

Under the 'Rent a Room' Scheme if a borrower lets furnished accommodation in his own home to a lodger, he does not have to pay tax provided that the total receipts (rent, plus any charges for meals or services) do not exceed certain amounts, currently £4,250 per year (£2,125, if letting jointly). The borrower will have to pay tax on anything over £4,250. These figures may rise over time.

Alternatively the borrower could choose not to use the 'Rent a Room' Scheme, if he would prefer to pay tax under the rules for other residential lettings.

19.5 REDUCING OUTGOINGS

At the same time as maximising income, advisers will wish to help borrowers to reduce their outgoings.

19.5.1 Reducing payments to unsecured creditors

Money from unsecured creditors will have come from many sources and will have been used for many different purposes. It may take the form of a bank loan being repaid by monthly instalments over a fixed period, payments under hire-purchase agreements for consumer goods, credit card debts, 'fringe' lending at high interest rates or informal loans from family, friends or acquaintances.

The common feature of unsecured creditors is that they often demand payment over considerably shorter periods than mortgage loans and the ratio of payments to the money owed is much greater. Advisers will therefore come across situations where borrowers are regularly paying hundreds of pounds per month to unsecured creditors, to whom relatively speaking only modest sums are owed, at the expense of their contractual monthly instalment payments to the mortgage lenders whose loans are secured on their homes.

Such behaviour by borrowers is extremely dangerous because, whilst the smaller debts are serviced, the borrower's home is at risk by ignoring the much larger debt owed to the mortgage lender.

Rescheduling payments

By means of the budget referred to at the head of this chapter, the adviser should take steps to reschedule the payments to the unsecured creditors and, where possible, to reduce them drastically in order to free up sufficient monies to pay the instalments on the main mortgage debt.

Help with rescheduling unsecured debts can be obtained from professional debt councillors, for example through the National Debtline, which provides a telephone advice service and an online money advice tool (see **www.nationaldebtline.co.uk**).

If the adviser takes on board the task of rescheduling debts, it would usually be necessary to provide unsecured creditors with an outline income and expenditure sheet, which will show the borrower's disposable income after they have paid the current monthly instalment on their mortgage loan(s). By allocating a certain proportion of the borrower's disposable income to the payment of unsecured creditors, and by apportioning that sum between the creditors in the proportions of the particular debt to the total debts owed, a payment scheme can be proposed which many unsecured creditors will accept, albeit with a review after 3, 6 or 12 months.

Payment holidays

Sometimes borrowers will simply have no disposable income with which to service unsecured creditors. If that is the case, the creditors may be advised of the 'temporary' position, with a request for a payment holiday until the position improves. Once again, unsecured creditors may accept that they will receive no payments for a period of time, if there is to be a structured review after three or six months.

Where the unsecured creditors are owed £750 or more, there is a risk of bankruptcy proceedings being brought against the borrower. However, this is a high-risk strategy for an unsecured creditor, particularly in circumstances where there is little or no equity in the borrower's home.

19.5.2   Council tax arrears and bailiffs

Borrowers are often under considerable pressure to pay off council tax arrears by unfeasibly high instalments. The pressure to pay arises from proceedings for liability orders and the threat of committal to prison, visits by bailiffs with the threat to remove the borrower's personal possessions and sell them at auction and from bankruptcy proceedings.

Faced with such an armoury of enforcement options and often aggressive tactics, borrowers find it very difficult to resist demands to pay council tax arrears. Nonetheless advisers can and should seek to negotiate reduced payments in respect of the arrears, in much the same way as unsecured creditors above. The budget statements should be presented to the courts when necessary, so that realistic payment terms can be imposed.

So far as bailiffs are concerned, the advice to borrowers in every case is never to let the bailiff into the home, under any circumstances. So long as the bailiff has not entered the home, their powers are very limited. However, once a bailiff has entered a home once, usually at the invitation of the borrower, on a return visit the bailiff has powers to force entry to remove the borrower's possessions. Advisers should be aware that there are currently proposals to increase bailiffs' powers.

19.5.3   Utilities and household insurance

The amounts payable for gas, electricity and household insurance can vary considerably from provider to provider. Borrowers may be paying more than they should if they are on an old payment plan, paying for gas and electricity separately or perhaps because they have remained with the same provider for many years.

Considerable savings can be achieved by changing payment arrangements, the energy tariff or the provider.

Detailed information about switching gas and electricity suppliers can be found on the internet, for example on the Citizens Advice website at **www.adviceguide. org.uk**. Assistance to switch suppliers can be obtained from **www.uswitch.com**.

There are numerous individual household insurers who will provide alternative quotes over the internet. Alternatively, borrowers may wish to use the services of an insurance broker.

By making savings to the reduction of utility and household insurance charges, borrowers can release money that will ease the pressure of maintaining mortgage payments.

19.5.4 Personal expenses

It is always a sensitive subject to question a borrower's personal expenditure on non-essential items. Advisers must be non-judgmental about a borrower's personal preferences. However, in the context of trying to reduce outgoings and maximising income to ease financial difficulties, it should be possible for advisers to discuss levels of personal expenditure without breaking the relationship of trust. In particular, it should be acceptable for an adviser to point out to a borrower that individual items of personal expenditure are much higher than the average and to ask the borrower whether there would not be a way to reduce that expenditure.

The Office for National Statistics (**www.statistics.gov.uk**) produces an annual report, which analyses household expenditure on goods and services by household income, composition, size, type and location. The latest report is called *Family Spending 2010 Edition: A Report on the Living Costs and Food Survey 2009* (20 April 2011). This shows that UK households spent an average of £455 a week, which included spending of £57.90 on recreation and culture (TVs, computers, newspapers, books, leisure activities and package holidays). In addition, food and non-alcoholic drink purchases contributed £52.20 to weekly household expenditure.

Obviously, the weekly expenditure will rise or fall depending on the composition of the household and its income. The report contains numerous tables which show such variations in expenditure, taking these factors into account.

19.6 DEALING WITH MORTGAGE PAYMENT SHORTFALLS

Even once income has been maximised and outgoings have been reduced, borrowers may find themselves in difficulties meeting the currently monthly instalment on the mortgage. There are several approaches to this situation.

19.6.1   Mortgage payment protection insurance

For many years it was common practice for borrowers to purchase mortgage payment protection insurance (MPPI) when the mortgage loan was first taken out.

Refunds for mis-sold policies

Sadly, a large number of such policies were mis-sold by lenders, including the four main high street banks, in circumstances where borrowers would never be able to make claims under the policies. For example, some policies were sold to borrowers who were self-employed and would not have been able to claim on them, to borrowers who were told wrongly that taking MPPI was a condition for being granted their loan and to borrowers who did not even realise they were taking out a policy.

Where policies have been mis-sold application may be made to the lender concerned for a refund of any premium paid, with interest. On 10 August 2010, the FSA took the lead by publishing Policy Statement 10/12 'The Assessment and Redress of Payment Protection Insurance Complaints' which, amongst other things, required lenders to go back over all their past sales to see if the borrowers had a claim for mis-selling. Court action to challenge the policy statement was lost in the High Court on 20 April 2011: see *R (on the application of British Bankers Association)* v. *Financial Services Authority* [2011] EWHC 999 (Admin). When the lenders decided not to appeal that decision in May 2011, banks and other lending institutions set aside literally billions of pounds to meet the expected repayments to borrowers.

In itself, a successful application for the return of the premium may provide useful capital that may be utilised in payment of mortgage arrears or to ease other financial problems. However, advisers should be aware that refunds may take several months and sometimes years to process. If a lender delays unreasonably or refuses to make a refund, the borrower can make a formal complaint to the lender and then complain to the FOS (see **Chapter 23**).

Claims under existing policies

In other situations MPPI may not have been mis-sold or, even where there is doubt about that, the mortgage borrower may wish to try to make a claim under the policy.

Typically, MPPI will cover situations where the borrower has lost income due to the loss or interruption of employment as a result of illness or redundancy. In its terms and conditions MPPI will set up circumstances in which a claim may be made, the evidence that is required, the amount which will be paid and the period of payment. Such policies are typically very complex and the obstacles that they create have in the past been used by insurers to refuse payment under the policy. In such circumstances a formal complaint to the insurer followed by a complaint to the FOS may resolve the reluctance of the insurer to pay under the policy (see **Chapter 23**).

Where payment is forthcoming, usually it will cover the whole of the mortgage instalment payment for one, or sometimes, two years or longer. Such payments would provide a welcome cushion to borrowers otherwise facing financial difficulties as a result of the loss of employment or reduction in pay.

19.6.2 Interaction with the Mortgage Pre-Action Protocol

Lenders should be advised at the earliest opportunity where a claim is made under an MPPI policy. Paragraph 6.1 of the Mortgage Pre-Action Protocol states that a lender should consider not starting a possession claim for mortgage arrears where the borrower can demonstrate to the lender that the borrower has submitted a claim to an insurer under a MPPI policy and has provided all the evidence required to process a claim. In addition, the borrower must demonstrate a reasonable expectation of eligibility for payment from the insurer and an ability to pay any part of the mortgage instalment not covered by a claim to the insurer (see **7.5** and **Appendix C5**).

Paragraph 8.1 of the Protocol goes on to say that the lender should consider whether to postpone the start of a possession claim where the borrower has made a genuine complaint to the FOS about the potential possession claim. It is submitted that this extends to a complaint to the FOS which may be made by a borrower in relation to the refusal of an MPPI insurer to meet mortgage payments under the policy, since the making of such payments might reduce or extinguish arrears on which any potential possession claim would be based.

19.7 NEGOTIATIONS WITH THE LENDER

There are several practical ways in which the level of the mortgage payments can be reduced. These include:

- extending the term of a repayment mortgage;
- deferring payment of interest or capital due under the mortgage (payment holidays);
- changing the type of a mortgage to interest only; and
- capitalising the arrears.

19.7.1 Extending the term of the mortgage

Lenders may be willing to extend the term of the mortgage where the borrower has a good record until the current financial difficulties arose, particularly where sufficient proposals are put forward for the future payment of arrears and mortgage instalments. Usually, lenders will not wish to extend the mortgage where the term will expire after the borrower's state retirement age.

By extending the term of the mortgage the monthly instalments are recalculated and spread over a longer period, so they will necessarily be lower than the existing instalment.

19.7.2 Deferring payments due under the mortgage

The lender may be willing to defer payment of interest, capital or both otherwise due under the mortgage. This is popularly known as a 'payment holiday'. This would be particularly suitable where there was a temporary interruption of income for a specified period, once again with adequate proposals for future payments. The suspension of payments due under the mortgage will prevent arrears accruing and allow the borrower to arrange his affairs in time for the recommencement of payments.

If the borrower has an interest-only mortgage linked to an endowment policy, but cannot afford payments to both, it is also possible to ask the endowment policy company to suspend payments for a period of time. Since the endowment will be used at the end of the term to repay the principal sum of the mortgage loan, it will be necessary to restart payments to the policy at some stage and this can be arranged with the company. Arrangements should also be made to catch up on the backlog of payments which were not paid during the period of suspension.

Another alternative might be to cash in or sell the endowment policy, to release money to pay the arrears. However, that might entail taking out a repayment mortgage for the remainder of the term. Since the value of the endowment policy could be considerably less if it were to be cashed in early, expert advice from a mortgage broker should be taken before taking this step.

19.7.3 Changing the type of a mortgage

Capital repayment mortgages are more expensive, because each month the borrower will be repaying interest on the monies borrowed, together with a small payment towards the capital loan. The payments are calculated so that at the end of the mortgage period all of the capital will have been repaid.

Interest-only mortgages tend to be much cheaper, because the borrower makes no monthly payment in reduction of the principal sum loaned. Instead, the borrower pays a small sum towards an endowment policy, which is then used at the end of the mortgage term to pay off the whole of the principal sum loaned in one go. Setting aside criticisms of this arrangement in recent years, where endowment policies have generated insufficient money to pay off the capital at the end of the mortgage term, the interest-only mortgage will be cheaper for the borrower to afford in terms of the monthly instalment payments.

Currently, interest-only mortgages are difficult to obtain for the ordinary homeowner. Some lenders no longer provide interest-only products at all. Where an existing borrower under a repayment mortgage seeks to change the type of mort-gage, lenders will often only permit this for relatively short periods, for example one or two years.

Although the change of type of mortgage is more difficult nowadays than in previous years, it remains a useful device to reduce monthly instalment payments, giving borrowers time to make other arrangements in relation to the mortgage arrears and future instalments.

19.7.4   Capitalising the arrears

Where arrears accrue, borrowers find themselves having to pay interest on the principal amount of the loan and additional interest on the arrears. The monthly instalments therefore increase, exacerbating financial problems which the bor-rower may already be experiencing. By capitalising the arrears, the lender adds them back into the principal sum loaned and then recalculates the instalment payments over the remaining period of the term. This will result in a reduction in the interest payments due each month from the borrower.

Again, lenders often set conditions before agreeing to capitalise arrears. It is very common for them to require the borrower to make six uninterrupted payments of the full amount of the monthly mortgage instalment, before agreeing to capitalisation. Notwithstanding this, capitalisation is a useful tool both practically to reduce the monthly instalments and psychologically to draw a line under past arrears and give the borrower a 'fresh start'. This is particularly so where capitalisation of the arrears can be combined at the same time with the change to an interest-only repayment basis, even if the latter is only for a couple of years.

19.8   GOVERNMENT INITIATIVES

In addition to Support for Mortgage Interest (SMI), which is a longstanding benefit for borrowers receiving certain state benefits (see **19.4.2**), in recent years the government has introduced two additional initiatives to help homeowners in financial difficulty: the Homeowners Mortgage Support Scheme and the Mortgage Rescue Schemes: see **Chapter 20**.

19.9   CONCLUSION

Advisers should not delay in utilising all available options to maximise the borrow-er's income and reduce his outgoings. By doing so, the adviser will strengthen the borrower's position significantly, not only in negotiations with the lender, but also in dealing with the court, all with the aim of keeping the borrower in his home.

CHAPTER 20

Government initiatives

20.1 HOMEOWNERS MORTGAGE SUPPORT SCHEME

The Homeowners Mortgage Support Scheme was designed to help households whose incomes had dropped temporarily, for example if there was a temporary reduction or loss of employment. The scheme worked by the lender delaying some of the monthly interest payments on the mortgage for up to two years.

However, this scheme was closed to new applicants from 21 April 2011, due to the very low take-up of the scheme after more than a year of operation, and therefore it is not covered any further in this book.

20.2 MORTGAGE RESCUE SCHEME – OVERVIEW

A Mortgage Rescue Scheme was introduced in Wales by the Welsh Assembly government (now known as the Welsh Government) in June 2008 and in England by the UK government in January 2009. Both schemes are aimed at protecting the most vulnerable households from the negative impacts of mortgage repossession and homelessness and are likely to continue at least until April 2013.

The schemes are targeted at households which, in the event that their homes are repossessed by mortgage lenders, would be accepted as homeless and whose local authority would therefore have a duty to secure accommodation for them.

While the schemes in England and Wales share similarities, there are sufficient differences in eligibility criteria and procedures, for the two to be dealt with separately in this chapter.

20.3 MORTGAGE RESCUE SCHEME – ENGLAND

20.3.1 Eligibility

In order to be eligible for the Mortgage Rescue Scheme the household under threat of repossession must be in 'priority need'.

Priority need

The categories of people in priority need are set out in the Housing Act (HA) 1996, s.189(1), with six additional categories added by the Homelessness (Priority Need for Accommodation) (England) Order 2002, SI 2002/2051, specifically for English local housing authorities (see **Appendix G** for more details about the law of homelessness).

In general terms persons who are in 'priority need' will include:

- a pregnant woman;
- someone with dependent children;
- someone who is vulnerable as a result of old age, mental illness or mental handicap or physical disability;
- some young people;
- people who are vulnerable as a result of various circumstances such as fostering, having served in the armed forces or having been imprisoned.

Any such household must be able to demonstrate that it has exhausted all other options and is at imminent risk of repossession.

Additional criteria

In England, the household will also need to meet the following criteria:

- the household must earn less than £60,000 a year;
- it must not own a second home, including a home abroad;
- the value of the mortgage and any other loans taken out against the home is less than 120 per cent of the value of the home; and
- the value of the home is not higher than certain levels set for each region.

20.3.2   Procedure

Application for assistance under the Mortgage Rescue Scheme in England is made to the local housing authority. Borrowers at risk of homelessness may apply directly or they may be referred to the scheme by advice agencies, such as Citizens Advice or Shelter, or by their mortgage lender or the courts.

The local housing authority will assess the borrower's eligibility for the scheme. This may include arranging for the borrower to meet with the council's money advisers to see if there are other ways of managing the debt and/or meeting the borrower's housing costs, and an assessment of the home at risk. The council will involve a housing association or 'private registered provider' to assess which kind of financial help may be best.

20.3.3 Options available to borrowers

The Mortgage Rescue Schemes in England and Wales both offer two separate options:

- a shared equity scheme; and
- a mortgage to rent scheme.

20.3.4 Shared equity scheme: England

Under the English shared equity scheme, the housing association provides an equity loan to the borrower to reduce the monthly mortgage repayments. The borrower remains the owner of the property, but in return grants an additional charge to the housing association to secure the equity loan. In order to come within this scheme, the borrower must:

- have at least 25 per cent equity in the property (which means that the mortgage must not be worth more than 75 per cent of the property's value); and
- be able to maintain payments on the original mortgage once the equity loan has been granted.

The borrower pays a low monthly interest-only charge on the equity loan, which must be repaid when the property is sold in the future.

20.3.5 Mortgage to rent scheme: England

The housing association may suggest that the borrower sells their home to the housing association. This is the government mortgage to rent scheme. The housing association will buy the borrower's home for 90 per cent of its market value. The borrower will remain in their home and pay a rent to the housing association as their tenant, at a rate which will be 20 per cent less than the market rate for the area.

20.4 MORTGAGE RESCUE SCHEME – WALES

20.4.1 Eligibility

In order to be eligible for the Mortgage Rescue Scheme the household under threat of repossession must be in 'priority need'.

Priority need

The categories of people in priority need are set out in the HA 1996, s.189(1), with six additional categories added by the Homeless Persons (Priority Need) (Wales) Order 2001, SI 2001/607 (W. 30), specifically for Welsh local housing authorities (see **Appendix G** for more details about the law of homelessness).

In general terms persons who are in 'priority need' will include:

- a pregnant woman;
- someone with dependent children;
- someone who is vulnerable as a result of old age, mental illness or mental handicap or physical disability;
- some young people;
- people who are vulnerable as a result of various circumstances such as fostering, having served in the armed forces or having been imprisoned.

Additionally, in Wales, mortgage rescue will be available to those applicants who are disabled and whose homes have been adapted to meet their needs.

Any such household must be able to demonstrate that it had exhausted all other options and is at imminent risk of repossession.

Additional criteria

In Wales, the household will also need to meet the following criteria:

- the property is the only or main residence of the family;
- the property is clear of any legal actions that would prevent it being sold; and
- it is not possible to sell the property and buy a cheaper home locally.

The Mortgage Rescue Scheme will not support properties where the debts of the household are greater than the open market value of the property. This will apply to cases of negative equity, but will also entail an assessment of the level of the household's unsecured debts and the cost of any works to the property in the event purchase takes place.

20.4.2   Procedure

In Wales, borrowers should contact the local housing authority or the housing directorate at the Welsh Government. The local authority housing options team, homeless team or housing strategy officers are equipped to explain how the scheme works in greater detail and whether it can assist the borrower facing repossession.

From April 2011, Welsh local authorities can decide whether to help borrowers with mortgage rescue. Once a borrower has been endorsed by the local authority for the scheme, it will be the responsibility of a housing association to carry out an assessment of the applicant's financial circumstances in terms of suitability for assistance under the scheme.

Funding for the scheme is limited. While help will be given to those in greatest need, when all the funds have been allocated in any particular financial year, the scheme will be unable to deal with any new applicants.

20.4.3 Options available to borrowers

The Mortgage Rescue Schemes in England and Wales both offer two separate options:

- a shared equity scheme; and
- a mortgage to rent scheme.

20.4.4 Shared equity scheme: Wales

Also known as a 'homebuy' equity loan, consideration will be given to:

- the open market value of the property;
- the level of debt of the applicant;
- the condition of the property and its appropriateness for social housing;
- the applicant's ability to maintain the property;
- the ability of the applicant to pay any ongoing mortgage commitments.

Where the scheme is available a housing association can provide an equity loan for an agreed percentage (usually 30 per cent, but up to a maximum of 50 per cent) of the equity in the property. The loan is repayable to the housing association when the property is sold in the future and is interest free.

The property value should be within limits which are published by the Welsh Government, although those limits may be waived in exceptional cases where the local authority and housing association consider that there are particular circumstances which would make access to the scheme appropriate.

20.4.5 Mortgage to rent: Wales

Under the mortgage to rent scheme, a local housing association will purchase the borrower's property at the market value and rent it back to them. The borrower will then become an assured tenant of their home.

CHAPTER 21

Selling the property

21.1 VOLUNTARY SALES

Despite a borrower's attempts to improve his financial position with regard to the mortgage, he may decide that he can no longer afford the monthly instalments and that he would prefer to sell the property. Usually, this will be on the open market.

However, certain local housing authorities operate a 'buy-back scheme' for properties originally bought under the right-to-buy scheme, where the borrower becomes a secure council tenant once again. This is a discretionary scheme, subject to conditions. Local authorities generally pay considerably less than the full market value of the property and often only the same amount as the borrower originally paid for it himself. While funds for buy-back schemes are limited, some borrowers in financial difficulty may find them an attractive way of retaining a home, albeit as tenants rather than homeowners.

21.1.1 By the borrower on the open market

Any sale on the open market is likely to achieve a higher price if the borrower remains in possession during the sale process, rather than vacate the premises and sell an empty property. For this reason, the borrower will need to persuade his lender to give him sufficient time to allow the sale to go ahead.

21.1.2 Marketing the property

Once the decision to sell has been reached, the borrower should arrange to put the property on the market promptly, with one or more estate agents. The lender should be notified of this step and provided with a copy of the agents' particulars. A solicitor will need to be instructed to handle the sale.

21.1.3 Mortgage Pre-Action Protocol

Paragraph 6.2 of the Mortgage Pre-Action Protocol (see **Appendix C5**) states that if a borrower can demonstrate that reasonable steps have been or will be taken to market a property at an appropriate price in accordance with reasonable professional advice, the lender should consider postponing starting a possession claim. The borrower must continue to take all reasonable steps actively to market the property where the lender has agreed to postpone starting a claim.

By paragraph 6.3, where the lender has agreed to postpone starting a possession claim the borrower should provide the lender with a copy of the particulars of sale and, where relevant, details of purchase offers received within a reasonable period of time specified by the lender. The Protocol also mentions the Home Information pack, but this has now been abolished.

The borrower should give the lender details of the estate agent and the conveyancer instructed to deal with the sale. The borrower should also authorise the estate agent and the conveyancer to communicate with the lender about the progress of the sale and the borrower's conduct during the process.

21.1.4 Asking the court for time to sell

If mortgage possession proceedings have already been issued and the matter comes before the court, an application can be made to the judge for an adjournment to enable the property to be sold. The court's powers are dealt with in detail in **Chapter 8**. However it is worth mentioning here that quite apart from the powers in AJA, the court has a residual and inherent jurisdiction to defer a possession order whilst the lender finds a buyer, with the borrowers in occupation up until the date of sale, see *Cheltenham & Gloucester* v. *Booker* (1997) 29 HLR 634.

It has been accepted at Court of Appeal level that a sale by the borrower is preferable to a forced sale by the lender, provided that the lender's position is protected, see *Target Home Loans* v. *Clothier* [1994] 1 All ER 439 (see **8.3.10**).

Some mortgage lenders rely on the case of *Mortgage Service Funding plc* v. *Steele* (1996) 72 P & CR D40 to rebut this assumption. In *Steele* Nourse LJ said:

> If the property has to be sold, it can just as well be sold by the mortgagee, whose duty is always to obtain the best price … at the date of sale.

Borrowers' advisers will want to point out that *Steele* was an application for leave to appeal, which carries less weight than a substantive decision. Furthermore, *Clothier*, which was a full decision on appeal, was not cited in *Steele*.

The court's approach will probably depend on the stage at which any sale has reached. If the sale process is quite advanced, the court may be willing to adjourn the possession hearing. However, the judge is likely to look for some certainty that the sale will go ahead. He will need some compelling evidence with regard to the sale process and/or confirmation that contracts have been exchanged.

In *National and Provincial BS* v. *Lloyd* [1996] 1 All ER 630, CA, clear evidence of completion of the sale 'in six or nine months, or even a year', was considered to be a reasonable period. However, this was rejected in *Bristol and West Building Society* v. *Ellis* (1997) 29 HLR 282, CA, where the borrower asked for a suspension of a possession warrant for three to five years in order to allow her children to finish their university education.

Valuation evidence

Where a lender objects to an adjournment, the judge will be concerned about the amount of equity in the property and whether the lender's interests would be prejudiced by an adjournment. This will require some valuation evidence in respect of the property. This might be provided by the particulars of sale. Alternatively, if the procedure is still at an early stage the borrower may wish to rely on a 'drive-by' valuation from an estate agent. This can usually be obtained free of charge and will be an approximate valuation deriving from an external viewing of the property concerned, combined with the estate agent's knowledge of the property market in that area for properties of that type and condition. An internet printout of agents' particulars of a similar property may also suffice.

If the court is not satisfied with the evidence produced about the progress of any sale, or if there is a concern about the equity in the property and, thus, the security for the loan, the court is more likely to make an outright possession order to take effect after an extended period of time – 56 days or two months is typical.

Such a delay may give time for the sale transaction to proceed. If there is insufficient time, but evidence of significant progress, the borrower can apply to the court to vary the terms of the possession order, to allow more time for the sale to proceed (see **13.4**).

Of course, if kept fully informed about progress of any sale, the lender may agree not to enforce any possession order that may have been granted by the court, which may make an application to vary unnecessary.

21.1.5 Proceeds of sale

Once a sale has completed, the proceeds of sale must be applied to discharge the first mortgage on the property and thereafter any subsequent mortgages or charges.

21.1.6 Dealing with second/subsequent charges

If a sale is to proceed without discharging the entirety of a first, second or subsequent charge, then the consent of the lender concerned will be required. Otherwise, once the sale has completed, the borrower will not be in a position to transfer the property free of encumbrances to the purchaser.

The borrower's options include trying to persuade the subsequent lender to accept a smaller sum to discharge the mortgage, or to consent to the sale going ahead and to certify discharge of the mortgage to the purchaser, but to come to some other arrangement for the repayment by the borrower of the unpaid amount after sale, by instalments.

If the subsequent charge lender refuses to give such consent, the borrower may ask the first charge lender to exercise its power of sale as the mortgagee under LPA 1925, s.101 and/or the first mortgage deed.

The effect of the first charge lender exercising its power of sale is to 'overreach' the subsequent charge lender's registered charge. This would remove the later charge from the property title at the Land Registry and any purchaser would take free from both the first and subsequent charges. The subsequent charge would effectively become unsecured, so that the subsequent charge lender would have to pursue its debt against the borrower as a normal creditor. First charge lenders may be willing to exercise their power of sale at the request of a borrower, where a controlled sale with the borrower in possession is likely to achieve a higher price than with an empty, repossessed property, where the proceeds of sale may leave a shortfall on the first lender's charge.

This situation where the likely proceeds of sale are less than the amounts secured is known as 'negative equity', see **21.6**.

21.2   ASSISTED VOLUNTARY SALES

Several mortgage lenders provide a structured scheme of 'assisted voluntary sale' (AVS). Such schemes may be appropriate either where the likely proceeds of sale will clear the first lender's charge, or more usually, in situations where there is likely to be a shortfall and hence negative equity. Generally, the borrower will be the seller under AVS, but AVS may be used to enable the lender to take over the sale, for example to overreach an unwilling second charge lender as described above.

The AVS scheme has several advantages to a borrower, offering:

- negotiated time to sell the property privately, to increase the chances of achieving the true market value;
- help with marketing and valuing the property;
- help with legal fees and estate agents' costs;
- in some cases, help in securing alternative accommodation;
- negotiation with unsecured creditors, in some cases achieving full and final settlements; and
- continuing support to help the borrower become debt free after the property is sold.

Several AVS schemes provide a dedicated case officer to support the borrower throughout the sale process. After selling the property, there may be sufficient equity to make settlement payments to other creditors. Otherwise, help may be provided to the borrower to arrange a structured payment plan, such as a debt management plan or an individual voluntary arrangement.

21.3 SALE AND RENT BACK ARRANGEMENTS

Sale and rent back schemes (SRB), sometimes known as 'sale and leaseback' or 'sell-to-rent-back', are relatively recent innovations, which are becoming increasingly popular with borrowers in difficulty. The adviser should beware of confusing them with equity release schemes, which are usually only available to people over 55 years of age. Some of the early SRB schemes were run by highly unscrupulous individuals, but since 25 June 2010, the sector has been regulated by the FSA.

The schemes work by a borrower entering into an arrangement with an individual or company (the provider) by which they sell them their home at a discount in return for being granted a tenancy of it. While this may allow the borrower to clear the mortgage and other debts, the borrower, as tenant, will face other significant risks. The tenancy offered is usually an assured shorthold under HA 1988 and once the fixed period has expired, the SRB provider will be able to regain possession by court order without difficulty. The provider is only likely to agree to a renewal of the tenancy if the property market makes it less advantageous to sell than to continue to rent. As soon as property prices start to rise, the provider will be keen to realise its asset by selling the property.

In the earlier schemes it was not uncommon for borrowers to give up their homes in exchange for a fixed-term tenancy of only 6 or 12 months. The FSA now requires that the tenancy term must be for at least five years.

Borrowers may still be evicted during the fixed term of the tenancy, for example if they fall behind with the new rental payments. The SRB provider is often financing the transaction with a buy-to-let mortgage and if it falls behind with its payments, the new lender may well seek possession.

Some schemes allow the SRB provider to increase the rent during the fixed term to a level as high as the previous mortgage instalments, in which case the former borrower is little better off than if they had kept their mortgage.

There may be defences open to former borrowers who are now tenants, particularly in some of the earlier schemes. The argument that such a former borrower has an overriding interest is dealt with at **4.4**.

A former borrower may also be able to prevent his eviction by relying on the equitable doctrine of proprietary estoppel, for example where he had been misled during the sale process as to how long he was going to be allowed to stay in the property. It is rare for the defence of misrepresentation to be of use because it requires rescission, i.e. the borrower would have ownership of his home returned to him, but would have to refund the sale proceeds to the SRB provider. Even so, it is sometimes the case that the borrower, if properly advised, could have remortgaged or extended the term of their existing mortgage to pay off their arrears. If so, they may be able to raise the finance to refund the discounted purchase price to the SRB provider. In such a case, when making an order for rescission, the court should be asked to make provision to allow a sufficient period for the borrower to put a remortgage in place.

Although in the short term an SRB scheme may appeal to a borrower, it should always be considered as a last resort.

21.4   EQUITY RELEASE SCHEMES

These schemes are usually only available to people over 55 and have a much better reputation than the sale and rent back schemes discussed above. There are two types of scheme, but only the home reversion type is relevant to this chapter. In such a scheme the borrower sells his home to an equity release provider in return for a lump sum, with which the borrower discharges his existing mortgage. The provider usually pays a heavily discounted price to reflect the fact that the borrower has a legal right to remain in their home for the rest of their life.

Particular problems arise where the former borrower has parted with 100 per cent of their home: it is usually a term of the equity release scheme that the former borrower remains responsible for repairs. If the borrower is on a low income, they may well not have the means to do this, in which case the provider may be able to terminate the borrower's life tenancy on the grounds that they have breached the agreement.

It follows that these schemes should be viewed as a last resort and the borrower would be better advised to solve arrears problems by means of one of the solutions set out in **Chapter 19**.

21.5   SALE BY THE LENDER

21.5.1   Duty to realise market value

A lender exercising its power of sale must exercise reasonable care to sell only at the proper market value. As Lord Moulton said in *McHugh* v. *Union Bank of Canada* [1913] AC 299 at 311:

> It is well settled law that it is the duty of a mortgagee when realising the mortgage property by sale to behave in conducting such realisation as a reasonable man would behave in the realisation of his own property, so that the mortgagor may receive credit for the fair value of the property sold.

More recently, it was held that where a lender exercises a power of sale it owes a duty to the borrower 'to take reasonable precautions to obtain the true market value of the mortgaged property at the date on which he decides to sell it': *Cuckmere Brick Co. Ltd* v. *Mutual Finance Ltd* [1971] Ch 949, per Salmon LJ.

Whilst some of the textbooks refer to the 'proper price' and others to the 'best price', Salmon LJ had difficulty in seeing any real different between them. He felt that 'proper price' was a little nebulous and 'the best price' may suggest an exceptionally high price. This is why he preferred to call it 'the true market value'.

In *Downsview Nominees Ltd* v. *First City Corporation Ltd* [1993] AC 295, Lord Templeman stated that 'if a mortgagee exercises power of sale in good faith and for the purpose of protecting his security, he is not liable to the mortgagor, even though he might have obtained a higher price'.

If a lender breaches its duty to take reasonable care to obtain the best price reasonably obtainable at the time, the borrower may bring an action seeking damages. However, the Court of Appeal in *Michael* v. *Miller* [2004] EWCA Civ 282 held that a mortgage lender will not breach its duty so long as the price obtained is within an acceptable bracket of market value estimates, even where the lender had agreed to a last-minute reduction in the purchase price.

In *Mortgage Express* v. *Mardner* [2004] EWCA Civ 1859 a lender in possession sold to an associated company. It was held that the connection between the mortgage lender and the purchaser put the lender under an evidential burden to show that it had taken all reasonable steps to comply with its duty to obtain the best price reasonably obtainable for the property. The lender's claim was limited by the court to the difference between the price which would have been obtained, on the balance of probability, had it discharged its duty, and the amount outstanding on the mortgage.

A similar decision was made in *Bradford & Bingley* v. *Ross* [2005] EWCA Civ 394.

21.6 NEGATIVE EQUITY

21.6.1 Definition

Borrowers are said to be with or in 'negative equity' where the amount of their mortgage exceeds the value of their home. It means that if the property is sold, the proceeds of sale would not discharge the mortgage, and there would be a shortfall owing to the lender.

The immediate problem for a borrower in negative equity is that they are unable to sell their property without the lender's permission.

21.6.2 Possible solutions

Several solutions are possible:

- obtain the lender's consent to a sale and reach agreement with the lender about paying any shortfall by instalments over time, after the sale;
- borrow money to discharge the balance by raising an unsecured loan (often at a higher interest rate) or a loan secured on another property, but only if the borrower can afford payments on both loans;
- discuss alternative options with the lender, for example obtaining consent to a sale and payment of a reduced, lump sum to settle the shortfall;

- if the first charge would be cleared, but the negative equity extends to a second, third or later charge, the first charge lender may be willing to carry out an assisted voluntary sale to overreach the later charges (see **21.2**).
- force a sale by obtaining a court order, see below.

21.6.3   Borrower applying for an order for sale

If the lender refuses to consent to a sale where there is negative equity, the borrower may apply to the court for an order for sale under LPA 1925, s.91(2) (see **Appendix A5**). This provision allows the court to direct a sale of the mortgage property 'on such terms as it thinks fit' even if the lender opposes the sale, for example because a shortfall would result. If a sale is ordered, the shortfall will still be repayable as an unsecured debt (see **21.6.4**).

Jurisdiction

The county court has jurisdiction where the amount owing in respect of the mortgage or charge at the commencement of the proceedings does not exceed £30,000 (LPA 1925, s.91(8)).

Therefore, the majority of applications are likely to be in the Chancery Division of the High Court.

Extent of the court's discretion

The leading case on the court's discretion is *Palk* v. *Mortgage Services Funding plc* [1993] Ch 330, CA. In that case the claimants, a husband and wife, were unable to pay the instalments under a mortgage of their house to a finance company, and negotiated the sale of the house for £283,000. However, the amount needed to redeem the mortgage was £358,587. The finance company refused to consent to the sale and obtained a suspended order for possession with a view to letting out the house and postponing the sale to achieve a better price in the future.

The borrowers applied for an order for sale under LPA 1925, s.91(2), since the sum due under the mortgage was increasing by about £43,000 a year (due to interest), but the lettings proposed by the finance company were unlikely to yield more than about £13,000 or £14,000 per year.

Despite the objection of the lender, the Court of Appeal allowed the sale to go ahead. Sir Donald Nicholls V-C held (at 340):

> Section 91(2) gives the court a discretion in wide terms. The discretion is unfettered. It can be exercised at any time. Self-evidently, in exercising that power the court will have due regard to the interests of all concerned. The court will act judicially. It cannot be right that the court should decline to exercise the power if the consequence will be manifest unfairness.

It was 'just and equitable' to order a sale notwithstanding that the sale price would be insufficient to redeem the mortgage 'because otherwise unfairness and injustice will follow'. The court summarised four factors which combined to produce this result:

- there was a substantial income shortfall, i.e. the rental under the proposed letting would fall significantly short of the interest that would be saved if the house was sold;
- the only prospect of recoupment of the shortfall lay in the hope that there would be a substantial rise in house prices generally. This was not a case where the sale was being postponed for a reason specific to that property, for example pending the outcome of an application for planning permission of development;
- the likelihood of the borrower suffering increased loss if the lender's plan proceeded was so high as to make the plan 'oppressive' to the borrower, whose liability was open-ended and would increase indefinitely. The risk of increased loss to the borrower was 'unacceptably disproportionate' to the prospect of any gain the lender may make from letting the house; and
- directing a sale would not preclude the lender from buying the property from the borrower, if it wished to have the opportunity to wait and see what happened to house prices.

In the subsequent case of *Barrett* v. *Halifax Building Society* (1996) 28 HLR 634 Evans-Lombe J in the Chancery Division of the High Court applied s.91(2) in a case where the building society lender had obtained an order for possession with a view to sale, rather than to letting. It was another case where the borrowers had negative equity and had negotiated a sale of the property for £252,000, where the amount required to redeem the mortgage, including the arrears, was £324,082. The court held that the discretion of the court as to whether to direct an order for sale of the mortgaged property will almost always be refused where the lender can demonstrate some tangible benefit of which he will be deprived if a sale is ordered. However, there was no discernible advantage to the lender in refusing to allow the sale, whereas there was an obvious advantage to the borrowers in being able to complete the proposed sale at a market price whilst occupied, where potential purchasers would not know that it was subject to a forced sale due to negative equity.

The judge also held that the borrowers should be entitled to deduct their reasonable costs and expenses arising from the sale from the gross proceeds of sale, before accounting to the lender for the balance.

Interaction of LPA 1925, s.91 with AJA 1970, s.36

In the case of *Cheltenham & Gloucester Building Society* v. *Krausz* (1996) 29 HLR 597, CA, the Court of Appeal considered the extent of the county court's jurisdiction to suspend a warrant for possession, pending an application for an order for sale under LPA 1925, s.91(2). Because of the value of the amount owing on the mortgage, the application had to be made to the High Court. The Court of Appeal accepted that the county court had power to suspend possession if the borrower intended to sell the mortgaged property and the county court was satisfied that the proceeds of sale would be sufficient to discharge the entirety of the mortgage debt. However, it held that s.36 does not empower the county court to suspend possession in order to permit the borrower to sell the mortgaged premises where the proceeds of sale will not suffice to discharge the mortgage debt, unless other funds will be available to the borrower to make up the shortfall. Giving the judgment of the court Phillips LJ stated (at 605):

> A mortgagor seeking relief in the circumstances of *Palk* is thus unable to invoke any statutory power to suspend the mortgagee's right to enter into possession.

As to whether the county court had an inherent power to suspend a possession order or warrant for possession Phillips LJ went on to say:

> Even if one assumed that the Chancery Court has power to order sale of mortgaged property on terms that displace the mortgagee's right to possession, I do not consider that it follows from this that the County Court, as part of its inherent jurisdiction can properly suspend an order or warrant for possession in order to enable a mortgagor to apply to the High Court for an Order under section 91.

However, he appeared to leave open the question whether the High Court was empowered to give such relief before the possession warrant takes effect.

Social considerations

The Chancery Division of the High Court considered the court's discretion under LPA 1925, s.91(2) again in the case of *Polonski* v. *Lloyds Bank Mortgages Ltd* (1999) 31 HLR 721. In this case the borrower had purchased a property in Mitcham, South London, described as a 'run-down area' with a history of problem families, drug dealers and violence nearby. The borrower negotiated a sale of the house to a housing association for £66,800. She wished to move to Salisbury to improve her employment prospects and better schooling for her small children. The bank refused to consent to the sale, because it would result in a shortfall of £12,000 due to the borrower being in negative equity. The borrower applied to the court for an order directing sale of the house pursuant to LPA 1925, s.91(2).

Applying the decision in *Palk*, Jacob J quoted Sir Michael Kerr in that case who said at 342:

> Are there any limits to the proper exercise of the court's discretion? The requirement of fairness to both sides goes without saying. But equality in giving effect to their wishes is manifestly impossible, since the plaintiffs request a sale and the company opposes it. The court must decide between them on the basis of what is just in all the circumstances. This will mean giving preference to the commercial interests of one over the other …

Jacobs J concluded (at 724) that the court's discretion was not limited to purely financial matters but:

> I think the court can take into account social matters and can look at all the reasons given by the mortgagor for wanting a sale.

He held that the borrower had shown perfectly good reasons why she would want to move; she had behaved 'thoroughly responsibly financially over the years as far as she can' and he could not see 'that it can be just in effect to require her to stay where she is'. He therefore made an order for sale under s.91(2).

Need for exceptional circumstances

The above cases all arose out of the economic recession in the mid-1990s. The various cases were revisited more recently in *Toor* v. *State Bank of India* [2010] EWHC 1097 in the Chancery Division District Registry (Birmingham). In that case the bank obtained a possession order against the borrowers, who then applied for an order under LPA 1925, s.91(2) compelling the bank to sell the property at a specified price to family friends.

The court refused to grant the application. It held that *prima facie* it was the right of a mortgage lender to determine how and when to exercise its security. While the courts had an unfettered discretion to interfere with that exercise as a result of the decision in *Palk* 'exceptional circumstances' would be required before a court could compel a lender to sell a property at a time when it did not wish to do so because of a shortfall in the sale value. The court could do so if there would otherwise be unfair prejudice or other unfairness to the borrower (as a result of *Polonski*), but it was for the borrower to make an application and to demonstrate, by evidence, that the requisite degree of prejudice or unfairness would result.

In the present case, it appeared that the principal motivation of the borrowers in forcing a sale to friends was not to achieve any financial benefit for themselves, but simply to avoid eviction and remain in occupation by arrangement with the proposed purchasers.

21.6.4   Residual debt owed to the lender

Whether the sale of a property in negative equity takes place with the consent of the lender, by order of the court under LPA 1925, s.91(2) or by a sale by the mortgagee under LPA 1925, s.101, there will be a shortfall owed by the borrower to the lender.

The sums involved may be considerable and the lender is likely to demand the borrower's urgent proposals for repayment of the debt.

Action to recover the shortfall

In the absence of agreement as to the repayment of the shortfall or the waiver of any part of it, the lender may issue proceedings for the shortfall, with statutory interest.

Any judgment obtained against the borrower can be enforced in the usual ways, including a charging order on other property, an attachment of earnings order or bankruptcy.

In *Mortgage Express* v. *Mardner* (see **21.5.1**), the lender's claim for the shortfall was limited by the court to the difference between the price which would have been obtained, on the balance of probability, had it discharged its duty to obtain the best price reasonably obtainable, and the amount outstanding on the mortgage.

Often the borrower will have been required to take out a mortgage indemnity policy to protect the lender from financial loss. In *Woolwich Building Society* v. *Brown* [1996] CLC 625, it was held that such a policy was not a contract of guarantee but an insurance contract. Accordingly the borrower's indebtedness was not discharged by the payment from the insurance company to the lender. The borrower was liable to the lender for the full amount owing and the lender did not have to give credit for any sums received from the insurers. It made no difference that the borrower had paid the premium.

Limitation periods

The time limit for actions to recover monies secured by a mortgage or charge or to recover proceeds of the sale of land is 12 years from the date on which the right to receive the money accrued (Limitation Act 1980, s.20(1)) (see **Appendix A6**).

In *West Bromwich Building Society* v. *Wilkinson* [2005] UKHL 44, [2005] 1 WLR 2303, it was held that the right to receive the money was the date on which the outstanding loan became due and payable. In this case the mortgage deed provided that the lender had the right to demand the full sum one month after the borrower first defaulted on a monthly instalment. This was considerably earlier than the date on which the lender relied, namely 12 years from the date of sale and as a result the lender's claim was statute-barred.

Any action to recover arrears of interest payable in respect of any sum of monies secured by a mortgage or other charge or payable in respect of proceeds of the sale of land, or to recover damages in respect of such arrears must be brought within six years from the date on which the interest became due (Limitation Act 1980, s.20(5)).

If the lender brings proceedings after the expiry of the relevant limitation period, the borrower will have an absolute defence to the claim.

Acknowledging the debt

A debtor's acknowledgement of his debt or other liquidated pecuniary claim, or part payment towards it, starts time running afresh under the Limitation Act 1980 (s.29(5)). To be effective for the purposes of s.29, an acknowledgement must be in writing and signed by the person making it (s.30(1)).

Mortgage lenders often rely on the decision in *Dungate* v. *Dungate* [1965] 3 All ER 818 to show that an acknowledgement of a debt by a borrower starts time running again under the Limitation Act 1980.

In the *Dungate* case, the Court of Appeal held that a claim on a debt was not statute-barred under the provisions of the previous Limitation Act 1939, where the debtor had sent a letter to the creditor in the following terms:

> Keep a check on totals and amounts I owe you and we will have account now and then ... sorry I cannot do you a cheque yet. Terribly short at the moment ...

The leading judgment by Diplock LJ held that the words in a letter amounted to an acknowledgement of the indebtedness to the creditor. The letter identified the creditor and there was no need to identify the amount of the debt. It was sufficient that the letter acknowledged a general indebtedness, provided that the amount of the debt could be ascertained by extraneous evidence. The words in the letter could plainly be construed as a statement: 'I owe you money which I cannot pay you at the moment.'

'Without prejudice' correspondence

The decision of the House of Lords in *Bradford & Bingley plc* v. *Rashid* [2006] UKHL 37, [2006] 1 WLR 2066 concerned a shortfall of some £15,583 arising following the sale of the property by the lender in 1991. The lender issued proceedings in 2003 and the sole defence advanced by the borrower was that of limitation pursuant to s.20(1) of the Limitation Act 1980 (allowing the period of 12 years for an action brought to recover 'any principal sum of monies secured by a mortgage') in respect of the debt, and s.20(5) (allowing six years for an action to recover arrears of interest payable in respect of any monies secured by a mortgage) in respect of the interest claim.

The debt would be statute-barred unless two letters written by an advice centre on the borrower's behalf in 2001 constituted acknowledgement of the debt under s.29(5), so as to start time running again. The first letter from the advice centre to the lender's solicitors enclosed the borrower's financial statement and asserted that 'at present he is not in a position to repay the outstanding balance, owed to you'. The lender's solicitors replied by suggesting that if the borrower were in a position to raise a lump sum payment in full and final settlement, the lender would be willing to consider writing off a substantial amount of the debt. To this the advice centre replied that the borrower 'is willing to pay approximately £500 towards the outstanding amount as a final settlement'.

The Law Lords all agreed that the two letters from the advice centre constituted clear acknowledgements of the debt owed by the borrower, confirming the decision in *Dungate* (above). However, there was some disagreement as to whether the letters were admissible in evidence as acknowledgements if they had been made as part of 'without prejudice' negotiations. As a matter of public policy without prejudice negotiations are not admissible at trial as evidence of their truth, nor in the opinion of Lord Brown could they be admitted as acknowledgements for the purpose of setting time running afresh under the 1980 Act.

In *Rashid*, the letters from the advice centre were not marked 'without prejudice', and treated the debt as an undisputed liability; they dealt only with whether, when and to what extent the borrower could meet that liability. The letters from the advice centre had the effect of acknowledging the debt and starting time running again under the Limitation Act, thus undermining the defence to the lender's action.

Had the letters sought to negotiate and compromise a disputed liability, they may have attracted protection of the without prejudice rule, without having started time running afresh.

Limitation – all monies charges

The application of the Limitation Act 1980 to a lender's right of possession of a dwelling-house occupied by the borrowers under an all monies legal charge was considered by the Court of Appeal in *National Westminster Bank plc* v. *Ashe* [2008] EWCA Civ 55. By s.15 of the 1980 Act there is a 12-year time limit for actions to recover land and by s.17 upon the expiration of that period the title of the lender to the land 'shall be extinguished'. Under the common form of all monies legal charge used in this case, the lending bank acquired an immediate right to possession of the borrowers' house on the execution of the charge which was more than 17 years before possession proceedings were brought. According to the borrowers, the bank's right of action had accrued more than 12 years before the action was brought, was therefore statute-barred and had been extinguished under the 1980 Act.

During the 12 years prior to the action the borrowers did nothing to cause time to run afresh: they neither made any payments to the bank in respect of the mortgage debt nor was there any acknowledgement of title (either of which would have given rise to a fresh right of action under ss.29 and 30 of the 1980 Act). In order for time to run against the bank in relation to its right of action to recover the land, the borrowers had to be in 'adverse possession' of the property within the meaning of Sched.1, Part I, para.8 of the 1980 Act. Giving the judgment of the court, Mummery LJ held that the borrowers' possession of their home was 'adverse possession' as against the bank within para.8; that the bank's cause of action had accrued and time had started to run from the granting of the legal charge. Since more than 12 years had elapsed since the borrowers had made any payment under the charge, the right to recover possession was barred and the legal charge was extinguished by reason of the operation of ss.15 and 17 of the 1980 Act.

21.6.5 Negotiating with the lender

Where on a sale a shortfall arises, it is common practice for lenders to negotiate with borrowers either for payment to be made in instalments or, more commonly, for a lump sum to be paid with a waiver by the lender of the balance.

Generally, the longer the period of time which passes between a sale and the negotiations, the smaller the lump sum required and, by comparison, the greater the sum that lenders are willing to waive in order to achieve finality.

Negotiations with regard to disputed liability should be conducted through 'without prejudice' correspondence and should not admit the debt, which may result in starting time running afresh for the purposes of the Limitation Act 1980 (see **21.6.4**). Any settlement achieved should be clearly expressed to be 'in full and final satisfaction of any outstanding debt, interest and costs'.

When negotiating with the lender about the payment of such shortfall, advisers should bear in mind that most first charge lenders are regulated in their actions by the FSA. In particular, lenders will be subject to the FSA's 'Mortgages and Home Finance: Conduct of Business sourcebook' (MCOB), which forms part of the 'Business Standards' section of the FSA Handbook (see **5.2**). Subsequent charge lenders are regulated in a similar way by the Office of Fair Trading (see **10.1.2**).

The MCOB sets out the requirements which apply to firms with mortgage business customers. MCOB 13.3.1 is explicit in stating that '[a] firm must deal fairly with any customer who (a) is in arrears on a regulated mortgage contract or home purchase plan; (b) has a sale shortfall, or (c) is otherwise in breach of a home purchase plan'. A 'sale shortfall' is defined as 'the outstanding amount due to the home finance provider, under a home finance transaction, following the sale of the property that is its subject'. MCOB 13.5.1 and 13.6.3 to 13.6.5 refer expressly to the steps that a lender must take where a shortfall arises on sale (see **http:// fsahandbook.info/FSA/html/handbook/MCOB**).

County court judgments

Where proceedings are brought by a lender and judgment entered, that county court judgment (CCJ) will be registered on the Register of Judgments, Orders and Fines, where it will remain for a period of six years.

Future lenders are likely to carry out a search of the CCJ register when deciding whether to offer credit. The existence of a registered CCJ is therefore likely to affect a person's creditworthiness and may make it more difficult to obtain a mortgage or loan in the future.

The impact of a registered CCJ can be minimised in the following ways:

- if the CCJ is paid off within a month of the day of judgment, it will be removed from the register;
- if the CCJ is paid after one month of the day of judgment, it will remain on the register, but be recorded as 'satisfied';
- if the judgment is set aside for any reason, the CCJ will be removed from the register; or
- entries on the register are removed automatically, six years from the date of judgment, pursuant to the Register of Judgments, Orders and Fines Regulations 2005, SI 2005/3595, reg.26(a).

21.6.6 Conclusion

When a borrower has lost his home and it has been sold, there are still numerous protections for him of which the adviser should be aware.

CHAPTER 22

Charging orders and bankruptcy

22.1 INTRODUCTION

The inability to pay a mortgage is usually a reflection of the borrower's other financial problems. Where the borrower is unable to meet payments on unsecured debts, whether arising from personal or business loans, there is a risk of a charging order or bankruptcy. This chapter will examine these related instances of home loss.

22.2 CHARGING ORDERS

A creditor of an unsecured debt will often protect his position by obtaining a court judgment against a borrower. The 'judgment creditor' can then apply to court for a charging order, under the Charging Orders Act 1979 and CPR Part 73. The application is a two-stage process involving an interim and a final charging order. At both stages the court has discretion as to whether to grant a charging order. If it does, the order can be registered against the borrower's property under the Charging Orders Act 1979.

If the debtor is the sole owner of the property, then the charge encumbers both the legal and the equitable estate of the property. If, on the other hand, the property is owned by the debtor along with at least one other person, then the charge will only attach to the equitable estate (that is the debtor's 'beneficial interest' in the sale proceeds of the property).

Once a creditor has the benefit of a charging order he may apply to court for an order for sale to realise what he is owed. The procedure can be found in CPR rule 73.10. The court has to balance the creditor's rights against the needs of the debtor and any of his dependants. If the debtor can demonstrate that he can repay the debt over a reasonable time or if he can make out a case of serious hardship, the court may refuse to order a sale.

If the property is owned by more than one person, the application for sale is made under the Trusts of Lands and Appointment of Trustees Act (TLATA) 1996, s.14. The fact that a property is jointly owned does not prevent an order for sale, but the court will take the co-owner's interests into account and will decide whether they override the creditor's entitlement to his money, see **22.4**.

22.3   BANKRUPTCY PETITIONS

A petition for a bankruptcy order to be made against an individual is usually presented to the court by one of the individual's creditors or by the individual himself. The application is made under the Insolvency Act (IA) 1986. The grounds for the petition will be that the debtor is unable to pay his debts, which in the case of a creditor's petition must exceed £750. If the court makes a bankruptcy order, the official receiver investigates the debtor's affairs and then either appoints a trustee in bankruptcy or carries out that function himself.

The function of the trustee in bankruptcy is to get in, realise and distribute the bankrupt's estate in accordance with IA 1986. Trustees in bankruptcy are often insolvency practitioners, who are authorised individuals who specialise in insolvency work.

22.3.1   The bankrupt's home

The bankrupt's interest in his home will form part of the estate which vests in the trustee. This applies whether the home is freehold or leasehold and whether it is owned solely by the bankrupt, or jointly with someone else, typically their spouse or civil partner.

If the bankrupt is the sole owner of the property, the legal title will usually be transferred to the trustee as well as the beneficial interest. If the home is jointly owned, the legal title remains with the bankrupt and the co-owner, but the trustee may still take action in relation to the property, such as applying for an order for possession or an order for sale to realise the beneficial interest of the bankrupt, to raise money to pay creditors. While such an application will be made under TLATA 1996, s.14 (see **22.4**), the matters for the court to take into account are those set out in IA 1986, s.335A, rather than TLATA 1996, s.15 (see s.15(4)).

Section 335A(2) provides that on such an application the court must have regard to:

- the interests of the bankrupt's creditors
- where the application is made in respect of a dwelling-house which is or has been the home of the bankrupt or the bankrupt's current or former spouse or civil partner: (i) the conduct of that spouse or partner so far as contributing to the bankruptcy, (ii) the needs and financial resources of that spouse or partner, and (iii) the needs of any children; and
- all the circumstances of the case other than the needs of the bankrupt.

Where the trustee makes an application to sell the bankrupt's interest in the family home, the court will generally only refuse an order to sell in exceptional circumstances (see IA 1986, s.335A(3)) or if the value of the bankrupt's interest in the property is worth less than £1,000.

However, with effect from 1 January 2011, where a bankrupt is living with his spouse or children in the family home, the trustee will no longer dispose of the bankrupt's interest in the family home until two years and three months after the bankruptcy order is made – except if an offer is received which is in the creditors' interests to accept. At that point a review is carried out which may result in:

- re-vesting the property interest in the bankrupt where it is valued at less than £1,000;
- offering the interest for sale to the bankrupt or a third party;
- the official receiver applying for a charging order; or
- the appointment of an insolvency practitioner trustee by the Secretary of State.

22.3.2   Position of the mortgage lender

Since the debt to the lender is secured on the property by way of a mortgage, the lender is relatively unaffected by the bankruptcy and the borrower remains liable for payment of the mortgage debt. If the bankrupt falls behind with his mortgage payments, the lender may seek to repossess the property and sell it in the normal way. Therefore, it may be in the borrower's interests to contact the lender at an early stage about his bankruptcy, with a view to making arrangements with regard to the monthly mortgage payments.

22.3.3   Effect of bankruptcy on court proceedings

At any time when proceedings on a bankruptcy petition are pending or an individual has been adjudged bankrupt, the court may stay any action, execution or other legal process against the property or against the debtor (IA 1986, s.285(1)).

After the making of a bankruptcy order no creditor has any remedy against the property or against the bankrupt himself in respect of a debt provable in bankruptcy, nor may the creditor commence any action or legal proceedings against the bankrupt except with the leave of the court and on such terms as the court may impose (IA 1986, s.285(3)). However, the restriction on proceedings and remedies does not affect the right of the secured creditor of the bankrupt to enforce his security (IA 1986, s.285(4)). Therefore, a lender may still bring possession proceedings or seek an order for sale in respect of the mortgaged property.

If one of two borrowers is made bankrupt (and, typically, it will be the husband) the other (again, typically, his wife) may still conduct proceedings in relation to the property and to the mortgage. So, for example, it was Mrs Palk who successfully appealed the decision to dismiss the joint application with her husband (before he was made bankrupt) for an order for sale under LPA 1925, s.91(2): *Palk* v. *Mortgage Services Funding plc* [1993] Ch 330 (see **21.6.3**).

Alternatively, proceedings may be brought in by the trustee in bankruptcy of the bankrupt husband, as happened in *National Westminster Bank plc* v. *Ashe* [2008] EWCA Civ 55 (see **21.6.4**).

22.4 POSITION OF CO-OWNERS

Until TLATA 1996 came into force on 1 January 1997, property owned by more than one person was normally held upon trust for sale and LPA 1925, s.30 applied. The presumption was that, unless there was an exceptional reason, the lender's right to recover money owed would prevail over the rights of a non-indebted co-owner; see, for example, *Re Citro* [1991] Ch 142 or *Lloyds Bank plc* v. *Byrne and Byrne* [1993] 1 FLR 369.

Section 1 of TLATA 1996 replaced the trust for sale with the simpler 'trust of land'. By TLATA 1996, s.14, where property is jointly owned, any person who is a trustee of the property or who has an interest in it can apply for an order declaring the nature or extent of a person's interest in property or for an order for sale. When considering an application under s.14 the court is to have regard to various matters set out in s.15 of the Act (except where the application is made by a borrower's trustee in bankruptcy, in which case the matters set out in IA 1986, s.335A(2) apply instead (TLATA 1996, s.15(4)) (see **22.3.1**)).

However, TLATA 1996, s.15 lists the interests of a secured creditor as only one of the matters, to which a court must have regard when deciding an application for an order for sale. Other matters include 'the intentions of the person who created the trust' (s.15(1)(a)) and 'the welfare of any minor who occupies or might reasonably be expected to occupy any land subject to the trust as his home' (s.15(1)(c)).

It was held in *Mortgage Corporation* v. *Shaire* [2000] EWHC Ch 452, [2001] 4 All ER 364 that a court now had greater flexibility when exercising its jurisdiction and this would operate for the benefit of families and to the detriment of banks and other chargees.

In *First National Bank plc* v. *Achampong* [2003] EWCA Civ 487, [2004] 1 FCR 18 the Court of Appeal set aside a legal charge signed by husband and wife, because the lender was put on inquiry of the husband's undue influence over his wife. However, the court went on to hold that the lender had an equitable charge over the husband's beneficial interest in the property by virtue of LPA 1925, s.63, which severed any beneficial joint tenancy. The lender was also entitled to an order for sale to realise the equitable charge over the husband's share of the property, pursuant to TLATA 1996, ss.14 and 15.

CHAPTER 23

Complaints about mortgage lenders

23.1 INTRODUCTION

Where the borrower is unhappy about his treatment by a lender with regard to any aspect of the handling of the loan, but, in particular, in relation to possession proceedings, the borrower may make a formal complaint. Initially this will be to the lender itself but, if that fails to resolve the matter satisfactorily, recourse may then be had to the independent Financial Ombudsman Service (FOS).

23.2 COMPLAINTS TO LENDERS – FSA REQUIREMENTS

The FSA Handbook (which contains the MCOB business standards referred to in Chapter 5) also contains detailed provisions for redress and dispute resolution. The full handbook can be accessed online at **http://fsahandbook.info/FSA/html/ handbook**.

The FSA Handbook is divided into several 'blocks', one of which is 'redress'. This in turn contains a chapter headed 'Dispute Resolution: Complaints' (or 'DISP' for short) which contains detailed requirements about how firms should handle complaints and the arrangements made by the FOS to deal with further complaints against firms at a higher level.

23.2.1 Information about internal complaints procedures

DISP 1.2 requires firms to publish appropriate information regarding their internal procedures for the reasonable and prompt handling of complaints. Such information should be provided in writing and free of charge to eligible complainants on request and when acknowledging a complaint.

Many lenders publish details of their complaints procedures on their websites or they will have provided written details with the mortgage documentation. If a borrower is considering a complaint, a request for the detailed procedure may be made either before or at the time that the complaint is made.

23.2.2 Mandatory rules

DISP 1.3 requires complaints to be handled reasonably and promptly. DISP 1.4 sets out mandatory rules as to how firms must resolve complaints. In particular, a firm must:

- investigate the complaint competently, diligently and impartially;
- assess the subject matter of the complaint and any remedial action fairly, consistently and promptly;
- offer redress or remedial action where a firm decides this is appropriate;
- explain to the complainant promptly, and in a way that is fair, clear and not misleading, its assessment of the complaint, its decision on it and any offer of remedial action or redress; and
- comply promptly with any offer of remedial action or redress accepted by the complainant.

A firm must send a final or other response to the complainant within eight weeks (DISP 1.6.2), after which a complainant may refer the matter to the FOS.

23.3 FINANCIAL OMBUDSMAN SERVICE

The FOS is a body of independent experts set up by Parliament to resolve individual complaints that consumers and financial businesses have not been able to resolve themselves. The Ombudsman Scheme was set up by Part XVI of the Financial Services and Markets Act (FSMA) 2000. Section 225 of the Act provides for a scheme 'under which certain disputes may resolve quickly and with minimum formality by an independent person'.

23.3.1 Compulsory jurisdiction of the FOS

The jurisdiction of the FOS is compulsory. That is to say that if the appropriate conditions in FSMA 2000, s.226 apply, complaints must be handled in the manner specified in the 'Dispute resolution: complaints' chapter of the FSA Handbook (see **23.2**).

The compulsory jurisdiction rules only apply to activities which are 'regulated activities' (FSMA 2000, s.226(4)). The activities of mortgage lenders will fall within the 'compulsory jurisdiction' of the FOS as these are regulated activities in accordance with FSMA 2000, s.22 and Sched.2, para.23. However, this is only the case in respect of mortgages which came into effect on or after 31 October 2004, which is the date from which the FSA first regulated mortgage loans under FSMA 2000.

By FSMA 2000, s.226A, the FOS has a similar compulsory jurisdiction to deal with complaints against lenders, which arise in relation to transactions under CCA 1974 – the so-called 'consumer credit jurisdiction'.

23.3.2   Determination of complaints

Where the FOS determines a complaint under the compulsory jurisdiction or under the consumer credit jurisdiction it must be determined 'by reference to what is in the opinion of the ombudsman, fair and reasonable in all the circumstances of the case'. The complainant will receive a written statement of the determination giving the ombudsman's reasons.

If the complainant notifies the ombudsman that he accepts the determination, it is binding on the respondent (i.e. on the lender) and the complainant (the borrower) and is final (FSMA 2000, s.228(5)).

23.3.3   Awards of compensation

Any determination by the ombudsman under the compulsory jurisdiction and the consumer credit jurisdiction may include an award against the respondent (i.e. against the lender) of such amount as the ombudsman considers fair compensation for loss or damage, or a direction that the lender take such steps in relation to the complainant as the ombudsman considers just and appropriate (whether or not a court could order those steps to be taken).

Any such direction is enforceable by injunction (FSMA 2000, s.229(9)(a)). The ombudsman also has power to award costs (FSMA 2000, s.230).

23.3.4   Detailed rules

The procedures of the FOS for investigating and determining complaints, the basis on which the ombudsman makes decisions and the awards which the ombudsman can make are found in DISP 3.1.

As will be seen above, the ombudsman will not consider a complaint until a lender has already had eight weeks to consider the complaint or has issued a final response.

23.3.5   Time limits for complaints

Certain time limits apply for borrowers to refer complaints to the ombudsman (DISP 2.8). Generally these time limits are:

- six months from the lender sending the borrower a final response (which has to mention the six-month time limit for making further complaint to the FOS); and
- six years from the event the borrower is complaining about (or – if later – three years from when the borrower knew, or could reasonably have known, he had cause to complain).

23.3.6   Complaints out of time

If a complaint falls outside these time limits the lender can choose to object to the ombudsman looking at the complaint, on the grounds that it is 'time-barred'. However, the FOS has discretion to look at complaints that fall outside these time limits in 'exceptional circumstances' (DISP 2.8.2). One example might be if the borrower was incapacitated through illness during the period when they could have complained.

The FOS can also look at a complaint that falls outside these time limits where the lender does not object.

23.3.7   Making a complaint

The FOS website (**www.financial-ombudsman.org.uk**) provides guidance to consumers and advisers about how to make complaints. In addition, there is a downloadable complaint form which can be printed off and posted to the FOS. The complaint form needs to be signed by the complainant and it should be returned to the FOS with any relevant paperwork. If the borrower needs any assistance with filling out the complaint form, there is a consumer helpline for this purpose on 0300 123 9 123 or 0800 023 4567 (Monday to Friday 8 am to 6 pm).

Upon receipt, the ombudsman will attempt to resolve the complaint at the earliest possible stage and by whatever means appear to him to be most appropriate, including mediation or investigation (DISP 3.5.1).

If necessary, the ombudsman will invite the parties to take part in a hearing if he considers that the complaint cannot be fairly determined without one. The ombudsman has powers to give directions in relation to the issues and evidence which the ombudsman may accept, and fix and extend time limits for any aspect of the consideration of the complaint.

23.3.8   Determination

As indicated above, the ombudsman's determination will be given in a written statement and, if accepted by the complainant, will be final and binding on both parties. It may include an award of compensation and/or costs. Any direction made by the ombudsman can be enforced by way of injunction.

23.4   MORTGAGE PRE-ACTION PROTOCOL

By para.8.1 of the Mortgage Pre-Action Protocol, a lender should consider whether to postpone the start of a possession claim where the borrower has made a genuine complaint to the FOS about the potential possession claim (see **7.5** and **Appendix C5**).

However, where a lender does not intend to await the decision of the FOS, it should give notice to the borrower with reasons that it intends to start a possession claim at least five business days before doing so (Protocol, para.8.2).

23.5 THE COURT'S GENERAL POWERS OF MANAGEMENT

By CPR rule 3.1(2)(f) the court has power in an appropriate case to stay the whole or part of any proceedings either generally or until a specified date or event.

Where a borrower has made a genuine complaint to the lender and/or to the FOS the outcome may have a bearing on possession proceedings, the court may be invited on application to stay the proceedings until such time as the complaint has been resolved.

CHAPTER 24

Tenants of borrowers

24.1 INTRODUCTION

Where a lender takes possession of residential property, any tenants of the borrower residing in the property may be at risk of losing their home. The position of the tenants and the approach of the lender may depend whether the mortgage was granted in respect of:

- a buy-to-let mortgage; or
- a residential owner-occupier mortgage.

24.2 BUY-TO-LET MORTGAGES

Unlike an owner-occupier, the buy-to-let borrower does not typically live in the property which is secured by the mortgage. The buy-to-let loan is a commercial arrangement by which, the borrower hopes, he will make a profit from the capital appreciation and/or rental stream of the property. Where the lender retakes possession of a buy-to-let property, the borrower will not lose their home.

However, by its very nature, it is highly likely that the borrower has let the property to one or more short-term tenants.

24.2.1 Implied consent to sub-letting

Most buy-to-let loans imply that the lender consents to the tenancy created, so long as it complies with the lender's terms and conditions. Most usually, these require that any tenancy granted is an assured shorthold tenancy, being the default tenancy under the Housing Act (HA) 1988, as amended. So long as that is the case, the tenancy will be binding on the lender, if the lender obtains a possession order against the borrower.

24.2.2 Lender retaking possession

Where the lender retakes possession of the property, it will effectively stand in the shoes of the borrower, as landlord of the tenants. The lender will then decide whether to allow the tenants to remain in possession, thereby benefiting from the rental stream which is part of the value of the property, or whether to serve notice to end the tenancy, either at the end of a fixed term or after two months if it is a periodic tenancy, with a view to bringing possession proceedings.

In these circumstances, the lender will not acquire any better rights than the borrower would have had as against the tenants.

24.2.3   Request for mortgage agreement

If the lender acts in a way which appears to be inconsistent with the above, the adviser should request information from the lender and/or the court as to the type of mortgage, and requesting a copy of the mortgage agreement itself. If this information is not forthcoming, then the court should be asked for a stay of proceedings and/or an adjournment until the agreement is produced, as the tenant's rights will be dependent on whether or not their tenancy is binding on the lender.

24.3   OWNER-OCCUPIER MORTGAGES

Where the borrower has taken out a mortgage for the purpose of buying his home, in which he lives, the basic position will be that the lender will not be bound by any tenancy of the property. As a result, the lender will be able to enforce the possession order obtained against the borrower against anyone in occupation.

24.3.1   Exceptions

There are exceptions, for example:

- where the tenancy was granted before the mortgage. This is unlikely for the original mortgage, but it may apply for a remortgage or if the proceedings are brought in respect of a second charge;
- the lender has specifically agreed to the creation of the tenancy at some point, although the adviser will have difficulty obtaining evidence of this fact; or
- the lender has recognised the tenancy in some way, indicating an intention to be bound by it. An example might be sending a demand for rent directly to the tenant.

Unless one of the exceptions apply, the tenancy will not be binding on the lender and it is highly likely that it will have been granted without the lender's permission.

24.4   PROTECTIONS FOR UNAUTHORISED TENANTS

The Mortgage Repossessions (Protection of Tenants etc) Act (MR(PT)A) 2010 came into force on 1 October 2010 (see **Appendix A8**). The purpose of the Act is to protect persons whose tenancies are not binding on lenders and it does so by requiring lenders to give notice of possession proceedings and of the proposed execution of possession orders to tenants.

The persons who benefit from MR(PT)A 2010 are tenants under an 'unauthorised tenancy'. This is defined in s.1(8) as an agreement which is or gives rise to:

- an assured tenancy within the meaning of HA 1988 – and this will include an assured shorthold tenancy; or
- a protected or statutory tenancy within the meaning of the Rent Act 1977,

and, in either case, where the lender's interest in the property is not subject to the tenancy.

24.4.1   Tenancies not covered by MR(PT)A 2010

Advisers should note that bare contractual tenancies are not included within the definition. A bare contractual tenancy might arise if one of the exemptions in HA 1988, Sched.1 applies to prevent the tenancy from being an assured tenancy. These include:

- a tenancy under which the dwelling-house consists of or comprises licensed premises (Sched.1, para.5),
- holiday lettings (Sched.1, para.9); and
- resident landlords (Sched.1, para.10).

This latter exemption is probably the one which will arise most commonly in practice. A tenancy of part of a building which is not a purpose-built block of flats (for example a converted house) where the landlord occupies as his only or principal home another part of the building (for example a basement flat) would be excluded under HA 1988, Sched.1, para.10.

24.4.2   Outline of the court's powers under MR(PT)A 2010

Section 1 of MR(PT)A 2010 gives the court power to postpone the giving of possession at two stages of the lender's original possession action against the borrower:

- before the making the possession order itself; and
- after the making of a possession order, but before execution of any warrant for possession.

MR(PT)A 2010 and regulations made under it also provide for notice to be given of intended execution of a possession order.

24.4.3   Power of court to postpone giving of possession

The lender should already have given notice to 'the tenant or the occupier' giving details of the possession claim against the borrower within five days of the lender receiving notification of the date of the hearing by the court (CPR rule 55.10). Copies of those notices, and evidence that the notices were sent, must be produced by the lender at the mortgage possession hearing (CPR rule 55.10(4)).

Assuming that tenants of the borrower have received such notices, they will be in a position to make an application under the MR(PT)A 2010, s.1(2), which provides:

> When making an order for delivery of possession of the property, the court may, on the application of the tenant, postpone the date for delivery of possession for a period not exceeding two months.

Alternatively, the tenants are entitled to make application at the stage when the lender seeks to enforce a possession order that it has obtained, by issue of a warrant for possession.

24.4.4 Power of court to postpone giving of possession

By MR(PT)A 2010, s.1(4) the court may, on the application of the tenant, stay or suspend execution of the order for a period not exceeding two months if:

- the court did not exercise its powers under s.1(2) when making the possession order or, if it did, the applicant was not the tenant when it exercised those powers;
- the applicant has asked the lender to give an undertaking in writing not to enforce the order for two months, beginning with the date the undertaking is given, and
- the mortgagee has not given such an undertaking.

Need to request an undertaking from the lender

From the point of view of the adviser, it is important to ensure that a written application is sent to the lender seeking such an undertaking and that evidence of that request, with confirmation that an undertaking has not been given, should be produced at the hearing of the application.

24.4.5 Exercise of the court's discretion

When considering whether to exercise its powers under s.1 (whether to postpone the date for delivery of possession or to stay or suspend execution of the possession order), the court must have regard to:

- the circumstances of the tenant; and
- if there is any outstanding breach by the tenant of a term of the unauthorised tenancy, then the nature of that breach and whether the tenant might reasonably be expected to have avoided breaching that term or to have remedied the breach.

Tenant's circumstances

The circumstances of the tenant will include the fact that they will be made homeless by the execution of a possession order against the borrower, and may emphasise the difficulty in obtaining alternative accommodation and the costs that will be involved.

The tenant would usually seek to maximise the time available to find somewhere else to live.

Breach of term of the tenancy

The most usual breach of a term of the unauthorised tenancy will be with regard to the payment of rent. It is possible that the tenant has withheld rent until the situation with regard to the lender's possession claim has been resolved.

In one reported county court decision, *GMAC RFC Ltd* v. *Jones* (unreported, Lambeth County Court, 15 November 2010; *Legal Action*, January 2011, p.36) the district judge held that, except for the recent setting aside of his rent, the tenant was not in default of his tenancy obligations. However, as he was at risk of losing his home, it was reasonable for him not to have remedied his breach by failing to pay rent. The tenant might have a claim against his landlord, presumably for breach of the covenant of quiet enjoyment.

24.4.6 Conditions that the court may impose

The court may make any postponement, stay or suspension under s.1 conditional on the making of payments to the lender in respect of the occupation of the property (or part of the property) during the period of postponement, stay or suspension.

Thus, the court may require the tenant to pay his rent in future to the lender rather than to the borrower.

24.4.7 Notice of execution of a possession order

Section 2 of MR(PT)A 2010 applies to any situation where a lender has obtained an order for possession of the mortgage property. It is not limited to situations where there may be a tenant of an unauthorised tenancy.

By MR(PT)A 2010, s.2(2) the possession order may only be executed:

- if the mortgagee gives notice at the property 'of any prescribed step' taken for the purpose of executing the order; and
- after the end of 'a prescribed period' beginning with the day on which such notice is given.

Regulations have been made with regard to the prescribed steps and prescribed period. The Dwelling Houses (Execution of Possession Orders by Mortgagees)

Regulations 2010, SI 2010/1809, which came into force with MR(PT)A 2010 on 1 October 2010, provide that:

- the 'prescribed step' is the mortgagee making an application to the court for a warrant for possession of the property; and
- the 'prescribed period' is 14 days.

Together, these provisions mean that the lender must give at least 14 days' notice of its application to the court for a warrant for possession of the property. The regulations are reproduced in **Appendix A9**.

Notice in prescribed form

Notice of execution of the possession order must be in a prescribed form, set out in the Schedule to the regulations. In addition, the notice must be given in any of the following ways:

- by sending the notice to the property by first class post or registered post in an envelope addressed to the tenant by name or, if that is not known, to 'the tenant or occupier';
- by leaving the notice at the property in an envelope addressed as above, or affixed to and displayed in a prominent place where its contents can be read by a person entering the property; or
- by personal service upon a person who appears to be in residence at the property.

The prescribed form of notice in the schedule to the regulations is directed to those people who are paying rent to live in the property. It advises such persons that they could be evicted from their home and that the law gives certain tenants the right to apply to the lender to ask it not to enforce the order for a period of two months. Should the lender refuse the request or if the tenants receive no reply, they may be able to make an application to court for a similar delay.

The provision of such notice under MR(PT)A 2010, s.2 will provide unauthorised tenants with an opportunity to make application under s.1(4) to stay or suspend execution of the order for a period not exceeding two months, if the mortgagee has failed to give an undertaking not to do so upon request by the tenant.

24.4.8 Joining the proceedings

In order to make an application under MR(PT)A 2010, the tenant will need to make an application at the same time to join the proceedings as an additional defendant.

If the application is opposed by the lender but is successful, the lender may be ordered to pay the tenant's legal costs of making the application. This was the result in *GMAC RFC Ltd* v. *Jones* (above). However, a potential consequence is that if the application fails, the tenant may be ordered to pay the lender's costs of opposing the application.

24.5   APPOINTMENT OF A RECEIVER

In exceptional circumstances the mortgagee of an owner-occupied residential mortgaged property may appoint a receiver. Where the receiver makes a claim for possession against the borrower, the provisions of MR(PT)A 2010 may not apply.

Advisers should request a copy of the deed of appointment of the receiver, to see whether he is acting as agent for the lender (in which case the protections may still apply) or, more likely, as agent for the borrower (in which case the protections are not likely to apply). The appointment of receivers by the lender is also dealt with at **Chapter 16**.

APPENDIX A

Statutes and statutory instruments

A1   ADMINISTRATION OF JUSTICE ACT 1970

36   Additional powers of court in action by mortgagee for possession of dwelling-house

(1) Where the mortgagee under a mortgage of land which consists of or includes a dwelling-house brings an action in which he claims possession of the mortgaged property, not being an action for foreclosure in which a claim for possession of the mortgaged property is also made, the court may exercise any of the powers conferred on it by subsection (2) below if it appears to the court that in the event of its exercising the power the mortgagor is likely to be able within a reasonable period to pay any sums due under the mortgage or to remedy a default consisting of a breach of any other obligation arising under or by virtue of the mortgage.

(2) The court –

    (a)   may adjourn the proceedings, or

    (b)   on giving judgment, or making an order, for delivery of possession of the mortgaged property, or at any time before the execution of such judgment or order, may –

        (i)   stay or suspend execution of the judgment or order, or

        (ii) postpone the date for delivery of possession,

    for such period or periods as the court thinks reasonable.

(3) Any such adjournment, stay, suspension or postponement as is referred to in subsection (2) above may be made subject to such conditions with regard to payment by the mortgagor of any sum secured by the mortgage or the remedying of any default as the court thinks fit.

(4) The court may from time to time vary or revoke any condition imposed by virtue of this section.

(5) [*repealed*]

(6) In the application of this section to Northern Ireland, 'the court' means a judge of the High Court in Northern Ireland, and in subsection (1) the words from 'not being' to 'made' shall be omitted.

A2   ADMINISTRATION OF JUSTICE ACT 1973

8   Extension of powers of court in action by mortgagee of dwelling-house

(1) Where by a mortgage of land which consists of or includes a dwelling-house, or by any agreement between the mortgagee under such a mortgage and the mortgagor, the mortgagor is entitled or is to be permitted to pay the principal sum secured by instalments or otherwise to defer payment of it in whole or in part, but provision is also made for earlier payment in the event of any default by the mortgagor or of a demand by

the mortgagee or otherwise, then for purposes of section 36 of the Administration of Justice Act 1970 (under which a court has power to delay giving a mortgagee possession of the mortgaged property so as to allow the mortgagor a reasonable time to pay any sums due under the mortgage) a court may treat as due under the mortgage on account of the principal sum secured and of interest on it only such amounts as the mortgagor would have expected to be required to pay if there had been no such provision for earlier payment.

(2) A court shall not exercise by virtue of subsection (1) above the powers conferred by section 36 of the Administration of Justice Act 1970 unless it appears to the court not only that the mortgagor is likely to be able within a reasonable period to pay any amounts regarded (in accordance with subsection (1) above) as due on account of the principal sum secured, together with the interest on those amounts, but also that he is likely to be able by the end of that period to pay any further amounts that he would have expected to be required to pay by then on account of that sum and of interest on it if there had been no such provision as is referred to in subsection (1) above for earlier payment.

(3) Where subsection (1) above would apply to an action in which a mortgagee only claimed possession of the mortgaged property, and the mortgagee brings an action for foreclosure (with or without also claiming possession of the property), then section 36 of the Administration of Justice Act 1970 together with subsections (1) and (2) above shall apply as they would apply if it were an action in which the mortgagee only claimed possession of the mortgaged property, except that –

    (a) section 36(2)(b) shall apply only in relation to any claim for possession; and
    (b) section 36(5) shall not apply.

(4) For purposes of this section the expressions 'dwelling-house', 'mortgage', 'mortgagee' and 'mortgagor' shall be construed in the same way as for the purposes of Part IV of the Administration of Justice Act 1970.

(5) [*repealed*]

(6) In the application of this section to Northern Ireland, subsection (3) shall be omitted.

A3 CONSUMER CREDIT ACT 1974

16 Exempt agreements

(1) This Act does not regulate a consumer credit agreement where the creditor is a local authority, or a body specified, or of a description specified, in an order made by the Secretary of State, being –

    (a) an insurer,
    (b) a friendly society,
    (c) an organisation of employers or organisation of workers,
    (d) a charity,
    (e) a land improvement company,
    (f) a body corporate named or specifically referred to in any public general Act,
    (ff) a body corporate named or specifically referred to in an order made under –

        section 156(4), 444(1) or 447(2)(a) of the Housing Act 1985,
        section 156(4) of that Act as it has effect by virtue of section 17 of the Housing Act 1996 (the right to acquire),
        section 2 of the Home Purchase Assistance and Housing Corporation Guarantee Act 1978 or section 31 of the Tenants' Rights, &c (Scotland) Act 1980, or Article 154(1)(a) or 156AA of the Housing (Northern Ireland) Order 1981 or Article 10(6A) of the Housing (Northern Ireland) Order 1983; or

(g)   a building society, or

(h)   a deposit-taker.

(2)   Subsection (1) applies only where the agreement is –

    (a)   a debtor-creditor-supplier agreement financing –

       (i)   the purchase of land, or

       (ii)   the provision of dwellings on any land,

    and secured by a land mortgage on that land, or

    (b)   a debtor-creditor agreement secured by any land mortgage; or

    (c)   a debtor-creditor-supplier agreement financing a transaction which is a linked transaction in relation to –

       (i)   an agreement falling within paragraph (a), or

       (ii)   an agreement falling within paragraph (b) financing –

    (aa)   the purchase of any land, or

    (bb)   the provision of dwellings on any land,

and secured by a land mortgage on the land referred to in paragraph (a) or, as the case may be, the land referred to in sub-paragraph (ii).

(3)   Before he makes, varies or revokes an order under subsection (1), the Secretary of State must undertake the necessary consultation.

(3A) The necessary consultation means consultation with the bodies mentioned in the following table in relation to the provision under which the order is to be made, varied or revoked:

TABLE

Provision of subsection (1)	Consultee
Paragraph (a) or (b)	The Financial Services Authority
Paragraph (d)	Charity Commission
Paragraph (e), (f) or (ff)	Any Minister of the Crown with responsibilities in relation to the body in question
Paragraph (g) or (h)	The Treasury and the Financial Services Authority

(4)   An order under subsection (1) relating to a body may be limited so as to apply only to agreements by that body of a description specified in the order.

(5)   The Secretary of State may by order provide that this Act shall not regulate other consumer credit agreements where –

    (a)   the number of payments to be made by the debtor does not exceed the number specified for that purpose in the order, or

    (b)   the rate of the total charge for credit does not exceed the rate so specified, or

    (c)   an agreement has a connection with a country outside the United Kingdom.

(6)   The Secretary of State may by order provide that this Act shall not regulate consumer hire agreements of a description specified in the order where –

    (a)   the owner is a body corporate authorised by or under any enactment to supply electricity, gas or water, and

    (b)   the subject of the agreement is a meter or metering equipment, or where the owner is a provider of a public electronic communications service who is specified in the order.

(6A) This Act does not regulate a consumer credit agreement where the creditor is a housing authority and the agreement is secured by a land mortgage of a dwelling.

(6B) In subsection (6A) 'housing authority' means –

    (a)   as regards England and Wales, the Regulator of Social Housing and an authority or body within section 80(1) of the Housing Act 1985 (the landlord condition for secure tenancies), other than a housing association or a housing trust which is a charity;

    (b)   as regards Scotland, a development corporation established under an order made, or having effect as if made under the New Towns (Scotland) Act 1968, the Scottish Special Housing Association or the Housing Corporation;

    (c)   as regards Northern Ireland, the Northern Ireland Housing Executive.

(6C) This Act does not regulate a consumer credit agreement if –

    (a)   it is secured by a land mortgage and entering into the agreement as lender is a regulated activity for the purposes of the Financial Services and Markets Act 2000; or

    (b)   it is or forms part of a regulated home purchase plan and entering into the agreement as home purchase provider is a regulated activity for the purposes of that Act.

(6D) But section 126, and any other provision so far as it relates to section 126, applies to an agreement which would (but for subsection (6C)(a)) be a regulated agreement.

(6E) Subsection (6C) must be read with –

    (a)   section 22 of the Financial Services and Markets Act 2000 (regulated activities: power to specify classes of activity and categories of investment);

    (b)   any order for the time being in force under that section; and

    (c)   Schedule 2 to that Act.

(7)   [repealed]

(7A) Nothing in this section affects the application of sections 140A to 140C.

(8)   In the application of this section to Scotland, subsection (3A) shall have effect as if the reference to the Charity Commission were a reference to the Lord Advocate.

(9)   In the application of this section to Northern Ireland subsection (3A) shall have effect as if any reference to a Minister of the Crown were a reference to a Northern Ireland department, and any reference to the Charity Commission were a reference to the Department of Finance for Northern Ireland.

(10) In this section –

    (a)   'deposit-taker' means –

        (i)   a person who has permission under Part 4 of the Financial Services and Markets Act 2000 to accept deposits,

        (ii)   an EEA firm of the kind mentioned in paragraph 5(b) of Schedule 3 to that Act which has permission under paragraph 15 of that Schedule (as a result of qualifying for authorisation under paragraph 12 of that Schedule) to accept deposits,

        (iii) any wholly owned subsidiary (within the meaning of the Companies Acts (see section 1159 of the Companies Act 2006)) of a person mentioned in sub-paragraph (i), or

        (iv) any undertaking which, in relation to a person mentioned in sub-paragraph (ii), is a subsidiary undertaking within the meaning of any rule of law in force in the EEA State in question for purposes connected with the implementation of the European Council Seventh Company Law Directive of 13 June 1983 on consolidated accounts (No 83/349/EEC), and which has no members other than that person;

(b) 'insurer' means –

    (i) a person who has permission under Part 4 of the Financial Services and Markets Act 2000 to effect or carry out contracts of insurance, or

    (ii) an EEA firm of the kind mentioned in paragraph 5(d) of Schedule 3 to that Act, which has permission under paragraph 15 of that Schedule (as a result of qualifying for authorisation under paragraph 12 of that Schedule) to effect or carry out contracts of insurance,

but does not include a friendly society or an organisation of workers or of employers.

(11) Subsection (10) must be read with –

    (a) section 22 of the Financial Services and Markets Act 2000;

    (b) any relevant order under that section; and

    (c) Schedule 2 to that Act.

16A Exemption relating to high net worth debtors and hirers

(1) The Secretary of State may by order provide that this Act shall not regulate a consumer credit agreement or a consumer hire agreement where –

    (a) the debtor or hirer is a natural person;

    (b) the agreement includes a declaration made by him to the effect that he agrees to forgo the protection and remedies that would be available to him under this Act if the agreement were a regulated agreement;

    (c) a statement of high net worth has been made in relation to him; and

    (d) that statement is current in relation to the agreement and a copy of it was provided to the creditor or owner before the agreement was made.

(2) For the purposes of this section a statement of high net worth is a statement to the effect that, in the opinion of the person making it, the natural person in relation to whom it is made –

    (a) received during the previous financial year income of a specified description totalling an amount of not less than the specified amount; or

    (b) had throughout that year net assets of a specified description with a total value of not less than the specified value.

(3) Such a statement –

    (a) may not be made by the person in relation to whom it is made;

    (b) must be made by a person of a specified description; and

    (c) is current in relation to an agreement if it was made during the period of one year ending with the day on which the agreement is made.

(4) An order under this section may make provision about –

    (a) how amounts of income and values of net assets are to be determined for the purposes of subsection (2)(a) and (b);

    (b) the form, content and signing of –

        (i) statements of high net worth;

        (ii) declarations for the purposes of subsection (1)(b).

(5) Where an agreement has two or more debtors or hirers, for the purposes of paragraph (c) of subsection (1) a separate statement of high net worth must have been made in relation to each of them; and paragraph (d) of that subsection shall have effect accordingly.

(6) In this section –

    'previous financial year' means, in relation to a statement of high net worth, the financial year immediately preceding the financial year during which the statement is made;

    'specified' means specified in an order under this section.

(7) In subsection (6) 'financial year' means a period of one year ending with 31st March.

(8) Nothing in this section affects the application of sections 140A to 140C.

16B Exemption relating to businesses

(1) This Act does not regulate –

    (a) a consumer credit agreement by which the creditor provides the debtor with credit exceeding £25,000, or

    (b) a consumer hire agreement that requires the hirer to make payments exceeding £25,000,

if the agreement is entered into by the debtor or hirer wholly or predominantly for the purposes of a business carried on, or intended to be carried on, by him.

(2) If an agreement includes a declaration made by the debtor or hirer to the effect that the agreement is entered into by him wholly or predominantly for the purposes of a business carried on, or intended to be carried on, by him, the agreement shall be presumed to have been entered into by him wholly or predominantly for such purposes.

(3) But that presumption does not apply if, when the agreement is entered into –

    (a) the creditor or owner, or

    (b) any person who has acted on his behalf in connection with the entering into of the agreement,

knows, or has reasonable cause to suspect, that the agreement is not entered into by the debtor or hirer wholly or predominantly for the purposes of a business carried on, or intended to be carried on, by him.

(4) The Secretary of State may by order make provision about the form, content and signing of declarations for the purposes of subsection (2).

(5) Where an agreement has two or more creditors or owners, in subsection (3) references to the creditor or owner are references to any one or more of them.

(6) Nothing in this section affects the application of sections 140A to 140C

16C Exemption relating to investment properties

(1) This Act does not regulate a consumer credit agreement if, at the time the agreement is entered into, any sums due under it are secured by a land mortgage on land where the condition in subsection (2) is satisfied.

(2) The condition is that less than 40% of the land is used, or is intended to be used, as or in connection with a dwelling –

    (a) by the debtor or a person connected with the debtor, or

    (b) in the case of credit provided to trustees, by an individual who is the beneficiary of the trust or a person connected with such an individual.

(3) For the purposes of subsection (2) the area of any land which comprises a building or

other structure containing two or more storeys is to be taken to be the aggregate of the floor areas of each of those storeys.

(4) For the purposes of subsection (2) a person is 'connected with' the debtor or an individual who is the beneficiary of a trust if he is –

    (a)   that person's spouse or civil partner;

    (b)   a person (whether or not of the opposite sex) whose relationship with that person has the characteristics of the relationship between husband and wife; or

    (c)   that person's parent, brother, sister, child, grandparent or grandchild.

(5) Section 126 (enforcement of land mortgages) applies to an agreement which would but for this section be a regulated agreement.

(6) Nothing in this section affects the application of sections 140A to 140C.

60   Form and content of agreements

(1) The Secretary of State shall make regulations as to the form and content of documents embodying regulated agreements, and the regulations shall contain such provisions as appear to him appropriate with a view to ensuring that the debtor or hirer is made aware of –

    (a)   the rights and duties conferred or imposed on him by the agreement,

    (b)   the amount and rate of the total charge for credit (in the case of a consumer credit agreement),

    (c)   the protection and remedies available to him under this Act, and

    (d)   any other matters which, in the opinion of the Secretary of State, it is desirable for him to know about in connection with the agreement.

(2) Regulations under subsection (1) may in particular –

    (a)   require specified information to be included in the prescribed manner in documents, and other specified material to be excluded;

    (b)   contain requirements to ensure that specified information is clearly brought to the attention of the debtor or hirer, and that one part of a document is not given insufficient or excessive prominence compared with another.

(3) If, on an application made to the OFT by a person carrying on a consumer credit business or a consumer hire business, it appears to the OFT impracticable for the applicant to comply with any requirement of regulations under subsection (1) in a particular case, it may, by notice to the applicant, direct that the requirement be waived or varied in relation to such agreements, and subject to such conditions (if any), as it may specify, and this Act and the regulations shall have effect accordingly.

(4) The OFT shall give a notice under subsection (3) only if it is satisfied that to do so would not prejudice the interests of debtors or hirers.

(5) An application may be made under subsection (3) only if it relates to –

    (a)   a consumer credit agreement secured on land,

    (b)   a consumer credit agreement under which a person takes an article in pawn,

    (c)   a consumer credit agreement under which the creditor provides the debtor with credit which exceeds £60,260,

    (d)   a consumer credit agreement entered into by the debtor wholly or predominantly for the purposes of a business carried on, or intended to be carried on, by him, or

    (e)   a consumer hire agreement.

(6) Subsections (2) to (5) of section 16B (declaration by the debtor as to the purposes of the agreement) apply for the purposes of subsection (5)(d).

61 Signing of agreement

(1) A regulated agreement is not properly executed unless –

    (a) a document in the prescribed form itself containing all the prescribed terms and conforming to regulations under section 60(1) is signed in the prescribed manner both by the debtor or hirer and by or on behalf of the creditor or owner, and

    (b) the document embodies all the terms of the agreement, other than implied terms, and

    (c) the document is, when presented or sent to the debtor or hirer for signature, in such a state that all its terms are readily legible.

(2) In addition, where the agreement is one to which section 58(1) applies, it is not properly executed unless –

    (a) the requirements of section 58(1) were complied with, and

    (b) the unexecuted agreement was sent, for his signature, to the debtor or hirer by an appropriate method not less than seven days after a copy of it was given to him under section 58(1), and

    (c) during the consideration period, the creditor or owner refrained from approaching the debtor or hirer (whether in person, by telephone or letter, or in any other way) except in response to a specific request made by the debtor or hirer after the beginning of the consideration period, and

    (d) no notice of withdrawal by the debtor or hirer was received by the creditor or owner before the sending of the unexecuted agreement.

(3) In subsection (2)(c), 'the consideration period' means the period beginning with the giving of the copy under section 58(1) and ending –

    (a) at the expiry of seven days after the day on which the unexecuted agreement is sent, for his signature, to the debtor or hirer, or

    (b) on its return by the debtor or hirer after signature by him,

whichever first occurs.

(4) Where the debtor or hirer is a partnership or an unincorporated body of persons, subsection (1)(a) shall apply with the substitution for 'by the debtor or hirer' of 'by or on behalf of the debtor or hirer'.

65 Consequences of improper execution

(1) An improperly-executed regulated agreement is enforceable against the debtor or hirer on an order of the court only.

(2) A retaking of goods or land to which a regulated agreement relates is an enforcement of the agreement.

87 Need for default notice

(1) Service of a notice on the debtor or hirer in accordance with section 88 (a 'default notice') is necessary before the creditor or owner can become entitled, by reason of any breach by the debtor or hirer of a regulated agreement, –

    (a) to terminate the agreement, or

    (b) to demand earlier payment of any sum, or

    (c) to recover possession of any goods or land, or

    (d) to treat any right conferred on the debtor or hirer by the agreement as terminated, restricted or deferred, or

(e)   to enforce any security.

(2)   Subsection (1) does not prevent the creditor from treating the right to draw upon any credit as restricted or deferred, and taking such steps as may be necessary to make the restriction or deferment effective.

(3)   The doing of an act by which a floating charge becomes fixed is not enforcement of a security.

(4)   Regulations may provide that subsection (1) is not to apply to agreements described by the regulations.

(5)   Subsection (1)(d) does not apply in a case referred to in section 98A(4) (termination or suspension of debtor's right to draw on credit under open-end agreement).

88   Contents and effect of default notice

(1)   The default notice must be in the prescribed form and specify –

    (a)   the nature of the alleged breach;

    (b)   if the breach is capable of remedy, what action is required to remedy it and the date before which that action is to be taken;

    (c)   if the breach is not capable of remedy, the sum (if any) required to be paid as compensation for the breach, and the date before which it is to be paid.

(2)   A date specified under subsection (1) must not be less than 14 days after the date of service of the default notice, and the creditor or owner shall not take action such as is mentioned in section 87(1) before the date so specified or (if no requirement is made under subsection (1)) before those 14 days have elapsed.

(3)   The default notice must not treat as a breach failure to comply with a provision of the agreement which becomes operative only on breach of some other provision, but if the breach of that other provision is not duly remedied or compensation demanded under subsection (1) is not duly paid, or (where no requirement is made under subsection (1)) if the 14 days mentioned in subsection (2) have elapsed, the creditor or owner may treat the failure as a breach and section 87(1) shall not apply to it.

(4)   The default notice must contain information in the prescribed terms about the consequences of failure to comply with it and any other prescribed matters relating to the agreement.

(4A) The default notice must also include a copy of the current default information sheet under section 86A.

(5)   A default notice making a requirement under subsection (1) may include a provision for the taking of action such as is mentioned in section 87(1) at any time after the restriction imposed by subsection (2) will cease, together with a statement that the provision will be ineffective if the breach is duly remedied or the compensation duly paid.

89   Compliance with default notice

If before the date specified for that purpose in the default notice the debtor or hirer takes the action specified under section 88(1)(b) or (c) the breach shall be treated as not having occurred.

127   Enforcement orders in cases of infringement

(1)   In the case of an application for an enforcement order under –

    (za)   section 55(2) (disclosure of information), or

    (zb)   section 61B(3) (duty to supply copy of overdraft agreement), or

    (a)   section 65(1) (improperly executed agreements), or

(b) section 105(7)(a) or (b) (improperly executed security instruments), or

(c) section 111(2) (failure to serve copy of notice on surety), or

(d) section 124(1) or (2) (taking of negotiable instrument in contravention of section 123),

the court shall dismiss the application if, but only if, it considers it just to do so having regard to –

(i) prejudice caused to any person by the contravention in question, and the degree of culpability for it; and

(ii) the powers conferred on the court by subsection (2) and sections 135 and 136.

(2) If it appears to the court just to do so, it may in an enforcement order reduce or discharge any sum payable by the debtor or hirer, or any surety, so as to compensate him for prejudice suffered as a result of the contravention in question.

(3) [*repealed, but may still apply to agreements made before 6 April 2007*] The court shall not make an enforcement order under section 65(1) if section 61(1)(a) (signing of agreements) was not complied with unless a document (whether or not in the prescribed form and complying with regulations under section 60(1)) itself containing all the prescribed terms of the agreement was signed by the debtor or hirer (whether or not in the prescribed manner).

(4) [*repealed*]

(5) [*repealed*]

129 Time orders

(1) Subject to subsection (3) below, if it appears to the court just to do so –

(a) on an application for an enforcement order; or

(b) on an application made by a debtor or hirer under this paragraph after service on him of –

(i) a default notice, or

(ii) a notice under section 76(1) or 98(1); or

(ba) on an application made by a debtor or hirer under this paragraph after he has been given a notice under section 86B or 86C; or

(c) in an action brought by a creditor or owner to enforce a regulated agreement or any security, or recover possession of any goods or land to which a regulated agreement relates,

the court may make an order under this section (a 'time order').

(2) A time order shall provide for one or both of the following, as the court considers just –

(a) the payment by the debtor or hirer or any surety of any sum owed under a regulated agreement or a security by such instalments, payable at such times, as the court, having regard to the means of the debtor or hirer and any surety, considers reasonable;

(b) the remedying by the debtor or hirer of any breach of a regulated agreement (other than the non-payment of money) within such period as the court may specify.

(3) Where in Scotland a time to pay direction or a time to pay order has been made in relation to a debt, it shall not thereafter be competent to make a time order in relation to the same debt.

135 Power to impose conditions, or suspend operation of order

(1) If it considers it just to do so, the court may in an order made by it in relation to a regulated agreement include provisions –

    (a) making the operation of any term of the order conditional on the doing of specified acts by any party to the proceedings;

    (b) suspending the operation of any term of the order either –

        (i) until such time as the court subsequently directs, or

        (ii) until the occurrence of a specified act or omission.

(2) The court shall not suspend the operation of a term requiring the delivery up of goods by any person unless satisfied that the goods are in his possession or control.

(3) In the case of a consumer hire agreement, the court shall not so use its powers under subsection (1)(b) as to extend the period for which, under the terms of the agreement, the hirer is entitled to possession of the goods to which the agreement relates.

(4) On the application of any person affected by a provision included under subsection (1), the court may vary the provision.

136 Power to vary agreements and securities

The court may in an order made by it under this Act include such provision as it considers just for amending any agreement or security in consequence of a term of the order.

140A Unfair relationships between creditors and debtors

(1) The court may make an order under section 140B in connection with a credit agreement if it determines that the relationship between the creditor and the debtor arising out of the agreement (or the agreement taken with any related agreement) is unfair to the debtor because of one or more of the following –

    (a) any of the terms of the agreement or of any related agreement;

    (b) the way in which the creditor has exercised or enforced any of his rights under the agreement or any related agreement;

    (c) any other thing done (or not done) by, or on behalf of, the creditor (either before or after the making of the agreement or any related agreement).

(2) In deciding whether to make a determination under this section the court shall have regard to all matters it thinks relevant (including matters relating to the creditor and matters relating to the debtor).

(3) For the purposes of this section the court shall (except to the extent that it is not appropriate to do so) treat anything done (or not done) by, or on behalf of, or in relation to, an associate or a former associate of the creditor as if done (or not done) by, or on behalf of, or in relation to, the creditor.

(4) A determination may be made under this section in relation to a relationship notwithstanding that the relationship may have ended.

(5) An order under section 140B shall not be made in connection with a credit agreement which is an exempt agreement by virtue of section 16(6C).

140B Powers of court in relation to unfair relationships

(1) An order under this section in connection with a credit agreement may do one or more of the following –

    (a) require the creditor, or any associate or former associate of his, to repay (in whole or in part) any sum paid by the debtor or by a surety by virtue of the agreement or any related agreement (whether paid to the creditor, the associate or the former associate or to any other person);

(b) require the creditor, or any associate or former associate of his, to do or not to do (or to cease doing) anything specified in the order in connection with the agreement or any related agreement;

(c) reduce or discharge any sum payable by the debtor or by a surety by virtue of the agreement or any related agreement;

(d) direct the return to a surety of any property provided by him for the purposes of a security;

(e) otherwise set aside (in whole or in part) any duty imposed on the debtor or on a surety by virtue of the agreement or any related agreement;

(f) alter the terms of the agreement or of any related agreement;

(g) direct accounts to be taken, or (in Scotland) an accounting to be made, between any persons.

(2) An order under this section may be made in connection with a credit agreement only –

(a) on an application made by the debtor or by a surety;

(b) at the instance of the debtor or a surety in any proceedings in any court to which the debtor and the creditor are parties, being proceedings to enforce the agreement or any related agreement; or

(c) at the instance of the debtor or a surety in any other proceedings in any court where the amount paid or payable under the agreement or any related agreement is relevant.

(3) An order under this section may be made notwithstanding that its effect is to place on the creditor, or any associate or former associate of his, a burden in respect of an advantage enjoyed by another person.

(4) An application under subsection (2)(a) may only be made –

(a) in England and Wales, to the county court;

(b) in Scotland, to the sheriff court;

(c) in Northern Ireland, to the High Court (subject to subsection (6)).

(5) In Scotland such an application may be made in the sheriff court for the district in which the debtor or surety resides or carries on business.

(6) In Northern Ireland such an application may be made to the county court if the credit agreement is an agreement under which the creditor provides the debtor with –

(a) fixed-sum credit not exceeding £15,000; or

(b) running-account credit on which the credit limit does not exceed £15,000.

(7) Without prejudice to any provision which may be made by rules of court made in relation to county courts in Northern Ireland, such rules may provide that an application made by virtue of subsection (6) may be made in the county court for the division in which the debtor or surety resides or carries on business.

(8) A party to any proceedings mentioned in subsection (2) shall be entitled, in accordance with rules of court, to have any person who might be the subject of an order under this section made a party to the proceedings.

(9) If, in any such proceedings, the debtor or a surety alleges that the relationship between the creditor and the debtor is unfair to the debtor, it is for the creditor to prove to the contrary.

140C   Interpretation of ss 140A and 140B

(1)   In this section and in sections 140A and 140B 'credit agreement' means any agreement between an individual (the 'debtor') and any other person (the 'creditor') by which the creditor provides the debtor with credit of any amount.

(2)   References in this section and in sections 140A and 140B to the creditor or to the debtor under a credit agreement include –

(a)   references to the person to whom his rights and duties under the agreement have passed by assignment or operation of law;

(b)   where two or more persons are the creditor or the debtor, references to any one or more of those persons.

(3)   The definition of 'court' in section 189(1) does not apply for the purposes of sections 140A and 140B.

(4)   References in sections 140A and 140B to an agreement related to a credit agreement (the 'main agreement') are references to –

(a)   a credit agreement consolidated by the main agreement;

(b)   a linked transaction in relation to the main agreement or to a credit agreement within paragraph (a);

(c)   a security provided in relation to the main agreement, to a credit agreement within paragraph (a) or to a linked transaction within paragraph (b).

(5)   In the case of a credit agreement which is not a regulated consumer credit agreement, for the purposes of subsection (4) a transaction shall be treated as being a linked transaction in relation to that agreement if it would have been such a transaction had that agreement been a regulated consumer credit agreement.

(6)   For the purposes of this section and section 140B the definitions of 'security' and 'surety' in section 189(1) apply (with any appropriate changes) in relation to –

(a)   a credit agreement which is not a consumer credit agreement as if it were a consumer credit agreement; and

(b)   a transaction which is a linked transaction by virtue of subsection (5).

(7)   For the purposes of this section a credit agreement (the 'earlier agreement') is consolidated by another credit agreement (the 'later agreement') if –

(a)   the later agreement is entered into by the debtor (in whole or in part) for purposes connected with debts owed by virtue of the earlier agreement; and

(b)   at any time prior to the later agreement being entered into the parties to the earlier agreement included –

(i)   the debtor under the later agreement; and

(ii)   the creditor under the later agreement or an associate or a former associate of his.

(8)   Further, if the later agreement is itself consolidated by another credit agreement (whether by virtue of this subsection or subsection (7)), then the earlier agreement is consolidated by that other agreement as well.

140D   Advice and information

The advice and information published by the OFT under section 229 of the Enterprise Act 2002 shall indicate how the OFT expects sections 140A to 140C of this Act to interact with Part 8 of that Act.

A4   HUMAN RIGHTS ACT 1998

6   Acts of public authorities

(1)   It is unlawful for a public authority to act in a way which is incompatible with a Convention right.

(2)   Subsection (1) does not apply to an act if –

    (a)   as the result of one or more provisions of primary legislation, the authority could not have acted differently; or

    (b)   in the case of one or more provisions of, or made under, primary legislation which cannot be read or given effect in a way which is compatible with the Convention rights, the authority was acting so as to give effect to or enforce those provisions.

(3)   In this section 'public authority' includes –

    (a)   a court or tribunal, and

    (b)   any person certain of whose functions are functions of a public nature,

but does not include either House of Parliament or a person exercising functions in connection with proceedings in Parliament.

(4)   [*repealed*]

(5)   In relation to a particular act, a person is not a public authority by virtue only of subsection (3)(b) if the nature of the act is private.

(6)   'An act' includes a failure to act but does not include a failure to –

    (a)   introduce in, or lay before, Parliament a proposal for legislation; or

    (b)   make any primary legislation or remedial order.

7   Proceedings

(1)   A person who claims that a public authority has acted (or proposes to act) in a way which is made unlawful by section 6(1) may –

    (a)   bring proceedings against the authority under this Act in the appropriate court or tribunal, or

    (b)   rely on the Convention right or rights concerned in any legal proceedings,

but only if he is (or would be) a victim of the unlawful act.

(2)   In subsection (1)(a) 'appropriate court or tribunal' means such court or tribunal as may be determined in accordance with rules; and proceedings against an authority include a counterclaim or similar proceeding.

(3)   If the proceedings are brought on an application for judicial review, the applicant is to be taken to have a sufficient interest in relation to the unlawful act only if he is, or would be, a victim of that act.

(4)   If the proceedings are made by way of a petition for judicial review in Scotland, the applicant shall be taken to have title and interest to sue in relation to the unlawful act only if he is, or would be, a victim of that act.

(5)   Proceedings under subsection (1)(a) must be brought before the end of –

    (a)   the period of one year beginning with the date on which the act complained of took place; or

    (b)   such longer period as the court or tribunal considers equitable having regard to all the circumstances,

but that is subject to any rule imposing a stricter time limit in relation to the procedure in question.

(6) In subsection (1)(b) 'legal proceedings' includes –

    (a)   proceedings brought by or at the instigation of a public authority; and

    (b)   an appeal against the decision of a court or tribunal.

(7) For the purposes of this section, a person is a victim of an unlawful act only if he would be a victim for the purposes of Article 34 of the Convention if proceedings were brought in the European Court of Human Rights in respect of that act.

(8) Nothing in this Act creates a criminal offence.

(9) In this section 'rules' means –

    (a)   in relation to proceedings before a court or tribunal outside Scotland, rules made by the Lord Chancellor or the Secretary of State for the purposes of this section or rules of court,

    (b)   in relation to proceedings before a court or tribunal in Scotland, rules made by the Secretary of State for those purposes,

    (c)   in relation to proceedings before a tribunal in Northern Ireland –

        (i)   which deals with transferred matters; and

        (ii)   for which no rules made under paragraph (a) are in force,

    rules made by a Northern Ireland department for those purposes,

and includes provision made by order under section 1 of the Courts and Legal Services Act 1990.

(10) In making rules, regard must be had to section 9.

(11) The Minister who has power to make rules in relation to a particular tribunal may, to the extent he considers it necessary to ensure that the tribunal can provide an appropriate remedy in relation to an act (or proposed act) of a public authority which is (or would be) unlawful as a result of section 6(1), by order add to –

    (a)   the relief or remedies which the tribunal may grant; or

    (b)   the grounds on which it may grant any of them.

(12) An order made under subsection (11) may contain such incidental, supplemental, consequential or transitional provision as the Minister making it considers appropriate.

(13) 'The Minister' includes the Northern Ireland department concerned.

8   Judicial remedies

(1) In relation to any act (or proposed act) of a public authority which the court finds is (or would be) unlawful, it may grant such relief or remedy, or make such order, within its powers as it considers just and appropriate.

(2) But damages may be awarded only by a court which has power to award damages, or to order the payment of compensation, in civil proceedings.

(3) No award of damages is to be made unless, taking account of all the circumstances of the case, including –

    (a)   any other relief or remedy granted, or order made, in relation to the act in question (by that or any other court), and

    (b)   the consequences of any decision (of that or any other court) in respect of that act,

the court is satisfied that the award is necessary to afford just satisfaction to the person in whose favour it is made.

(4) In determining –

    (a)   whether to award damages, or

(b)   the amount of an award,

the court must take into account the principles applied by the European Court of Human Rights in relation to the award of compensation under Article 41 of the Convention.

(5)   A public authority against which damages are awarded is to be treated –

(a)   in Scotland, for the purposes of section 3 of the Law Reform (Miscellaneous Provisions) (Scotland) Act 1940 as if the award were made in an action of damages in which the authority has been found liable in respect of loss or damage to the person to whom the award is made;

(b)   for the purposes of the Civil Liability (Contribution) Act 1978 as liable in respect of damage suffered by the person to whom the award is made.

(6)   In this section –

'court' includes a tribunal;
'damages' means damages for an unlawful act of a public authority; and
'unlawful' means unlawful under section 6(1).

9   Judicial acts

(1)   Proceedings under section 7(1)(a) in respect of a judicial act may be brought only –

(a)   by exercising a right of appeal;
(b)   on an application (in Scotland a petition) for judicial review; or
(c)   in such other forum as may be prescribed by rules.

(2)   That does not affect any rule of law which prevents a court from being the subject of judicial review.

(3)   In proceedings under this Act in respect of a judicial act done in good faith, damages may not be awarded otherwise than to compensate a person to the extent required by Article 5(5) of the Convention.

(4)   An award of damages permitted by subsection (3) is to be made against the Crown; but no award may be made unless the appropriate person, if not a party to the proceedings, is joined.

(5)   In this section –

'appropriate person' means the Minister responsible for the court concerned, or a person or government department nominated by him;
'court' includes a tribunal;
'judge' includes a member of a tribunal, a justice of the peace (or, in Northern Ireland, a lay magistrate) and a clerk or other officer entitled to exercise the jurisdiction of a court;
'judicial act' means a judicial act of a court and includes an act done on the instructions, or on behalf, of a judge; and
'rules' has the same meaning as in section 7(9).

SCHEDULE 1   THE ARTICLES

Section 1(3)

PART I   THE CONVENTION

Rights and Freedoms

Article 6
Right to a fair trial

1   In the determination of his civil rights and obligations or of any criminal charge against him, everyone is entitled to a fair and public hearing within a reasonable time by an independent and impartial tribunal established by law. Judgment shall be pronounced publicly but the press and public may be excluded from all or part of the trial in the interest of morals, public order or national security in a democratic society, where the interests of juveniles or the protection of the private life of the parties so require, or to the extent strictly necessary in the opinion of the court in special circumstances where publicity would prejudice the interests of justice.

2   Everyone charged with a criminal offence shall be presumed innocent until proved guilty according to law.

3   Everyone charged with a criminal offence has the following minimum rights:

    (a)   to be informed promptly, in a language which he understands and in detail, of the nature and cause of the accusation against him;

    (b)   to have adequate time and facilities for the preparation of his defence;

    (c)   to defend himself in person or through legal assistance of his own choosing or, if he has not sufficient means to pay for legal assistance, to be given it free when the interests of justice so require;

    (d)   to examine or have examined witnesses against him and to obtain the attendance and examination of witnesses on his behalf under the same conditions as witnesses against him;

    (e)   to have the free assistance of an interpreter if he cannot understand or speak the language used in court.

Article 8
Right to respect for private and family life

1   Everyone has the right to respect for his private and family life, his home and his correspondence.

2   There shall be no interference by a public authority with the exercise of this right except such as is in accordance with the law and is necessary in a democratic society in the interests of national security, public safety or the economic well-being of the country, for the prevention of disorder or crime, for the protection of health or morals, or for the protection of the rights and freedoms of others.

PART II   THE FIRST PROTOCOL

Article 1
Protection of property

Every natural or legal person is entitled to the peaceful enjoyment of his possessions. No one shall be deprived of his possessions except in the public interest and subject to the conditions provided for by law and by the general principles of international law.

The preceding provisions shall not, however, in any way impair the right of a State to enforce such laws as it deems necessary to control the use of property in accordance with the general interest or to secure the payment of taxes or other contributions or penalties.

A5   LAW OF PROPERTY ACT 1925

91   Sale of mortgaged property in action for redemption or foreclosure

(1)   Any person entitled to redeem mortgaged property may have a judgment or order for sale instead of for redemption in an action brought by him either for redemption alone, or for sale alone, or for sale or redemption in the alternative.

(2)   In any action, whether for foreclosure, or for redemption, or for sale, or for the raising and payment in any manner of mortgage money, the court, on the request of the mortgagee, or of any person interested either in the mortgage money or in the right of redemption, and, notwithstanding that –

   (a)   any other person dissents; or
   (b)   the mortgagee or any person so interested does not appear in the action;

   and without allowing any time for redemption or for payment of any mortgage money, may direct a sale of the mortgaged property, on such terms as it thinks fit, including the deposit in court of a reasonable sum fixed by the court to meet the expenses of sale and to secure performance of the terms.

(3)   But, in an action brought by a person interested in the right of redemption and seeking a sale, the court may, in the application of any defendant, direct the plaintiff to give such security for costs as the court thinks fit, and may give the conduct of the sale to any defendant, and may give such directions as it thinks fit respecting the costs of the defendants or any of them.

(4)   In any case within this section the court may, if it thinks fit, direct a sale without previously determining the priorities of incumbrancers.

(5)   This section applies to actions brought either before or after the commencement of this Act.

(6)   In this section 'mortgaged property' includes the estate or interest which a mortgagee would have had power to convey if the statutory power of sale were applicable.

(7)   For the purposes of this section the court may, in favour of a purchaser, make a vesting order conveying the mortgaged property, or appoint a person to do so, subject or not to any incumbrance, as the court may think fit; or, in the case of an equitable mortgage, may create and vest a mortgage term in the mortgagee to enable him to carry out the sale as if the mortgage had been made by deed by way of legal mortgage.

(8)   The county court has jurisdiction under this section where the amount owing in respect of the mortgage or charge at the commencement of the proceedings does not exceed £30,000.

101   Powers incident to estate or interest of mortgage

(1)   A mortgagee, where the mortgage is made by deed, shall, by virtue of this Act, have the

following powers, to the like extent as if they had been in terms conferred by the mortgage deed, but not further (namely): –

(i)   A power, when the mortgage money has become due, to sell, or to concur with any other person in selling, the mortgaged property, or any part thereof, either subject to prior charges or not, and either together or in lots, by public auction or by private contract, subject to such conditions respecting title, or evidence of title, or other matter, as the mortgagee thinks fit, with power to vary any contract for sale, and to buy in at an auction, or to rescind any contract for sale, and to re-sell, without being answerable for any loss occasioned thereby; and

(ii)   A power, at any time after the date of the mortgage deed, to insure and keep insured against loss or damage by fire any building, or any effects or property of an insurable nature, whether affixed to the freehold or not, being or forming part of the property which or an estate or interest wherein is mortgaged, and the premiums paid for any such insurance shall be a charge on the mortgaged property or estate or interest, in addition to the mortgage money, and with the same priority, and with interest at the same rate, as the mortgage money; and

(iii)   A power, when the mortgage money has become due, to appoint a receiver of the income of the mortgaged property, or any part thereof; or, if the mortgaged property consists of an interest in income, or of a rentcharge or an annual or other periodical sum, a receiver of that property or any part thereof; and

(iv)   A power, while the mortgagee is in possession, to cut and sell timber and other trees ripe for cutting, and not planted or left standing for shelter or ornament, or to contract for any such cutting and sale, to be completed within any time not exceeding twelve months from the making of the contract.

(1A) Subsection (1)(i) is subject to section 21 of the Commonhold and Leasehold Reform Act 2002 (no disposition of part-units).

(2)   Where the mortgage deed is executed after the thirty-first day of December, nineteen hundred and eleven, the power of sale aforesaid includes the following powers as incident thereto (namely): –

(i)   A power to impose or reserve or make binding, as far as the law permits, by covenant, condition, or otherwise, on the unsold part of the mortgaged property or any part thereof, or on the purchaser and any property sold, any restriction or reservation with respect to building on or other user of land, or with respect to mines and minerals, or for the purpose of the more beneficial working thereof, or with respect to any other thing:

(ii)   A power to sell the mortgaged property, or any part thereof, or all or any mines and minerals apart from the surface: –

(a)   With or without a grant or reservation of rights of way, rights of water, easements, rights, and privileges for or connected with building or other purposes in relation to the property remaining in mortgage or any part thereof, or to any property sold: and

(b)   With or without an exception or reservation of all or any of the mines and minerals in or under the mortgaged property, and with or without a grant or reservation of powers of working, wayleaves, or rights of way, rights of water and drainage and other powers, easements, rights, and privileges for or connected with mining purposes in relation to the property remaining unsold or any part thereof, or to any property sold: and

(c)   With or without covenants by the purchaser to expend money on the land sold.

(3)   The provisions of this Act relating to the foregoing powers, comprised either in this

section, or in any other section regulating the exercise of those powers, may be varied or extended by the mortgage deed, and, as so varied or extended, shall, as far as may be, operate in the like manner and with all the like incidents, effects, and consequences, as if such variations or extensions were contained in this Act.

(4) This section applies only if and as far as a contrary intention is not expressed in the mortgage deed, and has effect subject to the terms of the mortgage deed and to the provisions therein contained.

(5) Save as otherwise provided, this section applies where the mortgage deed is executed after the thirty-first day of December, eighteen hundred and eighty-one.

(6) The power of sale conferred by this section includes such power of selling the estate in fee simple or any leasehold reversion as is conferred by the provisions of this Act relating to the realisation of mortgages.

A6 LIMITATION ACT 1980

15 Time limit for actions to recover land

(1) No action shall be brought by any person to recover any land after the expiration of twelve years from the date on which the right of action accrued to him or, if it first accrued to some person through whom he claims, to that person.

(2) Subject to the following provisions of this section, where –

    (a)   the estate or interest claimed was an estate or interest in reversion or remainder or any other future estate or interest and the right of action to recover the land accrued on the date on which the estate or interest fell into possession by the determination of the preceding estate or interest; and

    (b)   the person entitled to the preceding estate or interest (not being a term of years absolute) was not in possession of the land on that date;

no action shall be brought by the person entitled to the succeeding estate or interest after the expiration of twelve years from the date on which the right of action accrued to the person entitled to the preceding estate or interest or six years from the date on which the right of action accrued to the person entitled to the succeeding estate or interest, whichever period last expires.

(3) Subsection (2) above shall not apply to any estate or interest which falls into possession on the determination of an entailed interest and which might have been barred by the person entitled to the entailed interest.

(4) No person shall bring an action to recover any estate or interest in land under an assurance taking effect after the right of action to recover the land had accrued to the person by whom the assurance was made or some person through whom he claimed or some person entitled to a preceding estate or interest, unless the action is brought within the period during which the person by whom the assurance was made could have brought such an action.

(5) Where any person is entitled to any estate or interest in land in possession and, while so entitled, is also entitled to any future estate or interest in that land, and his right to recover the estate or interest in possession is barred under this Act, no action shall be brought by that person, or by any person claiming through him, in respect of the future estate or interest, unless in the meantime possession of the land has been recovered by a person entitled to an intermediate estate or interest.

(6) Part I of Schedule 1 to this Act contains provisions for determining the date of accrual of rights of action to recover land in the cases there mentioned.

(7) Part II of that Schedule contains provisions modifying the provisions of this section in their application to actions brought by, or by a person claiming through, the Crown or any spiritual or eleemosynary corporation sole.

17 Extinction of title to land after expiration of time limit

Subject to –

    (a)   section 18 of this Act.

    (b)   [*repealed*]

at the expiration of the period prescribed by this Act for any person to bring an action to recover land (including a redemption action) the title of that person to the land shall be extinguished.

20 Time limit for actions to recover money secured by a mortgage or charge or to recover proceeds of the sale of land

(1)   No action shall be brought to recover –

    (a)   any principal sum of money secured by a mortgage or other charge on property (whether real or personal); or

    (b)   proceeds of the sale of land;

after the expiration of twelve years from the date on which the right to receive the money accrued.

(2)   No foreclosure action in respect of mortgaged personal property shall be brought after the expiration of twelve years from the date on which the right to foreclose accrued.

But if the mortgagee was in possession of the mortgaged property after that date, the right to foreclose on the property which was in his possession shall not be treated as having accrued for the purposes of this subsection until the date on which his possession discontinued.

(3)   The right to receive any principal sum of money secured by a mortgage or other charge and the right to foreclose on the property subject to the mortgage or charge shall not be treated as accruing so long as that property comprises any future interest or any life insurance policy which has not matured or been determined.

(4)   Nothing in this section shall apply to a foreclosure action in respect of mortgaged land, but the provisions of this Act relating to actions to recover land shall apply to such an action.

(5)   Subject to subsections (6) and (7) below, no action to recover arrears of interest payable in respect of any sum of money secured by a mortgage or other charge or payable in respect of proceeds of the sale of land, or to recover damages in respect of such arrears shall be brought after the expiration of six years from the date on which the interest became due.

(6)   Where –

    (a)   a prior mortgagee or other incumbrancer has been in possession of the property charged; and

    (b)   an action is brought within one year of the discontinuance of that possession by the subsequent incumbrancer;

the subsequent incumbrancer may recover by that action all the arrears of interest which fell due during the period of possession by the prior incumbrancer or damages in respect of those arrears, notwithstanding that the period exceeded six years.

(7)   Where –

    (a)   the property subject to the mortgage or charge comprises any future interest or life insurance policy; and

    (b)   it is a term of the mortgage or charge that arrears of interest shall be treated as part of the principal sum of money secured by the mortgage or charge;

interest shall not be treated as becoming due before the right to recover the principal sum of money has accrued or is treated as having accrued.

A7 UNFAIR TERMS IN CONSUMER CONTRACTS REGULATIONS 1999

Made 22nd July 1999
Laid before Parliament 22nd July 1999
Coming into force 1st October 1999

Whereas the Secretary of State is a Minister designated for the purposes of section 2(2) of the European Communities Act 1972 in relation to measures relating to consumer protection:

Now, the Secretary of State, in exercise of the powers conferred upon him by section 2(2) of that Act, hereby makes the following Regulations: –

1 Citation and commencement

These Regulations may be cited as the Unfair Terms in Consumer Contracts Regulations 1999 and shall come into force on 1st October 1999.

2 Revocation

The Unfair Terms in Consumer Contracts Regulations 1994 are hereby revoked.

3 Interpretation

(1) In these Regulations –

'the Community' means the European Community;
'consumer' means any natural person who, in contracts covered by these Regulations, is acting for purposes which are outside his trade, business or profession;
'court' in relation to England and Wales and Northern Ireland means a county court or the High Court, and in relation to Scotland, the Sheriff or the Court of Session;
'OFT' means the Office of Fair Trading;
'EEA Agreement' means the Agreement on the European Economic Area signed at Oporto on 2nd May 1992 as adjusted by the protocol signed at Brussels on 17th March 1993;
'Member State' means a State which is a contracting party to the EEA Agreement;
'notified' means notified in writing;
'qualifying body' means a person specified in Schedule 1;
'seller or supplier' means any natural or legal person who, in contracts covered by these Regulations, is acting for purposes relating to his trade, business or profession, whether publicly owned or privately owned;
'unfair terms' means the contractual terms referred to in regulation 5.

(1A) The references –

(a) in regulation 4(1) to a seller or a supplier, and
(b) in regulation 8(1) to a seller or supplier, include references to a distance supplier and to an intermediary.

(1B) In paragraph (1A) and regulation 5(6) –

'distance supplier' means –

    (a)   a supplier under a distance contract within the meaning of the Financial Services (Distance Marketing) Regulations 2004, or

    (b)   a supplier of unsolicited financial services within regulation 15 of those Regulations; and

'intermediary' has the same meaning as in those Regulations.

(2)   In the application of these Regulations to Scotland for references to an 'injunction' or an 'interim injunction' there shall be substituted references to an 'interdict' or 'interim interdict' respectively.

4 Terms to which these Regulations apply

(1)   These Regulations apply in relation to unfair terms in contracts concluded between a seller or a supplier and a consumer.

(2)   These Regulations do not apply to contractual terms which reflect –

    (a)   mandatory statutory or regulatory provisions (including such provisions under the law of any Member State or in Community legislation having effect in the United Kingdom without further enactment);

    (b)   the provisions or principles of international conventions to which the Member States or the Community are party.

5 Unfair Terms

(1)   A contractual term which has not been individually negotiated shall be regarded as unfair if, contrary to the requirement of good faith, it causes a significant imbalance in the parties' rights and obligations arising under the contract, to the detriment of the consumer.

(2)   A term shall always be regarded as not having been individually negotiated where it has been drafted in advance and the consumer has therefore not been able to influence the substance of the term.

(3)   Notwithstanding that a specific term or certain aspects of it in a contract has been individually negotiated, these Regulations shall apply to the rest of a contract if an overall assessment of it indicates that it is a pre-formulated standard contract.

(4)   It shall be for any seller or supplier who claims that a term was individually negotiated to show that it was.

(5)   Schedule 2 to these Regulations contains an indicative and non-exhaustive list of the terms which may be regarded as unfair.

(6)   Any contractual term providing that a consumer bears the burden of proof in respect of showing whether a distance supplier or an intermediary complied with any or all of the obligations placed upon him resulting from the Directive and any rule or enactment implementing it shall always be regarded as unfair.

(7)   In paragraph (6) –

'the Directive' means Directive 2002/65/EC of the European Parliament and of the Council of 23 September 2002 concerning the distance marketing of consumer financial services and amending Council Directive 90/619/EEC and Directives 97/7/EC and 98/27/EC; and

'rule' means a rule made by the Financial Services Authority under the Financial Services and Markets Act 2000 or by a designated professional body within the meaning of section 326(2) of that Act.

6 Assessment of unfair terms

(1) Without prejudice to regulation 12, the unfairness of a contractual term shall be assessed, taking into account the nature of the goods or services for which the contract was concluded and by referring, at the time of conclusion of the contract, to all the circumstances attending the conclusion of the contract and to all the other terms of the contract or of another contract on which it is dependent.

(2) In so far as it is in plain intelligible language, the assessment of fairness of a term shall not relate –

    (a) to the definition of the main subject matter of the contract, or

    (b) to the adequacy of the price or remuneration, as against the goods or services supplied in exchange.

7 Written contracts

(1) A seller or supplier shall ensure that any written term of a contract is expressed in plain, intelligible language.

(2) If there is doubt about the meaning of a written term, the interpretation which is most favourable to the consumer shall prevail but this rule shall not apply in proceedings brought under regulation 12.

8 Effect of unfair term

(1) An unfair term in a contract concluded with a consumer by a seller or supplier shall not be binding on the consumer.

(2) The contract shall continue to bind the parties if it is capable of continuing in existence without the unfair term.

9 Choice of law clauses

These Regulations shall apply notwithstanding any contract term which applies or purports to apply the law of a non-Member State, if the contract has a close connection with the territory of the Member States.

10 Complaints – consideration by OFT

(1) It shall be the duty of the OFT to consider any complaint made to it that any contract term drawn up for general use is unfair, unless –

    (a) the complaint appears to the OFT to be frivolous or vexatious; or

    (b) a qualifying body has notified the OFT that it agrees to consider the complaint.

(2) The OFT shall give reasons for its decision to apply or not to apply, as the case may be, for an injunction under regulation 12 in relation to any complaint which these Regulations require it to consider.

(3) In deciding whether or not to apply for an injunction in respect of a term which the OFT considers to be unfair, it may, if it considers it appropriate to do so, have regard to any undertakings given to it by or on behalf of any person as to the continued use of such a term in contracts concluded with consumers.

11 Complaints – consideration by qualifying bodies

(1) If a qualifying body specified in Part One of Schedule 1 notifies the OFT that it agrees to

consider a complaint that any contract term drawn up for general use is unfair, it shall be under a duty to consider that complaint.

(2)   Regulation 10(2) and (3) shall apply to a qualifying body which is under a duty to consider a complaint as they apply to the OFT.

12   Injunctions to prevent continued use of unfair terms

(1)   The OFT or, subject to paragraph (2), any qualifying body may apply for an injunction (including an interim injunction) against any person appearing to the OFT or that body to be using, or recommending use of, an unfair term drawn up for general use in contracts concluded with consumers.

(2)   A qualifying body may apply for an injunction only where –

    (a)   it has notified the OFT of its intention to apply at least fourteen days before the date on which the application is made, beginning with the date on which the notification was given; or

    (b)   the OFT consents to the application being made within a shorter period.

(3)   The court on an application under this regulation may grant an injunction on such terms as it thinks fit.

(4)   An injunction may relate not only to use of a particular contract term drawn up for general use but to any similar term, or a term having like effect, used or recommended for use by any person.

13   Powers of the OFT and qualifying bodies to obtain documents and information

(1)   The OFT may exercise the power conferred by this regulation for the purpose of –

    (a)   facilitating its consideration of a complaint that a contract term drawn up for general use is unfair; or

    (b)   ascertaining whether a person has complied with an undertaking or court order as to the continued use, or recommendation for use, of a term in contracts concluded with consumers.

(2)   A qualifying body specified in Part One of Schedule 1 may exercise the power conferred by this regulation for the purpose of –

    (a)   facilitating its consideration of a complaint that a contract term drawn up for general use is unfair; or

    (b)   ascertaining whether a person has complied with –

        (i)   an undertaking given to it or to the court following an application by that body, or

        (ii)   a court order made on an application by that body,

    as to the continued use, or recommendation for use, of a term in contracts concluded with consumers.

(3)   The OFT may require any person to supply to it, and a qualifying body specified in Part One of Schedule 1 may require any person to supply to it –

    (a)   a copy of any document which that person has used or recommended for use, at the time the notice referred to in paragraph (4) below is given, as a pre-formulated standard contract in dealings with consumers;

    (b)   information about the use, or recommendation for use, by that person of that document or any other such document in dealings with consumers.

(4) The power conferred by this regulation is to be exercised by a notice in writing which may –

    (a) specify the way in which and the time within which it is to be complied with; and

    (b) be varied or revoked by a subsequent notice.

(5) Nothing in this regulation compels a person to supply any document or information which he would be entitled to refuse to produce or give in civil proceedings before the court.

(6) If a person makes default in complying with a notice under this regulation, the court may, on the application of the OFT or of the qualifying body, make such order as the court thinks fit for requiring the default to be made good, and any such order may provide that all the costs or expenses of and incidental to the application shall be borne by the person in default or by any officers of a company or other association who are responsible for its default.

14 Notification of undertakings and orders to OFT

A qualifying body shall notify the OFT –

(a) of any undertaking given to it by or on behalf of any person as to the continued use of a term which that body considers to be unfair in contracts concluded with consumers;

(b) of the outcome of any application made by it under regulation 12, and of the terms of any undertaking given to, or order made by, the court;

(c) of the outcome of any application made by it to enforce a previous order of the court.

15 Publication, information and advice

(1) The OFT shall arrange for the publication in such form and manner as it considers appropriate, of –

    (a) details of any undertaking or order notified to it under regulation 14;

    (b) details of any undertaking given to it by or on behalf of any person as to the continued use of a term which the OFT considers to be unfair in contracts concluded with consumers;

    (c) details of any application made by it under regulation 12, and of the terms of any undertaking given to, or order made by, the court;

    (d) details of any application made by the OFT to enforce a previous order of the court.

(2) The OFT shall inform any person on request whether a particular term to which these Regulations apply has been –

    (a) the subject of an undertaking given to the OFT or notified to it by a qualifying body; or

    (b) the subject of an order of the court made upon application by it or notified to it by a qualifying body;

and shall give that person details of the undertaking or a copy of the order, as the case may be, together with a copy of any amendments which the person giving the undertaking has agreed to make to the term in question.

(3) The OFT may arrange for the dissemination in such form and manner as it considers appropriate of such information and advice concerning the operation of these Regulations as may appear to it to be expedient to give to the public and to all persons likely to be affected by these Regulations.

16 The functions of the Financial Services Authority

The functions of the Financial Services Authority under these Regulations shall be treated as functions of the Financial Services Authority under the Financial Services and Markets Act 2000.

Kim Howells
Parliamentary Under-Secretary of State for Competition and Consumer Affairs,
Department of Trade and Industry.
22nd July 1999

SCHEDULE 1   Qualifying Bodies

Regulation 3

PART ONE

1   The Information Commissioner.
2   The Gas and Electricity Markets Authority.
3   The Director General of Electricity Supply for Northern Ireland.
4   The Director General of Gas for Northern Ireland.
5   The Office of Communications.
6   The Water Services Regulation Authority.
7   The Office of Rail Regulation.
8   Every weights and measures authority in Great Britain.
9   The Department of Enterprise, Trade and Investment in Northern Ireland.
10 The Financial Services Authority.

PART TWO

11 Consumers' Association

SCHEDULE 2   Indicative and Non-exhaustive List of Terms which may be Regarded as Unfair

Regulation 5(5)

1   Terms which have the object or effect of –

    (a)   excluding or limiting the legal liability of a seller or supplier in the event of the death of a consumer or personal injury to the latter resulting from an act or omission of that seller or supplier;

    (b)   inappropriately excluding or limiting the legal rights of the consumer vis-à-vis the seller or supplier or another party in the event of total or partial non-performance or inadequate performance by the seller or supplier of any of the contractual obligations, including the option of offsetting a debt owed to the seller or supplier against any claim which the consumer may have against him;

    (c)   making an agreement binding on the consumer whereas provision of services by the seller or supplier is subject to a condition whose realisation depends on his own will alone;

    (d)   permitting the seller or supplier to retain sums paid by the consumer where the latter decides not to conclude or perform the contract, without providing for the consumer to receive compensation of an equivalent amount from the seller or supplier where the latter is the party cancelling the contract;

(e) requiring any consumer who fails to fulfil his obligation to pay a disproportionately high sum in compensation;

(f) authorising the seller or supplier to dissolve the contract on a discretionary basis where the same facility is not granted to the consumer, or permitting the seller or supplier to retain the sums paid for services not yet supplied by him where it is the seller or supplier himself who dissolves the contract;

(g) enabling the seller or supplier to terminate a contract of indeterminate duration without reasonable notice except where there are serious grounds for doing so;

(h) automatically extending a contract of fixed duration where the consumer does not indicate otherwise, when the deadline fixed for the consumer to express his desire not to extend the contract is unreasonably early;

(i) irrevocably binding the consumer to terms with which he had no real opportunity of becoming acquainted before the conclusion of the contract;

(j) enabling the seller or supplier to alter the terms of the contract unilaterally without a valid reason which is specified in the contract;

(k) enabling the seller or supplier to alter unilaterally without a valid reason any characteristics of the product or service to be provided;

(l) providing for the price of goods to be determined at the time of delivery or allowing a seller of goods or supplier of services to increase their price without in both cases giving the consumer the corresponding right to cancel the contract if the final price is too high in relation to the price agreed when the contract was concluded;

(m) giving the seller or supplier the right to determine whether the goods or services supplied are in conformity with the contract, or giving him the exclusive right to interpret any term of the contract;

(n) limiting the seller's or supplier's obligation to respect commitments undertaken by his agents or making his commitments subject to compliance with a particular formality;

(o) obliging the consumer to fulfil all his obligations where the seller or supplier does not perform his;

(p) giving the seller or supplier the possibility of transferring his rights and obligations under the contract, where this may serve to reduce the guarantees for the consumer, without the latter's agreement;

(q) excluding or hindering the consumer's right to take legal action or exercise any other legal remedy, particularly by requiring the consumer to take disputes exclusively to arbitration not covered by legal provisions, unduly restricting the evidence available to him or imposing on him a burden of proof which, according to the applicable law, should lie with another party to the contract.

2   Scope of paragraphs 1(g), (j) and (l)

(a) Paragraph 1(g) is without hindrance to terms by which a supplier of financial services reserves the right to terminate unilaterally a contract of indeterminate duration without notice where there is a valid reason, provided that the supplier is required to inform the other contracting party or parties thereof immediately.

(b) Paragraph 1(j) is without hindrance to terms under which a supplier of financial services reserves the right to alter the rate of interest payable by the consumer or due to the latter, or the amount of other charges for financial services without notice where there is a valid reason, provided that the supplier is required to inform the other contracting party or parties thereof at the earliest opportunity and that the latter are free to dissolve the contract immediately.

Paragraph 1(j) is also without hindrance to terms under which a seller or supplier reserves the right to alter unilaterally the conditions of a contract of indeterminate duration, provided that he is required to inform the consumer with reasonable notice and that the consumer is free to dissolve the contract.

(c) Paragraphs 1(g), (j) and (l) do not apply to:

– transactions in transferable securities, financial instruments and other products or services where the price is linked to fluctuations in a stock exchange quotation or index or a financial market rate that the seller or supplier does not control;

– contracts for the purchase or sale of foreign currency, traveller's cheques or international money orders denominated in foreign currency.

(d) Paragraph 1(l) is without hindrance to price indexation clauses, where lawful, provided that the method by which prices vary is explicitly described.

A8 MORTGAGE REPOSSESSIONS (PROTECTION OF TENANTS ETC) ACT 2010

An Act to protect persons whose tenancies are not binding on mortgagees and to require mortgagees to give notice of the proposed execution of possession orders.

8th April 2010

BE IT ENACTED by the Queen's most Excellent Majesty, by and with the advice and consent of the Lords Spiritual and Temporal, and Commons, in this present Parliament assembled, and by the authority of the same, as follows: –

1 Power of court to postpone giving of possession

(1) This section applies if –

(a) the mortgagee under a mortgage of land which consists of or includes a dwelling-house brings an action (other than an action for foreclosure) in which the mortgagee claims possession of the mortgaged property, and

(b) there is an unauthorised tenancy of all or part of the property.

(2) When making an order for delivery of possession of the property, the court may, on the application of the tenant, postpone the date for delivery of possession for a period not exceeding two months.

(3) Subsection (4) applies where an order for delivery of possession of the property has been made but not executed.

(4) The court may, on the application of the tenant ('the applicant'), stay or suspend execution of the order for a period not exceeding two months if –

(a) the court did not exercise its powers under subsection (2) when making the order or, if it did, the applicant was not the tenant when it exercised those powers,

(b) the applicant has asked the mortgagee to give an undertaking in writing not to enforce the order for two months beginning with the date the undertaking is given, and

(c) the mortgagee has not given such an undertaking.

(5) When considering whether to exercise its powers under this section, the court must have regard to –

(a) the circumstances of the tenant, and

    (b)   if there is an outstanding breach by the tenant of a term of the unauthorised tenancy –

        (i)   the nature of that breach, and

        (ii)   whether the tenant might reasonably be expected to have avoided breaching that term or to have remedied the breach.

(6)   The court may make any postponement, stay or suspension under this section conditional on the making of payments to the mortgagee in respect of the occupation of the property (or part of the property) during the period of the postponement, stay or suspension.

(7)   The making of any payment pursuant to –

    (a)   a condition of an undertaking of a kind mentioned in subsection (4)(c), or

    (b)   a condition imposed by virtue of subsection (6),

is not to be regarded as creating (or as evidence of the creation of) any tenancy or other right to occupy the property.

(8)   For the purposes of this section there is an 'unauthorised tenancy' if –

    (a)   an agreement has been made which, as between the parties to it (or their successors in title), is or gives rise to –

        (i)   an assured tenancy (within the meaning of the Housing Act 1988), or

        (ii)   a protected or statutory tenancy (within the meaning of the Rent Act 1977), and

    (b)   the mortgagee's interest in the property is not subject to the tenancy.

(9)   In this section 'the tenant', in relation to an unauthorised tenancy, means the person who is, as between the parties to the agreement in question (or their successors in title), the tenant under the unauthorised tenancy (or, if there is more than one tenant, any of them).

2   Notice of execution of possession order

(1)   This section applies where the mortgagee under a mortgage of land which consists of or includes a dwelling-house has obtained an order for possession of the mortgaged property.

(2)   The order may be executed –

    (a)   only if the mortgagee gives notice at the property of any prescribed step taken for the purpose of executing the order, and

    (b)   only after the end of a prescribed period beginning with the day on which such notice is given.

(3)   'Prescribed' means prescribed by regulations made by the Secretary of State.

(4)   Regulations made by the Secretary of State may prescribe the form of notices and the way in which they must be given.

(5)   The regulations may make supplementary, incidental, transitional or saving provision.

(6)   Regulations under this section may be made only with the consent of the Lord Chancellor.

(7)   Regulations under this section are to be made by statutory instrument.

(8)   A statutory instrument containing regulations made under this section is subject to annulment in pursuance of a resolution of either House of Parliament.

3   Interpretation

(1)   This section applies for the purposes of this Act.

(2) 'Dwelling-house' includes any building, or part of a building, that is used as a dwelling.

(3) The fact that part of the premises comprised in a dwelling-house is used as a shop or office, or for other business, trade or professional purposes, does not prevent the dwelling-house from being a dwelling-house for the purposes of this Act.

(4) 'Mortgage' includes a charge, and 'mortgagee' is to be read accordingly.

(5) 'Mortgagee' includes any person deriving title under the original mortgagee.

(6) 'Order' includes a judgment, and references to the making of an order are to be read accordingly.

4 Commencement, extent and short title

(1) This Act (except this section) comes into force on such day as the Secretary of State may by order made by statutory instrument appoint (and different days may be appointed for different purposes).

(2) An order under subsection (1) may make transitional or saving provision.

(3) This Act extends to England and Wales only.

(4) This Act may be cited as the Mortgage Repossessions (Protection of Tenants etc) Act 2010.

A9 DWELLING HOUSES (EXECUTION OF POSSESSION ORDERS BY MORTGAGEES) REGULATIONS 2010

Made 13th July 2010
Laid before Parliament 19th July 2010
Coming into force 1st October 2010

The Secretary of State makes the following Regulations in exercise of the powers conferred by section 2(2) to (5) of the Mortgage Repossessions (Protection of Tenants etc) Act 2010 ('the Act').
    The Lord Chancellor has consented to the making of these Regulations.

1 Citation and commencement

These Regulations may be cited as the Dwelling Houses (Execution of Possession Orders by Mortgagees) Regulations 2010 and come into force on 1st October 2010.

2 Notice of execution of possession order: prescribed step and prescribed period

The prescribed step referred to in section 2(2)(a) of the Act is the mortgagee making an application to the court for a warrant for possession of the property.

3 Notice of execution of possession order: prescribed step and prescribed period

The prescribed period referred to in section 2(2)(b) of the Act is fourteen days.

4 Prescribed form of notice of execution of possession order

The mortgagee's notice of execution of the possession order must be in the form set out in the Schedule to these Regulations.

5 Manner of giving notice

(1) The mortgagee's notice under regulation 4 may be given in any of the following ways –

255

(a)   by sending the notice to the property by first class post or registered post in an envelope addressed –

   (i)   to the tenant by name, or
   (ii) if the tenant's name is not known, to 'The Tenant or Occupier';

(b)   by leaving the notice at the property –

   (i)   in an envelope addressed as described in subparagraph (a), or
   (ii) affixed to and displayed in a prominent place where its contents can be read by a person entering the property; or

(c)   by personal service upon a person who appears to be in residence at the property.

Signed by authority of the Secretary of State for Communities and Local Government
Grant Shapps
Minister of State
Department for Communities and Local Government
12th July 2010

The Lord Chancellor consents to the making of these Regulations.
Jonathan Djanogly
Parliamentary Under Secretary of State
Ministry of Justice
13th July 2010

SCHEDULE

Regulation 4

Notice that your home is at risk

If you are paying rent to live in this property, please read the following carefully.

If you are an owner occupier, please seek advice on your
position as different rules apply

This notice is given under Section 2(4) of the Mortgage Repossessions (Protection of Tenants etc) Act 2010.

I give you notice that the Lender/the Lender's Agent has applied/will apply (delete as appropriate) to the court for a warrant for possession against this property on:
....

(Insert the date on which the application for the warrant for possession was made or will be made. The order will only be executed after the end of the 14 day prescribed period.)

At: ....
Tel: ....
Address: ....
....

(Insert the name, address and telephone number of the court at which the application has been or will be made.)

1.   This notice advises you that you could be evicted from your home. For tenants, be advised that your landlord's Lender has obtained an order for possession against the property. It is now seeking to enforce that order through the courts. Please read this notice carefully. If you need advice you should contact any of the following:

- a Citizens' Advice Bureau;
- a housing advice organisation, or charity such as Shelter;
- a housing aid centre;
- a Law Centre;
- a solicitor.

2. The law gives certain tenants the right to apply to the Lender to ask it not to enforce the order for a period of two months. You should contact the Lender or its Agent on the number given to ask for this delay if you require it. This is to give you time to find somewhere else to live. If you are unsure whether you may qualify, you should seek advice immediately from one of the organisations listed, or a similar organisation. If the Lender agrees to your request, they must confirm this to you in writing. If the Lender refuses your request, or if you receive no reply, you may be able to make an application to court for a similar delay. The Lender may make any agreement with you conditional on you continuing to pay to live at the property. An application to the Lender or to the court should be accompanied by any evidence you have to prove the existence of your tenancy.

3. This notice is not directed at owner occupiers. If you pay a mortgage to live at the property, you should urgently seek advice on your position as you have different rights.

4. If you do not ask for a delay, the Lender can go ahead to obtain possession of this property. Although the warrant for possession cannot be executed earlier than 14 days after the date on which the Lender sent you this notice **you must act quickly if you are seeking the delay, otherwise you may run out of time**.

Served on: ....

(Insert address of the property. Address to: 'Tenant/Occupier' or name of tenant(s) if known).

Served by: ....

('the Lender')

Tel: ....

Address: ....

....

....

(Insert full name of Lender, telephone number and address where enquiries about this notice can be made.)

If served by Lender's Agent:

Served on: ....

(Insert address of the property. Address to: 'Tenant/Occupier' or name of tenant(s) if known).

Served by: ....

('the Lender's Agent')

On behalf of: ....

('the Lender')

Tel: ....

Address: ....

....

....

(Insert full name of Lender's Agent, telephone number and address where enquiries about this notice can be made.)

Signed .... Date ....

To be signed and dated by the Lender or the Lender's Agent

257

APPENDIX B

Court forms

B1   FORM N123: MORTGAGE PRE-ACTION PROTOCOL CHECKLIST

Mortgage pre-action protocol checklist	Name of court		Claim no.
	Name of claimant		
	Name of defendant		
	Mortgage account number		

You must produce two copies of the Checklist on the day of the hearing.

Checklist

1. Is the possession claim within the scope of the Protocol? ☐ Yes ☐ No

2. Have you provided the defendant with the information/notice in the Protocol —

    (a) paragraph 5.1(1) ☐ Yes ☐ No If Yes, date provided: ☐☐/☐☐/☐☐☐☐

    (b) paragraph 5.1(2) ☐ Yes ☐ No If Yes, date provided: ☐☐/☐☐/☐☐☐☐

    (c) paragraph 5.7 ☐ Yes ☐ No If Yes, date of notice: ☐☐/☐☐/☐☐☐☐

3. Do you have evidence that the defendant has made a claim for —

    • Support for Mortgage Interest (SMI) ☐ Yes ☐ No

    • Mortgage Rescue Scheme (MRS), or ☐ Yes ☐ No

    • mortgage payment protection. ☐ Yes ☐ No

    If Yes, please explain why possession proceedings are continuing.

4. Is there an unresolved complaint by the defendant to the Financial Ombudsman Service that could justify postponing the possession claim? ☐ Yes ☐ No

    If Yes, please explain why possession proceedings are continuing.

5. Summarise the number and dates, in the three months prior to the date of this checklist, you attempted to discuss with the defendant ways of repaying the arrears.

N123 Pre-action protocol for possession claims based on mortgage or home purchase plan arrears in respect of residential property (04.10)   © Crown copyright 2010

6. In the three months prior to the date of this checklist have you rejected any proposals by the defendant to change the date or method of regular payments? ☐ Yes ☐ No

   If Yes, did you respond in accordance with paragraph 5.4 of the Protocol? ☐ Yes ☐ No

   If No, please explain why.

7. Have you rejected a proposal for repayment by the defendant in the three months prior to the date of this checklist? ☐ Yes ☐ No

   If Yes, have you responded in accordance with paragraph 5.5 of the Protocol? ☐ Yes ☐ No

   If No, please explain why.

8. Has the defendant indicated that the property will be or is being sold? ☐ Yes ☐ No

   If Yes, explain why possession proceedings are proceeding.

Statement of Truth

*I believe that the facts stated in this Checklist are true.

*I am duly authorised by the claimant to sign this statement.

Signed	Date
Full name	
Name of claimant's solicitor's firm	
Position or office held	

*Delete as appropriate

Guidance for the mortgage pre-action protocol checklist

The Checklist

This guidance is provided for those using the new Mortgage Pre-Action Protocol Checklist. Use of the Checklist came into effect on 1 October 2009 for all claims issued on or after that date in order to provide a uniform format for the provision of information to demonstrate compliance with the Protocol.

This guide must be read with the Mortgage Pre-Action Protocol, the Civil Procedure Rules and Practice Direction 55.

The Checklist (form N123), must be completed by all claimants (lenders) or their representatives making a possession claim. The claimant or their representative should be able to explain to the court the actions taken or not by the claimant, and the reason for issuing a possession claim.

Once the claimant and defendant (borrower) have been notified by the court of the date of the hearing, a Checklist must be completed indicating the action taken by the claimant within the previous three months to reach an agreement with the defendant, and comply with the Protocol.

The claimant must present two copies of the Checklist on the day of the hearing. No additional documents are necessary unless an issue arises.

Claimants can copy this form onto their systems but the form must not go beyond two sides.

Scope

The following mortgages fall within the scope of the Protocol and Checklist –

(i)   first charge residential mortgages and home purchase plans regulated by the Financial Services Authority under the Financial Services and Markets Act 2000;
(ii)   second charge mortgages over residential property and other secured loans regulated under the Consumer Credit Act 1974 on residential property; and
(iii)   unregulated residential mortgages.

Where a potential claim includes a money claim and a claim for possession, these are also within scope.

Q1 – requires confirmation of the type of mortgage and whether it is within scope of the Protocol as indicated above. If the answer is No, there is no need to compete the rest of the form. However, you must be prepared to explain to the court why you consider that the mortgage does not fall within the scope of the Protocol.

If the answer to Q1 is Yes, all the remaining questions must be answered in full.

Q2 – answer the questions Yes or No, as appropriate, and insert the dates where relevant. Where you have not complied with one or more of these requirements, you must be prepared to explain to the court in full why that is the case.

Q3 – answer the questions Yes or No, as appropriate. Where a claim, either for Support for Mortgage Interest (SMI), Mortgage Rescue Scheme (MRS) or under a mortgage payment protection policy, has been made, you must set out clearly and succinctly why you are proceeding with a claim for possession.

Q4 – answer the question Yes or No, as appropriate. If the defendant has an unresolved complaint you must set out clearly and succinctly why you are proceeding with a claim for possession.

Q5 – you should provide here a list of dates and details of the associated media (for example, letter, telephone, etc). Where use has been made of automated diallers, which do not necessarily keep an individual record of each attempted call, you should confirm the number of attempts and frequency that your system is programmed to make.

Q6 – answer the question Yes or No, as appropriate. Where you have answered:

- No, then no further information is required.
- Yes, you must also confirm whether or not you have complied with the requirements of paragraph 5.4 of the Protocol when notifying the defendant of your decision. If the answer to that question is:

    –   Yes – then no further information is required on the Checklist but you must be prepared to explain to the court what action you took if requested to do so.

– No – you should set out your reasons for non-compliance clearly and succinctly.

Q7 – answer the question Yes or No, as appropriate. Where you have answered:

- No, then no further information is required.
- Yes, you must also confirm whether or not you have complied with the requirements of paragraph 5.5 of the protocol when notifying the defendant of your decision. If the answer to that question is:
    - – Yes – then no further information is required on the Checklist but you must be prepared to explain to the court what action you took if requested to do so.
    - – No – you should set out your reasons for non-compliance clearly and succinctly.

Q8 – answer the question Yes or No, as appropriate. Where the defendant is trying to sell their property you need to explain clearly and succinctly why you are bringing proceedings including, specifically, whether or not the defendant has complied with the requirements of paragraphs 6.2 and 6.3 of the Protocol.

The statement of truth

The statement of truth must be signed and completed by the claimant or representative. This section must be completed in order to validate the information provided.

Service of the Checklist

Two copies of the Checklist must be brought to the hearing.

B2 FORM N5: CLAIM FORM FOR POSSESSION OF PROPERTY

Claim form for possession of property	In the	
	Claim No.	

Claimant
(name(s) and address(es))

SEAL

Defendant(s)
(name(s) and address(es))

The claimant is claiming possession of :

which (includes) (does not include) residential property. Full particulars of the claim are attached.
(The claimant is also making a claim for money).

This claim will be heard on: 20   at   am/pm

at

At the hearing
• The court will consider whether or not you must leave the property and, if so, when.
• It will take into account information the claimant provides and any you provide.

What you should do
• Get help and advice immediately from a solicitor or an advice agency.
• Help yourself and the court by **filling in the defence form** and **coming to the hearing** to make sure the court
  knows all the facts.

Defendant's name and address for service			
		Court fee	£
		Solicitor's costs	£
		Total amount	£
		Issue date	

N5 Claim form for possession of property (08.05)   HMCS

262

Claim No.	

Grounds for possession

The claim for possession is made on the following ground(s):

☐ rent arrears

☐ other breach of tenancy

☐ forfeiture of the lease

☐ mortgage arrears

☐ other breach of the mortgage

☐ trespass

☐ other *(please specify)* _____

Anti-social behaviour

The claimant is alleging:

☐ actual or threatened anti-social behaviour

☐ actual or threatened use of the property for unlawful purposes

Is the claimant claiming demotion of tenancy?   ☐ Yes   ☐ No

Is the claimant claiming an order suspending the right to buy?   ☐ Yes   ☐ No

See full details in the attached particulars of claim

Does, or will, the claim include any issues under the Human Rights Act 1998?   ☐ Yes   ☐ No

---

Statement of Truth

*(I believe)(The claimant believes) that the facts stated in this claim form are true.
* I am duly authorised by the claimant to sign this statement.

signed _____ date _____

*(Claimant)(Litigation friend *(where the claimant is a child or a patient)*)(Claimant's solicitor)
*delete as appropriate

Full name _____

Name of claimant's solicitor's firm _____

position or office held _____
        (if signing on behalf of firm or company)

Claimant's or claimant's solicitor's address to which documents or payments should be sent if different from overleaf.

	if applicable
Ref. no.	
fax no.	
DX no.	
e-mail	
Tel. no.	

Postcode

263

B3 FORM N120: PARTICULARS OF CLAIM FOR POSSESSION (MORTGAGED RESIDENTIAL PREMISES)

Particulars of claim for possession

(mortgaged residential premises)

In the

Claim No.

Claimant

Defendant

1. The claimant has a right to possession of:

About the mortgage

2. On   the claimant(s) and the defendant(s) entered into a mortgage of the above premises.

3. To the best of the claimant's knowledge the following persons are in possession of the property:

[Delete (a) or (b) as appropriate]

4   (a) The agreement for the loan secured by the mortgage (or at least one of them) is a regulated consumer credit agreement. Notice of default was given to the defendant(s) on   20 .

     (b) The agreement for the loan secured by the mortgage is not (or none of them is) a regulated consumer credit agreement.

5. The claimant is asking for possession on the following ground(s):

    (a) the defendant(s) (has)(have) not paid the agreed repayments of the loan and interest.
    Give details (as required under paragraph 2.5 of Practice Direction accompanying Part 55 of the Civil Procedure Rules):

N120 Particulars of claim for possession (mortgaged residential premises)(10.05)   HMCS

(b) because:

6. (a) The amount loaned was £

    (b) The current terms of repayment are: *(include any current periodic repayment and any current payment of interest)*

    (c) The total amount required to pay the mortgage in full as at   20   (not more than 14
    days after the claim was issued) would be £   taking into account any adjustment for
    early settlement. This includes £   payable for solicitor's costs and administration charges.

    (d) The following additional payments are also required under the terms of the mortgage:

    £   for   [not] included in 6(c)

    £   for   [not] included in 6(c)

    £   for   [not] included in 6(c)

    (e) Of the payments in paragraph 6(d), the following are in arrears:

    arrears of £

    arrears of £

    arrears of £

    [(f) The total amount outstanding under the regulated loan agreement secured by the mortgage is £   ]

    (g) Interest rates which have been applied to the mortgage:

    (i) at the start of the mortgage   % p.a.

    (ii) immediately before any arrears were accrued   % p.a.

    (iii) at the start of the claim   % p.a.

7. The following steps have already been taken to recover the money secured by the mortgage:

About the defendant(s)

8. The following information is known about the defendant's circumstances:
   (*in particular say whether the defendant(s) (is)(are) in receipt of social security benefits and whether any payments are made directly to the claimant*)

[Delete either (a) or (b) as appropriate]

9. (a) There is no one who should be given notice of these proceedings because of a registered interest in the property under section 31(10) of the Family Law Act 1996 or section 2(8) or 8(3) of the Matrimonial Homes Act 1983 or section 2(7) of the Matrimonial Homes Act 1967.

   (b) Notice of these proceedings will be given to   who has a registered interest in the property.

Tenancy

[Delete if inappropriate]

10. A tenancy was entered into between the mortgagor and the mortgagee on   .
    A notice was served on   .

What the court is being asked to do

11.   The claimant asks the court to order that the defendant(s):

(a) give the claimant possession of the premises;

(b) pay to the claimant the total amount outstanding under the mortgage.

Statement of Truth

*(I believe)(The claimant believes) that the facts stated in these particulars of claim are true.
* I am duly authorised by the claimant to sign this statement.

signed _____   date _____

*(Claimant)(Litigation friend *(where claimant is a child or a patient)*)(Claimant's solicitor)
delete as appropriate

Full name _____

Name of claimant's solicitor's firm _____

position or office held _____
                           (if signing on behalf of firm or company)

B4 FORM N7: NOTES FOR DEFENDANT (MORTGAGED RESIDENTIAL PREMISES)

The claimant has asked the court to make an order that you give up possession of the premises mentioned in the claim form. You should note that no-one can evict you from the property unless the court says that they can; the court will not make a decision before the hearing date. What you do may affect the court's decision. You should therefore take action immediately. These notes explain in more detail what you can do.

You should:

- get help and advice immediately from a solicitor or advice agency (see 'Getting help' below);
- fill in the attached defence form and return it to the court within 14 days of receiving the claim form;
- attend the hearing, even if you have agreed about repayment of any arrears with your mortgage lender.

What will happen at the hearing?

A judge will decide whether or not to make an order for possession. In making this decision, the judge will take account of the information provided by the claimant. The judge will also take account of any information you provide, such as details of your personal and financial circumstances, any proposal you have made to pay off any arrears, and any dispute you have about the amount owing. But the judge can only take the information into account if you provide it. Fill in these details on the defence form and attend the hearing. It is in your best interests to do both.

What kind of orders can the judge make?

The judge can:

- decide not to make an order
- make an order for possession but suspend it. This means that you will not have to give up possession so long as you can pay off any arrears in a reasonable time (the judge will decide how long) and pay the instalments as well;
- make a possession order for some future date to allow you time to move out or find somewhere else to live; or
- make an order that you give up possession a very short time ahead.
- if the loan agreement is 'regulated' (see paragraph 4 of the particulars of claim) the judge can make other orders which may help you.

Getting help

You should get help and advice immediately from a solicitor or an advice agency. This is particularly important whether or not you disagree with the claim. You may qualify for assistance from the Community Legal Service Fund (CLSF) to meet some or all of your legal costs. Ask about the CLSF at any county court office or any information or help point which displays this logo. Court staff can only help you complete the defence form and tell you about court procedures. **They cannot give legal advice.**

Replying to the claim

Although you should normally fill in the defence form and return it to the court within 14 days, the court will accept your defence at any time before, or even at, the hearing. You should note, however, that if you do return the form after the 14-day period, the court may order you to pay any costs caused by the delay.

Regulated consumer credit agreements

If you intend to apply to the court to consider or change the terms of your agreement, you should get advice immediately.

Paying any arrears

The court cannot accept payments. If you want to pay all or part of any arrears, send them to the claimant at the address for payment shown on the claim form, quoting the claimant's reference number, if one is given. Make sure you get receipts for all payments made. Proof may be required if there is any disagreement. Make sure you include on your defence form details of any payments you have made since the claim was issued, saying how much was paid, to whom and when.

Enforcement of a possession order

Where the court makes a possession order, the claimant can ask a bailiff or enforcement officer to evict you if:

- you do not give up possession on the date given in the order for possession; or
- you do not make payments in accordance with the suspended order for possession.

If your circumstances change after the possession order is made, you may apply to the court for the order to be varied. Use application form N244, which is available from any court office. You may have to pay a fee to make the application.

Registration of judgments

If a county court makes a money judgment (e.g. for the balance due under the mortgage) your name and address will be entered in the Register of Judgments, Orders and Fines if the claimant has to take steps to enforce the judgment. This may make it difficult for you to obtain credit.

B5   FORM N11M: DEFENCE FORM (MORTGAGED RESIDENTIAL PREMISES)

Defence form
(mortgaged residential premises)

Name of court	Claim No.
Name of Claimant	
Name of Defendant	
Date of hearing	

Personal details

1. Please give your:

   Title   ☐ Mr ☐ Mrs ☐ Miss ☐ Ms ☐ Other

   First name(s) in full

   Last name

   Date of birth   [D][D][M][M][Y][Y][Y][Y]

   Address *(if different from the address on the claim form)*

   Postcode

Disputing the claim

2. Do you agree with what is said about the property and the mortgage agreement in the particulars of claim?   ☐ Yes   ☐ No

   If No, set out your reasons below:

3. Do you agree that there are arrears of mortgage repayments as stated in the particulars of claim?   ☑ Yes   ☐ No

   If No, state how much the arrears are: £_____   ☐ None

N11M Defence form (mortgaged residential premises) (04.06)   HMCS

4. If the particulars of claim give any reasons for possession other than arrears of mortgage repayments, do you agree with what is said?   ☐ Yes   ☐ No

If No, give details below:

(Only answer these questions if the loan secured by the mortgage (or part of it) is a regulated consumer credit agreement)

5. Do you want the court to consider whether or not the terms of your original loan agreement are fair?   ☐ Yes   ☐ No

6. Do you intend to apply to the court for an order changing the terms of your loan agreement (a time order)?   ☐ Yes   ☐ No

Arrears

7. Have you paid any money to your mortgage lender since the claim was issued?   ☐ Yes   ☐ No

If Yes, state how much you have paid and when: £_____   date_____

8. Have you come to any agreement with your mortgage lender about repaying the arrears since the claim was issued?   ☐ Yes   ☐ No

I have agreed to pay £_____ each (week)(month).

9. If you have not reached an agreement with your mortgage lender, do you want the court to consider allowing you to pay the arrears by instalments?   ☐ Yes   ☐ No

10. How much can you afford to pay in addition to the current instalments?   £_____   per (week)(month)

About yourself

State benefits

11. Are you receiving Income Support? ☐ Yes ☐ No

12. Have you applied for Income Support? ☐ Yes ☐ No

   If Yes, when did you apply? _____

13. Does the Department of Social Security pay your mortgage interest? ☐ Yes ☐ No

Dependants (people you look after financially)

14. Have you any dependant children? ☐ Yes ☐ No

   If Yes, give the number in each age group below:

   ☐ under 11   ☐ 11-15   ☐ 16-17   ☐ 18 and over

Other dependants

15. Give details of any other dependants for whom you are financially responsible:

Other residents

16. Give details of any other people living at the premises for whom you are not financially responsible:

Money you receive

		Weekly	Monthly
17. Usual take-home pay or income if self-employed *including overtime, commission, bonuses*	£_____	☐	☐
Job Seekers allowance	£_____	☐	☐
Pension	£_____	☐	☐
Child benefit	£_____	☐	☐
Other benefits and allowances	£_____	☐	☐
Others living in my home give me	£_____	☐	☐
I am paid maintenance for myself (or children) of	£_____	☐	☐
Other income	£_____	☐	☐
Total income	**£_____**	☐	☐

Bank accounts and savings

18. Do you have a current bank or building society account? ☐ Yes ☐ No

   If Yes, is it

   ☐ in credit? If so, by how much? £_____

   ☐ overdrawn? If so, by how much? £_____

19. Do you have a savings or deposit account? ☐ Yes ☐ No

   If Yes, what is the balance? £_____

Money you pay out

20. Do you have to pay any court orders or fines? ☐ Yes ☐ No

Court	Claim/Case number	Balance owing	Instalments paid
		Total instalments paid £	per month

21. Give details if you are in arrears with any of the court payments or fines:

22. Do you have any loan or credit debts? ☐ Yes ☐ No

Loan/credit from	Balance owing	Instalments paid
	Total instalments paid £	per month

23. Give details if you are in arrears with any loan / credit repayments:

Regular expenses
(Do not include any payments made by other members of the household out of their own income)

24. What regular expenses do you have?
(List below)

		Weekly	Monthly
Council tax	£_____	☐	☐
Gas	£_____	☐	☐
Electricity	£_____	☐	☐
Water charges	£_____	☐	☐
TV rental & licence	£_____	☐	☐
Telephone	£_____	☐	☐
Credit repayments	£_____	☐	☐
Mail order	£_____	☐	☐
Housekeeping, food, school meals	£_____	☐	☐
Travelling expenses	£_____	☐	☐
Clothing	£_____	☐	☐
Maintenance payments	£_____	☐	☐
Other mortgages	£_____	☐	☐
Other	£_____	☐	☐
Total expenses	£_____	☐	☐

Priority debts

25. This section is for arrears only. Do not include regular expenses listed at Question 24.

		Weekly	Monthly
Council tax arrears	£_____	☐	☐
Water charges arrears	£_____	☐	☐
Gas account	£_____	☐	☐
Electricity account	£_____	☐	☐
Maintenance arrears	£_____	☐	☐

Others (give details below)

	Weekly	Monthly
£_____	☐	☐
£_____	☐	☐
£_____	☐	☐

26. If an order for possession were to be made, would you have somewhere else to live? ☐ Yes ☐ No

If Yes, say when you would be able to move in: _____

27. Give details of any events or circumstances which have led to your being in arrears with your mortgage (for example divorce, separation, redundancy, bereavement, illness, bankruptcy). If you believe you would suffer exceptional hardship by being ordered to leave the property immediately, say why.

Statement of Truth

*(I believe)(The defendant believes) that the facts stated in this defence form are true.
* I am duly authorised by the defendant to sign this statement.

signed_____ date _____
*(Defendant)(Litigation friend(where defendant is a child or a patient))(Defendant's solicitor)

delete as appropriate

Full name _____

Name of defendant's solicitor's firm _____

position or office held _____
(if signing on behalf of firm or company)

B6 FORM N440: NOTICE OF APPLICATION FOR A TIME ORDER

<table>
<tr><td>IN THE</td><td>COUNTY COURT</td></tr>
<tr><td></td><td>Claim no.</td></tr>
</table>

IN THE MATTER OF AN APPLICATION FOR A TIME ORDER

Between _____ **Applicant**
(Insert your full name in block capitals)

and _____ **Respondent**
(insert the full name in block capitals of the company to whom you make your payments)

1. I *(Name)*
_____

of *(Address)*

apply to the court for a time order

2. The following are the details of the regulated agreement in respect of which I am asking for a
time order.

a. The agreement is dated
_____

and the reference number is
_____

b. The names and addresses of the other parties
to the agreement are:

c. The name and address of the person (if any)
who acted as surety

is _____

of

d. *(Delete if not applicable)* The rights and duties of
the party named _____

at b. above passed to the respondent
on _____ when *(here give the reasons why you
now regard the respondent as your creditor)*

His address is

e. I signed the agreement at *(here give the address of
the shop or other place where you signed the agreement)*

_____

f. I agreed to pay instalments
of £ _____ a week ☐ a month ☐

g. ☐ The unpaid balance due under the
agreement is £ _____

or ☐ I do not know the unpaid balance

h. ☐ I am £ _____ in arrear
with my payments.

or ☐ I do not know how much the arrears
are.

N440 Notice of application for time order by debtor or hirer (4.99)

The Court Service Publications Unit

276

i. On   the Respondent served on
me:

☐   a default notice

☐   a notice given under section 76(1)

☐   a notice given under section 98(1)

or I attach a copy of the notice which the
Respondent served on me on

j. *You should complete this section if you are applying
for time to pay, if not cross it out.*

My proposals for payment are £ _____

to clear the arrears (if any) and then by instalments
of £ _____

k. *You should complete this section if you have failed to comply
with the agreement in any other respect.*

I am in breach of the following provisions of
the agreement:

And my proposals for remedying the breach(es)
are as follows:

_____

**3. I have answered the questions about my
financial circumstances set out in the schedule
to this application.**

_____

4. The names and addresses of the persons to be
served with this application are: *(You must include
any sureties)*

5. My address for service is:

_____

6. Signed _____

(Solicitor for the) Applicant.

Dated

_____

Civil Procedure Rules 1998 and Practice Directions

C1 CIVIL PROCEDURE RULES 1998

55.1 Interpretation

In this Part –

(a) 'a possession claim' means a claim for the recovery of possession of land (including buildings or parts of buildings);

(b) 'a possession claim against trespassers' means a claim for the recovery of land which the claimant alleges is occupied only by a person or persons who entered or remained on the land without the consent of a person entitled to possession of that land but does not include a claim against a tenant or sub-tenant whether his tenancy has been terminated or not;

(c) 'mortgage' includes a legal or equitable mortgage and a legal or equitable charge and 'mortgagee' is to be interpreted accordingly;

(d) 'the 1985 Act' means the Housing Act 1985;

(e) 'the 1988 Act' means the Housing Act 1988;

(f) 'a demotion claim' means a claim made by a landlord for an order under section 82A of the 1985 Act or section 6A of the 1988 Act ('a demotion order');

(g) 'a demoted tenancy' means a tenancy created by virtue of a demotion order; and

(h) 'a suspension claim' means a claim made by a landlord for an order under section 121A of the 1985 Act.

55.2 Scope

(1) The procedure set out in this Section of this Part must be used where the claim includes –

    (a) a possession claim brought by a –

        (i) landlord (or former landlord);

        (ii) mortgagee; or

        (iii) licensor (or former licensor);

    (b) a possession claim against trespassers; or

    (c) a claim by a tenant seeking relief from forfeiture.

(Where a demotion claim or a suspension claim (or both) is made in the same claim form in which a possession claim is started, this Section of this Part applies as modified by rule 65.12. Where the claim is a demotion claim or a suspension claim only, or a suspension claim made in addition to a demotion claim, Section III of Part 65 applies).

(2) This Section of this Part

    (a) is subject to any enactment or practice direction which sets out special provisions with regard to any particular category of claim;

(b)   does not apply where the claimant uses the procedure set out in Section II of this Part; and

(c)   does not apply where the claimant seeks an interim possession order under Section III of this Part except where the court orders otherwise or that Section so provides.

55.3   Starting the claim

(1)   The claim must be started in the county court for the district in which the land is situated unless paragraph (2) applies or an enactment provides otherwise.

(2)   The claim may be started in the High Court if the claimant files with his claim form a certificate stating the reasons for bringing the claim in that court verified by a statement of truth in accordance with rule 22.1(1).

(3)   Practice Direction 55A refers to circumstances which may justify starting the claim in the High Court.

(4)   Where, in a possession claim against trespassers, the claimant does not know the name of a person in occupation or possession of the land, the claim must be brought against 'persons unknown' in addition to any named defendants.

(5)   The claim form and form of defence sent with it must be in the forms set out in Practice Direction 55A.

55.4   Particulars of claim

The particulars of claim must be filed and served with the claim form.

(Part 16 and Practice Direction 55A provide details about the contents of the particulars of claim)

55.5   Hearing date

(1)   The court will fix a date for the hearing when it issues the claim form.

(2)   In a possession claim against trespassers the defendant must be served with the claim form, particulars of claim and any witness statements –

(a)   in the case of residential property, not less than 5 days; and

(b)   in the case of other land, not less than 2 days,

before the hearing date.

(3)   In all other possession claims –

(a)   the hearing date will be not less than 28 days from the date of issue of the claim form;

(b)   the standard period between the issue of the claim form and the hearing will be not more than 8 weeks; and

(c)   the defendant must be served with the claim form and particulars of claim not less than 21 days before the hearing date.

(Rule 3.1(2)(a) provides that the court may extend or shorten the time for compliance with any rule)

55.7   Defendant's response

(1)   An acknowledgment of service is not required and Part 10 does not apply.

(2)   In a possession claim against trespassers rule 15.2 does not apply and the defendant need not file a defence.

(3)   Where, in any other possession claim, the defendant does not file a defence within the

time specified in rule 15.4, he may take part in any hearing but the court may take his failure to do so into account when deciding what order to make about costs.

(4) Part 12 (default judgment) does not apply in a claim to which this Part applies.

55.8 The hearing

(1) At the hearing fixed in accordance with rule 55.5(1) or at any adjournment of that hearing, the court may –

    (a) decide the claim; or

    (b) give case management directions.

(2) Where the claim is genuinely disputed on grounds which appear to be substantial, case management directions given under paragraph (1)(b) will include the allocation of the claim to a track or directions to enable it to be allocated.

(3) Except where –

    (a) the claim is allocated to the fast track or the multi-track; or

    (b) the court orders otherwise,

any fact that needs to be proved by the evidence of witnesses at a hearing referred to in paragraph (1) may be proved by evidence in writing.

(Rule 32.2(1) sets out the general rule about evidence. Rule 32.2(2) provides that rule 32.2(1) is subject to any provision to the contrary)

(4) Subject to paragraph (5), all witness statements must be filed and served at least 2 days before the hearing.

(5) In a possession claim against trespassers all witness statements on which the claimant intends to rely must be filed and served with the claim form.

(6) Where the claimant serves the claim form and particulars of claim, the claimant must produce at the hearing a certificate of service of those documents and rule 6.17(2)(a) does not apply.

55.9 Allocation

(1) When the court decides the track for a possession claim, the matters to which it shall have regard include –

    (a) the matters set out in rule 26.8 as modified by the relevant practice direction;

    (b) the amount of any arrears of rent or mortgage instalments;

    (c) the importance to the defendant of retaining possession of the land;

    (d) the importance of vacant possession to the claimant; and

    (e) if applicable, the alleged conduct of the defendant

(2) The court will only allocate possession claims to the small claims track if all the parties agree.

(3) Where a possession claim has been allocated to the small claims track the claim shall be treated, for the purposes of costs, as if it were proceeding on the fast track except that trial costs shall be in the discretion of the court and shall not exceed the amount that would be recoverable under rule 46.2 (amount of fast track costs) if the value of the claim were up to £3,000.

(4) Where all the parties agree the court may, when it allocates the claim, order that rule 27.14 (costs on the small claims track) applies and, where it does so, paragraph (3) does not apply.

55.10 Possession claims relating to mortgaged residential property

(1) This rule applies where a mortgagee seeks possession of land which consists of or includes residential property.

(2) Within 5 days of receiving notification of the date of the hearing by the court, the claimant must send a notice to –

    (a) the property, addressed to 'the tenant or the occupier';

    (b) the housing department of the local authority within which the property is located; and

    (c) any registered proprietor (other than the claimant) of a registered charge over the property.

(3) The notice referred to in paragraph (2)(a) must –

    (a) state that a possession claim for the property has started;

    (b) show the name and address of the claimant, the defendant and the court which issued the claim form; and

    (c) give details of the hearing.

(3A) The notice referred to in paragraph 2(b) must contain the information in paragraph (3) and must state the full address of the property.

(4) The claimant must produce at the hearing –

    (a) a copy of the notices; and

    (b) evidence that they have been sent.

(4A) An unauthorised tenant of residential property may apply to the court for the order for possession to be suspended.

55.10A Electronic issue of certain possession claims

(1) A practice direction may make provision for a claimant to start certain types of possession claim in certain courts by requesting the issue of a claim form electronically.

(2) The practice direction may, in particular –

    (a) provide that only particular provisions apply in specific courts;

    (b) specify –

        (i) the type of possession claim which may be issued electronically;

        (ii) the conditions that a claim must meet before it may be issued electronically;

    (c) specify the court where the claim may be issued;

    (d) enable the parties to make certain applications or take further steps in relation to the claim electronically;

    (e) specify the requirements that must be fulfilled in relation to such applications or steps;

    (f) enable the parties to correspond electronically with the court about the claim;

    (g) specify the requirements that must be fulfilled in relation to electronic correspondence;

    (h) provide how any fee payable on the filing of any document is to be paid where the document is filed electronically.

(3) The Practice Direction may disapply or modify these Rules as appropriate in relation to possession claims started electronically.

C2   PRACTICE DIRECTION 55A – POSSESSION CLAIMS

This Practice Direction supplements Part 55

Section I – General rules

55.3 – Starting the claim

1.1   Except where the county court does not have jurisdiction, possession claims should normally be brought in the county court. Only exceptional circumstances justify starting a claim in the High Court.

1.2   If a claimant starts a claim in the High Court and the court decides that it should have been started in the county court, the court will normally either strike the claim out or transfer it to the county court on its own initiative. This is likely to result in delay and the court will normally disallow the costs of starting the claim in the High Court and of any transfer.

1.3   Circumstances which may, in an appropriate case, justify starting a claim in the High Court are if –

(1)   there are complicated disputes of fact;

(2)   there are points of law of general importance; or

(3)   the claim is against trespassers and there is a substantial risk of public disturbance or of serious harm to persons or property which properly require immediate determination.

1.4   The value of the property and the amount of any financial claim may be relevant circumstances, but these factors alone will not normally justify starting the claim in the High Court.

1.5   The claimant must use the appropriate claim form and particulars of claim form set out in Table 1 to Practice Direction 4. The defence must be in form N11, N11B, N11M or N11R, as appropriate.

1.6   High Court claims for the possession of land subject to a mortgage will be assigned to the Chancery Division.

1.7   A claim which is not a possession claim may be brought under the procedure set out in Section I of Part 55 if it is started in the same claim form as a possession claim which, by virtue of rule 55.2(1) must be brought in accordance with that Section.

(Rule 7.3 provides that a claimant may use a single claim form to start all claims which can be conveniently disposed of in the same proceedings)

1.8   For example a claim under paragraphs 4, 5 or 6 of Part I of Schedule 1 to the Mobile Homes Act 1983 may be brought using the procedure set out in Section I of Part 55 if the claim is started in the same claim form as a claim enforcing the rights referred to in section 3(1)(b) of the Caravan Sites Act 1968 (which, by virtue of rule 55.2(1) must be brought under Section I of Part 55).

1.9   Where the claim form includes a demotion claim, the claim must be started in the county court for the district in which the land is situated.

55.4 – Particulars of claim

2.1   In a possession claim the particulars of claim must:

(1)   identify the land to which the claim relates;

(2)   state whether the claim relates to residential property;

   (3)   state the ground on which possession is claimed;

   (4)   give full details about any mortgage or tenancy agreement; and

   (5)   give details of every person who, to the best of the claimant's knowledge, is in possession of the property.

Land subject to a mortgage

2.5   If the claim is a possession claim by a mortgagee, the particulars of claim must also set out:

   (1)   if the claim relates to residential property whether:

        (a)   a land charge of Class F has been registered under section 2(7) of the Matrimonial Homes Act 1967;

        (b)   a notice registered under section 2(8) or 8(3) of the Matrimonial Homes Act 1983 has been entered and on whose behalf; or

        (c)   a notice under section 31(10) of the Family Law Act 1996 has been registered and on whose behalf; and

   if so, that the claimant will serve notice of the claim on the persons on whose behalf the land charge is registered or the notice or caution entered.

   (2)   the state of the mortgage account by including:

        (a)   the amount of:

            (i)   the advance;

            (ii)   any periodic repayment; and

            (iii)   any payment of interest required to be made;

        (b)   the amount which would have to be paid (after taking into account any adjustment for early settlement) in order to redeem the mortgage at a stated date not more than 14 days after the claim started specifying the amount of solicitor's costs and administration charges which would be payable;

        (c)   if the loan which is secured by the mortgage is a regulated consumer credit agreement, the total amount outstanding under the terms of the mortgage; and

        (d)   the rate of interest payable:

            (i)   at the commencement of the mortgage;

            (ii)   immediately before any arrears referred to in paragraph (3) accrued;

            (iii)   at the commencement of the proceedings.

   (3)   if the claim is brought because of failure to pay the periodic payments when due:

        (a)   in schedule form, the dates and amounts of all payments due and payments made under the mortgage agreement or mortgage deed for a period of two years immediately preceding the date of issue, or if the first date of default occurred less than two years before the date of issue from the first date of default and a running total of the arrears;

        (b)   give details of:

            (i)   any other payments required to be made as a term of the mortgage (such as for insurance premiums, legal costs, default interest, penalties, administrative or other charges);

        (ii)   any other sums claimed and stating the nature and amount of each such charge; and

        (iii)   whether any of these payments is in arrears and whether or not it is included in the amount of any periodic payment.

(4) whether or not the loan which is secured by the mortgage is a regulated consumer credit agreement and, if so, specify the date on which any notice required by sections 76 or 87 of the Consumer Credit Act 1974 was given;

(5) if appropriate details that show the property is not one to which section 141 of the Consumer Credit Act 1974 applies;

(6) any relevant information about the defendant's circumstances, in particular:

        (a)   whether the defendant is in receipt of social security benefits; and

        (b)   whether any payments are made on his behalf directly to the claimant under the Social Security Contributions and Benefits Act 1992;

(7) give details of any tenancy entered into between the mortgagor and mortgagee (including any notices served); and

(8) state any previous steps which the claimant has taken to recover the money secured by the mortgage or the mortgaged property and, in the case of court proceedings, state:

        (a)   the dates when the claim started and concluded; and

        (b)   the dates and terms of any orders made.

2.5A If the claimant wishes to rely on a history of arrears which is longer than two years, he should state this in his particulars and exhibit a full (or longer) schedule to a witness statement.

Possession claim against trespassers

2.6 If the claim is a possession claim against trespassers, the particulars of claim must state the claimant's interest in the land or the basis of his right to claim possession and the circumstances in which it has been occupied without licence or consent.

Possession claim in relation to a demoted tenancy by a housing action trust or a local housing authority

2.7 If the claim is a possession claim under section 143D of the Housing Act 1996 (possession claim in relation to a demoted tenancy where the landlord is a housing action trust or a local housing authority), the particulars of claim must have attached to them a copy of the notice to the tenant served under section 143E of the 1996 Act.

55.5 – Hearing date

3.1 The court may exercise its powers under rules 3.1(2)(a) and (b) to shorten the time periods set out in rules 55.5(2) and (3).

3.2 Particular consideration should be given to the exercise of this power if:

(1) the defendant, or a person for whom the defendant is responsible, has assaulted or threatened to assault:

        (a)   the claimant;

        (b)   a member of the claimant's staff; or

        (c)   another resident in the locality;

(2) there are reasonable grounds for fearing such an assault; or

(3) the defendant, or a person for whom the defendant is responsible, has caused serious damage or threatened to cause serious damage to the property or to the home or property of another resident in the locality.

3.3 Where paragraph 3.2 applies but the case cannot be determined at the first hearing fixed under rule 55.5, the court will consider what steps are needed to finally determine the case as quickly as reasonably practicable.

55.6 – Service in claims against trespassers

4.1 If the claim form is to be served by the court and in accordance with rule 55.6(b) the claimant must provide sufficient stakes and transparent envelopes.

55.8 – The hearing

5.1 Attention is drawn to rule 55.8(3). Each party should wherever possible include all the evidence he wishes to present in his statement of case, verified by a statement of truth.

5.2 If relevant the claimant's evidence should include the amount of any rent or mortgage arrears and interest on those arrears. These amounts should, if possible, be up to date to the date of the hearing (if necessary by specifying a daily rate of arrears and interest). However, rule 55.8(4) does not prevent such evidence being brought up to date orally or in writing on the day of the hearing if necessary.

5.3 If relevant the defendant should give evidence of:

(1) the amount of any outstanding social security or housing benefit payments relevant to rent or mortgage arrears; and

(2) the status of:

(a) any claims for social security or housing benefit about which a decision has not yet been made; and

(b) any applications to appeal or review a social security or housing benefit decision where that appeal or review has not yet concluded.

5.4 If:

(1) the maker of a witness statement does not attend a hearing; and

(2) the other party disputes material evidence contained in his statement,

the court will normally adjourn the hearing so that oral evidence can be given.

5.5 The claimant must bring 2 completed copies of Form N123 to the hearing.

Consumer Credit Act claims relating to the recovery of land

7.1 Any application by the defendant for a time order under section 129 of the Consumer Credit Act 1974 may be made:

(1) in his defence; or

(2) by application notice in the proceedings.

Enforcement of charging order by sale

7.2 A party seeking to enforce a charging order by sale should follow the procedure set out in rule 73.10 and the Part 55 procedure should not be used.

C3 PRACTICE DIRECTION 55B – POSSESSION CLAIMS ONLINE

This Practice Direction supplements CPR rule 55.10A.

Scope of this practice direction

1.1 This practice direction provides for a scheme ('Possession Claims Online') to operate in specified county courts –

(1) enabling claimants and their representatives to start certain possession claims under CPR Part 55 by requesting the issue of a claim form electronically via the PCOL website; and

(2) where a claim has been started electronically, enabling the claimant or defendant and their representatives to take further steps in the claim electronically as specified below.

1.2 In this practice direction –

(1) 'PCOL website' means the website **www.possessionclaim.gov.uk** which may be accessed via Her Majesty's Courts Service website (**www.hmcourts-service.gov. uk**) and through which Possession Claims Online will operate; and

(2) 'specified court' means a county court specified on the PCOL website as one in which Possession Claims Online is available.

Information on the PCOL website

2.1 The PCOL website contains further details and guidance about the operation of Possession Claims Online.

2.2 In particular the PCOL website sets out –

(1) the specified courts; and

(2) the dates from which Possession Claims Online will be available in each specified court.

2.3 The operation of Possession Claims Online in any specified court may be restricted to taking certain of the steps specified in this practice direction, and in such cases the PCOL website will set out the steps which may be taken using Possession Claims Online in that specified court.

Security

3.1 Her Majesty's Courts Service will take such measures as it thinks fit to ensure the security of steps taken or information stored electronically. These may include requiring users of Possession Claims Online –

(1) to enter a customer identification number or password;

(2) to provide personal information for identification purposes; and

(3) to comply with any other security measures,

before taking any step online.

Fees

4.1 A step may only be taken using Possession Claims Online on payment of the prescribed fee where a fee is payable. Where this practice direction provides for a fee to be paid electronically, it may be paid by –

(1) credit card;

(2) debit card; or

(3) any other method which Her Majesty's Courts Service may permit.

4.2   A defendant who wishes to claim exemption from payment of fees must do so through an organisation approved by Her Majesty's Courts Service before taking any step using PCOL which attracts a fee. If satisfied that the defendant is entitled to fee exemption, the organisation will submit the fee exemption form through the PCOL website to Her Majesty's Courts Service. The defendant may then use PCOL to take such a step.

(Her Majesty's Courts Service website contains guidance as to when the entitlement to claim an exemption from payment of fees arises. The PCOL website will contain a list of organisations through which the defendant may claim an exemption from fees).

Claims which may be started using Possession Claims Online

5.1   A claim may be started online if –

(1) it is brought under Section I of Part 55;

(2) it includes a possession claim for residential property by –

     (a)   a landlord against a tenant, solely on the ground of arrears of rent (but not a claim for forfeiture of a lease); or

     (b)   a mortgagee against a mortgagor, solely on the ground of default in the payment of sums due under a mortgage,

    relating to land within the district of a specified court;

(3) it does not include a claim for any other remedy except for payment of arrears of rent or money due under a mortgage, interest and costs;

(4) each party has an address for service in England and Wales; and

(5) the claimant is able to provide a postcode for the property.

5.2   A claim must not be started online if a defendant is known to be a child or protected party.

Starting a claim

6.1   A claimant may request the issue of a claim form by –

(1) completing an online claim form at the PCOL website;

(2) paying the appropriate issue fee electronically at the PCOL website or by some other means approved by Her Majesty's Courts Service.

6.2   The particulars of claim must be included in the online claim form and may not be filed separately. It is not necessary to file a copy of the tenancy agreement, mortgage deed or mortgage agreement with the particulars of claim.

6.2A In the case of a possession claim for residential property that relies on a statutory ground or grounds for possession, the claimant must specify, in section 4(a) of the online claim form, the ground or grounds relied on.

6.3   Subject to paragraphs 6.3A and 6.3B, the particulars of claim must include a history of the rent or mortgage account, in schedule form setting out –

(1) the dates and amounts of all payments due and payments made under the tenancy agreement, mortgage deed or mortgage agreement either from the first date of default if that date occurred less than two years before the date of issue or for a period of two years immediately preceding the date of issue; and

(2) a running total of the arrears.

6.3A Paragraph 6.3B applies where the claimant has, before commencing proceedings, provided the defendant in schedule form with –

(1) details of the dates and amounts of all payments due and payments made under the tenancy agreement, mortgage deed or mortgage account –

    (a) for a period of two years immediately preceding the date of commencing proceedings; or

    (b) if the first date of default occurred less than two years before that date, from the first date of default; and

(2) a running total of the arrears.

6.3B Where this paragraph applies the claimant may, in place of the information required by paragraph 6.3, include in his particulars of claim a summary only of the arrears containing at least the following information –

(1) The amount of arrears as stated in the notice of seeking possession served under either section 83 of the Housing Act 1985 or section 8 of the Housing Act 1988, or at the date of the claimant's letter before action, as appropriate;

(2) the dates and amounts of the last three payments in cleared funds made by the defendant or, if less than three payments have been made, the dates and amounts of all payments made;

(3) the arrears at the date of issue, assuming that no further payments are made by the defendant.

6.3C Where the particulars of claim include a summary only of the arrears the claimant must –

(1) serve on the defendant not more than 7 days after the date of issue, a full, up-to-date arrears history containing at least the information required by paragraph 6.3; and

(2) either –

    (a) make a witness statement confirming that he has complied with sub-paragraph (1) or (2) of paragraph 6.3A as appropriate, and including or exhibiting the full arrears history; or

    (b) verify by way of oral evidence at the hearing that he has complied with sub-paragraph (1) or (2) of paragraph 6.3A as appropriate and also produce and verify the full arrears history.

(Rule 55.8(4) requires all witness statements to be filed and served at least 2 days before the hearing.)

6.4 If the claimant wishes to rely on a history of arrears which is longer than two years, he should state this in his particulars and exhibit a full (or longer) schedule to a witness statement.

6.5 When an online claim form is received, an acknowledgment of receipt will automatically be sent to the claimant. The acknowledgment does not constitute notice that the claim form has been issued or served.

6.6 When the court issues a claim form following the submission of an online claim form, the claim is 'brought' for the purposes of the Limitation Act 1980 and any other enactment on the date on which the online claim form is received by the court's computer system. The court will keep a record, by electronic or other means, of when online claim forms are received.

6.7 When the court issues a claim form it will –

(1) serve a printed version of the claim form and a defence form on the defendant; and

(2) send the claimant notice of issue by post or, where the claimant has supplied an e-mail address, by electronic means.

6.8 The claim shall be deemed to be served on the fifth day after the claim was issued irrespective of whether that day is a business day or not.

6.9 Where the period of time within which a defence must be filed ends on a day when the court is closed, the defendant may file his defence on the next day that the court is open.

6.10 The claim form shall have printed on it a unique customer identification number or a password by which the defendant may access the claim on the PCOL website.

6.11 PCOL will issue the proceedings in the appropriate county court by reference to the post code provided by the claimant and that court shall have jurisdiction to hear and determine the claim and to carry out enforcement of any judgment irrespective of whether the property is within or outside the jurisdiction of that court.

(CPR 30.2(1) authorises proceedings to be transferred from one county court to another.)

Defence

7.1 A defendant wishing to file –

(1) a defence; or

(2) a counterclaim (to be filed together with a defence) to a claim which has been issued through the PCOL system,

may, instead of filing a written form, do so by –

(a) completing the relevant online form at the PCOL website; and

(b) if the defendant is making a counterclaim, paying the appropriate fee electronically at the PCOL website or by some other means approved by Her Majesty's Courts Service.

7.2 Where a defendant files a defence by completing the relevant online form, he must not send the court a hard copy.

7.3 When an online defence form is received, an acknowledgment of receipt will automatically be sent to the defendant. The acknowledgment does not constitute notice that the defence has been served.

7.4 The online defence form will be treated as being filed –

(1) on the day the court receives it, if it receives it before 4 p.m. on a working day; and

(2) otherwise, on the next working day after the court receives the online defence form.

7.5 A defence is filed when the online defence form is received by the court's computer system. The court will keep a record, by electronic or other means, of when online defence forms are received.

Statement of truth

8.1 CPR Part 22 requires any statement of case to be verified by a statement of truth. This applies to any online claims and defences and application notices.

8.2 CPR Part 22 also requires that if an applicant wishes to rely on matters set out in his application notice as evidence, the application notice must be verified by a statement of truth. This applies to any application notice completed online that contains matters on which the applicant wishes to rely as evidence.

8.3 Attention is drawn to –

(1) paragraph 2 of Practice Direction 22, which stipulates the form of the statement of truth; and

(2) paragraph 3 of Practice Direction 22, which provides who may sign a statement of truth; and

(3) CPR 32.14, which sets out the consequences of making, or causing to be made, a false statement in a document verified by a statement of truth, without an honest belief in its truth.

Signature

9.1 Any provision of the CPR which requires a document to be signed by any person is satisfied by that person entering his name on an online form.

Communication with the court electronically by the messaging service

10.1 If the PCOL website specifies that a court accepts electronic communications relating to claims brought using Possession Claims Online the parties may communicate with the court using the messaging service facility, available on the PCOL website ('the messaging service').

10.2 The messaging service is for brief and straightforward communications only. The PCOL website contains a list of examples of when it will not be appropriate to use the messaging service.

10.3 Parties must not send to the court forms or attachments via the messaging service.

10.4 The court shall treat any forms or attachments sent via the messaging service as not having been filed or received.

10.5 The court will normally reply via the messaging service where –

(1) the response is to a message transmitted via the messaging service; and

(2) the sender has provided an e-mail address.

Electronic applications

11.1 Certain applications in relation to a possession claim started online may be made electronically ('online applications'). An online application may be made if a form for that application is published on the PCOL website ('online application form') and the application is made at least five clear days before the hearing.

11.2 If a claim for possession has been started online and a party wishes to make an online application, he may do so by –

(1) completing the appropriate online application form at the PCOL website; and

(2) paying the appropriate fee electronically at the PCOL website or by some other means approved by Her Majesty's Courts Service.

11.3 When an online application form is received, an acknowledgment of receipt will automatically be sent to the applicant. The acknowledgment does not constitute a notice that the online application form has been issued or served.

11.4 Where an application must be made within a specified time, it is so made if the online application form is received by the court's computer system within that time. The court will keep a record, by electronic or other means, of when online application forms are received.

11.5 When the court receives an online application form it shall –

(1) serve a copy of the online application endorsed with the date of the hearing by post on the claimant at least two clear days before the hearing; and

(2) send the defendant notice of service and confirmation of the date of the hearing by post; provided that

(3) where either party has provided the court with an e-mail address for service,

service of the application and/or the notice of service and confirmation of the hearing date may be effected by electronic means.

Request for issue of warrant

12.1 Where –

(1) the court has made an order for possession in a claim started online; and
(2) the claimant is entitled to the issue of a warrant of possession without requiring the permission of the court

the claimant may request the issue of a warrant by completing an online request form at the PCOL website and paying the appropriate fee electronically at the PCOL website or by some other means approved by Her Majesty's Courts Service.

12.2 A request under paragraph 12.1 will be treated as being filed –

(1) on the day the court receives the request, if it receives it before 4 p.m. on a working day; and
(2) otherwise, on the next working day after the court receives the request.

(CCR Order 26 rule 5 sets out certain circumstances in which a warrant of execution may not be issued without the permission of the court. CCR Order 26 rule 17(6) applies rule 5 of that Order with necessary modifications to a warrant of possession.)

Application to suspend warrant of possession

13.1 Where the court has issued a warrant of possession, the defendant may apply electronically for the suspension of the warrant, provided that:

(1) the application is made at least five clear days before the appointment for possession; and
(2) the defendant is not prevented from making such an application without the permission of the court.

13.2 The defendant may apply electronically for the suspension of the warrant, by –

(1) completing an online application for suspension at the PCOL website; and
(2) paying the appropriate fee electronically at the PCOL website or by some other means approved by Her Majesty's Courts Service.

13.3 When an online application for suspension is received, an acknowledgment of receipt will automatically be sent to the defendant. The acknowledgment does not constitute a notice that the online application for suspension has been served.

13.4 Where an application must be made within a specified time, it is so made if the online application for suspension is received by the court's computer system within that time. The court will keep a record, by electronic or other means, of when online applications for suspension are received.

13.5 When the court receives an online application for suspension it shall –

(1) serve a copy of the online application for suspension endorsed with the date of the hearing by post on the claimant at least two clear days before the hearing; and
(2) send the defendant notice of service and confirmation of the date of the hearing by post; provided that
(3) where either party has provided the court with an e-mail address for service, service of the application and/or the notice of service and confirmation of the hearing date may be effected by electronic means.

Viewing the case record

14.1 A facility will be provided on the PCOL website for parties or their representatives to view –

    (1) an electronic record of the status of claims started online, which will be reviewed and, if necessary, updated at least once each day; and

    (2) all information relating to the case that has been filed by the parties electronically.

14.2 In addition, where the PCOL website specifies that the court has the facility to provide viewing of such information by electronic means, the parties or their representatives may view the following information electronically –

    (1) court orders made in relation to the case; and

    (2) details of progress on enforcement and subsequent orders made.

C4   PRACTICE DIRECTION 7B – CONSUMER CREDIT ACT 2006 – UNFAIR RELATIONSHIPS

This Practice Direction supplements CPR rule 7.9

1.1 In this practice direction 'the Act' means the Consumer Credit Act 1974, a section referred to by number means the section with that number in the Act, and expressions which are defined in the Act have the same meaning in this practice direction as they have in the Act.

1.2 'Consumer Credit Act procedure' means the procedure set out in this practice direction.

When to use the Consumer Credit Act procedure

2.1 A claimant must use the Consumer Credit Act procedure where he makes a claim under a provision of the Act to which paragraph 3 of this practice direction applies.

2.2 Where a claimant is using the Consumer Credit Act procedure the CPR are modified to the extent that they are inconsistent with the procedure set out in this practice direction.

2.3 The court may at any stage order the claim to continue as if the claimant had not used the Consumer Credit Act procedure, and if it does so the court may give any directions it considers appropriate.

2.4 This practice direction also sets out matters which must be included in the particulars of claim in certain types of claim, and restrictions on where certain types of claim may be started.

The provisions of the Act

3.1 Subject to paragraph 3.2 and 3.3 this practice direction applies to claims made under the following provisions of the Act:

    (1) section 141 (claim by the creditor to enforce regulated agreement relating to goods etc),

    (2) section 129 (claim by debtor or hirer for a time order),

    (3) section 90 (creditor's claim for an order for recovery of protected goods),

    (4) section 92(1) (creditor's or owner's claim to enter premises to take possession of goods),

    (5) section 140B(2)(a) (debtor's or surety's application for an order relating to an unfair relationship);

    (6) creditor's or owner's claim for a court order to enforce a regulated agreement relating to goods or money where the court order is required by –

    (a)   section 65(1) (improperly executed agreement),

    (b)   section 86(2) (death of debtor or hirer where agreement is partly secured or unsecured),

    (c)   section 111(2) (default notice etc not served on surety),

    (d)   section 124(1) or (2) (taking of a negotiable instrument in breach of terms of section 123), or

    (e)   section 105(7)(a) or (b) (security not expressed in writing, or improperly executed).

3.2   This practice direction does not apply to any claim made under the provisions listed in paragraph 3.1 above if that claim relates to the recovery of land.

3.3   This practice direction also does not apply to a claim made by the creditor under section 141 of the Act to enforce a regulated agreement where the agreement relates only to money. Such a claim must be started by the issue of a Part 7 claim form.

Restrictions on where to start some Consumer Credit Act claims

4.1   Where the claim includes a claim to recover goods to which a regulated hire purchase agreement or conditional sale agreement relates, it may only be started in the county court for the district in which the debtor, or one of the debtors:

(1)   resides or carries on business, or

(2)   resided or carried on business at the date when the defendant last made a payment under the agreement.

4.2   In any other claim to recover goods, the claim may only be started in the court for the district:

(1)   in which the defendant, or one of the defendants, resides or carries on business, or

(2)   in which the goods are situated.

4.3   A claim of a debtor or hirer for an order under section 129(1)(b) or 129(1)(ba) of the Act (a time order) may only be started in the court where the claimant resides or carries on business.

(Costs rule 45.1(2)(b) allows the claimant to recover fixed costs in certain circumstances where such a claim is made.)

(Paragraph 7 sets out the matters the claimant must include in his particulars of claim where he is using the Consumer Credit Act procedure.)

The Consumer Credit Act procedure

5.1   In the types of claim to which paragraph 3 applies the court will fix a hearing date on the issue of the claim form.

5.2   The particulars of claim must be served with the claim form.

5.3   Where a claimant is using the Consumer Credit Act procedure, the defendant to the claim is not required to:

(1)   serve an acknowledgment of service, or

(2)   file a defence, although he may choose to do so.

5.4   Where a defendant intends to defend a claim, his defence should be filed within 14 days of service of the particulars of claim. If the defendant fails to file a defence within this period, but later relies on it, the court may take such a failure into account as a factor when deciding what order to make about costs.

5.5   Part 12 (default judgment) does not apply where the claimant is using the Consumer Credit Act procedure.

5.6 Each party must be given at least 28 days' notice of the hearing date.
5.7 Where the claimant serves the claim form, he must serve notice of the hearing date at the same time, unless the hearing date is specified in the claim form.

Powers of the court at the hearing

6.1 On the hearing date the court may dispose of the claim.
6.2 If the court does not dispose of the claim on the hearing date:

(1) if the defendant has filed a defence, the court will:

(a) allocate the claim to a track and give directions about the management of the case, or
(b) give directions to enable it to allocate the claim to a track,

(2) if the defendant has not filed a defence, the court may make any order or give any direction it considers appropriate.

6.3 Rule 26.5 (3) to (5) and rules 26.6 to 26.10 apply to the allocation of a claim under paragraph 6.2.

Matters which must be included in the particulars of claim

7.1 Where the Consumer Credit Act procedure is used, the claimant must state in his particulars of claim that the claim is a Consumer Credit Act claim.
7.2 A claimant making a claim for the delivery of goods to enforce a hire purchase agreement or conditional sale agreement which is:

(1) a regulated agreement for the recovery of goods, and
(2) let to a person other than a company or other corporation, must also state (in this order) in his particulars of claim:

(a) the date of the agreement,
(b) the parties to the agreement,
(c) the number or other identification of the agreement (with enough information to allow the debtor to identify the agreement),
(d) where the claimant was not one of the original parties to the agreement, the means by which the rights and duties of the creditor passed to him,
(e) the place where the agreement was signed by the defendant (if known),
(f) the goods claimed,
(g) the total price of the goods,
(h) the paid up sum,
(i) the unpaid balance of the total price,
(j) whether a default notice or a notice under section 76(1) or section 88(1) of the Act has been served on the defendant, and, if it has, the date and the method of service,
(k) the date on which the right to demand delivery of the goods accrued,
(l) the amount (if any) claimed as an alternative to the delivery of goods, and
(m) the amount (if any) claimed in addition to –

(i) the delivery of the goods, or
(ii) any claim under sub paragraph (l) above with the grounds of each such claim.

7.3 A claimant who is a debtor or hirer making a claim for an order under section 129(1)(b) or 129(1)(ba) of the Act (a time order) must state (in the following order) in the particulars of claim:

(1) the date of the agreement,
(2) the parties to the agreement,
(3) the number or other means of identifying the agreement,
(4) details of any sureties,
(5) if the defendant is not one of the original parties to the agreement then the name of the original party to the agreement,
(6) the names and addresses of the persons intended to be served with the claim form,
(7) the place where the claimant signed the agreement,
(8) details of the notice served by the creditor or owner giving rise to the claim for the time order,
(9) the total unpaid balance the claimant admits is due under the agreement, and –

> (a) the amount of any arrears (if known), and
> (b) the amount and frequency of the payments specified in the agreement,

(10) the claimant's proposals for payments of any arrears and of future instalments together with details of his means;
(11) where the claim relates to a breach of the agreement other than for the payment of money the claimant's proposals for remedying it.

7.3A A claimant who is a debtor or hirer making a claim for an order under section 129(1)(ba) of the Act must attach to the particulars of claim a copy of the notice served on the creditor or owner under section 129A(1)(a) of the Act.

7.4 (1) This paragraph applies where a claimant is required to obtain a court order to enforce a regulated agreement by:

> (a) section 65(1) (improperly executed agreement),
> (b) section 105(7)(a) or (b) (security not expressed in writing, or improperly executed),
> (c) section 111(2) (default notice etc. not served on surety),
> (d) section 124(1) or (2) (taking of a negotiable instrument in breach of terms of section 123), or
> (e) section 86(2) of the Act (death of debtor or hirer where agreement is partly secured or unsecured).

(2) The claimant must state in his particulars of claim what the circumstances are that require him to obtain a court order for enforcement.

Admission of certain claims for recovery of goods under regulated agreements

8.1 In a claim to recover goods to which section 90(1)**[1]** applies:

(1) the defendant may admit the claim, and
(2) offer terms on which a return order should be suspended under section 135(1)(b).

8.2 He may do so by filing a request in practice form N9C.
8.3 He should do so within the period for making an admission specified in rule 14.2(b). If the defendant fails to file his request within this period, and later makes such a request, the court may take the failure into account as a factor when deciding what order to make about costs.
8.4 On receipt of the admission, the court will serve a copy on the claimant.
8.5 The claimant may obtain judgment by filing a request in practice form N228.

8.6 On receipt of the request for judgment, the court will enter judgment in the terms of the defendant's admission and offer and for costs.

8.7 If:

(1) the claimant does not accept the defendant's admission and offer, and

(2) the defendant does not appear on the hearing date fixed when the claim form was issued,

the court may treat the defendant's admission and offer as evidence of the facts stated in it for the purposes of sections 129(2)(a)**[2]** and 135(2)**[3]**.

Additional requirements about parties to the proceedings

9.1 The court may dispense with the requirement in section 141(5) (all parties to a regulated agreement and any surety to be parties to any proceedings) in any claim relating to the regulated agreement, if:

(1) the claim form has not been served on the debtor or the surety, and

(2) the claimant either before or at the hearing makes an application (which may be made without notice) for the court to make such an order.

9.2 In a claim relating to a regulated agreement where –

(1) the claimant was not one of the original parties to the agreement, and

(2) the former creditor's rights and duties under the agreement have passed to him by –

    (a) operation of law, or

    (b) assignment,

the requirement of section 141(5) (all parties to a regulated agreement and any surety to be parties to any proceedings) does not apply to the former creditor, unless the court otherwise orders.

9.3 Where a claimant who is a creditor or owner makes a claim for a court order under section 86(2) (death of debtor or hirer where agreement is partly secured or unsecured) the personal representatives of the deceased debtor or hirer must be parties to the proceedings in which the order is sought, unless no grant of representation has been made to the estate.

9.4 Where no grant of representation has been made to the estate of the deceased debtor or hirer, the claimant must make an application in accordance with Part 23 for directions about which persons (if any) are to be made parties to the claim as being affected or likely to be affected by the enforcement of the agreement.

9.5 The claimant's application under paragraph 9.4:

(a) may be made without notice, and

(b) should be made before the claim form is issued.

Notice to be given to re-open a consumer credit agreement

10.1 Paragraph 10.2 applies where –

(1) a debtor or any surety intends to seek an order relating to an unfair relationship between a creditor and that debtor, arising out of a credit agreement (taken together with any related agreement);

(2) a claim relating to that agreement or any related agreement has already begun; and

(3) section 140B(2)(b) or section 140B(2)(c) applies.

10.2 The debtor or surety must serve written notice of intention on the court and every other party to the claim within 14 days of service of the claim form.

10.3 A debtor or surety (as the case may be) who serves a notice under paragraph 10.2 will be treated as having filed a defence for the purposes of the Consumer Credit Act procedure.

Footnotes

1. Section 90(1) provides that:

At any time when –

(a) the debtor is in breach of a regulated hire-purchase or a regulated conditional sale agreement relating to goods, and

(b) the debtor has paid to the creditor one-third or more of the total price of the goods, and

(c) the property in the goods remains in the creditor, the creditor is not entitled to recover possession of the goods from the debtor except on an order of the court.

2. Section 129(2) provides that –

A time order shall provide for one or both of the following, as the court considers just –

(a) the payment by the debtor or hirer or any surety of any sum owed under a regulated agreement or a security by such instalments, payable at such times, as the court, having regard to the means of the debtor or hirer and any surety, considers reasonable;

(b) the remedying by the debtor or hirer of any breach of a regulated agreement (other than non-payment of money) within such period as the court may specify.

3. Section 135(2) provides that –

The court shall not suspend the operation of a term [in an order relating to a regulated agreement] requiring the delivery up of goods by any person unless satisfied that the goods are in his possession or control.

C5 PRE-ACTION PROTOCOL FOR POSSESSION CLAIMS BASED ON MORTGAGE OR HOME PURCHASE PLAN ARREARS IN RESPECT OF RESIDENTIAL PROPERTY

I INTRODUCTION

1 Preamble

1.1 This Protocol describes the behaviour the court will normally expect of the parties prior to the start of a possession claim within the scope of paragraph 3.1 below.

1.2 This Protocol does not alter the parties' rights and obligations.

1.3 It is in the interests of the parties that mortgage payments or payments under home purchase plans are made promptly and that difficulties are resolved wherever possible without court proceedings. However in some cases an order for possession may be in the interest of both the lender and the borrower.

2 Aims

2.1 The aims of this Protocol are to –

(1) ensure that a lender or home purchase plan provider (in this Protocol collectively referred to as 'the lender') and a borrower or home purchase plan customer (in this Protocol collectively referred to as 'the borrower') act fairly and reasonably with each other in resolving any matter concerning mortgage or home purchase plan arrears; and

(2) encourage more pre-action contact between the lender and the borrower in an effort to seek agreement between the parties, and where this cannot be reached, to enable efficient use of the court's time and resources.

2.2 Where either party is required to communicate and provide information to the other, reasonable steps should be taken to do so in a way that is clear, fair and not misleading. If the lender is aware that the borrower may have difficulties in reading or understanding the information provided, the lender should take reasonable steps to ensure that information is communicated in a way that the borrower can understand.

3 Scope

3.1 This Protocol applies to arrears on –

(1) first charge residential mortgages and home purchase plans regulated by the Financial Services Authority under the Financial Services and Markets Act 2000;

(2) second charge mortgages over residential property and other secured loans regulated under the Consumer Credit Act 1974 on residential property; and

(3) unregulated residential mortgages.

3.2 Where a potential claim includes a money claim and a claim for possession this protocol applies to both.

4 Definitions

4.1 In this Protocol –

(1) 'possession claim' means a claim for the recovery of possession of property under Part 55 of the Civil Procedure Rules 1998 (CPR);

(2) 'home purchase plan' means a method of purchasing a property by way of a sale and lease arrangement that does not require the payment of interest;

(3) 'bank holiday' means a bank holiday under the Banking and Financial Dealings Act 1971;

(4) 'business day' means any day except Saturday, Sunday, a bank holiday, Good Friday or Christmas day; and

(5) 'Mortgage Rescue Scheme' means the shared equity and mortgage to rent scheme established either –

(a) by the UK Government to help certain categories of vulnerable borrowers avoid repossession of their property in England, announced in September 2008 and opened in January 2009; or

(b) by the Welsh Assembly Government to help certain categories of vulnerable borrowers avoid repossession of their property in Wales, first announced in June 2008.

II   ACTIONS PRIOR TO THE START OF A POSSESSION CLAIM

5   Initial contact and provision of information

5.1   Where the borrower falls into arrears the lender must provide the borrower with –

(1)   where appropriate, the required regulatory information sheet or the National Homelessness Advice Service booklet on mortgage arrears; and

(2)   information concerning the amount of arrears which should include –

    (a)   the total amount of the arrears;

    (b)   the total outstanding of the mortgage or the home purchase plan; and

    (c)   whether interest or charges will be added, and if so and where appropriate, details or an estimate of the interest or charges that may be payable.

5.2   The parties must take all reasonable steps to discuss with each other, or their representatives, the cause of the arrears, the borrower's financial circumstances and proposals for repayment of the arrears (see 7.1). For example, parties should consider whether the causes of the arrears are temporary or long term and whether the borrower may be able to pay the arrears in a reasonable time.

5.3   The lender must advise the borrower to make early contact with the housing department of the borrower's Local Authority and, should, where necessary, refer the borrower to appropriate sources of independent debt advice.

5.4   The lender must consider a reasonable request from the borrower to change the date of regular payment (within the same payment period) or the method by which payment is made. The lender must either agree to such a request or, where it refuses such a request, it must, within a reasonable period of time, give the borrower a written explanation of its reasons for the refusal.

5.5   The lender must respond promptly to any proposal for payment made by the borrower. If the lender does not agree to such a proposal it should give reasons in writing to the borrower within 10 business days of the proposal.

5.6   If the lender submits a proposal for payment, the borrower must be given a reasonable period of time in which to consider such proposals. The lender must set out the proposal in sufficient detail to enable the borrower to understand the implications of the proposal.

5.7   If the borrower fails to comply with an agreement, the lender should warn the borrower, by giving the borrower 15 business days notice in writing, of its intention to start a possession claim unless the borrower remedies the breach in the agreement.

6   Postponing the start of a possession claim

6.1   A lender must consider not starting a possession claim for mortgage arrears where the borrower can demonstrate to the lender that the borrower has –

(1)   submitted a claim to –

    (a)   the Department for Works and Pensions (DWP) for Support for Mortgage Interest (SMI); or

    (b)   an insurer under a mortgage payment protection policy; or

    (c)   a participating local authority for support under a Mortgage Rescue Scheme,

and has provided all the evidence required to process a claim;

(2)   a reasonable expectation of eligibility for payment from the DWP or from the insurer or support from the local authority; and

(3)   an ability to pay a mortgage instalment not covered by a claim to the DWP or the insurer in relation to a claim under paragraph 6.1(1)(a) or (b).

6.2 If a borrower can demonstrate that reasonable steps have been or will be taken to market the property at an appropriate price in accordance with reasonable professional advice, the lender must consider postponing starting a possession claim. The borrower must continue to take all reasonable steps actively to market the property where the lender has agreed to postpone starting a possession claim.

6.3 Where the lender has agreed to postpone starting a possession claim the borrower should provide the lender with a copy of the particulars of sale, the Energy Performance Certificate (EPC) or proof that an EPC has been commissioned and (where relevant) details of purchase offers received within a reasonable period of time specified by the lender. The borrower should give the lender details of the estate agent and the conveyancer instructed to deal with the sale. The borrower should also authorise the estate agent and the conveyancer to communicate with the lender about the progress of the sale and the borrower's conduct during the process.

6.4 Where the lender decides not to postpone the start of a possession claim it must inform the borrower of the reasons for this decision at least 5 business days before starting proceedings.

7 Further matters to consider before starting a possession claim

Starting a possession claim should normally be a last resort and such a claim must not normally be started unless all other reasonable attempts to resolve the position have failed. The parties should consider whether, given the individual circumstances of the borrower and the form of the agreement, it is reasonable and appropriate to do one or more of the following –

(1) extend the term of the mortgage;

(2) change the type of mortgage;

(3) defer payment of interest due under the mortgage;

(4) capitalise the arrears; or

(5) make use of any Government forbearance initiatives in which the lender chooses to participate.

8 Complaints to the Financial Ombudsman Service

8.1 The lender must consider whether to postpone the start of a possession claim where the borrower has made a genuine complaint to the Financial Ombudsman Service (FOS) about the potential possession claim.

8.2 Where a lender does not intend to await the decision of the FOS it must give notice to the borrower with reasons that it intends to start a possession claim at least 5 business days before doing so.

9 Compliance

9.1 Parties must be able, if requested by the court, to explain the actions that they have taken to comply with this protocol.

C6 PRACTICE DIRECTION – PRE-ACTION CONDUCT

SECTION I – INTRODUCTION

1. Aims

1.1 The aims of this Practice Direction are to –

(1) enable parties to settle the issue between them without the need to start proceedings (that is, a court claim); and

(2) support the efficient management by the court and the parties of proceedings that cannot be avoided.

1.2 These aims are to be achieved by encouraging the parties to –

(1) exchange information about the issue, and

(2) consider using a form of Alternative Dispute Resolution ('ADR').

2. Scope

2.1 This Practice Direction describes the conduct the court will normally expect of the prospective parties prior to the start of proceedings.

2.2 There are some types of application where the principles in this Practice Direction clearly cannot or should not apply. These include, but are not limited to, for example –

(1) applications for an order where the parties have agreed between them the terms of the court order to be sought ('consent orders');

(2) applications for an order where there is no other party for the applicant to engage with;

(3) most applications for directions by a trustee or other fiduciary;

(4) applications where telling the other potential party in advance would defeat the purpose of the application (for example, an application for an order to freeze assets).

2.3 Section II deals with the approach of the court in exercising its powers in relation to pre-action conduct. Subject to paragraph 2.2, it applies in relation to all types of proceedings including those governed by the pre-action protocols that have been approved by the Head of Civil Justice and which are listed in paragraph 5.2 of this Practice Direction.

2.4 Section III deals with principles governing the conduct of the parties in cases which are not subject to a pre-action protocol.

2.5 Section III of this Practice Direction is supplemented by two annexes aimed at different types of claimant.

(1) Annex A sets out detailed guidance on a pre-action procedure that is likely to satisfy the court in most circumstances where no pre-action protocol or other formal pre-action procedure applies. It is intended as a guide for parties, particularly those without legal representation, in straightforward claims that are likely to be disputed. It is not intended to apply to debt claims where it is not disputed that the money is owed and where the claimant follows a statutory or other formal pre-action procedure.

(2) Annex B sets out some specific requirements that apply where the claimant is a business and the defendant is an individual. The requirements may be complied with at any time between the claimant first intimating the possibility of court proceedings and the claimant's letter before claim.

2.6 Section IV contains requirements that apply to all cases including those subject to the pre-action protocols (unless a relevant pre-action protocol contains a different provision). It is supplemented by Annex C, which sets out guidance on instructing experts.

3. Definitions

3.1 In this Practice Direction together with the Annexes –

(1) 'proceedings' means any proceedings started under Part 7 or Part 8 of the Civil Procedure Rules 1998 ('CPR');

(2) 'claimant' and 'defendant' refer to the respective parties to potential proceedings;

(3) 'ADR' means alternative dispute resolution, and is the collective description of methods of resolving disputes otherwise than through the normal trial process; (see paragraph 8.2 for further information); and

(4) 'compliance' means acting in accordance with, as applicable, the principles set out in Section III of this Practice Direction, the requirements in Section IV and a relevant pre-action protocol. The words 'comply' and 'complied' should be construed accordingly.

SECTION II – THE APPROACH OF THE COURTS

4. Compliance

4.1 The CPR enable the court to take into account the extent of the parties' compliance with this Practice Direction or a relevant pre-action protocol (see paragraph 5.2) when giving directions for the management of claims (see CPR rules 3.1(4) and (5) and 3.9(1)(e)) and when making orders about who should pay costs (see CPR rule 44.3(5)(a)).

4.2 The court will expect the parties to have complied with this Practice Direction or any relevant pre-action protocol. The court may ask the parties to explain what steps were taken to comply prior to the start of the claim. Where there has been a failure of compliance by a party the court may ask that party to provide an explanation.

Assessment of compliance

4.3 When considering compliance the court will –

(1) be concerned about whether the parties have complied in substance with the relevant principles and requirements and is not likely to be concerned with minor or technical shortcomings;

(2) consider the proportionality of the steps taken compared to the size and importance of the matter;

(3) take account of the urgency of the matter. Where a matter is urgent (for example, an application for an injunction) the court will expect the parties to comply only to the extent that it is reasonable to do so. (Paragraph 9.5 and 9.6 of this Practice Direction concern urgency caused by limitation periods.)

Examples of non-compliance

4.4 The court may decide that there has been a failure of compliance by a party because, for example, that party has –

(1) not provided sufficient information to enable the other party to understand the issues;

(2) not acted within a time limit set out in a relevant pre-action protocol, or, where no specific time limit applies, within a reasonable period;

(3) unreasonably refused to consider ADR (paragraph 8 in Part III of this Practice Direction and the pre-action protocols all contain similar provisions about ADR); or

(4) without good reason, not disclosed documents requested to be disclosed.

Sanctions for non-compliance

4.5 The court will look at the overall effect of non-compliance on the other party when deciding whether to impose sanctions.

4.6 If, in the opinion of the court, there has been non-compliance, the sanctions which the court may impose include –

(1) staying (that is suspending) the proceedings until steps which ought to have been taken have been taken;

(2) an order that the party at fault pays the costs, or part of the costs, of the other party or parties (this may include an order under rule 27.14(2)(g) in cases allocated to the small claims track);

(3) an order that the party at fault pays those costs on an indemnity basis (rule 44.4(3) sets out the definition of the assessment of costs on an indemnity basis);

(4) if the party at fault is the claimant in whose favour an order for the payment of a sum of money is subsequently made, an order that the claimant is deprived of interest on all or part of that sum, and/or that interest is awarded at a lower rate than would otherwise have been awarded;

(5) if the party at fault is a defendant, and an order for the payment of a sum of money is subsequently made in favour of the claimant, an order that the defendant pay interest on all or part of that sum at a higher rate, not exceeding 10% above base rate, than would otherwise have been awarded.

5. Commencement of pre-action protocols

5.1 When considering compliance, the court will take account of a relevant pre-action protocol if the proceedings were started after the relevant pre-action protocol came into force.

5.2 The following table sets out the pre-action protocols currently in force and the dates that they came into force –

Pre-Action Protocol	Came into force
Personal Injury	26 April 1999
Clinical Disputes	26 April 1999
Construction and Engineering	2 October 2000
Defamation	2 October 2000
Professional Negligence	16 July 2001
Judicial Review	4 March 2002
Disease and Illness	8 December 2003
Housing Disrepair	8 December 2003

Possession Claims based on rent arrears	2 October 2006
Possession Claims based on Mortgage Arrears etc.	19 November 2008

SECTION IV – REQUIREMENTS THAT APPLY IN ALL CASES

9. Specific Provisions

9.1 The following requirements (including Annex C) apply in all cases except where a relevant pre-action protocol contains its own provisions about the topic.

Disclosure

9.2 Documents provided by one party to another in the course of complying with this Practice Direction or any relevant pre-action protocol must not be used for any purpose other than resolving the matter, unless the disclosing party agrees in writing.

Information about funding arrangements

9.3 Where a party enters into a funding arrangement within the meaning of rule 43.2(1)(k), that party must inform the other parties about this arrangement as soon as possible and in any event either within 7 days of entering into the funding arrangement concerned or, where a claimant enters into a funding arrangement before sending a letter before claim, in the letter before claim.

(CPR rule 44.3B(1)(c) provides that a party may not recover certain additional costs where information about a funding arrangement was not provided.)

Experts

9.4 Where the evidence of an expert is necessary the parties should consider how best to minimise expense. Guidance on instructing experts can be found in Annex C.

Limitation Periods

9.5 There are statutory time limits for starting proceedings ('the limitation period'). If a claimant starts a claim after the limitation period applicable to that type of claim has expired the defendant will be entitled to use that as a defence to the claim.

9.6 In certain instances compliance may not be possible before the expiry of the limitation period. If, for any reason, proceedings are started before the parties have complied, they should seek to agree to apply to the court for an order to stay (i.e. suspend) the proceedings while the parties take steps to comply.

Notifying the court

9.7 Where proceedings are started the claimant should state in the claim form or the particulars of claim whether they have complied with Sections III and IV of this Practice Direction or any relevant protocol.

Transitional Provision

9.8   The amendments to paragraph 9.3 do not apply to a funding arrangement entered into before the 1st October 2009 and paragraph 9.3 in force immediately before that date will continue to apply to that funding arrangement as if paragraph 9.3 had not been amended.

APPENDIX D

Other regulatory material

D1   LSC MANUAL: FINANCIAL ELIGIBILITY (VOLUME 2E)

4.   General Principles of Assessment

4.1   Period of Calculation

1.   The period of calculation when determining income is the calendar month up to and including the date of the application for funding. For example, if the application is made on December 8 then the period of calculation will commence on November 9. In practical terms when income/allowances do not vary month on month then the relative amounts can be taken by reference to the most recent month's or week's payments, e.g. the most recent monthly wage.

4.2   Aggregation of Means

1.   Regulation 11 contains a general provision that the income and capital of the client's partner must be taken into account and added to those of the client. Partner is defined as anyone (including a person of the same sex) with whom the applicant lives as a couple, and includes a person with whom the person concerned is not living but from whom he is not living separate and apart.
2.   This means that just because the client and their partner are physically separated i.e. they live in separate properties, does not necessarily mean that they are living separate and apart for the purpose of the regulations. The fact that both terms are used (i.e. 'separate' and 'apart') means that more than mere physical separation is required if the partners' means are not to be aggregated. Living separate and apart is well defined in the context of matrimonial law and refers to a breakdown in the relationship. In other words, the parties must be living separate and apart because at least one of them regards the relationship as at an end and not due purely to financial or practical reasons e.g. job location or the fact that one of the parties is in prison, hospital, residential care etc. In many asylum cases there may be occasions where the client is physically separated from their partner due to the partner still being abroad, but the relationship is still intact. In such cases the normal rules of aggregation still apply and the client and their partner will still be treated as a couple for aggregation purposes. However in such cases it may be necessary to consider whether the assets and income of the partner, together with any of the client's assets that have been left behind, are currently truly 'disposable' as far as the client is currently concerned. In such cases the supplier should make reasonable enquiries of the client to determine to what extent that income and those assets are available. If it is decided in an individual case that the partner's income and assets are not available to the client and therefore excluded from the assessment then it would not be appropriate to make any dependant's allowance for the partner (see section 6 below).
3.   Further in general the term separate and apart refers to physical separation i.e. the parties are living in separate properties. However, this may not always be the case. It is

possible for former partners to live separate and apart in the same household. This would be the case if they regarded their relationship as at an end but remained living in the same property simply waiting for the property to be sold before going their separate ways.

4. In addition for unmarried couples, although not conclusive it would be usual for there to be some evidence of a pooling of financial resources and they must regard themselves as a couple. It would not be appropriate to aggregate the resources of say a brother and sister, or flatmates who are not living as a couple. Further evidence of living as a couple may include joint care of a child of the couple. Issues may arise where a couple are married according to English law but have not undergone their traditional cultural ceremony and thus are not and never have been actually living together. In the eyes of each other and their family and community they are not yet married. In such cases it would be appropriate to treat them as though they were not married and therefore not to aggregate the resources in the assessment.

5. However, there is an important exception to this rule and means are not aggregated where the partner has a contrary interest in the matter in respect of which the client is seeking funding.

Contrary interest in the most obvious sense will mean that the partner is the opponent or potential opponent in proceedings. However, this will not necessarily be the case – the client and their partner could in theory have a contrary interest in a claim made by a third party, such as in the case of a mortgagee seeking possession where undue influence by the partner may be a defence.

In disputes between divorcing or separating couples, whether as to children or property, one partner will by definition have a contrary interest to the other. However, if a client has left his or her spouse and has gone to live with a new partner as a couple in the same household, then the means of the new partner should be aggregated with those of the applicant.

7. Assessing Disposable Capital

7.4   Value of property

1. Provided it is not the subject matter of the dispute (see section 7.3 above for details), a client's main or only dwelling in which he resides must be taken into account as capital subject to the following rules:

   (a) The dwelling should be valued at the amount for which it could be sold on the open market;

   (b) The amount of any mortgage or charge registered on the property must be deducted but the maximum amount that can be deducted for such a mortgage or charge is £100,000; and

   (c) The first £100,000 of the value of the client's interest after making the above mortgage deduction must be disregarded.

Example:

The applicant has a home worth £215,000 and the mortgage is £200,000:

Value of home:	£215,000
Deduct mortgage up to maximum allowable:	£100,000
Deduct exemption allowance:	£100,000
Amount to be taken into account in assessing financial eligibility:	£15,000

In this example the client is ineligible.

2. Where the applicant has more than one property the value of all other properties should be taken into account but the total amount which can be allowed in respect of mortgages and charges on all the properties cannot exceed £100,000. In applying this rule the mortgage for the main dwelling is deducted last. There is no equity disregard for second properties.

    Example:

    The client has a main dwelling worth £150,000 and a second dwelling worth £100,000. Each has a mortgage of £80,000.

Value of second dwelling:	£100,000
Deduct mortgage up to maximum allowable:	£80,000
Amount to be taken into account in assessing financial eligibility:	£20,000

    Only £20,000 of the £100,000 mortgage allowance remains:

Value of home:	£150,000
Deduct mortgage up to maximum allowable:	£20,000
Deduct exemption allowance:	£100,000
Amount to be taken into account in assessing financial eligibility:	£30,000

    In this example the client is ineligible.

Checklist and precedents

E1   DUTY ADVISER MORTGAGE SCHEME CHECKLIST

Order ADVISER is seeking:	
Order LENDER is seeking:	

Claim no.:	
DJ:	
Hearing date:	(First or adjourned hearing?)
NAME:	**Type of property:**
ADDRESS:	**Who lives at property:**
Phone no.:	**Priority need?**
Claimant:	**Mortgage type:**
	(1st / 2nd / 3rd charge?)
	Endowment payment up to date?
Monthly instalment:	Capital / Interest
Last payment made (and date):	
Date of mortgage:	
Regulated by CCA:	Yes / No
All monies charge:	Yes / No
Amount borrowed:	
Total arrears to date:	Admitted / Disputed
Amount of arrears at summons:	
Remaining terms of mortgage (years):	
Minimum *Norgan* order:	
Outstanding balance:	
Current value of property:	
Mortgage payment protection policy?	
How much can pay off arrears:	
Working / Benefits / Income / Debts / Lump sum payments	
Claim for Support for Mortgage Interest:	Date(s) applied

Agreement(s) to clear arrears: Date(s) / Whether kept to / Amount / In writing?
Reason for arrears / Compliance with Pre-Action Protocol / Notes for hearing:

E2   DEFENCE AND COUNTERCLAIM (TO ANNEX TO FORM N11M)

IN THE SUBURBAN COUNTY COURT   Claim no.: _____

B E T W E E N

MIDLAND CITIES PROVIDENTIAL LENDING LTD

Claimant/
Part 20 Defendant

and

MR BRIAN MORGAN-ORR

First Defendant

MRS JULIA MORGAN-ORR

Second Defendant/
Part 20 Claimant

DEFENCE AND COUNTERCLAIM
OF THE SECOND DEFENDANT
(to be annexed to Form N11M)

---

1. The Second Defendant denies that the Claimant has a right to possession as alleged in paragraph 1 of the Particulars of Claim.
2. The Second Defendant admits that on the 25 August 2007 she signed a mortgage deed in favour of the Claimant as referred to in paragraph 2 but for the reasons set out in paragraphs 6 to 10 below, she denies that she is bound by it.
3. The Second Defendant admits that she lives in the premises known as 11 Park Hall Road, Suburbia with the First Defendant and their 11-year-old son, as stated in paragraph 3 of the Particulars of Claim.
4. The Second Defendant admits that the mortgage referred to in paragraph 4 of the Particulars of Claim is not a regulated consumer credit agreement.
5. The Second Defendant does not admit the arrears alleged in paragraphs 5 and 6 of the Particulars of Claim and requires the Claimant to prove the existence and extent of the arrears that it is claiming.
6. The Second Defendant did not understand the transaction into which she was entering when she signed the mortgage deed and which was manifestly disadvantageous to her.
7. Furthermore, the Second Defendant was induced to sign the mortgage deed by misrepresentations of fact made by the First Defendant.
8. Furthermore, the Second Defendant reposed trust and confidence in the First Defendant and was subject to undue influence and duress from him. She signed the mortgage deed as a result of that pressure.
9. The Second Defendant relies on the following particulars:

Particulars

9.1 The Second Defendant has lived with the First Defendant continuously since 1992 and is the mother of his son.
9.2 The Second Defendant is a hairdresser by trade and has little experience of business or financial matters. She has always relied heavily upon the First Defendant in this regard.

9.3 The Second Defendant did not understand that the transaction was to be secured upon the premises which are the family home.

9.4 The First Defendant told the Second Defendant that the transaction was a short-term bridging loan to pay off debts that he had incurred. He assured her that the bridging loan would be cleared within three months by a conventional remortgage of the premises at affordable interest rates. He said that the Claimant was also a mortgage broker and had guaranteed to arrange the said remortgage.

9.5 The Second Defendant was aware that the First Defendant was under pressure to pay off his debts and that he was receiving treatment from his doctor for anxiety and depression. The First Defendant told the Second Defendant that if he were made bankrupt he would commit suicide and that the only way to avoid bankruptcy was to arrange the loan with the Claimant and then remortgage the premises.

10. The Claimant knew or had constructive notice of the particulars set out in paragraph 9 above. It took no steps to ensure that the Second Defendant was independently advised so that she understood the nature and consequence of the transaction. It did not attempt to protect her from the duress and undue influence being exercised by the First Defendant when it knew of the close relationship between them. It failed to protect her from the misrepresentations made by the First Defendant.

Particulars

10.1 Two weeks before the mortgage deed was signed the Second Defendant attended a meeting at the Claimant's office in the company only of the First Defendant. She played no part in the discussions. When asked if she had any questions, she stated that she found the whole matter confusing and would discuss it in detail with the First Defendant after the meeting.

10.2 The mortgage deed was then sent by the Claimant to the First Defendant with instructions that he and the Second Defendant should execute it. No requirement was made that the Second Defendant should take independent advice and the Claimant did not write to her separately.

10.3 The Second Defendant's signature was witnessed by a lay person, who had also witnessed the First Defendant's signature.

11. Accordingly, the Second Defendant denies that she owes any money to the Claimant and denies that the Claimant is entitled to enforce the mortgage against her or that it is entitled to a possession order.

Counterclaim

12. The Second Defendant repeats the Defence set out above and Counterclaims for:

(i)   An order rescinding the mortgage as between her and the Claimant; or
(ii) A declaration that the mortgage is unenforceable against her;
(iii) Damages of not more than £[ ];
(iv) Interest on damages as provided by statute; and
(v)   Costs.

Statement of truth
*[I believe][The Defendant believes] that the facts stated in this Defence and Counterclaim are true.
*I am duly authorised by the Defendant to sign this statement.
Full name:

Name of Claimant's firm of solicitors: Friendly Solicitors

Signed: _____   **Position or office held:** _____
*[Defendant][Litigation   (if signing on behalf of firm or
friend][Defendant's solicitor]   company)

delete as appropriate

Date: _____

Address to which notices about this case can be sent to you:

Friendly Solicitors   **Tel:**
Station Approach
Suburbia CC5 5TT   **Fax:**

                             Ref:

E3   APPLICATION TO SET ASIDE POSSESSION ORDER (FORM N244)

Application notice

For help in completing this form please read
the notes for guidance form N244Notes.

Name of court	SUBURBAN COUNTY COURT
Claim no.	1 XZ 30092
Warrant no. (if applicable)	
Claimant's name (including ref.)	BANK OF WALES t/a HABILAX
Defendant's name (including ref.)	MR HARVEY WILSON MRS JANE WILSON
Date	26 August 2011

1. What is your name or, if you are a solicitor, the name of your firm?

   JANE WILSON

2. Are you a   ☐ Claimant   ☑ Defendant   ☐ Solicitor

   ☐ Other (please specify)

   If you are a solicitor whom do you represent?

3. What order are you asking the court to make and why?

   That the suspended possession order dated 8 March 2011 be set aside pursuant to CPR Part 3.1(2)(m), as it was obtained in my absence. I have a good reason for not having attended the hearing and I acted promptly as soon as I learned of it. Further details are set out in my witness statement (attached).

4. Have you attached a draft of the order you are applying for?   ☑ Yes   ☐ No

5. How do you want to have this application dealt with?   ☑ at a hearing   ☐ without a hearing

   ☐ at a telephone hearing

6. How long do you think the hearing will last?   [   ] Hours   30 Minutes

   Is this time estimate agreed by all parties?   ☐ Yes   ☑ No

7. Give details of any fixed trial date or period

8. What level of Judge does your hearing need?   District Judge

9. Who should be served with this application?   The Claimant

10. What information will you be relying on, in support of your application?

☑ the attached witness statement

☐ the statement of case

☐ the evidence set out in the box below

If necessary, please continue on a separate sheet.
Please see attached witness statement and draft order.

Statement of Truth

(I believe) (The applicant believes) that the facts stated in this section (and any continuation sheets) are true.

Signed _____ Dated _26 August 2011_

        Applicant('s Solicitor)('s litigation friend)

Full name __JANE WILSON_____

Name of applicant's solicitor's firm _____

Position or office held _____

(if signing on behalf of firm or company)

11. Signature and address details

Signed _____ Dated _26 August 2011_

        Applicant('s Solicitor)('s litigation friend)

Position or office held _____

(if signing on behalf of firm or company)

Applicant's address to which documents about this application should be sent

MRS JANE WILSON c/o 10 Brannigan Close London Postcode S E 2 9 5 J L	If applicable	
	Phone no.	
	Fax no.	
	DX no.	
	Ref no.	

E-mail address	

2

315

E4   DRAFT ORDER TO SET ASIDE POSSESSION ORDER

Draft Order

In the SUBURBAN COUNTY COURT	
Claim no.	1 XZ 30092
Warrant no. (if applicable)	
Claimant (including ref)	BANK OF WALES T/A HABILAX
Defendant(s) (including ref)	MR HARVEY WILSON MRS JANE WILSON
Date	

Before District Judge [*name*]

Upon hearing [*name*] for the Claimant and [*name*] for the Defendant

IT IS ORDERED THAT:

1.   The possession order in these proceedings dated [*date*] is set aside.
2.   The Claim for possession be adjourned generally on terms that the Second Defendant pay the Claimant the unpaid instalments under the mortgage at the rate of £300 per month in addition to the current instalments due under the said mortgage. The first payment to be made on or before [*date*].
3.   The Claimant has permission on written request to the court to restore this action if the Second Defendant fails to comply with the terms set out in paragraph 2 above.
4.   Costs [*to be decided by the court*]

E5 WITNESS STATEMENT TO SET ASIDE POSSESSION ORDER

Made on behalf of:	the Second Defendant
Witness:	Jane Wilson
No. of statement:	1
Exhibits:	3
Date:	26 August 2011

IN THE SUBURBAN COUNTY COURT   Claim no.: 1 XZ 20092

BETWEEN:

BANK OF WALES
t/a HABILAX

Claimant

and

(1) MR HARVEY WILSON
(2) MRS JANE WILSON

Defendants

WITNESS STATEMENT
OF SECOND DEFENDANT

I, **JANE WILSON** of 33 Suburban Road, London SE29 0TD (temporarily of 10 Brannigan Close, London SE29 5JL) make this statement in support of my application for a possession order made in these proceedings on 15 March 2011 to be set aside. Except where I state otherwise, this statement is made from my own knowledge.

1. In February 2007 I bought the property known as 33 Suburban Road, London SE29 0TD with my estranged husband, Harvey Wilson, with the benefit of a mortgage from the Claimant.

2. As far as I was aware the mortgage was being maintained. Our arrangement was that Harvey paid the mortgage and I paid all the other household bills and outgoings. Unknown to me Harvey was often failing to pay the instalments. The Claimant bank took the matter to court. I now know that Harvey did not attend the hearing but agreed with the Claimant that they would ask for a suspended possession order, on terms that we pay the current monthly mortgage instalments, plus £200 per month to clear the arrears, which were then £4,417.

3. Harvey kept all the court papers from me including the suspended possession order. I have now learned that he was having an affair and was spending our mortgage money on his new girlfriend.

4. On Friday 17 June 2011 I returned home after work with the children to find the locks changed and security screens on the windows and doors. I rang Harvey and he told me everything and said that he was leaving me. I had to spend the weekend with friends; the children went and stayed with my mother.

5. I took action as promptly as I could. In particular, on Monday morning 20 June 2011 I called the Claimant bank to explain the situation to them. I followed this up with a letter and a copy to the court, as I did not know exactly what to do.

6. I wrote to the Claimant to let it know that I would continue the monthly payments as well as the £200 towards the arrears. I took a second job and **there is now shown to me marked 'JW1'** a bundle of receipts showing all the payments that I have made. These show that I made payments every month from June 2011 to date.

7. On 16 August 2011 I received a letter back from the court telling me to seek legal advice. I eventually managed to find a solicitor who could see me. I was advised that to regain possession of my home I have to apply to set the possession order aside. I am told that the court will want to know that I have acted promptly when I found out that the court had made an order against me, that I had good reason for not attending the hearing and that I have a reasonable prospect of success. I will deal with these three points in turn.

8. I did act promptly as soon as I learned that the possession order had been made. In particular, I contacted the Claimant and took over responsibility for the mortgage payments. I made this application as soon as I became aware that I could apply to this court.

9. As explained, I had a very good reason for not attending the possession hearing, because my husband failed to tell me that it was taking place.

10. I would argue that had I attended the hearing, it is very likely that the possession proceedings would have been adjourned on condition that I paid the current mortgage instalments, together with £200 per month. Without either me or my husband at court, a suspended possession order was made in these terms. If I had attended and explained that I had been trusting my husband, but that I was now taking over responsibility for the mortgage, I believe that the court would have given me a chance to prove myself by adjourning the proceedings.

11. I am now divorcing my husband, because I cannot continue in a marriage where I had been so badly deceived and let down.

12. I have two children aged 12 and 15 and if we lose our home I will have nowhere else to live and all of us will be homeless.

13. I work as theatre manager and my gross salary is £35,000 per annum. **I am now shown marked 'JW2'** a copy of my last three months of payslips. In addition, I have a second, part-time job working for an estate agent earning £12,000 per annum. **I am now shown marked 'JW3'** a form with a breakdown of my income and outgoings. The current arrears are £6,245. If I paid these off over the remaining 21 years left on the mortgage, I would have to pay about £25 per month; however, I am offering to pay £200 per month. The house was bought in 2007 for £200,000, so there is therefore sufficient equity in the property and sufficient time for me to clear the arrears within a reasonable period.

14. In all these circumstances I ask that the possession order be set aside and that the possession proceedings be adjourned on condition that I pay the current mortgage instalments, together with £200 per month towards the arrears.

I believe that the facts set out in this witness statement are true.

Signed:

Dated: 26 August 2011

E6 APPLICATION TO SUSPEND WARRANT OF EVICTION (FORM N244)

[*Note: To be combined with Form N245 (application for suspension of a warrant and/or variation of an order) – see* **14.3.1**.]

Application notice

For help in completing this form please read
the notes for guidance form N244Notes.

Name of court	CENTRAL TOWN COUNTY COURT
Claim no.	1 QP 45477
Warrant no. (if applicable)	30000123
Claimant's name (Including ref.)	WREXBURY FINANCE LTD
Defendant's name (including ref.)	MRS GLORIA ANNUNZIATA
Date	

1. What is your name or, if you are a solicitor, the name of your firm?

GLORIA ANNUNZIATA

2. Are you a ☐ Claimant ☑ Defendant ☐ Solicitor

☐ Other *(please specify)*

If you are a solicitor whom do you represent?

3. What order are you asking the court to make and why?

That the warrant for possession in these proceedings due to be executed on   be stayed and that
the suspended possession order be varied, in the terms of the draft order attached.

4. Have you attached a draft of the order you are applying for? ☑ Yes ☐ No

5. How do you want to have this application dealt with? ☑ at a hearing ☐ without a hearing
☐ at a telephone hearing

6. How long do you think the hearing will last? [   ] Hours [10] Minutes

Is this time estimate agreed by all parties? ☐ Yes ☐ No

7. Give details of any fixed trial date or period

8. What level of Judge does your hearing need? District Judge

9. Who should be served with this application? The Claimant

10. What information will you be relying on, in support of your application?

- ☑ the attached witness statement
- ☐ the statement of case
- ☐ the evidence set out in the box below

If necessary, please continue on a separate sheet.

Please see attached witness statement and draft order.

Fuller details about my finances will be found in the attached form N245, which I have also completed.

Statement of Truth

(I believe) (The applicant believes) that the facts stated in this section (and any continuation sheets) are true.

Signed _____   Dated _____
Applicant('s Solicitor)('s litigation friend)

Full name GLORIA ANNUNZIATA _____

Name of applicant's solicitor's firm _____

Position or office held _____
(if signing on behalf of firm or company)

11. Signature and address details

Signed _____   Dated _____
Applicant('s Solicitor)('s litigation friend)

Position or office held _____
(if signing on behalf of firm or company)

Applicant's address to which documents about this application should be sent

Mrs Gloria Annunziata 44, Green Gardens Suburbia Postcode S E 2 9 3 L H	If applicable	
	Phone no.	
	Fax no.	
	DX no.	
	Ref no.	

E-mail address	

E7   DRAFT ORDER TO SUSPEND WARRANT OF EVICTION

Draft Order

In the CENTRAL TOWN COUNTY COURT	
Claim no.	1 QP 45477
Warrant no. (if applicable)	30000123
Claimant (including ref)	WREXBURY FINANCE LTD
Defendant(s) (including ref)	MRS GLORIA ANNUNZIATA
Date	

Before District Judge [*name*]

And upon hearing [*name*] for the Claimant and [*name*] for the Defendant

IT IS ORDERED THAT:

1. Warrant for Eviction No. [*number*] be suspended so long as the Defendant pay to the Claimant the arrears due under the mortgage of £[*amount*] by the payments set out below **in addition** to the regular mortgage payments that fall due from time to time, as follows:

    Payments in respect of arrears

    £[*amount*] on or before the [*date*]

    [*or*]

    £[*amount*] per calendar month, the first such payment being made on or before the [*date*] for [*number*] months and then £[*amount*] per calendar month
2. The court orders that the Claimant's costs of this action be assessed in the sum of £[*amount*] and added to the amount owing under the mortgage.

E8   WITNESS STATEMENT TO SUSPEND WARRANT OF EVICTION

Made on behalf of:	Defendant
Witness:	Gloria Annunziata
No. of statement:	1
Exhibits:	4
Date:	[*date*]

IN THE CENTRAL TOWN COUNTY COURT   Claim no. 1: QP 45477
                                        Warrant no.: 30000123

BETWEEN:

WREXBURY FINANCE LTD

Claimant

and

MRS GLORIA ANNUNZIATA

Defendant

WITNESS STATEMENT OF GLORIA ANNUNZIATA

---

1.   My name is Gloria Annunziata of 44, Green Gardens, Suburbia, SE29 3LH. I am the Defendant in these proceedings. I make this witness statement in support of my applications:

   (a)   to suspend a warrant of eviction due to be executed on [*date*] at 10.30 am; and
   (b)   to vary the terms of the possession order dated [*date*], to suspend it and to allow me time to pay off the arrears by instalments.

2.   The main grounds for my application are:

   (a)   The arrears arose because I was off work due to an accident and I fell into debt during that time. I am soon to start work again and I will be able to pay the mortgage;
   (b)   I have a compensation claim for the accident and I am expecting to receive £[*amount*] within the next 3 months;
   (c)   Since the notice of eviction, there have been payments of Support for Mortgage Interest to the mortgage account and I have reduced the arrears by £[*amount*];
   (d)   If the eviction goes ahead, I will be made homeless together with my two young children. I will have nowhere to go and will suffer great hardship.

3.   I live at 44, Green Gardens, Suburbia, SE29 3LH. This is a two-bedroom house. I live there with my son John, whose date of birth is [*date*] and who is therefore 6 years old, and my daughter Katie, whose date of birth is [*date*] and who is therefore just 3 years old.

4.   My mortgage account shows that until 2009 I was paying my mortgage on a fairly regular basis. I had missed the occasional instalment but I was coping. I was working as a legal secretary earning £[*amount*] per year.

5.   Then on 26 January 2011 I was knocked over by a hit and run driver. I was very badly injured and have not been able to return to work. My employment contract does not

provide for sick pay, so I have been living on statutory sick pay and more recently on income support. I did not apply for income support as quickly as I could have because I did not realise that I would qualify. I have now received advice and have applied for a backdated payment. If this is successful I will receive £[*amount*] which I will pay onto the mortgage account.

6. No payments were made to the mortgage for [*number*] months after which the sum of £[*amount*] per month was paid by the Department for Work and Pensions (DWP) by way of Support for Mortgage Interest (SMI). I have applied for a back payment of SMI.

7. I have now received a letter telling me that I will be evicted on Wednesday, [*date*]. Since receiving this letter my benefits adviser has been in constant touch with the DWP. As a result of her pressure, the DWP says that it has paid £[*amount*] to the Claimant by way of back mortgage interest. This is in respect of the period between [*date*] and [*date*]. In addition, I am told that a further payment of about £[*amount*] will be made on [*date*], in respect of the period between [*date*] and [*date*].

8. Taking into account all of the payments the DWP has made and is likely to make, I believe that the mortgage arrears will be reduced by around £[*amount*] to £[*amount*] in total. I will then be able to reduce them over time at the rate of £[*amount*] per month when I return to work.

9. I am now mostly recovered from my injuries and I have found a new job starting work on [*date*]. It is part-time work and not as well paid as my last job. **There is now shown to me marked GA1** a letter from my new employer offering me the job. **There is now shown to me marked GA2** a statement of what my income will be when I start work and a statement of my outgoings. It will be seen that although things will be tight, I will be able to pay the current mortgage plus a small amount towards the arrears each month.

10. There are 18 years still to run on the mortgage. **I am now shown marked GA3** two computer print outs of estate agents' details of houses in my area that are for sale. From these it can be seen that the house is worth about £[*amount*] and, as shown in the Claim Form, the outstanding mortgage is £[*amount*], so if I pay the current mortgage plus £[*amount*] per month the arrears will be clear long before the end of the mortgage term.

11. I have made a claim for my injuries arising from the car accident. I am told that it is worth about £[*amount*]. The Motor Insurer's Bureau has accepted that I am entitled to compensation and **there is now shown to me marked GA4** a copy of a letter from my solicitor telling me that the compensation should arrive within the next [*number*] months. I would like to keep this for myself given what I have been through but if the court wants to make it a condition of staying this warrant that I pay all of it onto the mortgage account, I will do so.

12. I am extremely concerned about my situation and terrified that if the eviction goes ahead, I will be homeless along with my children. Although I have received a great deal of support from my mother, I do not think I can live permanently with her with my two children. They need their own home and space and so does my mother, since her flat only has two bedrooms.

13. I will be in priority need for re-housing from the council but it is by no means certain that they will re-house me; I am worried that they may argue that I have made myself homeless intentionally by allowing the arrears to accrue. I would strongly dispute this but I will not be eligible for legal aid once I start work again and I am told that homelessness appeals are very hard to win, especially without legal representation.

14. In all the circumstances, I humbly ask this honourable court to grant the relief requested in my notice of application.

I believe that the facts stated in this witness statement are true.

Signed:
Dated:

E9   DEFENCE TO CCA POSSESSION ACTION

IN THE SUBURBAN COUNTY COURT   Claim no.: _____

BETWEEN

READY FINANCE LIMITED

Claimant

and

MR COLIN SUMMER

Defendant

DEFENCE
(to be annexed to Form N11M)

[*Note: This precedent only applies to agreements made on or after 31 May 2005. It may be combined with the defence and counterclaim (unfair relationship), depending on the facts in the case (see **Appendix E10**).*]

1. The Defendant denies that the Claimant has a right to possession of the leasehold flat at 29 Trusting Drive, Suburbia ('the premises') as alleged in paragraph 1 of the Particulars of Claim.
2. The Defendant admits that he entered into the mortgage ('the agreement') referred to in paragraph 2 of the particulars of claim, but denies that the agreement is valid or enforceable against him, or that the Claimant has a right to possession of the premises.
3. The Defendant admits and avers that he is in possession of the premises with the persons stated in paragraph 3 of the Particulars of Claim.
4. The agreement purports to be an 'all monies charge' but the Defendant avers that in reality it is an agreement regulated by the Consumer Credit Act 1974 ('the Act') and regulations made under the Act, in particular, the Consumer Credit (Agreement) Regulations 1983 as amended ('the Regulations').

    [*or*]

    The Defendant admits and avers that the agreement is regulated by the Consumer Credit Act 1974 ('the Act') and by the Consumer Credit (Agreements) Regulations 1983, as amended ('the Regulations').
5. The agreement has failed to comply with numerous requirements of the Act and Regulations. In particular:

    Particulars

    5.1 Before the agreement was made the Claimant failed to provide a copy of the unexecuted agreement or a notice in the prescribed form indicating the right of the Defendant to withdraw, as required by s.58(1) of the Act and regulation 2(3) and Schedule 2, Part 1 of the Regulations; accordingly, by virtue of s.61(2) of the Act the agreement was not executed properly .
    5.2 The agreement was not in the prescribed form, did not contain all the prescribed terms and did not conform to regulations under s.60(1), contrary to s.61(1)(a). In particular, the agreement did not contain terms stating the amount of credit, the rate

of interest or how the Defendant was to discharge his obligations under the agreement to make the repayments, contrary to Schedule 6 to the Regulations;

5.3 The agreement did not embody all the terms of the agreement, contrary to s.61(1)(b) [e.g. In particular, the agreement did not record the agreement of the parties before the document was signed, that the Defendant was entitled upon giving one month's notice to take a 'payment holiday' of up to one year, at any time during the first 10 years of the agreement];

5.4 The agreement, when presented to the Defendant for signature, was not in such a state that all its terms were readily legible, contrary to s.61(1)(c);

5.5 The agreement did not contain the information, statements of the protection and remedies available under the Act, forms of signature boxes and separate boxes, which the Regulations require regulated agreements to contain in the order set out in paragraphs (a) to (f) of regulation 2(4) and as specified in Schedules 1, 2 and 5 of the Regulations

6. By reason of the above, the purported agreement is unenforceable by the Claimant against the Defendant under s.65 of the Act.[1]

[or, where the agreement was made before 6 April 2007:]

By reason of the above, the purported agreement is unenforceable by the Claimant against the Defendant under s.65 of the Act and the court has no power to make an enforcement order under s.65(1) by reason of the provisions of s.127(3) of the Act.[2]]

[Additional clause where a default notice has not been served, or is defective:]

7. The Claimant has failed to serve the Defendant with any default notice in respect of any alleged breach of the regulated agreement, contrary to ss.87 and 88 of the Act [or] the default notice which the Claimant has served on the Defendant did not comply with the requirements of s.88 of the Act or regulation 2 of and Schedule 2 to the Consumer Credit (Enforcement, Default and Termination Notices) Regulations 1983, as amended [*identify the precise failing and quote the exact provision in the Regulations*]; and therefore the Claimant is not entitled by reason of any breach to demand earlier payment of any sum, to recover possession of the premises or to enforce any security under s.87 of the Act.

Statement of truth
*[I believe][The Defendant believes] that the facts stated in this Defence are true.
*I am duly authorised by the Defendant to sign this statement.
Full name:
Name of Claimant's firm of solicitors: Friendly Solicitors
Signed: _____   **Position or office held:** _____   *[Defendant][Litigation   (if signing on behalf of firm or   friend][Defendant's solicitor]   company)

---

[1] See **10.4.1**.

[2] This extremely powerful provision deprives the court of any discretion to order that the agreement is enforceable; it is only available if the loan agreement was signed before 6 April 2007 and the agreement omits a 'prescribed term'. Agreements made after that date are unenforceable unless the court orders otherwise, see **10.4.1**. The likelihood therefore is that the claimant will respond to this defence by requesting that the court orders in its favour. There is no presumption that the court will consent, but it will depend on the facts of each case. Also see **Appendix E10**.

325

*delete as appropriate

Date: _____

Address to which notices about this case can be sent to you:

Friendly Solicitors

Station Approach

Suburbia CC5 5TT

Tel:

Fax:

Ref:

E10   DEFENCE AND COUNTERCLAIM – UNFAIR RELATIONSHIP

IN THE SUBURBAN COUNTY COURT   Claim no.: _____

B E T W E E N

READY FINANCE LIMITED

Claimant/
Part 20 Defendant

and

MR YUSUF TUZMAN

Defendant/
Part 20 Claimant

DEFENCE AND COUNTERCLAIM
(to be annexed to Form N11M)

[*Notes: This precedent may be combined with the defence to a CCA possession action, depending on the facts in the case (see **Appendix E9**).*

This precedent may also be adapted to form the basis of a free-standing claim by the borrower for an order pursuant to CCA 1974, s.140B(1), in circumstances where the lender has not yet issued possession proceedings.]

1.   The Defendant admits that he is the owner of the leasehold flat at 29 Trusting Drive, Suburbia ('the property'), but denies that the Claimant has a right to possession of the premises as alleged in paragraph 1 of the Particulars of Claim.

2.   The Defendant admits that on the 20 May 2009 he entered into a mortgage in favour of the Claimant as referred to in paragraph 2, but for the reasons set out in paragraph 4, he challenges the level of the alleged arrears and denies that he is bound by the terms of the agreement.

3.   The Defendant admits that the agreement for the loan secured by the mortgage is regulated by the Consumer Credit Act 1974 ('the Act'), as amended by the Consumer Credit Act 2006, as referred to in paragraph 4, but avers that it must be read in conjunction with the terms of a related offer letter dated 23 April 2009.

4.   The Defendant claims relief from the court under sections 140A to 140D of the Act, by reason that the relationship between the Claimant (as creditor) and the Defendant (as debtor) arising out of the agreement is unfair to the Defendant.

Particulars

4.1   The following terms of the agreement taken with the related agreement in the offer letter dated 23 April 2009 were unfair:

4.1.1   The offer letter contained an unfair term within the meaning of the Unfair Terms in Consumer Contracts Regulations 1999 (UTCCR), which stated that the Defendant would be subject to a penalty if, having invited an offer in the form of the letter dated 23 April 2009, he then decided not to proceed with the agreement;

4.1.2   The agreement also contained unfair terms within the UTCCR, by which it sought (at para.5) to bind the Defendant to terms in a third document entitled 'Rights and Obligations' which the Defendant has never seen, but which the Claimant relies upon to charge an fee of £75 for every 'late payment letter' it sends; (at para.11) to vary the charges payable under the agreement at the discretion of the Claimant after the Defendant was bound, and (at para.19) to a duty on the Defendant to notify the Claimant of all absences from the premises of more than 14 days, whereupon an unspecified charge for 'empty property top-up insurance' is levied;

4.1.3 The rates of interest charged in the agreement are excessively high, oppressive and exploitative, being several times higher that those applicable generally in the market sector, or payable by borrowers in similar situations, particularly when the sums advanced are secured on a property with substantial equity, so that there is little or no risk to the Claimant;

4.1.4 The Claimant's employee or agent, Mr Henshaw, insisted on additional security for the loan, taking custody of £5,000 worth of premium bond certificates at the time the loan agreement was signed by the Defendant.

4.2 The way in which the Claimant has exercised or enforced any of its rights under the agreement or any related agreement are unfair, in that:

4.2.1 The Claimant's employees or agents, including Mr Henshaw, have bombarded the Defendant with notices of default, accompanied by aggressive letters and followed up by threatening telephone calls, all of which have caused the Defendant great distress;

4.2.2 The Claimant has ignored requests by the Defendant and his daughter-in-law for information as to how monies owing by the Defendant might be paid and how to put an end to the notices, letters and telephone calls detailed above;

4.2.3 The Claimant has rushed to proceedings to enforce its security, with no regard for the Defendant's circumstances or his attempts to put matters right.

4.3 The following other things done (or not done) by, or on behalf of, the Claimant (either before or after the making of the agreement or any related agreement) were unfair to the Defendant:

4.3.1 The Claimant's employee or agent, Mr Henshaw, exploited the Defendant's vulnerability as a single, elderly, disabled, partially-sighted individual with a poor command of English and yet pressurised the Defendant, to his detriment, to enter into a complex, onerous and unsuitable agreement, which the Defendant did not understand;

4.3.2 The Defendant was subject to aggressive marketing calls from the Claimant's employees and agents, including Mr Henshaw;

4.3.3 After the agreement was made, the Claimant acted unfairly by failing to provide key information about the agreement in a clear and timely manner, particularly when requested by the Defendant and his daughter-in-law by telephone and by letter, and by failing to disclose material facts about the way charges are applied to the account;

4.3.4 The Claimant's employee or agent, Mr Henshaw, visited the Defendant in his home on at least six occasions, ostensibly to discuss the alleged arrears, but on each occasion he demanded and the Defendant paid a 'consultation fee' of £100 cash from his savings.

5.   The Defendant therefore seeks an order from the court pursuant to s.140B(1) of the Act
     [*delete as appropriate*]:

5.1 to require the Claimant or any associate or former associate of his to repay the
     following sum paid by the Defendant or by a surety, namely: an order that the
     Claimant repays £600 to the Defendant;

5.2 to require the Claimant or any associate or former associate of his to do or not to do
     (or to cease doing) the following steps, namely: an order that the Claimant desists
     from contacting the Defendant by telephone or by visits to his home, and desists
     from sending the Defendant aggressive and/or threatening letters;

5.3 to reduce or discharge the following sum payable by the Defendant or by a surety,
     namely: an order to reduce to nil the fees levied for 'late payment letters';

5.4 to direct the return of the following property provided by the Defendant for the
     purposes of a security, namely: an order for the return to the Defendant of the
     premium bond certificates taken by Mr Henshaw as an additional security for the
     loan;

5.5 to set aside any duty imposed on the Defendant or on a surety, namely: an order to
     set aside the duty to notify the Claimant of all absences from the premises of more
     than 14 days;

5.6 to alter the terms of the agreement or of any related agreement in the following
     way: an order reducing the rate of interest to no more than 0.5% above the Bank of
     England base lending rate;

5.7 to direct accounts to be taken between the following persons, namely: an account
     of all charges and interest levied by the Claimant and payments made on or behalf
     of the Defendant.

Counterclaim

6.   The Defendant repeats the above Defence and counterclaims:

6.1 for an order pursuant to s.140B(1) of the Act as may be appropriate;

6.2 interest on any sums found due or payable by the Claimant as a result of the order,
     pursuant to s.69 of the County Courts Act 1984; and

6.3 costs.

Statement of truth
*[I believe][The Defendant believes] that the facts stated in this Defence and Counterclaim are true.
*I am duly authorised by the Defendant to sign this statement.
Full name:
Name of Claimant's firm of solicitors: Friendly Solicitors
Signed: _____   **Position or office held:** _____   *[Defendant][Litigation   (if signing on behalf of firm or   friend][Defendant's solicitor]   company)
delete as appropriate
Date: _____
Address to which notices about this case can be sent to you:

Friendly Solicitors Station Approach Suburbia CC5 5TT	**Tel:** **Fax:** **Ref:**

E11 DUTY ADVICE SCHEME – STANDARD POST-HEARING LETTER TO BORROWER

Dear

Re: Hearing at [*town*] County Court

I am writing to confirm the outcome of the court hearing on [ ] day [ ] 2011, when I represented you as duty solicitor.

Explanation of what happened at court

Your lender [*name*] brought possession proceedings against you on the basis of mortgage arrears of £[*amount*] at the date of the hearing.

At the hearing the lender's representative asked for an outright possession order. After making representations on your behalf (set out later in this letter), District Judge [*name*] made the following order [*delete as appropriate*]:

1. Your case is adjourned to the first available date after 28 days on condition that:
2. you pay your current monthly instalment (presently £[*amount*] per month) plus £[*amount*] per month towards the current arrears of £[*amount*]; and
3. **you must file and serve witness evidence by [*date*]** confirming your proposals for future payment of your mortgage, including evidence of any other agency or person responsible for meeting your monthly payments.

[*or*]

1. You are to give up possession of your home to the lender in 28 days;
2. The date on which you are to give up possession of the property to the lender is **suspended** so long as you comply with the following terms:
3. you must pay your current monthly instalments of £[*amount*] on the due date plus £[*amount*] each month towards the current arrears of £[*amount*].

All of this means that so long as you continue to pay your current monthly instalments and £[*amount*] towards your arrears, the lender will take no further action to evict you.

What will happen next: action by the court or by the lender?

You will receive an order from the court confirming the order made by the District Judge.

[*or*]

You will receive an order from the court giving you the next hearing date, when you **must** attend court once again.

The next steps for you to take

You must seek advice from a solicitor or an advice centre in order to [*set out necessary steps, e.g.* prepare a witness statement to prove your ability to pay the mortgage, with evidence from your brother about his means and ability to assist you].

[*Or, if it is a CCA regulated agreement:*]

Since this charge on your property is regulated by the Consumer Credit Acts you should seek advice from a solicitor or an advice centre in order to see whether you can challenge the level of the arrears, the interest rate and other terms of the charge. In particular, it may be possible for you to challenge the agreement on the basis that it is an 'unfair relationship', and you may be able to apply to the court to vary the terms of the agreement and/or apply for a 'time order' to give you an extended period in which to repay the arrears.

You must make the payments ordered by the court. If you fail to meet the payments the lender will apply for an eviction warrant and you should seek further legal advice at that stage, to try to prevent the eviction going ahead.

After making regular payments for 6 or 12 months you can ask your lender to 'capitalise' the arrears, which means add them to the outstanding balance of the mortgage. If your lender agrees to do this, a new monthly repayment is calculated. You then pay the new monthly payment for the remaining term of the mortgage. You should seek advice if your lender does not agree to do this and/or if you need help to reduce your monthly payments and/or if you need debt counselling.

Important issues in your case

[*Set out information obtained from client at court relevant to the case/representations to the judge/issues requiring further advice, e.g.* Having taken instructions from you at court, I told the District Judge that you were currently receiving income support and that the Department for Work and Pensions (DWP) was paying Support for Mortgage Interest (SMI) to the lender at the rate of £450 per month. As this was less than the current monthly instalment of your mortgage, your brother was willing to pay another £450 per month, which was confirmed by letter, and you could afford to pay £50 per month, so that the mortgage and some of the arrears would be paid each month. Recently, you had made a £850 payment to the lender and in six months' time your fixed-term high-interest rate would end, and a lower interest rate would then apply to your account. I also emphasised that you had vulnerability due to a head injury when you fell in a bus some time ago and that you had been seeking advice from the CAB about your entitlement to SMI. I asked for your case to be adjourned for six months.

The lender's representative strongly opposed any adjournment, but the judge said that she could not make a decision until she had evidence of your brother's means and your ability to pay future instalments and arrears. The District Judge therefore adjourned your case to give you time to provide this evidence, as indicated above.]

If you need debt advice or counselling you can contact the National Debtline on 0808 808 4000 or seek advice online at: **www.nationaldebtline.co.uk**.

Mortgage payment protection insurance

It may be that you took out a mortgage protection policy at the same time as your mortgage, to pay the mortgage instalments in the event of unemployment or illness. If you have such a policy, it is important that you lodge the necessary claim form with the insurers as soon as possible. You should do this even though you may be outside the timescale in the policy for making a claim, because insurance companies have discretion to extend time. If the insurance company refuses do so in your case, you can complain to the Financial Ombudsman Service.

Where to get further help

I attach a list of solicitors and advice centres that you can contact if you wish to obtain further advice. However, if you would like me to help you with this problem, please telephone my office to make an appointment. You should explain that I represented you as duty solicitor and that I invited you to telephone for an appointment.

Alternatively, you may be able to find a local solicitor by calling Community Legal Advice on 0845 345 4345.

Do you qualify for further legal help?

Since you are receiving income support/jobseeker's allowance you should qualify for free legal help wherever you go.

[*or*]

Since you are receiving a low income, you should qualify for free legal help wherever you go, but a future adviser will carry out a more detailed check of your means if you seek advice.

[*or*]

The level of your income probably means that you will not qualify for free legal help or free legal aid, but a future adviser will carry out a more detailed check of your means, if you seek advice.

Extent of duty advice scheme

I assisted you as a duty adviser under a scheme funded by the Legal Services Commission. Please note that there is no provision for the same duty adviser to attend court when adjourned cases return to court. Although you may find that there is another duty adviser at court on the next hearing date, there is no guarantee of this. Therefore, if you need representation at further hearings, this should be arranged in advance with an advice centre or solicitor's firm which has agreed to take on your case. Further public funding may be available to assist with the preparation of your case or representation at court.

Quality control

If there is anything you want to clarify about today, or about this letter, please do contact me by phone. If you have any complaint about the duty advice scheme service provided at court, please contact [*name*], who has overall responsibility for this scheme.

Yours sincerely,

Case studies

The case studies below are taken from real mortgage possession claims, mostly arising from a county court duty advice scheme. They have been adapted to guarantee anonymity. They are included to illustrate aspects of the law and procedure covered in this book. In each case, the adviser was doing the best he or she could on limited information, often without documentation and in a short timescale. The results show what advisers can sometimes achieve for borrowers even in difficult and unpromising circumstances.

F1 PROCEDURAL DEFICIENCIES

Case study 1 – PCOL

The mortgage borrower was in very high arrears. He needed time to find lodgers. There was a very high risk of an outright possession order, because there was little to go on. The adviser looked at the court documents, which had been issued by Possession Claim Online (PCOL), to find that only the odd pages had been printed.

The adviser applied for an adjournment for the court documents to be re-served and the judge agreed to this. The case came back more than eight weeks later, giving the borrower time to find lodgers and therefore improve his position.

Case study 2 – No mortgage terms at court

The same PCOL case (above) came back to court for a second hearing when the borrower produced evidence that he had now found lodgers, who would be moving in at the weekend. The lender's representative countered by saying that sub-letting was not allowed under the terms of the mortgage.

The adviser argued (a) that having lodgers was not 'sub-letting', because it did not involve 'parting with possession', but merely granting a personal right to the lodgers to remain in the property; and (b) the adviser asked to see the mortgage conditions.

The lender's representative did not have a copy of the mortgage conditions at court, so the adviser applied for a second adjournment, which was granted by the district judge, giving the borrower even more time to install the lodgers, receive 'rent' and start payment to his mortgage account.

Case study 3 – Technical breaches (notice to occupiers)

The owner of a buy-to-let property turned up to a mortgage possession hearing, and so did his tenants. The judge asked to see all of the relevant documents in support of the possession claim, including the witness statement and the notice to occupiers.

Under the old rules, it was a mandatory requirement to serve a notice to occupiers 14 days before the hearing (now the notice must be served within five days of receiving notice of the hearing). The adviser applied for an adjournment because of short service of the notice to occupiers.

The lender's representative argued strenuously against such an adjournment, citing the court's case management powers to extend or abridge any time limits and arguing that even if the occupiers had not had 14 days to take advice, they still had actual notice of the hearing because they had actually attended court, and there was no prejudice.

The counter argument was that the CPR case management powers to abridge time do not apply to the mandatory requirement to give 14 days' notice to occupiers. The judge agreed. The notice period was a mandatory requirement, so the claim was adjourned 28 days for proper notice to be given.

F2 ADJOURNMENTS

Case study 4 – Buying time for SMI claim

Mr S lived in a two-bedroom flat with his partner and their five-year-old child. He lost his job as a mortgage consultant when he travelled to West Africa, because his mother was seriously ill and fell into a coma. He left his partner to pay the mortgage, which she failed to do. When he returned to the UK after four months, he owed mortgage arrears of £3,600. The relationship with his partner broke down and she moved out of the property with their child.

He applied for jobseeker's allowance and Support for Mortgage Interest (SMI).

The lender sought an outright possession order. With very little to go on, and with no possibility of paying the mortgage, the adviser applied for an adjournment to allow time for the claim for SMI to be processed and paid.

The district judge adjourned the case to the first open date after six weeks on condition that the borrower paid £20 per month towards the arrears whilst his claim for SMI was processed.

Comment: This was a surprising result, but shows what can be achieved simply by relaying the facts of the case and asking for an adjournment, even with very little to go on.

Case study 5 – Buying time for a general improvement in borrower's position

Mr A was a 50-year-old teacher, who had slipped at work and badly injured his knee. He lost his job and could not pay the mortgage instalments on his right-to-buy flat (which he had originally occupied as a tenant, before buying it from the council).

He owed £10,000 mortgage arrears and the lender sought an outright possession order.

Mr A was receiving employment and support allowance and had applied for SMI. With monthly instalments of more than £1,000, he could pay neither his mortgage, nor any arrears.

The adviser applied for a three-month adjournment on ground that there were several unknown factors that needed to be investigated. In particular, the borrower:

- had a mortgage payment protection policy, but had not yet made a claim;
- was on employment and support allowance and his claim for SMI was still pending;
- was due to have a knee operation in two months' time, and should return to work in four to six months after that;
- was due to receive a legacy from a parent's will in the sum of £250,000, that he would use to clear the mortgage and all arrears.

Very reluctantly, the district judge said that there may be merit in the submissions. She granted an adjournment for 28 days, to give time for the borrower to progress all matters and to produce documentary evidence at the next hearing. The borrower was not ordered to make any payments pending the next hearing.

Case study 6 – adjournment to obtain documentary proof

The borrower came to court saying that he had very recently obtained a new job as a bus driver and he therefore now had the ability to pay not only his mortgage instalments, but also to start to reduce the very substantial arrears. When told, the lender's representative expressed disbelief and indicated his intention to apply for an outright possession hearing.

The borrower had no letters, payslips or bank statements to confirm that he was in work. The adviser pressed him further, but all that he could produce was an identity card from the bus company, which had been dangling on a lanyard around his neck.

The adviser relied upon the identity card at the hearing to support the borrower's story. The district judge accepted that as evidence that the borrower was now in work and he adjourned the possession claim, so that proper documentary evidence of earnings could be filed at court.

F3   USING THE MORTGAGE PRE-ACTION PROTOCOL

Case study 7 – using the Protocol

For the first case study, see **7.8.5**.

Case study 8 – using the Protocol

Ms J was a council employee living in a two-bedroom right-to-buy flat with three children. She remortgaged and had a good, unbroken payment record for more than three years.

Ms J then became pregnant and went on maternity leave from work on a reduced income, resulting in a break in payments for a period of four months and in mortgage arrears of about £2,000.

While she could gather together sufficient resources from maternity pay, working tax credit and child benefit to pay the current monthly instalment (CMI), she was unable to make any payments towards the arrears. She needed an adjournment of the possession hearing for three months, at which point she would return to work, her pay would increase and she could then afford to pay the arrears by instalments.

The adviser made representations that the borrower had asked the lender for reduced payments and/or a payment holiday until she returned to work, but this had been turned down by the lender, apparently without reasons being given. The adviser argued this was a breach of paras.5.4 and 5.5 of the Mortgage Pre-Action Protocol for mortgage possession claims (which require a lender to consider a reasonable request from the borrower to change the date of regular payment and to respond promptly to any proposal by the borrower, and to give written reasons for refusal).

Having heard these representations the district judge made an order that the possession claim should be adjourned to the first open date after 12 weeks on terms that the borrower pay her CMI plus £20 per month off the arrears.

F4   THE HEARING

Case study 9 – Changing prior agreements

On the telephone the borrower had offered to pay the CMI plus £100 per month towards the arrears. On these terms the lender was willing to accept a suspended possession order.

At court it was clear that the borrower would struggle to meet the £100 per month payments and was likely to breach the suspended possession order quite quickly. In negotiations before the court hearing the lender's representative threatened to ask for an outright possession order if the borrower tried to change the terms of the agreement on the telephone.

The borrower wanted finality and instructed the adviser not to apply for an adjournment in this case.

With the borrower's consent, the adviser put it to the district judge that whilst the lender had agreed in principle to a suspended possession order, it was not realistic to order arrears payments at £100 per month and that, despite the agreement out of court, a lower figure of CMI plus £30 per month should be made. The judge agreed and made an order on this basis.

Summary of the law relating to homelessness

The complexities of homelessness law are beyond the scope of this book. However, this note summarises the key provisions of the law relating to homelessness, with particular reference to mortgage borrowers who may be faced with the loss of their home.

G1 THE LAW

The main provisions which govern a local housing authority's responsibilities towards the homeless are found in Part VII of the Housing Act (HA) 1996, as amended by the Homelessness Act 2002 and as supplemented by Codes of Guidance published from time to time by relevant government departments.

In England, the most recent guidance will be found in the Homelessness Code of Guidance for Local Authorities issued in July 2006, which has been updated by the Supplementary Guidance on Intentional Homelessness, published in August 2009. In Wales, the relevant document is the Code of Guidance to Local Authorities on Allocation of Accommodation and Homelessness, issued in April 2003 by the Welsh Assembly Government (now known as the Welsh Government). Copies of the guidance can be found at: **www.communities.gov.uk** and **http://wales.gov.uk** respectively.

G2 DEFINITION OF HOMELESSNESS

A person is defined as homeless under HA 1996, s.175(1) if he has no accommodation available for his occupation, in the United Kingdom or elsewhere, which he:

- is entitled to occupy by virtue of an interest in it or by virtue of an order of the court,
- has an express or implied licence to occupy, or occupies as a residence by virtue of any enactment or rule of law giving him the right to remain in occupation or restricting the right of another to recover possession.

A person is threatened with homelessness if it is likely that he will become homeless within 28 days (s.175(4)).

G3 MAIN HOMELESSNESS DUTIES

If a person applies to a local authority for accommodation, or for assistance in obtaining accommodation, and the authority has reason to believe that he is or may be homeless or threatened with homelessness, then by HA 1996, s.184(1) the authority is under a duty to make inquiries in order to satisfy itself:

- whether the person is eligible for assistance (i.e. is not a 'person from abroad' pursuant to HA 1996, s.185) and, if so,
- whether any duty is owed to that person and, if so,
- what duty is owed.

Interim duty to accommodate

If the local housing authority has reason to believe that an applicant may be homeless, eligible for assistance and have a priority need, it shall secure temporary accommodation until a final decision has been made in his case (s.188(1)). Priority need is dealt with below.

Duty to persons with priority need, who are not homeless intentionally

Where the local housing authority is satisfied that an applicant is homeless, eligible for assistance and has a priority need, and is not satisfied that he became homeless intentionally, the authority 'shall secure that accommodation is available for occupation by the applicant' (s.193(1)). This is the main housing duty, which homeless persons rely upon to be rehoused by the council.

Duty to persons not in priority need, who are not homeless intentionally

Where the local housing authority is satisfied that the applicant is homeless and eligible for assistance and is not satisfied that he became homeless intentionally, but is not satisfied that he has a priority need, a lesser duty is owed. The authority is only under a duty to 'provide the applicant with (or secure that he is provided with) advice and assistance in any attempts he may make to secure that accommodation becomes available for his occupation' (s.192(2)), although there is a power to secure that accommodation is available.

Duty to persons becoming homeless intentionally

By HA 1996, s.190, if the local housing authority is satisfied that an applicant is homeless and is eligible for assistance, but is also satisfied that he became homeless intentionally, it has the following duties:

- if the authority is satisfied that the applicant has a priority need, it shall secure temporary accommodation for such period as it considers will give him a reasonable opportunity of securing accommodation and provide him with advice and assistance to this end, but
- if it is not satisfied that he has a priority need, the duty is only to provide him with advice and assistance.

G4 PRIORITY NEED

An applicant may have a priority need either by fulfilling one of the categories of priority need, or if a member of his or her household is pregnant or vulnerable. HA 1996, s.189(1) sets out four categories of people who have a priority need in both England and Wales:

- a pregnant woman or a person with whom she resides or might reasonably be expected to reside;
- a person with whom dependent children reside or might reasonably be expected to reside;

- a person who is vulnerable as a result of old age, mental illness or handicap or physical disability or other special reason, or with whom such person resides or might reasonably be expected to reside; and
- a person who is homeless or threatened with homelessness as a result of an emergency such as flood, fire or other disaster.

Additional categories in England

Six additional categories have been added for English local housing authorities by the Homelessness (Priority Need for Accommodation) (England) Order 2002, SI 2002/2051:

- most children aged 16 or 17;
- young people under 21, who have been looked after, accommodated or fostered, but are not students in full-time education;
- people who are vulnerable as a result of having been looked after, accommodated or fostered;
- people who are vulnerable as a result of having served in the armed forces;
- people who are vulnerable as a result of having been imprisoned; and
- people who are vulnerable as a result of ceasing to occupy accommodation because of actual or threatened violence.

Additional categories in Wales

There are also six additional categories added for Welsh local housing authorities added by the Homeless Persons (Priority Need) (Wales) Order 2001, SI 2001/607 (W.30):

- young people aged 18, 19 or 20 who have been looked after, accommodated or fostered;
- young people aged 18, 19 or 20 who are at particular risk of sexual or financial exploitation;
- 16- and 17-year-olds;
- anyone who has been subject to domestic violence or is at risk of domestic violence;
- a person who is homeless after leaving the armed forces; and
- a former prisoner who is homeless after being released from custody.

G5   BECOMING HOMELESS INTENTIONALLY

HA 1996, s.191(1) states that a person becomes homeless intentionally 'if he deliberately does or fails to do anything in consequence of which he ceases to occupy accommodation which is available for his occupation and which it would have been reasonable for him to continue to occupy'.

An act or omission in good faith on the part of the person who was unaware of any relevant fact is not to be treated as deliberate (s.191(2)).

The greatest concern for mortgage borrowers is that the fact of losing their home due to mortgage arrears might be considered as a deliberate act or omission, leading to a finding by the local authority that the borrower has made himself homeless intentionally.

The position in England

At paras.11.18 to 11.20 of the 2006 Code of Guidance for England local authorities are given the following guidance on this issue:

> **11.18.** An applicant's actions would not amount to intentional homelessness where he or she has lost his or her home, or was obliged to sell it, because of rent or

mortgage arrears resulting from significant financial difficulties, and the applicant was genuinely unable to keep up the rent or mortgage payments even after claiming benefits, and no further financial help was available.

11.19. Where an applicant has lost a former home due to rent arrears, the reasons why the arrears accrued should be fully explored. Similarly, in cases which involve mortgagors, housing authorities will need to look at the reasons for mortgage arrears together with the applicant's ability to pay the mortgage commitment when it was taken on, given the applicant's financial circumstances at the time.

11.20. Examples of acts or omissions which may be regarded as deliberate (unless any of the circumstances set out in paragraph 11.17 apply) include the following, where someone:

(i) chooses to sell his or her home in circumstances where he or she is under no risk of losing it;

(ii) has lost his or her home because of wilful and persistent refusal to pay rent or mortgage payments;

(iii) could be said to have significantly neglected his or her affairs having disregarded sound advice from qualified persons;

(iv) voluntarily surrenders adequate accommodation in this country or abroad which it would have been reasonable for the applicant to continue to occupy

....

The position in Wales

In the 2003 Welsh Code of Guidance for Local Authorities on Allocation of Accommodation and Homelessness the position is as follows:

15.6. Other circumstances in which the applicant's actions may not amount to intentional homelessness include:

(i) where imprudence or lack of foresight on the part of an applicant led to homelessness, but the applicant's act or omission was in good faith;

(ii) where an applicant has lost his or her home, or was obliged to sell it because he or she got into rent or mortgage arrears because of real financial difficulties (for example because he or she became unemployed or ill or suffered greatly reduced earnings or family breakdown), and genuinely could not keep up the rent payments or loan repayments even after claiming benefits, and for whom no further financial help was available. In the case of mortgagors, authorities need to look at the applicant's ability to pay the mortgage commitment when it was taken on, given his or her financial circumstances at the time ...

Case law

In several cases, mortgage borrowers have been found to have been intentionally homeless. For example, in *William* v. *London Borough of Wandsworth* [2006] EWCA Civ 535, [2006] HLR 42, the borrower remortgaged his home, but failed to meet his increased commitments under the mortgage out of the monies borrowed, which were spent on other things. The borrower ran into financial difficulties within nine months of the remortgage and eventually lost his home. The local authority held that the failure to pay monies due under the mortgage was to be treated as deliberate act within the meaning of HA 1996, s.191(1), and the Court of Appeal upheld the authority's finding that he was homeless intentionally as a result.

In *Watchman* v. *Ipswich Borough Council* [2007] EWCA Civ 348, [2007] HLR 33 the borrower was a council tenant with a history of rent arrears, who bought the house with her husband. The monthly mortgage repayments were considerably higher than the rent they had been paying, although initially at a discounted rate. They took out a further loan for improvements, the husband then lost his job and interest rates rose. They fell into arrears with the mortgage and the lender repossessed the house. The Court of Appeal upheld the local authority's finding that the borrower was intentionally homeless as a result of her deliberate actions, i.e. knowingly taking on a mortgage where she would be unable to meet the monthly repayments.

However, the position of mortgage borrowers has been mitigated to an extent by the 2009 Supplementary Guidance on Intentional Homelessness.

Supplementary guidance

To assist borrowers in the current economic climate, the government published the Homelessness Code of Guidance for Local Authorities: Supplementary Guidance on Intentional Homelessness in August 2009, to give guidance on how local housing authorities should apply the various statutory criteria, when considering whether applicants who are homeless because of difficulties in meeting mortgage commitments are intentionally homeless or not. This provides some relief to borrowers by stating:

9.   Intentionality does not depend on whether applicants have behaved wisely or prudently or reasonably. Where an applicant's failure to seek help may have been foolish, imprudent or even unreasonable, this would not necessarily mean his or her conduct was not in good faith.

10.   As mentioned above, some former homeowners may seek housing assistance from a local housing authority having lost their home in one of the following circumstances:

(i)   having voluntarily surrendered the property (handed the keys back);

(ii)   having sold the property;

(iii)   where the property was repossessed after the applicant refused an offer under the Mortgage Rescue Scheme (MRS);

(iv)   where the property was repossessed after the applicant refused an offer of Homeowners Mortgage Support scheme (HMS);

(v)   where the property was repossessed and the applicant had not sought help.

There should be no general presumption that a homeowner will have brought homelessness on him or herself in any of the above scenarios. A person cannot be found to have become intentionally homeless from a property where he or she was already statutorily homeless, e.g. because it was not reasonable for him to continue to occupy the property (see paras.8.18 et seq of the Homelessness Code of Guidance for Local Authorities). Consequently, where someone was already homeless before surrendering or selling their home or refusing an offer under MRS or HMS, the 'acts' of surrender or sale, and the 'omission' of refusing an offer of MRS or HMS cannot be treated as the cause of homelessness.

G6   REMEDIES

In the face of an adverse decision from a local authority concerning his or her application for homelessness assistance or accommodation, the homeless borrower must request a review of the decision within 21 days of being notified of the decision (HA 1996, s.202(3)). If the review decision is also unfavourable, appeal has to be made to the county court, once again within 21 days of being notified of the adverse review decision (s.204). Advisers on mortgage matters should be sure to refer borrowers to a homelessness specialist, well before these time limits become a factor.

Useful organisations

Advice Services Alliance
Tel: 020 7378 6428
www.asauk.org.uk

Association for Research in the Voluntary and Community Sector (ARVAC)
www.arvac.org.uk

Business Debtline
Tel: 0800 197 6026
www.bdl.org.uk

Citizens Advice
www.citizensadvice.org.uk
www.adviceguide.org.uk

Community Legal Advice
Directory of agencies providing legal advice
Tel: 0845 345 4345
www.legalservices.gov.uk/public/
community_legal_advice.asp
http://legaladviserfinder.justice.gov.uk/
AdviserSearch.do

Consumer Credit Counselling Service
Tel: 0800 138 1111
www.cccs.co.uk

Consumer Direct
Helpline for consumer problems
Tel: 0845 404 0506
www.consumerdirect.gov.uk

Council of Mortgage Lenders
www.cml.org.uk

Debt Advice Foundation
Free debt advice telephone helpline and online self-help tools
Tel: 0800 043 40 50
www.debtadvicefoundation.org

Department for Work and Pensions
www.dwp.gov.uk

Dial UK
Network of 139 local disability information and advice organisations
Tel: 01302 310 123
enquiries@dialuk.org.uk

Disability Benefits Enquiry Line
Tel: 0800 88 22 00
www.dwp.gov.uk

Disability Living Allowance and Attendance Allowance
Tel: 08457 123 456

Disability Rights Commission
Tel: 08457 622 633
www.drc-gb.org

Enforcement Services Association (formerly Certificated Bailiffs Association)
Tel: 0117 907 4771
www.ensas.org.uk

Financial Ombudsman Scheme
Tel: 0845 080 1800
www.financial-ombudsman.org.uk

Financial Services Authority
Consumer Helpline
Tel: 0845 606 1234
www.fsa.gov.uk

Financial Services
Compensation Scheme
Tel: 020 7892 7300
www.fscs.org.uk

Gamblers Anonymous
Tel: 0870 050 8880
www.gamblersanonymous.org.uk

Gamcare
Advice on gambling issues
Tel: 0845 600 0133
www.gamcare.org.uk

IFA Promotions for a list of Independent
Financial Advisers
Tel: 0800 0853 250
www.unbiased.co.uk

Insolvency Practitioners Association
www.insolvency-practitioners.org.uk

Jobcentre Plus
www.jobcentreplus.gov.uk

Law Centres Federation
Tel: 020 7387 8570
www.lawcentres.org.uk

Local Government Ombudsman
Advice Line
Tel: 0845 602 1983
www.lgo.org.uk

Money Advice Association (MAA)
Tel: 01476 594 970
www.m-a-a.org.uk

Money Advice Service Health Check
A free, unbiased personal action plan
designed to help consumers make the most
of their money now and plan for future goals
https://healthcheck.moneyadviceservice.
org.uk

Money Advice Trust: Information Hub
Access to a range of information for people
with an interest in money advice, credit, debt
and debt remedies and recovery
www.infohub.moneyadvicetrust.org

MoneyBasics
Independent information about money
www.moneybasics.co.uk

Mortgage Help
Government website giving mortgage
advice to those in arrears
http://mortgagehelp.direct.gov.uk

My Money Steps
Online debt advice tool provided by
National Debtline
www.mymoneysteps.org

National Consumer Council
Tel: 020 7730 3469
www.ncc.org.uk

National Debtline
Source of money and debt advice
Tel: 0808 808 4000
www.nationaldebtline.co.uk

Office of Fair Trading (OFT)
Tel: 0845 722 4499
www.oft.gov.uk

Payplan
Source of free debt advice
Tel: 0800 917 7823
www.payplan.com

Pension Credit Claim Line
Tel: 0800 99 1234
www.thepensionservice.gov.uk

Shelter
Free housing advice helpline
Tel: 0808 800 4444
www.shelter.org.uk

Taxaid
Tel: 0845 120 3779
www.taxaid.org.uk

Tax Credits Helpline
Tel: 0845 300 3900
www.hmrc.gov.uk

Telephone Helplines Association
Provides information on helplines
Tel: 0845 120 3767
www.helplines.org.uk

Trading Standards
To complain to the local Trading Standards
service on line
www.consumercomplaints.org.uk

Turn2us
Calculator to help work out entitlement to
benefits and tax credits
www.turn2us.org.uk/benefits_search.aspx

Which?
Tel: 0845 307 4000
www.which.net

Winter Fuel Payments Helpline
Tel: 0845 915 1515
www.thepensionservice.gov.uk/winterfuel

Index